Creating Classrooms for Authors

Jerome C. Harste
Indiana University

Kathy G. Short
Goshen College

With

Carolyn Burke
Indiana University

---

and contributing
teacher researchers

Gloria Kauffman
Fairfield Community Schools

Myriam Revel-Wood
Monroe County
Community Schools

Susan Robinson
Indianapolis Public Schools

Deborah W. Rowe
Peabody College
of Vanderbilt University

Mary Lynn Woods
Eagle-Union Public Schools

Virginia Woodward
Indiana University

and Others

Creating Classrooms for Authors

The Reading–Writing Connection

Heinemann
Portsmouth, NH

Heinemann Educational Books, Inc.
70 Court Street   Portsmouth, NH 03801
Offices and agents throughout the world

Portions of Chapter 1 are based on Deborah W. Rowe and Jerome C. Harste, "Reading and Writing in a System of Knowing: Curricular Implications," in *The Pursuit of Literacy*, ed. by Michael Sampson (Dubuque, Iowa: Kendall/Hunt, 1986), pp. 126-44. Reprinted by permission.

Figure CC22.1:   Poem from *Blackberry Ink* by Eve Merriam. Copyright © 1985 by Eve Merriam. All rights reserved. Reprinted by permission of Marian Reiner for the author.

Library of Congress Cataloging-in-Publication Data

Harste, Jerome C. (Jerome Charles)
    Creating classrooms for authors : the reading-writing connection /
Jerome C. Harste, Kathy G. Short, with Carolyn Burke.
        p. cm.
    Bibliography: p.
    Includes index.
    ISBN 0-435-08465-8
    1. English language—Composition and exercises—Study and
teaching.   2. Language arts.   I. Short, Kathy Gnagey.   II. Burke,
Carolyn L.   III. Title.
LB1576.H26 1988
372.6—dc19   88-696
                                                                           CIP

Prepress production work by G&H SOHO, Ltd.
Printed in the United States of America.
10 9 8 7 6 5 4 3 2 1

Contents

Preface   ix

SECTION ONE / The Authoring Cycle: Let's Think Curriculum   1

Chapter 1

The Authoring Cycle: A Theoretical and Practical Overview   3
Deborah W. Rowe / Jerome C. Harste / Kathy G. Short

Introduction
Authoring: Children as Informants
The Authoring Cycle as a Learning Cycle
The Authoring Cycle in Action
A Guided Tour Through an Authoring Cycle with Corey
Extending the Cycle to Reading, Art, and Units of Study
Conclusion

Feature Article 1

Teaching as Curriculum Development   39
Mary Lynn Woods

Introduction
Written Conversation
Uninterrupted Reading and Writing
Conclusion

Chapter 2

Starting an Authoring Cycle   51

Introduction
Life Experiences
Uninterrupted Reading and Writing
Author's Folder
Authors' Circle
Semantic Revision and Self-Editing
Editors' Table
Publishing/Celebrating Authorship
Language Strategy Instruction/Invitations
Conclusion

Feature Article 2

Reading as a Process of Authorship   105

Kathy G. Short / Gloria Kauffman

Introduction
The Authoring Cycle as a Curricular Framework
Literature Circles in the Classroom
Conclusion

Chapter 3

Creating a Classroom for Authors and Authorship   117

Introduction
Work Time
Author Sharing Time
Authors' Chair
Classroom Library
Writing-Reading Center
Readers' Theatre
Shared Reading
Authors Meeting Authors
Literature Response Activities
Journals
Pen Pals
Message Board
Conclusion

Feature Article 3

Invitations to Read, to Write, to Learn   169

Myriam Revel-Wood

Introduction
Invitations to Read
Invitations to Write
Invitations to Use Reading and Writing to Learn
Conclusion

Chapter 4

Keeping the Cycle Going   181

Introduction
Multimedia Blitz
Science and Social Studies Clubs
Environmental Print Walks, Books, and Recipes
Teachers and Students as Resident Artists
Parents' Day

Units of Study: The Teacher as Learner
Conclusion

SECTION TWO / The Authoring Cycle: Curricular Components 213

Anomalies	215
Authors' Chair	219
Authors' Circle	221
Author's Folder	227
Authors Meeting Authors	232
Bookmaking	238
Choose Your Own Story	243
Classroom Newspaper	246
Cloning an Author	253
Editors' Table	257
Family Stories	263
Generating Written Discourse	268
Getting to Know You	274
Group Composed Books	277
Journals	280
Learning Logs	286
Literature Circles	293
Literature Response Activities	305
Message Board	309
Mine, Yours, and Ours	313
Picture Setting	318
Poetry in Motion	323
Readers' Theatre	329
Save the Last Word for Me	332
Say Something	336
Schema Stories	340
Shared Reading	346
Sketch to Stretch	353
Text Sets	358
Theme Cycles	366
Wordless Picture Books	372
Written Conversation	375
Bibliography	381
Suggested Reading	387
Index	391

Preface

This volume presents a curricular framework for classroom reading and writing experiences that help students understand how reading and writing relate to reasoning and learning. Through this curriculum, students will come to see reading and writing as composing, composing as a form of learning, and learning as a form of authorship.

Although this book is meant to be practical, we believe it is important that teachers have a theoretical frame. Chapter 1, "The Authoring Cycle: A Theoretical and Practical Overview," summarizes the profession's current knowledge about reading, writing, and reasoning as they relate to curriculum and learning. Readers who wish to examine this theoretical base more carefully are referred to our book, *Language Stories & Literacy Lessons* (Harste, Woodward & Burke 1984), as well as to the videotape series, *The Authoring Cycle: Read Better, Write Better, Reason Better* (Harste & Jurewicz 1985) and the viewing guide that accompanies that series, *The Authoring Cycle: A Viewing Guide* (Harste, Pierce & Cairney 1985). This volume is a companion to as well as an extension of these works.

The videotape series was an attempt to develop and implement a theoretically based curriculum using what we had learned about the evolution of literacy as reported in *Language Stories & Literacy Lessons*. The videotape series focuses on three classrooms in three Indiana settings—inner city (Sue Robinson, Grade 6, School 39, Indianapolis Public Schools), suburban (Mary Lynn Woods, K-8, multi-age/grade classroom, Eagle-Union Public Schools, Zionsville), and small town/city (Myriam Revel-Wood, Grade 4, Monroe County Community Schools, Bloomington). The present volume also includes reference to Kathy Short's work with Gloria Kauffman in Grades 1 and 3, Fairfield Community Schools, Millersburg, Indiana. This book essentially grew out of sharing the curriculum we developed with other teachers through inservices and the videotape series. Teachers still felt they needed a handbook—a reference or guide to take back to the classroom.

The two sections of this volume are organized around three major components of curriculum and how each component was realized in the classrooms in which we worked. Although these components overlap, they involve how to begin an authoring cycle (Chapter 2, "Starting an Authoring Cycle"), creating a conducive context for exploring literacy in the classroom (Chapter 3, "Creating a Classroom for Authors and Authorship"), and using this frame for communicating and extending curriculum (Chapter 4, "Keeping the Cycle Going"). For each component, we share one set of options worked out among us, Carolyn Burke, and the teachers. We used italic type to signal the titles of these strategy lessons at their first mention in Section One. Full lesson plans for each strategy are included in Section Two. Earlier versions of many of these strategy lessons have appeared in mimeographed materials. Judith Newman from Nova Scotia, for example, spent her sabbatical with us; after she returned home, she and other teachers in the area wrote an initial version of some of these strategy lessons (see Newman 1983). The TAWL Group (Teachers Applying Whole Language) in Columbia, Missouri, under the leadership of Dorothy Watson, also compiled strategy lessons. To date they have produced two books, one for elementary teachers and another for secondary teachers (Hulett 1982; Mid-Missouri TAWL 1983). Lynn Rhodes and some teachers in Denver have written several volumes showing how specific children's books might be extended (Rhodes 1983). Because all these sources include strategy lessons other than those suggested in this volume, readers may wish to consult these volumes for additional ideas. Authors of the various strategy lessons in this volume are credited in the reference section of each lesson.

In all instances the curricular strategies we have elected to discuss reflect the particular strengths of teachers with whom we have worked—Gloria Kauffman knows children's literature and how to excite children about books and authorship; Mary Lynn Woods probably knows more than any other teacher we have ever met about working with and successfully communicating curriculum to parents, school officials, and the media; Myriam Revel-Wood understands at a very fundamental and powerful level that schools ought to focus on learning and that reading and writing are vehicles for learning—she opens new worlds to children and they love her for it; Sue Robinson understands reading and writing as functional activities—she trusts learners and learning, she knows how to plan, when to abandon plans, which learning invitation is the right one to make. We've seen her engage a group of sixth graders in a year-long study of China, prompted by a basal reading lesson!

At the end of the first three chapters, readers have the opportunity to hear directly from the teachers involved in classrooms using the authoring cycle as a curricular frame. The intent of these Feature Articles is to present key insights as well as various portrayals of how to begin.

The reporting in this volume, then, is the result of a group of people who have worked and thought together, and built from the thinking and work of others over time. Ludwik Fleck ([1935] 1979) calls such a like-minded group a "thought collective." Thought collectives hold some values in common, but this does not mean that everyone thinks exactly alike. That's why we must assume responsibility for this book and the curriculum it presents, though within it you will meet and see reflected the theory and practice of many others.

Readers need to understand that this volume is but one attempt to organize curriculum around an authoring cycle. Many other options exist. We see this attempt as a "conceptual starter kit." We assume teachers will build on this base by modifying and reshaping what is presented.

To highlight as well as to acknowledge Carolyn Burke's conceptual input in the origination, development, and implementation of the authoring cycle, we elected to list her as a contributing author as well as a co-editor for the volume itself. In addition, we want to acknowledge Virginia Woodward, with whom we have conversed over the years about the authoring cycle and its implications for curriculum.

We acknowledge the teachers with whom we worked by making them contributing authors. We want to thank both them and their children for allowing us to use their work in this volume. In closing, a special thanks also is given to Kathryn Mitchell Pierce (Webster College, St. Louis), Diane Stephens (University of North Carolina, Wilmington), Jean Anne Clyde (University of Louisville), and Deborah Rowe (Peabody College of Vanderbilt University, Nashville) for their contributions and work on earlier versions of this volume and to Trevor Cairney (Riverina-Murray Institute of Higher Education, Wagga Wagga, New South Wales, Australia) for encouraging us to keep moving forward with this project.

THE
AUTHORING CYCLE:
LET'S THINK
CURRICULUM

CHAPTER 1

The Authoring Cycle: A Theoretical and Practical Overview

Deborah W. Rowe / Jerome C. Harste / Kathy G. Short

Introduction

At 6 years of age, Alison had a telephone conversation with her friend, Jennifer (Harste, Woodward & Burke 1984). They decided to get together after church on Sunday and play "ballerina." Alison would get her leotard, slippers, and hair ribbons from her dresser; Jennifer would bring her leotard, slippers, and hair ribbons with her in a bag from church. When Alison got off the phone, she went to her room and recorded her conversation. As seen in Figure 1.1, she uses art, math, and language to do so.

If we define literacy as the processes by which we, as humans, mediate the world for the purpose of learning, this language story demonstrates that Alison is clearly engaged in "real" literacy. To mediate the world is to create sign systems—mathematics, art, music, dance, language—that stand between the world as it is and the world as we perceive it. These sign systems act as prisms that, through reflection, permit us better to understand ourselves and our world.

We asked 4-year-old Michelle to write her name and anything else she could write (Harste, Woodward & Burke 1984). She wrote three sets of letters in three rows (see Figure 1.2). When we asked her to read what she had written she pointed to the first set of letters and said, "This says Michelle; [moving to the second

Figure 1.1   Uninterrupted Writing (Alison, Age 6).

Figure 1.2 Uninterrupted Writing (Michelle, Age 4).

set of letters] Jay, that's my daddy's name; [moving to the third set] and Nancy, that's my mother's name." Michelle paused at this point, thought a moment, then snatched up the pen and drew a circle around the names, as shown in Figure 1.2. Putting down the pen she announced, "And together these say Morrison"—her family name.

The function of the sign systems we create is learning. The sign systems permit new insights and understandings and, in the process of their creation and use, expand humankind's potential to *mean*. Michelle uses language not only to record and communicate her thinking, but also to grow—to find new patterns that connect. To be truly literate is to take ownership of this process, to use sign systems such as art, music, mathematics, and drama as tools for learning.

This definition of literacy has important implications for us as teachers. It suggests that if we want students to understand what it really means to be literate, we need to provide certain kinds of classroom experiences. We can select and plan these experiences only by becoming careful observers of children's intentions and behaviors within the context of classroom experiences. As educators, we are interested in what is learned today, as well as how this learning provides an environment that fosters and extends learning tomorrow. Only by using children as our curricular informants—by studying the mental trips they take as a function of the curricular experiences we provide—can we judge whether a set of instructional activities has achieved what we hoped.

We will begin by introducing some of the children and experiences that have led us to see expressions in all modes of language (i.e., reading, writing, listening, speaking) as *authorship,* and our young informants as *authors. Webster's Ninth New Collegiate Dictionary* provides two definitions of *author.* The first definition is "the writer of a literary work (as a book)," but the second is more general—"one that originates or gives existence." Although the creation of written texts is certainly important, children have repeatedly shown us that authoring means much more. Authoring and literacy involve "making" meanings through any of the available communication systems (language, art, drama, etc.) to achieve personal and social goals.

This chapter will also relate authoring to learning. Current theories of cognition (Anderson & Pearson 1984; Neisser 1976; Spiro et al. in press) have shown that learning is not simply a matter of transferring information from the outside world to some sort of in-head storehouse. Instead, learners must actively construct knowledge for themselves—a process that is affected by learners' current beliefs, hypotheses, interests, needs, and purposes.

In the final analysis, our interest in reading and writing is also an interest in learning. Researchers studying the mental processes involved in reading and writing have found that these activities have much in common. Even more important from an educational perspective, they have found that both reading and writing support the process of learning. We will argue that this is so because reading and writing, like all forms of communication, involve authoring. They are processes in which we *originate, negotiate,* and *revise* ideas. For us, meaning generation is the essence of learning. This belief has led us to propose that a curricular model that highlights authoring will also facilitate learning. In this chapter, we will introduce the authoring cycle as one such model and provide several illustrations of how, together with some excellent classroom teachers, we have used this framework to plan and evaluate activities with our students.

Authoring: Children as Informants

In our studies of young children's reading and writing (Harste, Burke & Woodward 1981, 1983; Harste, Woodward & Burke 1984), we often asked our informants to write a story. When we gave 5-year-old Beth pen and paper she produced the product seen in Figure 1.3A. If we had not watched and listened to Beth as she wrote her story, we might have followed the path already blazed by many others and called Beth's product "scribbling." However, partly because we had designed our study to focus on writing and reading *processes,* and partly because we had available the technology of video recording, we were able to arrive at a different conclusion. We believe that Beth is, in every sense of the word, an author.

By examining Beth's story as it looked at different points in the process, it is easier to see how we came to this conclusion. Beth began her story by drawing a picture of a sun and a house (Figure 1.3B). Then she proceeded to write her name, first near the top

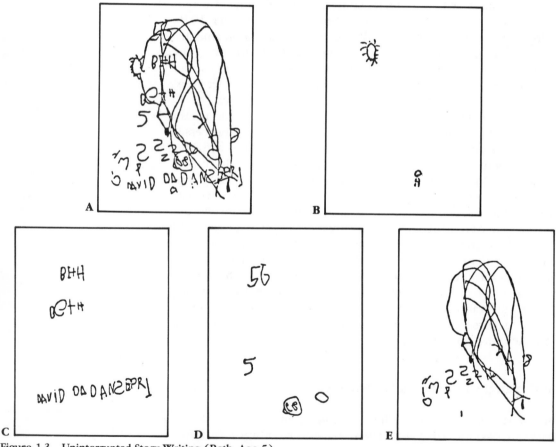

Figure 1.3 Uninterrupted Story Writing (Beth, Age 5).

of the page and then near the center as she announced, "I can write my name another way." Near the bottom of the page she wrote *David Dansberger* and told us it was her brother's name (Figure 1.3C). Shown in Figure 1.3D is Beth's attempt to write her other brother's name, *Jeff.* She decided her *J* didn't look right and said so, "That doesn't look right!" as she tried to erase it with her finger. Farther down the page she drew a picture of David and announced, "This is David." Next she began to draw a picture of Jeff, but remembered she hadn't finished his name earlier. With an exclamation of "Oops!" she decided not to finish his picture either. Her next effort was an attempt to write her age, *5,* near the abandoned *J* at the top of the page, but once again she was dissatisfied with the product. So she immediately produced the *5* located near the middle of the page.

After a pause, Beth began saying and writing her numbers backward: "Eight, seven, six, five" (Figure 1.3E). Once again she was displeased with her *5* and said "Five, five, five, five" as she made a series of forms in an attempt to produce one she could accept. Finally she shrugged her shoulders and continued by saying and writing, "Four, three, two, one, zero, blast off!" At this point Beth drew the rocket seen in the center of the page complete with plumes of smoke and accompanied by sound effects, "Varoom! Varoom! Varoom! Varoom!" Upon request, Beth read her story: "Well, this is a story about what me and my brothers do at home, play rockets and things like that."

The processes Beth used in writing her story share much in common with those of older authors whose finished texts appear more conventional. Beth has truly constructed meanings in the course of this experience. She is not merely transcribing images from her linguistic and visual stores onto the paper. Like adult authors (e.g., Eisner 1982; Graves 1984), Beth experiences the influence of the already produced work on subsequent meanings. Her decision to abandon writing Jeff's name has the effect of eliminating his picture as well!

We are fortunate that Beth gives us so many clues to her meaning-making processes. Her spontaneous verbalizations serve both a social and a personal function. At times she directs her comments to the adult researcher to clarify and extend her work, as in her comment, "I can write my name another way." This serves to share her newest discovery about language with us (i.e., *Beth* and *BEth* both spell "Beth"), and to clarify her intentions in writing her name twice. Language also serves to fill in details that are not signed in the text, such as the fact that *David Dansberger* is the author's brother. At other times, her comments seem to accompany the realization that her product is not meeting her intentions and needs to be revised. Though many researchers (e.g., Piaget 1976; Vygotsky 1962; Hakes 1980) have suggested that 5-year-olds have limited metalinguistic awareness, Beth seems to us to demonstrate many of the same kinds of awarenesses of both language features and processes that are observed in adult writers. All of us have muttered to ourselves, "That doesn't look right," as we have attempted a difficult spelling or tried to address a difficult concept. And whether or not our "Oops!" has been expressed aloud, we have also experienced the necessity of deleting an idea because it did not fit well in the current text.

Beth also uses other strategies that demonstrate her engagement in authoring. First, she shows that she understands and uses "keep-going" strategies. By this we mean that she keeps foremost in her mind the task of getting the meaning down and refuses to get hopelessly sidetracked in details. While dissatisfaction with her 5 leads her momentarily to test several ways of creating a more pleasing symbol, after a few tries she returns to the main task of writing her story. She marks this decision with a shrug that seems to mean, "I'll have to return to that later." In any case, at age 5, Beth has discovered a "keep-going" strategy also used by adult authors.

The second strategy Beth demonstrates is the orchestration of alternate communication systems to produce a message. She creates a unified meaning using written language, oral language, art, and math. Her first act is to use art to produce the setting for her story—"home." She then deftly identifies herself using written language and the mathematical symbol "5," and uses writing and drawing to identify her brother. Finally Beth completes her story by combining mathematical symbols to stand for the countdown, with a swirl of energetic drawing to represent the rocket's blast-off. Her story, though scripted unconventionally from an adult perspective, was created using components of a well-formed story—setting, characters, attempt, and so on (Stein & Glenn 1978).

Actually, children like Beth have forced us to see that there is never a "pure" act of reading or writing even for adults. Writing always involves some amount of reading during production, and reading always involves speaking and listening to either real or imagined audiences. Beth and children like her demonstrate to us that alternate communication systems such as language, art, drama, math, and music are commonly combined to create meaning. After all, how frequently do adults' written texts include drawings, diagrams, or photographs? How often do television commercials include drama, art, and written and oral language? We propose that children, too, see the potential usefulness of combining these various communication systems. After all, each is a way to "mean." For us as adults this recognition comes harder, probably because we were taught to see each system as a separate "subject" in school. But most successful communicators have rediscovered the power of using alternate communication systems (or have hired advertising agencies or editors to do this for them).

To sum up, we have seen that Beth creates meanings as she writes. She uses this literacy event to test her current language hypotheses. She uses the social aspects of language to support and elaborate her story, and the personal aspects to express awareness of her own language products and processes. This awareness allows her to self-correct and to direct the subsequent course of her story. It allows her to shift stances from actually communicating to thinking about communicating. She uses "keep-going" strategies and approaches the task of story writing as a multimodal event. She orchestrates art, oral language, written language, and math to produce a unified meaning. Beth has taken ownership of the literacy process. Beth is an author.

The Authoring Cycle as a Learning Cycle

Authoring is a form of learning. As we use language, art, or drama to communicate ideas, the process of working with the words, paints, or gestures allows us to construct and generate meanings for ourselves as well as for others. As Elliot Eisner (1982) has commented, "the demands of the occasion motivate the creation" (p. 52). Literacy is a process of outgrowing our current selves to solve our communicative problems. Reading and writing are transactions whereby language users begin with concepts and beliefs, but in the process free themselves from what they presently think, feel, and perceive. The same is true for other forms of literacy.

In the writing process, authors often produce multiple, mental drafts even before they begin the document that is usually considered the first rough draft. Some researchers (e.g., Donaldson 1978) believe that forms of authoring that actually produce lasting traces are especially important in the learning process because they allow us to work analytically on our present understandings. For example, as readers of our own writing or the writing of others we can check the logic, fine-tune the message, or even overcode the message with yet another layer of meaning. When we write, the text is never wholly conceived beforehand. The authoring process allows us not only to clarify and add details but also to produce an interim text that serves as the basis for forming new ideas and discovering new connections between existing ideas. In a real sense, through reading and writing we often outgrow both the author and ourselves—gaining a new understanding in the process. We would argue that the element of the authoring process that is most important for learning is not meaning maintenance, but meaning generation.

We have used the diagram seen in Figure 1.4 to depict the authoring cycle as a model for curriculum (Harste, Woodward & Burke 1984). Learners bring to the cycle a stock of life experiences that are the basis for engaging in personally meaningful communicative events. The oval that surrounds the cycle represents the situational context in which all instances of authoring are embedded, and the activities listed outside the oval represent the multitude of culture-specific contexts in which literacy events can be enacted.

The path of the cycle crisscrosses between the alternate communication systems of language, art, drama, music, and math. This is a recognition that both authoring and learning are multimodal processes and that authors shift stances from reader to writer to artist to speaker and so on. As authors move between communi-

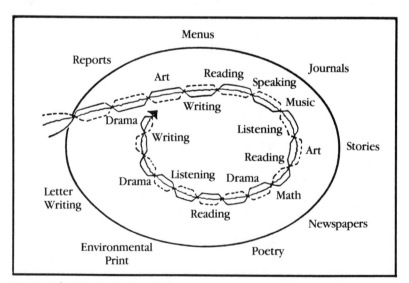

Figure 1.4   The Authoring Cycle.

cation systems they are able to expand the range of meanings they can express. Eisner (1982) has cogently reminded us that "not everything can be said through anything" (p. 49). Communication systems have varying potentials to express particular ideas. If we encourage only those forms of communication that highlight language, many types of meanings will necessarily be neglected because they simply are not amenable to linguistic expression. Attempts to express messages in alternate media also encourage authors to generate new meanings and to expand existing ones because learners are required to take a new psychological stance toward their knowledge. They are encouraged to reflect on their concepts in the process of inventing forms to express them. A final aspect of the cycle depicted in this diagram is the regenerative nature of authoring. Neither authoring nor learning is seen as having an end point. When meanings are expressed or created, they metaphorically become fuel for the next cycle. On the basis of our current understandings, we approach tomorrow's communication events.

In the following subsections, we will list and briefly discuss some principles that are most important for guiding curricular decisions. Because we believe that authoring creates important opportunities for learning, we will argue that curricula should be designed to provide supportive environments in which the strategies of successful authoring can be experienced, demonstrated, and valued. We will also describe some of our experiences in designing and implementing such a curriculum for children.

Experiencing Authorship

To experience authorship, children must have multiple opportunities to engage in activities such as reading, writing, drawing, drama, and math for a variety of reasons each day in the classroom. Because we can learn a process only through engagement in that process, the opportunities and activities we provide are important.

1. *Activities should be functional.* Because communication is learned through use and authoring is motivated by the need to "mean," students should feel they are communicating for real purposes. If children engage in a muted form of the process, they come to understand what literacy is like under such conditions. Often "school literacy" is something quite different from "real literacy." It ought not to be. Functional activities allow children to experience literacy as it occurs in the world outside school. This

means that we have to provide children ample opportunities to use writing and drawing to organize their thinking as well as to use reading, writing, and drawing to get things done. For example, we need to provide opportunities for children to communicate with absent friends and parents, to send notes to their teachers and classmates, and to create signs used in the classroom. When children understand the purpose of communicating, they are motivated to author their own texts. They also learn how literacy may be used as a form of social action.

2. *Activities should encourage social interaction.* Learning is a socio-psycholinguistic event. Vygotsky (1978) helped us understand that learning begins in social interaction and that these social processes become internalized and determine our thinking processes. Through an exchange of meanings in conversation we begin to explain things to ourselves and to clarify our thinking. As we experience the perspectives of others, we extend and elaborate our current notions. In addition, social interaction serves as an important source of ideas and assistance with authoring problems. Reading and writing only look like private, silent acts. In actuality, real readers and writers argue with themselves and others both alone and in public. What was external becomes internal. Literacy in alternate systems is learned in the same way. For example, artists also argue with themselves and others about the meanings they are creating through art.

3. *Activities should be rich in texts and contexts.* Students should have opportunities to experience a variety of forms of communication under a variety of circumstances. Because different communication systems are used to express different concepts, the authoring cycle must be multimodal. And because learning is largely context-specific, authoring should occur in a variety of culturally relevant settings. For example, students should be presented with opportunities to experience both public communication (where the product is meant for formal presentation to others) and private communication (where the audience is the author).

4. *Activities should encourage transmediation.* Transmediation occurs when meanings formed in one communication system are moved to an alternate communication system (e.g., from reading to art). Knowledge is recast in a new form of expression. This process of recasting our knowing is the essence of literacy. Through transmediation students are provided the opportunity to reflect consciously on their concepts (Eisner 1982) and to elaborate and form new connections between existing concepts (Siegel 1984).

5. *Activities should link conventional forms to their functions in different communicative tasks.* Students should always focus first on getting their meanings down. Activities should highlight the distinction between the production of public documents that require careful attention to conventional form, and private documents—such as rough drafts, notes, sketches, and informal class assignments—where such attention is of secondary importance. Students should recognize that the importance of convention varies with the communication system and context involved. Second, activities should help students recognize conventions as social agreements among communicators in a particular setting. For example, students should come to recognize that we have made a social agreement that letters will open with *Dear Aunt Jane* and stories with *Once upon a time,* and that books are closed with *The End,* but phone conversations are ended with *Good-bye.* Students should also come to understand that conventions change from one location to another and across time. In curricular activities, convention should not be confused with communication.

6. *Activities should provide a variety of audiences for authors.* Children need audiences other than the teacher and themselves (Barnes 1975). They need the opportunity to explain their ideas to others who do not understand the concepts they are presenting. Addressing different audiences has the potential for encouraging authors to become aware of their own thinking and also of their communication strategies.

7. *Activities should allow learners to explore the complexity of natural communication.* It seems logical that limiting the complexity of literacy demonstrations would aid children's literacy learning. But although making things simple may help children master a particular rule quickly, this type of instruction does little to help children understand and use communication systems in the complex interactive contexts they encounter outside school. As amazing as it is, even very young children are able to build knowledge of a complex world by interacting with others in meaningful contexts. Literacy learning is no exception. Children are capable of monitoring and directing their own literacy learning when they have many opportunities to encounter literacy used in familiar situations (Rowe 1986). The complexity of literacy actually supports this learning. For example, the multimodal nature of literacy provides multiple entry points for understanding messages and for learning about literacy. When children have opportunities to experience natural communication, they are able to form hypotheses that reflect its irregularity as well as its systematicity.

Because learning is context-specific, children need opportunities to experience literacy as it occurs in nonschool settings.

Demonstrating Authorship

Classrooms must be places where children can see the strategies of successful communication demonstrated. In instructional activities, children should be free to select and attend to the demonstrations for which they are ready. Demonstrating is not modeling. A careful look at those instances of learning that some people call modeling will reveal that the child has not imitated or modeled everything present. Learners, even very young learners, are selective. They imitate or model some dimensions of what they see, but not others. This suggests that they are actively deciding what they will attend to in a literacy event. If language was "modeled," children would imitate or model *all* features of their language encounters. Instead, they select particular aspects to incorporate when constructing their own rules of language comprehension and production. This is equally true for learning in other communication systems. For example, very young children's drawings of the human figure have the characteristic "tadpole" shape not because the children are deficient in their ability to copy a model, but because they have selected only some aspects of the model for inclusion in their graphic sign for the human figure (Arnheim 1954).

From Smith (1982) we learn that any literacy event provides a complex set of demonstrations. For example, in seeing their parents read a newspaper, children see many things demonstrated, such as how to turn pages, what things to read first, and when and where one reads newspapers. If adults read or talk to children about the content of the paper, children may see demonstrations that newspapers contain information about what interesting things are happening in the world, what is going to be on television, and what is on sale in the stores. Children in environments where music, drama, art, or math are used for real purposes also have access to demonstrations of the potentials of these media for communication. Attention to demonstrations is generative. It is a means of learning how something *might* be done, rather than how it *must* be done (Gardner 1980; Smith 1982). It is a means of exploring the potentials of the various communication systems for meeting personal and social goals.

1. *Activities should be open-ended so that children are free to choose which demonstrations they will attend to in a particular*

activity. Open-ended activities allow children to enter and exit at their own level of interest and involvement. No one attends to all the demonstrations that are present in a communicative event. Because of cognitive limits, only a selected number of demonstrations can be attended to at any given moment. Which demonstrations are selected is a function of experience and interest, given the potentials inherent in an instance of language, art, math, music, or drama in use. In the classroom, although teachers and children participate in the same activity, their attention will likely be focused on different aspects of the event. Even though teachers may specifically plan activities to highlight particular features or processes of literacy, children must be given the choice to focus on those demonstrations they find interesting. Teachers must not only accept the right of children to attend to things they find interesting, but also realize that learning occurs through this process of relating current demonstrations to existing hypotheses. The child's readiness is never an issue with open-ended activities. The real issue is whether we, as teachers, can accept and value varying responses.

2. *Activities should be presented as invitations.* Choice is central in curriculum because students test different hypotheses according to their different needs, interests, and experiences. Children should be invited rather than forced to engage in specific literacy activities. When authors retain ownership of the process, they are more likely to focus their efforts on meaning generation rather than solely on meaning maintenance.

3. *Teachers and other adults should engage in the same communicative activities in which they ask children to engage.* When teachers and other adults engage in the same activities in which they ask their students to participate, they provide demonstrations of the strategies of successful readers, writers, and artists. They also demonstrate the kinds of problems faced by adult authors and how those problems are solved. Teachers gain, too, in that they share literacy experiences with their students. Adults engaging in these activities learn how the "real curriculum" of firsthand experiences relates to the "planned curriculum"; this understanding facilitates curriculum development. Because it is important that children see the strategies of successful written language use and learning demonstrated, teachers should consider inviting parents, administrators, professional authors, and others to involve themselves in the classroom on a regular basis.

4. *Children should be given opportunities to learn from one another.* Literacy and literacy learning are social events. Authors

have different strengths and areas of expertise. As children watch each other and talk together about their work, they provide important demonstrations for one another. The opportunity must therefore be provided for children to read together, write together, and learn from one another. Authors in all media support one another by talking together and reacting to rough drafts, whether the product is a storybook, a speech, or a painting. Teachers need to set up their classrooms so that children rely on their own personal and social resources rather than solely on the teacher. When they use their own support networks, children develop cooperative social patterns that are likely to be functional outside school. Most learners will always have a network of peers willing to react to their ideas, but the continual presence of a teacher is less certain.

Valuing Authorship

In our research, we found that young children, before instruction, have proficient literacy strategies (Harste, Woodward & Burke 1984). We also found that after only 20 days of phonics instruction, all too many of these successful language users were willing to exchange their strategies for the ones taught in school. If what learners know is not valued, that knowledge will atrophy. This is as true for adults as it is for children.

1. *Opportunities should be available for discussion and interaction.* Group sharing times allow authors to share their creations and to discuss the problems they faced and the strategies they used to surmount them. Discussions should center around how they *used* language, art, math, and so on; what they learned about the communication system itself; and what they learned through its use. Teachers can suggest that good ideas be tried by others the next time they read, write, draw, act, or create a tune. Teachers, too, should discuss their own problems in creating or responding to a text, along with the processes they used to solve them.

2. *Children's work should be treated as the "real" thing.* If teachers introduce only published works, children will learn that their own writing, drawing, or tunes are not the "real" thing. Teachers can solve this problem by sharing children's work during *Author Sharing Times* (see Chapter 3) or by using one of the children's texts as the focus for other activities. Celebrating authors and authorship through publication, plays, exhibitions, and readings should be an integral part of the daily class routine.

3. *Children should be helped to value literacy and the work of authoring.* If children come to the classroom having had few

opportunities to test their own hypotheses, they will need encouragement in getting started. Little things make a difference. A kind word or a note from the teacher complimenting students for discussing their understandings of a story with friends legitimizes these attempts and clarifies for the children what attitudes and actions are encouraged and valued in the classroom. For example, sometimes children will feel that it is cheating to use the illustrations in a picture book to aid comprehension during reading. This attitude has been learned. A word of encouragement can let them know the teacher understands that these are legitimate cues in reading, and that "meaning" in a picture book is allocated among multiple systems. Through discussion, children come to re-value old strategies and to evaluate their own learning in terms of how the different communication systems operate in their personal system of learning.

4. *Teachers should expect and value variation in responses.* If authoring is truly constructive, variation in both processes and products will be the norm. Because children have different cultural and instructional histories, they will approach the task of authoring differently. They will form different concepts and attend to different demonstrations. If the authoring cycle is to be successful as a curricular model, the diversity that results when individuals truly engage in the authoring process must be celebrated and valued.

5. *"Rough draft" thinking and communicating should be respected.* Writing, like oral reading and drawing, leaves the language user vulnerable in that the visible trail it produces is often abused. It is very easy to intimidate learners. On the other hand, we have much to learn about how to support them. Teachers can start by respecting in-process thinking as much as they do final efforts. The classroom should provide an open and supportive environment in which students feel free to explore their newest ideas with peers and teachers (Barnes 1975). If students feel pressure to present only fully formed ideas, they will be unlikely to take the risk of exploring creative solutions to problems. Further, there is a need for "rough draft" interpretation as well as "rough draft" expression; that is, authors need the freedom to construct tentative meanings from the art, written texts, and music of others just as much as they require freedom to produce successive drafts of their own drawings, stories, or songs. When "rough draft" thinking is combined with social interaction, authors have the maximum opportunity to encounter new perspectives on their work and to clarify and develop their understandings.

Occasionally children should be asked to compare various drafts of their pieces to document their own growth. If reading, writing, drama, art, and so on are presented as tools for learning, documenting the changes in these processes is an important criterion for success in the classroom.

6. *A wide variety of types of authorship should be expected and respected.* There are many forms of authorship. As Eisner (1982) points out, students are unlikely to be fooled into believing that alternate literacies are valued and valuable if the school segregates and confines them to a brief period each week such as is now generally done with music, art, and movement. Students should be encouraged to use a variety of communication forms to express themselves in all "subject" areas. Instead of everyone giving an oral presentation or written report on a certain topic, students can express their understandings through drama, art, music, movement, and so on. The choice of alternate communication systems should be respected, as should the more traditional choice of language as a mode of expression.

7. *Activities should be regenerative.* Activities should encourage students to review and revise past ideas and past products. As suggested earlier, the most fruitful learning comes when students are encouraged to re-engage in the authoring process on repeated occasions to expand and revise earlier hypotheses and conclusions.

The Authoring Cycle in Action

We have attempted in the preceding sections to build a notion of authorship that entails both expressive and interpretive modes of communication and encompasses not only language but also art, movement, drama, music, and math. We have described the authoring cycle as a model for curriculum and listed some of the principles we believe are most important for guiding curricular decisions. What remains to be done, then, is to provide some real-life examples of the authoring cycle in action. Our aim in the next section is to present the general features of the authoring cycle by describing a series of curricular events we (Deborah Rowe and Kathy Short) helped to plan and implement in a summer school program that based its curriculum on the authoring cycle. We will also demonstrate how the authoring cycle functions as a learning cycle for students and teachers alike, using as an example Gloria Kauffman's first-grade classroom where Kathy Short (1986) participated as a researcher and teacher.

A Publishing Cycle

Figure 1.5 demonstrates one way the authoring cycle can be implemented in a publishing program. This activity cycle (Burke 1984) had been developed through our experiences working with students and has benefited immeasurably from our collaborative relationships with several excellent teachers who have implemented and revised this model to fit their classroom needs. We want to stress at the outset that, like learning, curriculum is context-specific; it must be modified to address the needs of teachers and students in particular situations.

Briefly, we start the cycle by announcing that the students will be publishing a newspaper, magazine, or book, and that everyone can participate as an author or editor or both. During the first

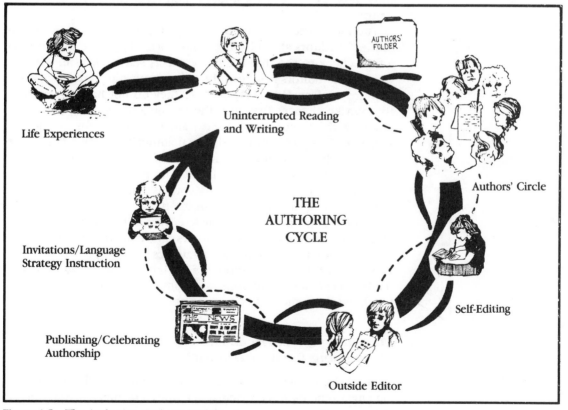

Figure 1.5   The Authoring Cycle: Publishing.

weeks of school students engage in uninterrupted reading and writing activities. As they write, they place their work in their *Author's Folders*. When several students have pieces they want to publish, they gather in small groups we call *Authors' Circles;* only teachers and students who would like reactions to a piece participate. Of course, this implies that teachers have been writing, too. Each author reads his or her piece aloud and receives feedback on its content. Meaning is the focus of the Authors' Circle. Concerns about conventional form (spelling, punctuation, and so on) are left for later periods of editing.

After receiving feedback, authors usually engage in revision and self-editing. They may respond directly to their listeners' comments, but because they maintain ownership of their piece they need not follow suggestions. After revision and self-editing, if authors still want to publish their pieces, they put them in the editors' box, to be read by students and teachers acting as outside editors.

The job of the outside editors is patterned after the responsibilities of editors at publishing companies. They serve primarily as a final check to see that the piece makes sense and is in conventional form. Editors first read the text for meaning, marking points that are unclear. However, because they do not have the authority to make changes that alter the meaning of the text, they must confer with the author to discuss any suggestions for changes in meaning. This gives authors the final authority to make (or refuse to make) changes that affect the sense of their pieces. When these changes have been negotiated, the editors make routine corrections in conventional form, just as a professional copy editor would, before sending the manuscript to the typist. A book manuscript is assembled and bound with sturdy covers; a newspaper or magazine piece is combined with others and copied. The cycle continues as teachers demonstrate strategies that are pertinent to the hypotheses particular children are testing, and begins again as students accept new invitations and continue to write—sometimes for themselves, and sometimes for publication.

Evaluating the Curriculum: "I am aping for the cartonist"

As teachers, we are authors in a special sense—authors of learning environments and curricular activities. Planning curriculum requires creative adaptation of ideas and methods to meet the needs of learners in particular classroom settings. Like other instances of authoring, curriculum planning requires a two-pronged evaluation. First we must examine the fit between our beliefs and intentions and the activities we have planned. Here we ask ourselves whether our plans *provide opportunities* for students to experience authoring firsthand, to see it demonstrated by others, and to value it as a learning process. Second, we must gauge students' responses to the curriculum. Just as readers of written texts create their own understandings of the linguistic structures presented by the author, students construct their own meanings about the learning process during their transactions with curricular activities. The question is whether students are *actually* having the experiences, seeing the demonstrations, and coming to value literacy as we had hoped.

The following episode illustrates how this evaluation process occurred in one curricular setting. This setting was a summer school for students in Grades 1-6 who were experiencing difficulty with reading and writing. As a staff, we decided to publish a school newspaper as one way to encourage and celebrate authorship.

Before the summer program began at School 39, our staff meetings were filled with discussions about the match between our curricular beliefs and the plans we were making. We began this first type of evaluation long before children ever entered the building. However, the most important evaluation of the curriculum could only be made by observing the students' reactions to the authoring cycle in use. We knew we were on the right curricular track one hot summer morning after school had been in session about two weeks, and after the first issue of the newspaper had been distributed. Two second graders rushed up to the big table where we were preparing for the day's editorial board meeting, and almost in unison announced, "We're here to be cartoonists!" As members of the newspaper staff we were pleased, but as teachers we were thrilled. This incident assured us that the publication program was truly allowing students to engage in the authoring cycle.

Figure 1.6 shows two notes received in the editors' mailbox later that day. Obviously, both Bobby and Brian were using authoring as a means of social action; they saw their writing and art as serving important purposes in a specific social situation. They also demonstrated an acute awareness of the form of expression that might be most persuasive when applying for a position as an illustrator. Each included a drawing as evidence of his qualifications for the job. Also, their use of functional spelling indicates an awareness that, in this setting, getting the message down was most

Figure 1.6   Applications for Positions as Cartoonists (Bobby and Brian, Grade 2).

important. Their identical decisions about the form of the notes suggest that writing was a collaborative effort. By themselves these observations are exciting, but the notes also indicated to us that the authoring cycle was succeeding on a more general level.

To explain, we must turn to the first issue of the newspaper. After a week of hard work, the student editors had proudly distributed an 18-page, single-spaced paper, completely filled with stories written about and by the School 39 students and teachers. Like many publications, it was met with enthusiasm tempered by a bit of criticism. The first critical comment we heard was, "Where are the pictures?" In a casual way one of the teachers responded, "Don't talk to us. Send a letter to the editors!" This incident began one of the most exciting (and unplanned) aspects of the publishing program.

Within the day the editors received the note seen in Figure 1.7 from Mai Xia, a sixth grader. When the editorial board met, they talked about the note, its merit, and what actions should be taken. From this meeting grew several decisions. First, the editors posted an advertisement for cartoonists. Second, the board discussed how to respond to Mai Xia's note. Some suggested writing her a note or going to tell her of the board's decision. Following a teacher's suggestion, the editors decided to look at magazines and newspapers to see how other editors handled letters from their readers. They finally settled on a format that published readers' letters followed by the editors' replies. Figure 1.7 also shows the reply drafted by the editors.

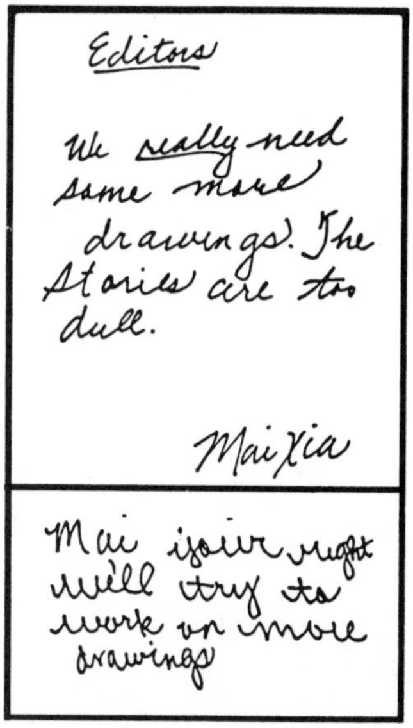
Editors

We really need same more drawngs. The Stories are too dull.

Mai Xia

Mai your right well try to work on more drawings

Figure 1.7 Letter to the Editors (Mai Xia, Grade 6) and Draft of Editors' Reply.

Once word spread that complaints and comments should be sent to the editors, several other notes were received. Keith, a first grader, suggested page numbers (Figure 1.8). But fifth-grader Cathy's irate note concerning an error in the story about her pets provided an even stronger demonstration to the editors of the power of publishing—to please and to displease. Figure 1.9 contains her note and the editors' reply. They read:

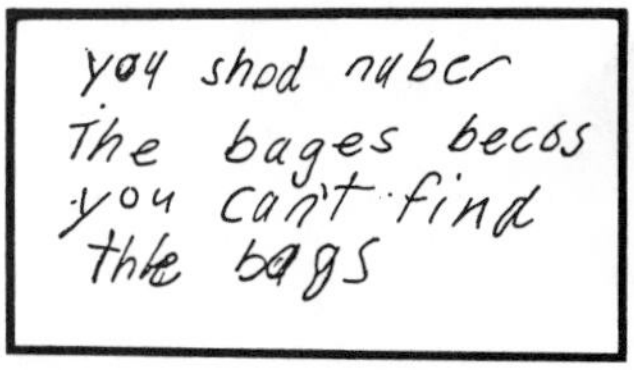
you shod nuber The bages becos you can't find the bags

Figure 1.8 Letter to the Editors (Keith, Grade 1).

Editors The person who edited my story lied. They said I had a parrot instead of [a] ferret. They should have asked me about it. Cathy

Dear Cathy We're sorry about the mistake about the parrot and the ferret. We found out that Cathy really has [a] ferret instead of a parrot. From the Editors

Once the "letters to the editors" phenomenon began, there was no doubt in anyone's mind that the newspaper had a real audience of discriminating readers who demanded not only conventional forms but also accuracy in reporting.

The authoring cycle came full circle when Bobby and Brian applied for the cartoonists' positions. In the course of a real

Editors

The person who editing story lied. They said if had a parrot instead of ferrot. They should have asked me about it

Cathy

Dear Cathy were sorry about the Mistake about the Parrot and the Farrot.
We found out that cathy really has Farrat instead of a parrot,

From the Editors

Figure 1.9   Letter to the Editors (Cathy, Grade 5) and Reply.

literacy event both students and teachers had found it necessary to attend to available demonstrations to make functional decisions about their use of language. They had chosen to issue invitations that would regenerate the cycle and those invitations had been accepted.

A Guided Tour Through an Authoring Cycle with Corey

The authoring cycle also provided the curricular frame that Gloria Kauffman used to organize writing experiences for her first-grade students. In her classroom, children were involved in many different kinds of reading and writing experiences, including personal journals, pen pal letters, the message board, note taking, shared reading, class read-aloud sessions, literature response activities, written stories and reports, and the publication of class books, newspapers, and individual books. Although much of the children's writing was informal and so never went through a revision process, children selected some of their writing to go through the authoring cycle and be published in some way.

To illustrate how the authoring cycle was developed in Gloria's classroom, we will follow one piece of writing through the entire cycle. Corey, the author, was repeating first grade and so began the year with little confidence in his ability as a learner and as a language user. As the year progressed, Corey's confidence in his own learning increased and other children came to admire his work and to borrow ideas from him for their own writing and illustrating.

One day in February, after finishing a story, Corey could not think of any ideas for a new piece. He looked at books in the classroom and talked with others, but still he could not find an idea he liked. Finally he sat down with Gloria, his teacher, and together they generated a list of topics and experiences that he might be able to write about (Figure 1.10).

During the next month, Corey wrote stories based on several of these ideas, as well as on other topics. When, in the middle of March, he again needed a new story idea, he consulted his list of topics in his Author's Folder and decided to write about the time he had "smashed my toe on the door."

Corey quickly produced a short story about his smashed toe

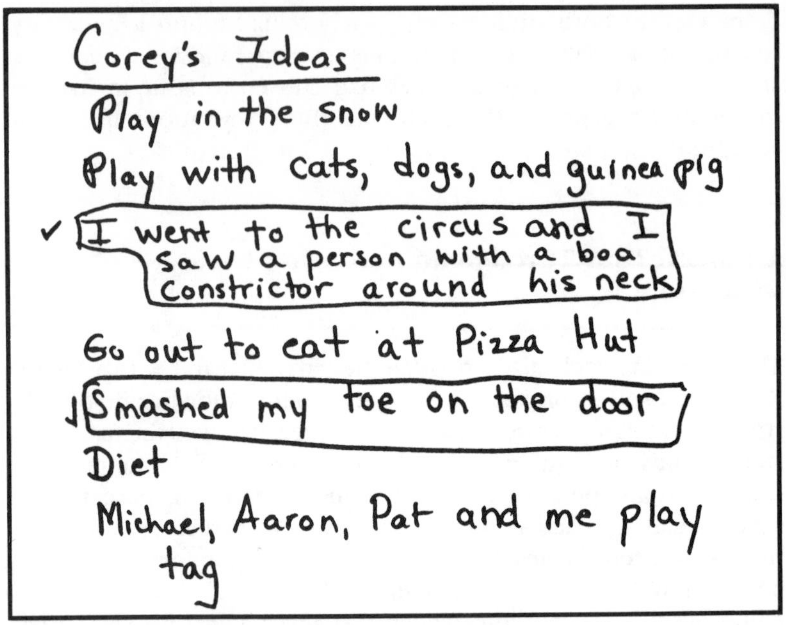

Corey's Ideas
Play in the snow
Play with cats, dogs, and guinea pig
✔ I went to the circus and I saw a person with a boa constrictor around his neck
Go out to eat at Pizza Hut
✔ Smashed my toe on the door
Diet
Michael, Aaron, Pat and me play tag

Figure 1.10   List of Writing Topics (Corey, Grade 1).

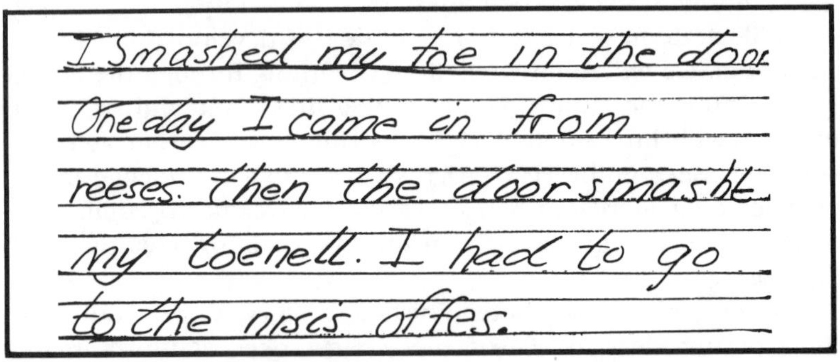

I smashed my toe in the door
One day I came in from
reeses. then the door smasht
my toenell. I had to go
to the nrscs offes.

Figure 1.11   First Draft of "Smashed Toe" Story (Corey, Grade 1).

(Figure 1.11). He took the piece to Gloria, who was informally conferencing with children as they wrote. Gloria read his story and commented that she hadn't known that he had once stubbed his toe and that she would find the story more interesting if he told more about what had happened. Gloria began talking with another child and Corey returned to his desk. He reread his story for a few minutes, then got some paper and began writing.

Corey continued writing on the piece the next day until he had filled three pages (Figure 1.12). He excitedly read his story to

I Smashed my toe in the door

One day I came in from
reeses. then the door smasht
my toenell. I had to go
to the nrsis offes.

I thot. I just spraned my
toe antell I looked at
it? it was bleeting and
it had little bits of
toenell peeses in my .ok.
Wen I saw it. I tried
not to cry "but" I cudet
help it. filly Chuck and

I went down to the nrsis
offes. they called my mom.
My mom came and sied,
what did you do to your
self?and I dident say
inny thing. and then I
had to go home. I had
to have it bandij up for th
munth.

Figure 1.12   Second Draft of "Smashed Toe" Story (Corey, Grade 1).

several children and to Gloria and then put it in the revision box. An Authors' Circle for writers to discuss their pieces with each other would meet as soon as three or four pieces of writing were in the box.

The next day four pieces were in the box, so Gloria met with Corey and the other writers. When it was Corey's turn to share, he read his story aloud to the group. As he read, he realized he wanted to say "Then they called my mom" instead of "They called my mom," so he quickly added the word "then" and continued reading.

After Corey had finished, Jessica commented that she liked the way he described the pieces of toenail stuck in his sock. Sherri added that she liked the way he had said that he tried not to cry but couldn't help it. After the children had commented on what they had heard in his story, they began asking questions about parts that were unclear. "How did it happen that the door hit your toe?" asked Erin. "Well, I was opening the outside door to come in from recess. It started shutting. I was trying to be sneaky and go in the other door when the teacher couldn't see me and it shut on my toe," Corey explained to the group. Sherri suggested that he might want to add how he had gotten home with his mom. Gloria pointed out that the first page didn't make sense to her because he had written about going to the nurse's office and then described the door shutting on his toe. Corey reread his story and realized that he no longer needed the sentence that had been the first ending of his story and so crossed it out. He talked about the revisions he planned to make after the Authors' Circle and decided he would add the part about how the accident happened, but not how he had gotten home.

After he left the Authors' Circle, Corey read through his piece again and added a section about sneaking in the door. He then put the story in the editors' box, but just before it was time to go home he reclaimed his story to write another section describing what had happened when his mom took him home. He decided he wanted more feedback on his story because he had made so many changes, so he put his piece back in the revision box (Figure 1.13).

The next day, Corey again met in an Authors' Circle. As he read his story aloud to the group, he realized that he had written "she could carry my" when he meant "she could carry me," and that he wanted his story to end with "I haven't broke my toenail," not "I have broke my toenail." After he made these changes, the other authors in the group commented on what they had heard as they listened to his story, and then Sheila asked him why he had written this story. "I wanted to remember it all the time," he responded. Amy said that she was confused by the part about "two months." "It should be at a different place in the story," she commented. Gloria

I smashed my toe in the door
One day I came in from
reeses. then the door smasht
my toenell. ~~I had to go~~
~~to the nrics office.~~
I was going to sneek
in the ather door wen
it hit my toenell.

I thot I just spraned my
toe antell I looked at
it? it was blecting and
it had little buts of
toenell peeses in my sk.
Wen I saw it I tried
not to cry "but" I cudet
help it. filly Chuck and

(continued)

Figure 1.13   Third Draft of "Smashed Toe" Story (Corey, Grade 1).

I went down to the nrsis offes. ~~they~~ then →they called my mom. My mom came and sied, what did you do to your self? and I diden't say inny thang. and then I had to go home.*(I had to have it bandij up for tu ~~munth.~~)

I was borl so she cod cary me. Wen my brother and sister got back from school they "ased" what hapedpind. I "sead" I hart my toe on the door. *
One day my toenell gruy back again. after that I haveen't broke my toenell agan. the end.
March 19
By Corey F.

Figure 1.13 *Continued*

30

pointed out that this was where he had ended the story before, and suggested that he might either cross it out or move it if he didn't think it made sense. Corey decided to move this sentence to a position just before the section describing his toenail growing back. He also decided that he did not want to make any other changes in his story and that he wanted to get it published, so he placed it in the editors' box.

The story was edited for meaning and conventions such as spelling and punctuation by an outside editor. Each week, three children from the classroom served as outside editors for any pieces submitted that week for publication. After editing, the story was then typed by a parent volunteer and returned to Corey. He cut his story apart according to what he wanted on each page and glued the parts into a book. The next step was for Corey to work on his illustrations. Illustrating his published books was an important part of the cycle for Corey, and he often spent a great deal of time creating pictures that extended his story. His illustrations were usually brightly colored and filled the entire page. Other children in the room admired his illustrating style and emulated it in their own books. For this book, Corey tried a new art medium, using colored pencils rather than crayons.

After Corey had illustrated his story, he read his finished book (Figure 1.14) to the entire group during the class read-aloud time. They responded by telling him their favorite parts and asking questions about how he had written it and what he liked about it. This was a time of celebration as Corey proudly presented his book to the class. After this, the book went into the classroom library for the rest of the school year, and children often read it during their shared reading time.

Following the publication of this book, we talked with Corey about the processes he had used to extend his story and make it more interesting for others to read. We chose to focus on this aspect of his experience because we felt it had the most potential for pushing him to grow as a writer. However, we could have also explored the function of quotation marks or question marks with him. This strategy lesson was intended to help Corey reflect on the processes he had used in authoring the "smashed toenail" book so that he would become aware of writing strategies he could use in later experiences.

As this example illustrates, the authoring cycle provided a framework that children in Gloria's classroom used to guide their activities as they authored their own books. It allowed them to connect their life experiences with their school experiences. During many

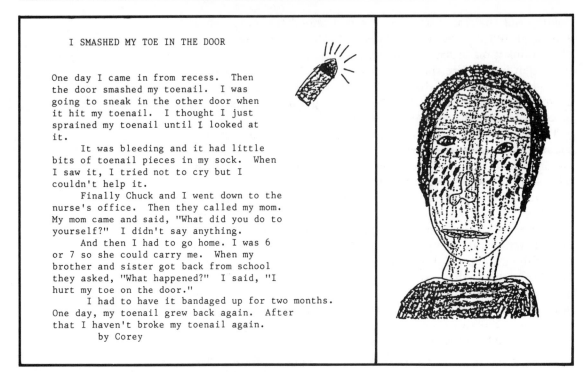

I SMASHED MY TOE IN THE DOOR

One day I came in from recess. Then
the door smashed my toenail. I was
going to sneak in the other door when
it hit my toenail. I thought I just
sprained my toenail until I looked at
it.
     It was bleeding and it had little
bits of toenail pieces in my sock. When
I saw it, I tried not to cry but I
couldn't help it.
     Finally Chuck and I went down to the
nurse's office. Then they called my mom.
My mom came and said, "What did you do to
yourself?" I didn't say anything.
     And then I had to go home. I was 6
or 7 so she could carry me. When my
brother and sister got back from school
they asked, "What happened?" I said, "I
hurt my toe on the door."
     I had to have it bandaged up for two months.
One day, my toenail grew back again. After
that I haven't broke my toenail again.
          by Corey

Figure 1.14   Published Version of "Smashed Toe" Story (Corey, Grade 1).

periods of uninterrupted writing and reading, they wrote for both private and public purposes and chose some of their public documents to be rethought and revised in order to be published for others to read. As they shared their stories with others through informal interactions and Authors' Circles, the children shifted from taking the perspective of an author to taking the perspective of reader and critic. These shifts occurred as they read their pieces aloud and listened to the comments other authors made about their stories. As children became aware of their audience, they were able to see their writing in a different light.

The presence of an outside editor at the end of the cycle helped children put aside concerns about convention until later in the cycle and to focus, instead, on meaning. Because conventions exist to support readers, not writers, it was important that the editors were outside readers, rather than the authors who already knew what their pieces said. The celebration of authorship created a purpose for publication. Children saw others reading the books they had written, and their work took on new importance. The opportunity to reflect on their learning processes during and after writing helped them to gain greater control and understanding of their writing processes so they could continue to grow and to push themselves as authors.

Extending the Cycle to Reading, Art, and Units of Study

Originally the authoring cycle served only as a framework for the writing curriculum in Gloria's classroom. As we worked together, however, we came to see the authoring cycle as a general framework for curriculum, and to see authoring as a metaphor for a more general process of meaning construction that occurs regardless of the communication system or field of study involved. Several examples illustrating these insights are presented below (see Figure 1.15).

For a month Gloria and the children had been exploring a unit on fairy tales. The children had read and listened to many different fairy tales and had created dramas, murals, dioramas, and other pieces of art related to these stories. Some children had begun using the fairy-tale form in their writing. In this unit, the children

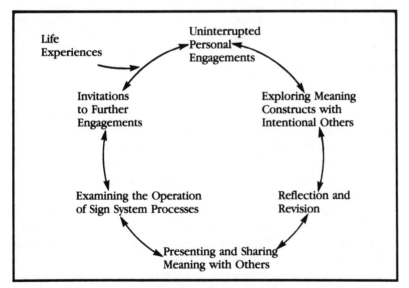

Figure 1.15 The Authoring Cycle: A Curricular Framework (Short & Burke 1988).

had been involved in many extensive reading experiences; that is, they had read widely from the fairy-tale genre. But they also had intensive reading experiences with some of the folktales during whole-class book discussions and small-group book discussions, called *Literature Circles*. Each week children could sign up for one of four folktales that they wanted to explore with others in a small group. The Literature Circles usually lasted two or three days. These intensive reading experiences gave children the opportunity to examine their understandings closely and to negotiate the meanings they were constructing from reading fairy tales.

The potential of intensive reading experiences to generate new literacy knowledge is illustrated by a Literature Circle in Gloria's classroom on the folktale about Hansel and Gretel. As the discussion of this folktale progressed, one of the children, Pat, suddenly came up with the idea that the witch was actually the stepmother in disguise. In response to Gloria's skeptical request that he support this interpretation, he pointed out that after the children had killed the witch and returned home, they found out that the stepmother had died while they were gone. Several other children agreed with Pat, and pointed out that the witch was "weird." She did not act or look like a witch, and the children felt that this was further evidence that she wasn't a witch, but the stepmother in disguise. They pointed out that witches are magic and that when a witch touches you, something is supposed to happen to you. The witch touched both Hansel and Gretel, but nothing had happened to them. Another source of this interpretation was the story of Snow White, which had been read aloud to the class a week earlier.

The entire group, including Gloria, excitedly explored this alternative interpretation of the Hansel and Gretel story. Several months later in another discussion, Pat proudly referred back to this Literature Circle by talking about "my idea" of the witch.

In this Literature Circle, Pat and the other participants authored a new interpretation for a familiar story and continued to celebrate that meaning in later classroom experiences. As this episode illustrates, the role of Literature Circles in the reading process was similar to the role of Authors' Circles in the writing process. Both helped children share and revise meanings they had authored—whether the meanings had been constructed through reading the texts of others or through writing their own texts.

In this classroom, the teachers and children also valued texts authored in other communication systems, as demonstrated by a group of children who explored space and rockets. After looking at books and talking together, several of the children began using their knowledge of rockets to make paper rockets. All but Aaron used the same process of paper folding and gluing in their rocket constructions. While they all had used a paper cylinder for the rocket body, Aaron had devised a different way to fold and attach fins to the rocket body than the other boys. When they met together to share their "rough draft" rockets, the other boys made fun of Aaron's rocket, which looked different from theirs. Aaron, however, explained why and how he was making his rocket, and as he talked, the other boys realized that he had some good ideas. Following their Authors' Circle on the rocket constructions, the other boys made modifications in their rockets. The finished products later became part of a classroom display about space. Although the boys in this example were using paper sculptures rather than language to construct meaning, their progress through the authoring cycle is similar to the events that occurred as Corey worked to draft, discuss, revise, edit, and eventually publish his "smashed toe" book.

In addition to using the authoring cycle to construct meaning in a variety of communication systems, the children in Gloria's classroom also used the authoring cycle to construct meaning in units of study. For example, in a unit on dinosaurs, a small group of children was involved in many uninterrupted experiences with reading and writing about dinosaurs as well as in constructing art projects such as murals, dioramas, and milk carton sculptures, and in composing a song about dinosaurs. Some of these constructions never went beyond the "rough draft" stage, but others were shared and revised so that they could be formally presented to the class. These presentations included displays, published books, and oral presentations to other members of the class. In this event, the children's understandings about dinosaurs were first explored widely through many communication systems. These understandings were then shared and explored intensively with others so that they could be revised and publicly presented to the rest of the class. The cycle that the group moved through in the exploration of dinosaurs was discussed and became, for the children, an important demonstration of how they might explore their own units of study.

These experiences with authoring through writing, reading, art, and units of study allowed us to see the authoring cycle as a general framework for curriculum and to expand our definition of authoring. We observed that, regardless of the communication system involved, we had (1) constructed meaning from our experiences, (2) engaged in many uninterrupted attempts to construct meaning, (3) informally explored and negotiated some of our constructions with others, (4) revised and reflected on our constructions, (5) shared and presented our authoring to others in a public form, (6) examined through reflection the processes we used to construct meaning and (7) moved ahead to accept new invitations to form still other texts. Both children and teachers came to see these activities as a *learning cycle,* not just a *writing cycle* (see Figure 1.15).

Conclusion

In this chapter, reading and writing, together with alternate communication systems such as art, drama, and dance, have been proposed as the core of curriculum. By using the authoring cycle as an organizational frame for social studies, science, math, and the other content areas, these media become vehicles for learning rather than objects of study in their own right.

How we, as educators, conceptualize education and literacy is important. Similarly, *how* we teach determines *what* we teach. As a curricular frame, the authoring cycle represents an attempt to orchestrate the how and what of teaching, so that children can experience mental trips associated with using literacy as a vehicle for exploring and expanding their world. In the instructional settings we have described, the authoring cycle was implemented through activities that were functional, social, and rich in texts and contexts. Over time, these activities encouraged expression of meanings in alternate communication systems and provided a strong sense of audience for authors, editors, readers, and listeners. They provided chances for students to focus on meaning in the creation of texts and on convention when and if they decided to publish their work. Conversations in the Authors' Circles and elsewhere allowed students the freedom to explore their "rough draft" ideas with others and to seek demonstrations of how problems were solved by others. And, perhaps most exciting, as students took ownership of the publishing program and the research projects, they joined teachers in issuing invitations to participate in the cycle. The authoring cycle, as implemented in these programs, was truly regenerative. It provided students and teachers with rich experiences in authoring—and in learning. Demonstrations of successful authoring were abundant. These classrooms sent the message that risk taking and active engagement were valued. In the authoring cycle, learning is what literacy is all about.

An understanding of the active nature of communication helps us clarify its role in the learning process and design activities that allow the natural richness of communicative events to support and motivate learning. When children see authoring as a central experience, they develop functional notions of what it means to be literate. Through participation in a wide variety of literacy events they come to experience both the meaning maintenance and meaning generation potentials of the various communication systems. As they shift stances from listener to speaker, to reader, to writer, to artist, to actor, students come to view their knowledge and the communication systems themselves in a new way.

The authoring process is a fundamental part of the learning process. Moreover, when a broad definition of *author* is used, the relation of learning and authoring is closer to synonym than metaphor. Thus, it is important to acknowledge the central role of communication in curriculum. We have presented the authoring cycle as one curricular model that celebrates authors and authorship. As teachers, it is our responsibility to plan and implement curricular activities in which students can experience authoring as the construction of new meanings and the reorganization of existing ones. To do this we must provide invitations for children to engage in literacy events along with many demonstrations of the strategies used by successful authors. Finally, throughout the curriculum, the message must be clear that authoring is valued, and that even very young students are truly respected as authors. The authoring cycle is a curricular model that puts the responsibility and ownership of authoring—and learning, for that matter—in the hands of *students*. We believe this is theoretically sound given what we now know about the role of reading and writing in the learning process.

Teaching as Curriculum Development

Mary Lynn Woods

Introduction

Over an 11-year period I had taught fourth graders, fifth graders, preschoolers, remedial readers, and preservice and inservice teachers. During the course of those years I had implemented a wide variety of programs by essentially following the manual. Curriculum, for me, was a course of study. At best I altered these prepackaged programs to reflect my beliefs about curriculum by adding creative touches—a special unit of study here, a language experience activity there. I was considered a good teacher yet, not surprisingly, I felt unsatisfied.

Deep down I believed that teaching ought to provide meaningful learning experiences that invited students to assume responsibility for and ownership of learning. I saw my role as supporting the learning process. In my mind the curriculum packages I had used did not seem to foster self-motivated learning.

In the spring of 1981 the Eagle-Union School Board decided to initiate a summer school program for students needing remedial work in reading and mathematics. Because I was, at the time, Director of Chapter 1, I was approached and asked to develop a curriculum for that program. I decided to develop a curriculum that better reflected what I believed.

During the school year I had taken a graduate course on reading comprehension with Dr. Jerome Harste. Building on my understanding of the relationship between reading, writing, and reasoning, I proposed a summer course of study entitled WRITE (Writing Reading Intuitive Thinking Experiences). My intent was to use this opportunity to explore the potential of a comprehensive language arts curriculum as well as to identify new instructional strategies that supported children using reading and writing to learn.

Dr. Carolyn Burke asked me if the WRITE program might be a field site for a graduate level practicum being offered at Indiana University. I agreed. I told her I planned to develop an innovative program that her students would find beneficial. What I did not know at the time was that I would gain far more from the bargain than I had originally envisioned.

That first summer nineteen children, Grades 1-8, enrolled in the program. Carolyn and I agreed on a set of goals: (1) to teach reading and writing as process-oriented events; (2) to design strategies that did not fragment language; and (3) to generate a curriculum that involved students, teachers, and parents. We began by thinking about an authoring cycle as a curricular frame and about uninterrupted reading and writing experiences that might start that cycle.

Analysis of an issue after the fact can often deceive one into believing that the decision-making process was effortless. In actuality, decisions related to theoretically based instruction occur in a trial and error fashion, gleaning credibility from teacher/student feedback and a sense of knowing what constitutes valuable learning. Over the course of the summer I learned how to observe what happened with students while they were involved in a language activity and to evaluate that experience in relation to my beliefs about learning. The knowledge I gained helped me clarify my beliefs about language and learning, view the child as a co-author of curriculum, and understand curriculum and curriculum development as the essence of the teaching experience. Some examples of this learning process may be helpful.

Written Conversation

The first day of class teachers and students alike participated in a language activity called *Written Conversation*. Written Conversation is both a reading and writing activity. Two learners sit with one piece of paper and a pencil between them. No words are spoken. To communicate with each other they must write.

As I observed students engaged in this experience, I was surprised to find learners reading and writing with ease and confidence. Here were students who were having difficulty in their regular academic program, yet when presented with the opportunity to write and to begin writing at their own level, they not only succeeded but excelled. Under our classroom conditions disabled learners did not look disabled! After observing and experiencing the dynamics of this activity on the first day, I could see that it was process-oriented, served as a clear demonstration of our intention not to fragment language, and called for involvement from everyone. The following conversation is an example of the interactions that took place between a pair of reluctant fourth and sixth graders in the class (also see Figure FA1.1):

Hi, Chris. How are you doing?
Just fine!

Are you enjoying this class?
Yes

Is it funny sitting on the floor?
Well, I didn't wear any good clothes . . . and at least it is carpeted.
Yes, it's nice.

Did you see the big letter to your right? It's from Judy. She visited us. If you want to you can go look.
Judy who? Is she an owl?

You can go see it.
Yes, I read it.

Good. You start reading it.
Okay!

How is the program helping you.
Increasing my reading and writing abilities.

Will this help you in school? EXPLAIN!
Yes, it will help me understand words and language more!

Uninterrupted Reading and Writing

Tyler, who had completed first grade, was an experienced reader but an inexperienced writer. The first day of class he let us know quite clearly that he was apprehensive about the idea of

Hi, Chris. How are you doing?
Just fine! Are you enjoying this class? yes

Is it funny sitting on the floor?
    Well I didn't wear any good clothes...and at least it is carpeted
yes it's nicer

Did you see the big letter better to you're right? It's from Judy. She visited us if you want to you can go look.

    Judy whooo? Is she an owl?

            you can go see it.
        yes I read it. good you start ready I

        Okay!

~~what is your name? (first, middle, last)~~
How is this program helping you?
Increasing my reading and writing abilities.
Will this help you in school? EXPLAIN!

        yes, it will help me understand words & language more!

Figure FA1.1   Written Conversation.

joining in our writing adventures. Aware of his reluctance, I initially suggested that we take dictation from Tyler and invite him to write when the opportunity arose.

One language activity that we had introduced in the classroom was personal *Journals.* Each day we wrote in our Journals. Occasionally we shared entries with each other.

Because I knew Tyler was a reluctant writer, I volunteered to work with him during Work Time. As he shared various entries in his journal, 6-year-old Tyler began to assume ever-increasing responsibility for his own writing. He was beginning to feel comfortable with writing and to discover that he had lots of experiences to write about. Figure FA1.2 shows the series of entries that Tyler shared and illustrates the growth I saw; the following is what he wrote:

Journal Entry (Tyler, June 10).
One time I was down at my Grandma and Grandpa's house and when my Mom and Dad came. We celebrated my Mom's birthday.

Figure FA1.2 Journal Entries of Tyler (Age 6).

(continued)

June 17

The Carpet people came and then my Dad took me to get a donot at the Donot Don. Then he took me to my friends house and then we played a little and then another friends mom came and picked us up and took us. my friend Adam. my friend Scott and Re TO French CLASS AND ON THE TWAY WE HAD To Cross A VERY OILY rOAD And Has we had to go back because I forgot my bag and we had to go back when the oiby read.

June 22

CLIMBING LIKE MONKIE'S!

When we went to the Art museum it was closed but there was a big yard WJTH METAL sculptures. AND I

CLIMBED with my feet on the bars and my hands holding on to the bars.

And one of the sculptures LOOKED LIKE This And then after that we took a walk along A looololeno PATH and then it was time to gIM HoMe.

Figure FA1.2   *Continued*

And then my cousin Tim came and my other cousin Joanie and Tim and I played outside for a little while and then it was time for me to go. We went home back to Zionsville. The next day I came to class and had some fun.

Journal Entry (Tyler, June 14).
One time I was at my friend's house to stay over night. And then in the morning Chrissy snored so much that we had to get up and then that afternoon we play sky-do (Frisbee with a hole in the middle) and then on accident I got the sky-do right up in a tree.

June 25

AT SWIMING CLASS
TODAY I could not touch in
my regular class so I went over to a
different class and went to a
diffent PaIT AN DAK
teacher's name is Amy

I back floated out to my
kicking and RACLeR al:
then I floated on my stomach
AICKING
IN MY CLASS are

Shannon, Erin, Tracy, Jennifer
2 Boys & the other girls

July 1

BIKE
My Dad went to the lumber store
and I asked MY MOM if i
COUD TAKE MY
TRANING WEELS
Off. I COVDEL
AT first I didn't do
too well but then I did SuPER! at the
back of the church PARKING loT
TO EASTER
I TOOK FAST.
A BIKE.TIde
dOWNtoWNToDO.

WiTh . MY DAD
i fell ON MY BIKE.
AND MY DAD SAD
foroiT PoP AWELees.

The eND

Figure FA1.2 *Continued*

Then we tried to get it down with Chris's baseball. That didn't work.
So then we tried my friend's Frisbee. That didn't work. Then we
talked a little and just forgot about it. Then we played a little and
came inside for supper. And then we went to bed. And then the
next morning after breakfast we went outside and [the] sky-do was
out of the tree.

Journal Entry (Tyler, June 17).
The carpet people came and then my Dad took me to get a donut at
the Donut Dan. Then he took me to my friend's house and then we
played a little and then another friend's Mom came and picked us up
and took us, my friend Adam, my friend Scott and me to French class
and on the way we happened to cross a very oily road and then we
had to go back because I forgot my bag and we had to go back over
the oily road.

Journal Entry (Tyler, June 22).
Climbing like monkeys. When we went to the art museum it was closed but there was a big yard with metal sculptures. And I climbed with my feet on the bars and my hands holding on to the bars. And one of the sculptures looked like this [picture]. And then after that we took a walk along a long, long path and then it was time to go home.

Journal Entry (Tyler, June 25).
At swimming class today I could not touch in my regular class so I went over to a different class and went to a different part and my teacher's name is Amy. I back floated out to my teacher kicking and then I floated on my stomach kicking. In my class are Shannon, Erin, Tracy, Jennifer, 2 boys and the other girls.

Journal Entry (Tyler, July 1).
Bike. My Dad went to the lumber store and I asked my Mom if I could take my training wheels off. I could. At first I didn't do too well but then I did super! At the back of the church parking lot, it is easier to go fast. I took a bike ride downtown today with my Dad. I fell on my bike and my Dad said, "Forget pop-a-wheelies." The end.

As the days progressed, I found I was learning both from the planned curriculum and from unplanned events. Curriculum, rather than being fixed or prepackaged before instruction, became negotiated. For example, ten days after the program began, Tuck came into the room with a story he had written at home. Tuck, a fifth grader, usually behaved in a guarded and reserved manner in the classroom, often holding back from class participation. For the first time, he seemed anxious to share something with us, asking me if he could in fact read it to the class. One glance at his text and his face told me that the time to do this was right now. Spontaneously, our first order of business became *Authors' Chair*. Everyone gathered together to hear Tuck's remarkable tale (see Figure FA1.3):

The Lost Animal
One day this ostrich got lost. He had lived in the City Zoo. But he hated all the city noises. So he ran away to the wilderness. He was looking for a home. The ostrich found a lake. So he stayed there.

The next day he found some blueberries to eat. All the sudden, it got very quiet. The ostrich got scared. The ostrich decided he'd rather be in the city. So he decided he wanted to go back, but he

The Last animal

One day this ostrich ~~ostreg~~ got lost.
He had lived in the City Zoo.
But he hated all the city noises.
So he ran away to the wilderness.
He was looking for a home. The
osteg found a lake. So he stayed
thayr. ~~He found some bennessas~~
The next day he found some blacber
-ies to eat. All the suden, it got very
quiet. The ostreg got scared. The
ostreg decided he'd rather be in
the city. So he decided he wanted to
go back, but he didnt so the
way back. Then, this eagle dashed
along. He said, "What is your name?
The ostreg said "I dont have a
name". She said that's ok because
I dont have a name. The ostreg
told the eagle his problem. The eagle
said "I no the way to the zoo.
But I t is a long way. But, the eagle
took him back It took him 40 days
and 40 nights

Tuck

Figure FA1.3 Tuck's Story.

didn't know the way back. Then this eagle dashed along. He said, "What is your name?" The ostrich said, "I don't have a name." She said, "That's okay because I don't have a name." The ostrich told the eagle his problem. The eagle said, "I know the way to the zoo, but, it is a long way." But the eagle took him back. It took them 40 days and 40 nights. Tuck

The class received Tuck's piece, asked him some questions for clarification, and encouraged him to publish his story in book form. Through this process Tuck took ownership of literacy and learned how to use the group to support his own growth as a writer. Tuck became an author. The demonstrations he provided spurred several other children to draft stories for possible publication.

Conclusion

At the end of the summer, I tried to take inventory of what had happened. I knew I felt good about my teaching. I knew that both the students and the teachers in the class had enjoyed themselves. I had watched myself, students, and other teachers explore reading and writing in new ways. Many students had worked outside of class writing stories, journal entries, conversations, and notes for the message board. Several had brought books from home to share. Many students arrived early for class and often lingered after dismissal to talk, read, or write. Many parents made an extra effort to come inside the building when they picked up their children. Some stopped by to ask what they might do at home to continue to support the growth in reading and writing that they felt their children were experiencing. Some just stopped by to tell me how much their children were enjoying the class. On Parents' Day, the final week of class, every child had a least one guest; some had two—both of their parents had taken time off from work to be with us!

Before leaving school that summer I took some time to think reflectively about what I had learned about language learning, language teaching, and curriculum. I listed the following four beliefs:

1. Language learning occurs quite naturally when meaningful contexts are provided. Activities selected should be open, allowing students to get in and out at their level.
2. Language learning is a social process. This means that everyone in a classroom is both a teacher and a learner. Children learn much from being in the presence of others using reading and writing to learn.
3. Parents play a vital role in the development of their children as language users. School/home relationships are an important part of a good language arts program.
4. Curriculum is not so much a course of study as it is a transaction between learners in a language setting. Curriculum is negotiated rather than given and only reaches fruition over time and with repeated opportunities for engagement.

Reflecting upon my list, I realized that as a result of my decision to develop a new curriculum both the children and I had grown. Not only could I now more clearly articulate what it was that I knew, but I had gained new insights and developed a new sense of professionalism. The transition I made that summer of 1981 affected what I believed not only about curriculum, but also about language, learning, and children. The beliefs I had articulated would change my approach to teaching. Somehow, deep inside, I suddenly knew why I loved teaching and why curriculum development was not only an opportunity to learn about the dynamics of teaching but a professional right as well. Based on my own experiences, I strongly encourage others to begin.

CHAPTER 2

Starting an Authoring Cycle

Introduction

Recently we had the opportunity to sit in the classrooms of 36 teachers for purposes of understanding the current state of reading comprehension instruction in the United States (Harste & Stephens 1985). One of the more depressing findings was that often children had no clear idea about how the activities they were engaged in related to becoming a proficient reader. Sometimes not even the teachers understood. Children often completed worksheets without understanding how the skill they were working on related to their becoming a more strategic reader. Teachers gave students the worksheet because it presented the next skill they were teaching, not because they saw this skill as central to being a strategic reader or because they understood the relationship between strategic reading and strategic learning. Even in whole language classrooms, teachers and children often seemed to be engaged in activities for the sake of activity, not because they saw how journal writing contributed to becoming a more successful user and learner of written language. Our report concluded that in way too many classrooms, "curriculum has fallen through the cracks."

"The function of curriculum," Carolyn Burke (1985b) says, "is to give perspective." For curriculum to work, teachers have to have a sense of what successful users and learners of written language do. The activities they select for inclusion in their curriculum are seen as invitations for their children to engage in, to see demonstrated, and to come to value the social and mental strategies that successful language users employ. If the curricular activity they se-

51

lect does not support the child taking the mental trip they had envisioned, a new invitation needs to be offered. This process is called curriculum development. It's why children, not activities and tests, must be the teacher's curricular informant. It's why curriculum is negotiated and why curriculum must be in the hands of teachers and children.

It's also why it is not good enough if the teacher is the only person in the classroom who understands how an activity relates to proficiency or success as a user and learner of written language. Children need to have a curricular perspective, too. They need to understand how what they are doing here and now in the classroom relates to becoming a strategic user of written language for purposes of learning. In short, curriculum needs to be made visible to both teachers and students in classrooms.

The authoring cycle provides such a curricular frame. It is an attempt to make curriculum visible to both teachers and students. We sometimes introduce the cycle in our classrooms by selecting activities that highlight writing because we have found that writing encourages even children in academic trouble in reading to develop and find their own voice as well as to take (or retake) ownership of the process of literacy itself. It is important to remember, however, that the authoring cycle is our metaphor for the learning cycle, and although the activities we select highlight reading, writing, speaking, and listening, this does not give us as teachers of the language arts a right to be verbocentric. There are many forms of knowing. A good language arts curriculum expands communication potential rather than shuts it down. The focus of a good language arts curriculum is on the social and psychological strategies of successful learners as they employ the language arts as both tools and toys for learning.

In regard specifically to written language literacy, then, researchers studying the process of reading and the process of writing have found that both processes bear much in common. Even more importantly they have found that both reading and writing support the process of learning.

Figure 2.1, the authoring cycle, summarizes many of the insights into the process of reading and writing by suggesting the following.

1. Reading and writing are events that involve the making and shaping of ideas (or meaning) over time.
2. Cognitively, both reading and writing are driven by a search for a unified meaning, or "text"; learning is defined socially and psychologically as a search for "patterns that connect."

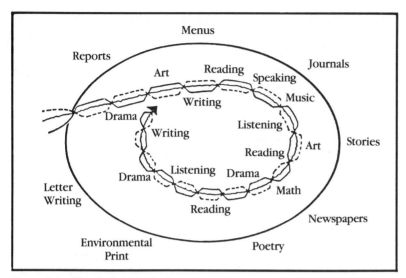

Figure 2.1 The Authoring Cycle.

3. In this search for a unified meaning or patterns that connect, readers and writers begin with what they know, but involvement in this process generates learning (i.e., takes the learner beyond what is known).

4. Readers and writers do this by constantly shifting perspectives from reader to writer, from speaker to listener, from participant to spectator, from monitor to critic, in the very process of reading and writing itself.

5. There is in this sense no "pure" act of reading or writing—writers talk, read, write, listen, draw, and gesture, all in the name of writing; readers discuss ideas they find problematic, listen, sketch, underline, and do a number of other things, all in the name of reading.

6. The multimodal and social nature of the reading and writing process make reading and writing complex events, but this very complexity supports learning when language users are allowed to shift perspective from reader to writer, speaker to listener, participant to spectator, monitor to critic.

7. In their specific detail, reading and writing vary by the circumstances of use; both in function and form, journals are different from letters, letters from stories, stories from poetry. To be strategic, readers and writers must vary the strategies they use by content and context.

8. To find literacy empowering, users must do more than just connect; they must reflectively be able to decide what stance they will or will not take.

The authoring cycle as a curricular frame (see Figure 2.2) builds from these insights but moves one step further to a curriculum. Using the major components of this cycle as a frame, what follows is a detailed description of how Carolyn Burke, Sue Robinson, Mary Lynn Woods, Myriam Revel-Wood, Gloria Kauffman and we have used the authoring cycle to organize the language arts curriculum in school settings.

Life Experiences

Some persons talk about teaching without ever mentioning the word *learning*. Others talk about learning without talking about teaching. Both of these perspectives are wrong. Teaching and learning are a relationship. You cannot talk about one without talking about the other.

From this frame, curriculum is defined as a reflexive look at the relationship between teaching and learning. Although we have a responsibility to plan activities to foster the kinds of learning we see as central to literacy, we do not have the right to do this in disregard of the children. What the children know—their life experiences—becomes a touchstone upon which curriculum is negotiated. By keeping our focus on life experiences our curriculum is made vital and ever alive. Because we build curriculum upon experience our classrooms look different, and no formula or magic set of activities will guarantee an authoring curriculum. In fact, to the extent that teachers just apply published materials in disregard of the specific children they teach, the whole process movement in education is in jeopardy. The activities we suggest in this book are open and should allow children to make the activities their own.

Children have no place to begin a unit of study other than from what they currently know, perceive, and feel. Curriculum has no other place to begin than with children's current concepts and language. In starting the authoring cycle it is important, therefore, to select open activities that permit all students—the underachievers as well as the most proficient written language users in the class—to connect; they should be able to begin and achieve, given their current level of proficiency.

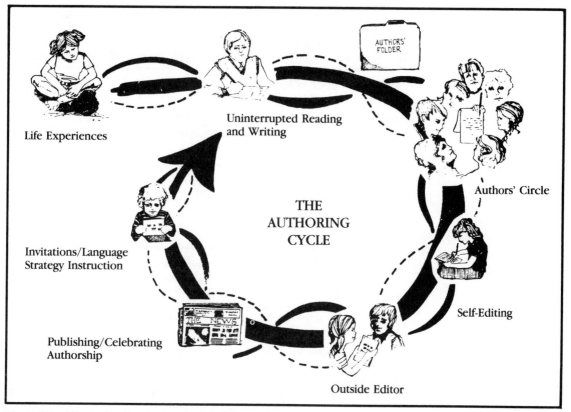

Figure 2.2 The Authoring Cycle as Curricular Frame.

One way we start the cycle is by announcing that the class will be publishing a class magazine or newspaper and that the first articles will be written interviews of everyone in the class. These interviews, we explain, are articles written to introduce someone to others who haven't had the pleasure of meeting the person. The class magazine will be distributed to parents and classroom visitors, and the final product will include each child's article introducing someone in the class as well as a drawing or a photograph of that person, which we either take or have the child bring in. The final product will be useful in getting to know each other.

An activity called *Getting to Know You* supports the children's development of their interviews. In this activity children are asked to jot down some questions that they wish to ask the person they have elected to interview. (We used to ask children to interview

Rob is going to be ten years old. He has one brother and one sister. In his spare time he likes to play sports. His favorite sport is football. His favorite color is blue. He hates pink. He also hates green peppers. He wears braces. His favorite food is pizza. His favorite subject is reading.

Figure 2.3   Rob's Character Sketch (Andy, Grade 4).

someone they didn't know, but often better articles result when friendship pairs are permitted to interview each other.) Children are encouraged to take notes during their interviews and to use the notes in writing their rough drafts.

Typically, Getting to Know You is introduced by reading an example of the kind of article a student their age has written (see Figure 2.3) or one we have written in a previous setting (see

I would like to introduce Dr. Dorothy Watson from the University of Missouri. Dr. Watson and I have laughed our way through many workshops together. I not only thoroughly enjoy Dorothy, but consider her one of the best teachers I have ever met. It is my intent to introduce Dorothy to you in such a way that you too can come to appreciate and understand her as I do.

To do this you need to meet Dorothy on personal grounds. It is these grounds that establish her as forever the teacher; forever the comic. One story should suffice. It personifies Dorothy—who she is; what she is like. It is the story of "Dorothy and the Mugger."

As Dorothy was walking home one night in Detroit, a young man attempted to grab her purse. With a tight grip on the purse, Dorothy managed to abort his efforts, though she was knocked down in the process. This, of course, did not please her.

"Young man! What do you think you are doing? . . . You ought to be ashamed of yourself!"

After Dorothy convinced the mugger that he "owed it to her" to help her up and adjust her wig—this was the early '70s and wigs were the mark of liberation—she proceeded to extract why it was he was out roaming the streets harassing young women. Dorothy responded to his excuse "for bus fare" by giving him five dollars, patting him on the butt, and telling him to "behave himself."

"Yes, madam," was his response as he went off into the night.

It is this bringing out the best in people, this laughing at life, this let's-let-bygones-be-bygones that makes her such a wonderful teacher and friend. Her humor breaks down defenses. Her foibles make her approachable. Her attitude speaks to the possibility of a better life.

Who, I ask, dare ask more of a friend . . . a colleague . . . a teacher?

Figure 2.4   Character Sketch (Adult).

Figure 2.4). After reading the student's selection we share the procedure the student used in writing the article via overheads of the notes that were taken and the student's first draft (see Figure 2.5). We explain that Andy, the author, took notes, wrote a rough draft, took this to Authors' Circle, got some new ideas, revised, and finally sent it to *Editors' Table* where it was reread, proofed, and finally typed for publication. We talk about the fact that Andy gathered more information than he actually used, that he changed his mind, that he moved ideas around, and that his final draft was quite different from his first draft.

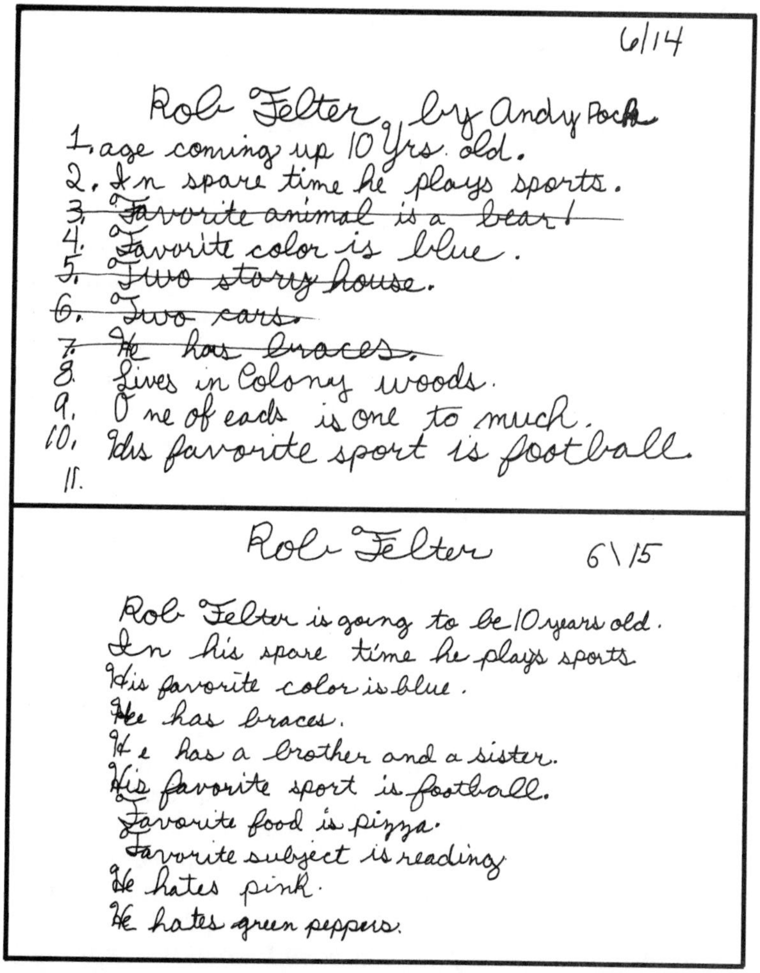
6/14

Rob Felter, by Andy

1. age coming up 10 Yrs. old.
2. In spare time he plays sports.
3. ~~Favorite animal is a bear!~~
4. Favorite color is blue.
5. ~~Two story house.~~
6. ~~Two cars.~~
7. ~~He has braces.~~
8. Lives in Colony woods.
9. One of each is one to much.
10. His favorite sport is football.
11.

Rob Felter 6\15

Rob Felter is going to be 10 years old.
In his spare time he plays sports
His favorite color is blue.
He has braces.
He has a brother and a sister.
His favorite sport is football.
Favorite food is pizza.
Favorite subject is reading
He hates pink.
He hates green peppers.

Transcription:

1. Age coming up 10 yrs. old.
2. In spare time he plays sports.
3. Favorite animal is bear.
4. Favorite color is blue.
5. five story house.
6. two cars.
7. He has braces.
8. Lives in Colony Woods.
9. One of each is one too much.
10. His favorite sport is football.

Figure 2.5 Notes for Interview (with Transcription) and Rough Draft (Andy, Grade 4).

Once we have introduced the activity in this fashion, students pair up, conduct interviews, and, if time permits, begin drafting their articles. By the end of the first day some children will have finished their articles while others may still be interviewing each other or writing their rough drafts. At Author Sharing Time on the first day it is important to assure students that no matter where they are in the process this is okay. Children can be invited to share their first drafts with the group whether they have finished them or not. Students who do manage to finish their rough drafts place them in their Author's Folder and either select their own topic to write about on the second day, or pick up on another invitation.

A variation of Getting to Know You that we have successfully used with young children was developed in Gloria Kauffman's first-grade classroom. The children were introduced to the strategy on the second day of school as a way to create a newspaper about themselves that they could send to introduce themselves to a class of students who were going to be their new pen pals. After a discussion of good questions to ask in an interview, each person, including the teacher, chose a partner and went off to conduct the interviews. The children were told to take notes of what the person they were interviewing said and to use their notes later to dictate their interview to the teacher. When several children said, "But I can't spell," we answered that they were the only ones who would read their notes and they could use words, letters, or pictures—whatever would help them remember what had been said in the interview when it came time to dictate their article.

When later we began having the children dictate their interviews for the newspaper from their notes, we were excited by their notes and by how well they were able to use them to retrieve the information shared with them. Children had freely moved across communication systems using various combinations of written language and pictures in their notes. Figure 2.6 contains several of the children's notes and copies of the interviews dictated from these notes.

Once a child had dictated an interview to us, we read it back to the author and several other children sitting nearby to see if they thought it made sense to other readers. Following these informal Authors' Circles, the interviews were typed and published in a newspaper that was distributed to the children and their pen pals. Using the interviews to produce a newspaper for their pen pals gave this activity a purpose that went beyond the immediate classroom. The children got to know each other better as well as introduce themselves to their new pen pals. This strategy could therefore be used anytime a classroom begins exchanging letters with a new group of pen pals.

Later on in the year, when Getting to Know You may no longer be appropriate because the children already know each other well, an activity that can be used to introduce the authoring cycle to children is *Family Stories.* We developed this activity along with Gloria Kauffman as a way for children to explore the stories that their families told over and over again about earlier events that happened to various family members. The children were told that each of us has important stories that we carry around inside us and that one kind of these stories is family stories. These family stories

DOG

PAT

Pat drank two glasses of grapefruit juice this morning for breakfast. Pat ate bacon and eggs and toast. Pat likes dogs. He played with his 4 × 4 last night.

by Aaron

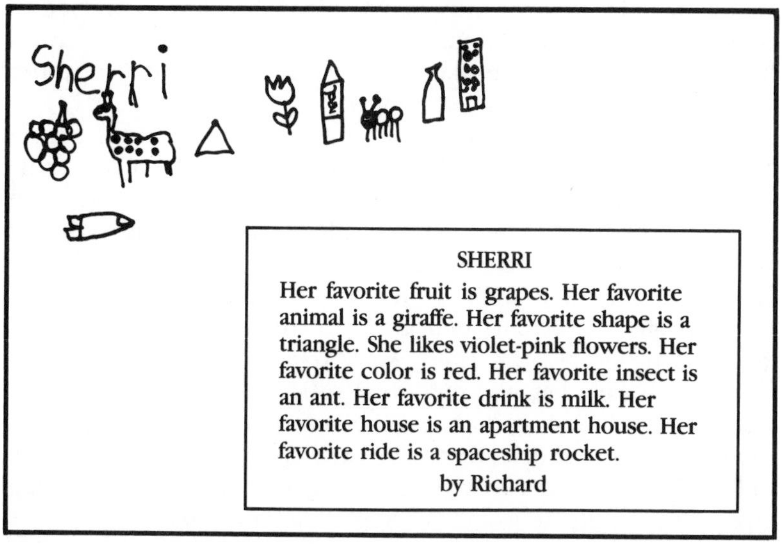

Sherri

SHERRI

Her favorite fruit is grapes. Her favorite animal is a giraffe. Her favorite shape is a triangle. She likes violet-pink flowers. Her favorite color is red. Her favorite insect is an ant. Her favorite drink is milk. Her favorite house is an apartment house. Her favorite ride is a spaceship rocket.

by Richard

(continued)

Figure 2.6   First-Grade Interview Notes and Articles.

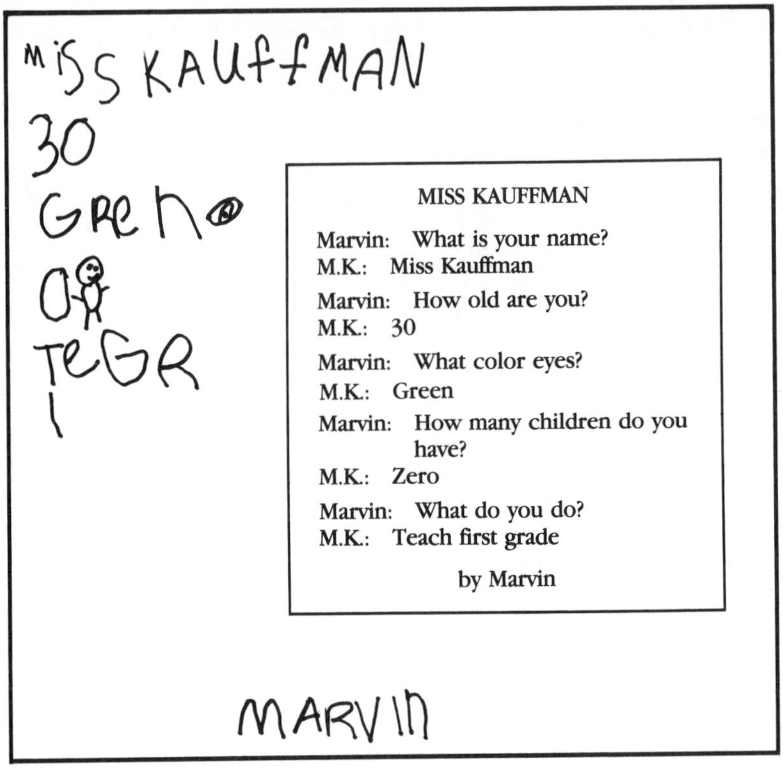

```
MiSS KAUffMAN
30
GReho
O Y
TeGR
|
```

> **MISS KAUFFMAN**
>
> Marvin: What is your name?
> M.K.:   Miss Kauffman
>
> Marvin: How old are you?
> M.K.:   30
>
> Marvin: What color eyes?
> M.K.:   Green
>
> Marvin: How many children do you have?
> M.K.:   Zero
>
> Marvin: What do you do?
> M.K.:   Teach first grade
>
> by Marvin

MARVIN

Figure 2.6   *Continued*

are "remember when" stories about things that have happened to people in their family and that family members share at gatherings and reunions. They were asked to interview their parents or other family members to begin gathering some of these stories.

For the next week or two, children brought in their notes from these interviews on scraps of paper and shared their stories orally with the group. Each day, several children had new stories to tell to the class. The children were then asked to make a list of their stories and to decide which ones they wanted to write. The children wrote their family stories, took them to Authors' Circles, and published individual collections of their stories. Each child then chose one favorite family story to include in a newspaper of family stories that was published to share with parents. If we were using this activity to begin the authoring cycle midyear, we would have the children first each write their favorite family story and publish these in a newspaper. We would then invite children to continue collecting and writing their family stories in their

Author's Folders to create individual books or to go on to other kinds of writing invitations.

Both Getting to Know You and Family Stories allow children to make immediate connections with their past experiences as they begin exploring authoring through writing. Because these writing activities build so directly on their past experiences and lead quickly to a publication, children come to understand the cycle as a curricular frame for authoring in the classroom.

Uninterrupted Reading and Writing

Once Getting to Know You has been introduced, children should be given uninterrupted time to conduct their interviews and to begin to draft their articles. Having a period of time each day for uninterrupted reading and writing is the key to a successful reading and writing program.

In many ways uninterrupted reading and writing is the heart of the language arts curriculum. Because children can learn a process only through engagement in that process, children must be given invitations to engage in reading and writing each day. Without invitations, there will be limited engagement. Without engagement, children cannot make connections. Without making connections, children cannot reflectively grow. Invitations to engage—time for uninterrupted reading and writing—is a "firstness;" a prerequisite to growth and learning.

Invitations and choice are important. A true invitation, however, is more than just a choice between two activities you propose. An invitation means that the children have the right to turn down an option and to justify how their own idea is an equally valid experience.

Choice is an integral part of the literacy learning process. In many ways choice is the propeller that gets the whole process started. It is in making the decision to read this book rather than that book, or to write this story rather than that story, that ownership of the process occurs. To make any decision, the learner needs to weigh and think about a variety of information. This thinking about available options is crucial; it allows one to focus on a topic and, because alternatives have been weighed and rejected, to know what can be done with a topic before really beginning. If and when topics and books are assigned rather than chosen, no such personal weighing has taken place. The orientation of the language user is other-directed (what does "the teacher" want?).

By allowing real choices, students have to decide and then begin composing. In so doing, they take ownership of the literacy process.

To these ends, children need to be informed that although they will be reading and writing each day, only a small portion of what they read or write will be presented to others. The language arts curriculum in the classroom is more than just publishing. Uninterrupted time for reading and writing allows readers and writers the opportunity to test, confirm, and revise their latest language hypotheses and thus to grow. Through time for uninterrupted reading and writing, language users try various strategies and come to see written language as a tool for learning. In a curriculum organized around an authoring cycle, first drafts are valued as much as final drafts. Students need time to explore meaning before they are expected to present meaning. Without a first draft there can be no second draft or final draft. Without risk there is no growth. Carolyn Burke (1986) says it this way, "Within every professional there once was an amateur." Her quote should be shared and discussed with children.

We have used several instructional strategies to support students as they move toward choosing and writing on their own topics during uninterrupted writing. One is to have students create a list of possible writing ideas. We use the technique suggested by Graves (1983) and Atwell (1987) of demonstrating how we make our own list of experiences and ideas to write about. We then brainstorm with students about possible topics and experiences from their lives and ask them to make their own lists. They can use these lists to choose the topic they want to begin writing about in their first piece. These lists of possible writing topics are kept in the student's Author's Folder so that ideas can be added later whenever students think of new possible topics.

In addition to having students make a list of topics, we also introduce specific writing invitations. Some students find it difficult to begin with a list of ideas and instead need the support of writing invitations. We offer invitations that allow students to build from their own life experiences but that give them some support in generating story and language structures.

As soon as some students finish their rough drafts of their interviews, we have them make lists of ideas so they can begin other pieces of writing while they are waiting to meet in an Authors' Circle on their interviews. We also begin offering writing invitations so that students can decide either to write on their own topics or to accept one of the invitations. We typically introduce

Picture Setting as a writing invitation by suggesting that if students are having difficulty thinking of something they wish to write about, they can go home and look through a series of magazines to find a picture of a setting (void of characters) that reminds them of some experience in their lives. To make sure they understand what they are to do, we share some picture settings we have selected and tell the children what we are reminded of by these settings. It is important to assure the children that they are free to write about anything they wish during uninterrupted reading and writing time, and that they need not accept this invitation if they already have another idea for a story.

On the next day we begin Work Time—our official name for uninterrupted reading and writing each day—by finding out how many children are still drafting their written interviews (we recommend they finish these first). We then ask how many accepted our invitation to find a background picture setting to create a new story; these children are invited to bring their pictures and assemble at a table in the back. We also find out how many others have their own ideas and are ready to begin drafting new selections. Students who have not taken our invitation, who have finished the rough draft of their interview, and who do not feel they have a story just waiting to be written, are reminded of other writing opportunities available in the room—such as Pen Pals (see Chapter 3), *Message Board,* and Journals—or are invited to look through the books in the classroom library to find something to read. During uninterrupted time for reading and writing, everyone is expected to engage in such activities, though the particular reading and writing activity is a matter of choice.

There is nothing magical about Picture Settings as a first invitation. Instead, teachers might offer an invitation to write a text for a wordless book or to write a text based on a patterned language story. The key is to offer students specific invitations to get them started while providing them the option of turning down the invitation and going with their own topic.

During Work Time, students are seldom engaged in the same activity. Instead they are engaged in various kinds of reading and writing experiences as well as in Authors' Circle or Editors' Table. Teachers who have conducted only whole-group instruction may feel uncomfortable starting with so many options. Instead, they may want to begin by offering students two or three options.

A safe way to move to three or more options is to create a pocket chart using a piece of tagboard and a series of library pocket card holders labeled with the options available for children. For example, if four people can be at the Writing-Reading Center (see Chapter 3), place four passes in this pocket. Children going to that center pick up a pass from the chart and replace it when they are done. If there are no more passes in a pocket, a student must wait until someone returns one before going to this center.

If you decide you do not need this amount of control to make invitations and choice work in your classroom, it's still not a bad idea to start with some kind of organizational structure. Students bring a history of literacy and literacy instruction with them, and they need time to get used to taking an increasing amount of responsibility for their use of time. A pocket chart can help by giving just the right amount of structure, but allowing more choice than they are used to. Myriam Revel-Wood uses neither of these techniques but simply lists all the available activities on the blackboard as a ready reference for children as they plan their morning. Other teachers ask everyone to take five minutes at the start of the day to plan their morning and post their planned schedule at their work area. During Author Sharing Time at the end of the morning, achievements and intentions are compared and discussed.

During Work Time, teachers should be constantly introducing new invitations for reading and writing activities. Uninterrupted reading and writing experiences can include Pen Pals, Journals, Message Board, *Shared Reading, Readers' Theatre,* Getting to Know You, Family Stories, Picture Setting, Written Conversation, *Choose Your Own Story, Wordless Picture Books, Learning Logs,* Literature Logs, *Group Composed Books,* or stories that students choose to read or write about on their own topics.

Author's Folder

Invitations to write are issued daily. Some are informal (Journals, Learning Logs, letters, etc.), while others are formal (stories or articles that the child perceives as publishable). It is not uncommon for children to think that they are going to publish the story they wrote in conjunction with the Picture Setting invitation, only to find that on another day they write something they like even better and elect instead to publish that piece. Students soon have a variety of rough drafts, some complete and others in process at the same time. All drafts of formal writing experiences are dated and kept in a manila folder with the child's name on it. We call this our Author's Folder.

In Mary Lynn Woods's room, Author's Folders are kept on a

library book return cart. The upper shelf on this cart forms a V that is a nice holder for the folders. Sue Robinson uses a cardboard box covered with contact paper. Children date their work, staple together all draft copies of a single piece, and file their work from oldest to newest. New folders are created as needed, and old folders are filed and kept. Gloria Kauffman has two sets of folders for each child. One set holds pieces the child is currently working on, and the second set holds pieces that are completed and have been published or that the student has decided not to publish. Both sets are stored in cardboard boxes and are always available to the students.

Author's Folders support the role of the author as a decision maker in choosing what to write, how to write, and how long to write. Because authors keep current and past drafts of writing and lists of writing ideas in their folders, they can continue to work on current pieces of writing and to return to earlier drafts. Authors use the folders to revisit past drafts, to continue work in the present, and to plan for future drafts. Author's Folders thus provide the organizational support that authors need for writing over time.

The folders provide a cumulative record of an author's pieces of writing, both published and unpublished, throughout the year. These folders thus give both the student and the teacher a way to monitor growth over time in writing processes and mechanics. As students look back through their writing, they are able to see how much they've grown as writers. We have found it helpful to ask students occasionally to look through their folders and write a self-evaluation of their writing growth.

Both student self-evaluations and teacher evaluations will be more insightful and complete if the teacher and the student use an evaluation form of some type to record comments about the student's behavior during writing, conferencing, and editing as well as comments on the actual pieces of writing. The evaluation form we use is stapled to the inside front cover of the Author's Folder. Although we have continued to work on new and better forms of evaluation (see Mills 1986), we will share here the procedure we have most frequently used.

Our evaluation form has been a single sheet of typing paper divided in thirds. The upper third is labeled "Mechanics." In this area we record any growth we see in the area of writing mechanics as a function of our having looked through the work in the folder. We date each observation and refer to a particular child's piece by using the date the child wrote on the draft. Our observations can be as simple as:

"Is using complete sentences."

"Knows how to use quotation marks."

"Used the exclamation point appropriately."

We make no attempt to record all the mechanical aspects of writing that the child knows, only those things that we see as new understandings and uses, given what we currently know about that child's control of mechanics. Students also add their own comments on the sheet when they feel they've learned a new convention.

The middle section of the form is entitled "Strategies." In this section we or the student record strategies that the student has not been seen using before. Observations recorded could include:

"Was able to revise by inserting new information in an old paragraph."

"Moved information in draft around rather than just tagging new information onto the end."

"Is learning how to support fellow authors—helped Stephanie by listening to her story and then asking her what things she was having problems with."

"Did not ask for spelling help during her draft today."

"Showed evidence of reading like a writer—during Readers' Theatre announced, 'Oh, this story gives me an idea for a story I can write.'"

"Reread journal to get ideas for writing to pen pal."

"Reread piece to self before going to Author's Chair."

Process observations come from our perusal of the Author's Folder as well as from our observations of the child throughout the day. Rather than running back and forth to the Author's Folders recording these observations, we use a clipboard with a sheet of self-adhesive 1″ labels. On these labels we record the student's name and our process observations as we make them throughout the day. At the end of the day, we use these to write the child a note saying how pleased we are to see this new progress. Each morning we post these notes on the Message Board and stick the label with the observations in the appropriate slot on the evaluation sheet in the child's Author's Folder.

The last third of the evaluation form is entitled "Insights." In this section we record sudden "aha experiences" that the child has had, insights we have had into what the child knows, and things we think the child still needs to learn or connections the child is ready to make, given our observation of his or her work and behavior. Children add their own comments about new things they've discovered or are exploring and want to know more about. We use these observations to guide our selection of books and writing experiences and to plan strategy instruction for individual students or groups. Ariel, for example, was forever asking for words to be pronounced when reading things on her own. To help her, we talked with her about the fact that readers will always encounter new words, and gave her several strategies she might try (skip the troublesome word and read ahead to see if it will make sense later; put in a synonym that seems to fit). If two or more children seem to be having the same or similar problems, we call them together, announce to the group that we are going to talk about some strategies successful readers use when they encounter something unknown in reading or writing, and invite these children and anyone else who would like help to join the group. These are fairly direct instructional settings following the format of a strategy lesson as outlined by Goodman, Burke, and Sherman (1980). On occasion an open-ended lesson can be planned for the whole group. We have, for example, used Choose Your Own Story as a generic activity to help children begin to take ownership of the reading process. Some children read these books by themselves, others paired up, discussed alternatives, and took turns reading selected pages. Still others were encouraged to try their hand at writing their own Choose Your Own Story.

When a section of the evaluation form fills up, we staple another form on top of it and continue our observational record. Because what we record can be and is read by the students themselves, often they approach us: "Didn't you see that I used a semicolon in this story?" "Didn't you see that Stephen and I used *Say Something* when we were reading the hard article on salamanders yesterday?" As children bring up things we missed, we add them, but, more importantly, we encourage children to date and add their own observations to the form. We explain that they need to be interested in evaluation because they are the ones who need to be constantly learning. Because there is no attempt to hide what we are looking for, goals and objectives are clear to them as well as to us.

One of the side benefits of this procedure is that it keeps us alerted to those children to whom we are not as attentive as we should be. Students in our classroom rarely "slip through the cracks" because as we write notes and stick our observations in Author's Folders, we are constantly reminded of whom we have not observed.

The Edmonton Public Schools, under the guidance of Margaret Stevenson, have been moving to a process approach of evaluation for some time now. Currently the central office has developed legal-sized pocket folders in five different colors that teachers can order for use as Author's Folders. At the end of the year a composite folder is forwarded to the child's new teacher with selected samples of the child's work, documenting what growth occurred over the year, as well as the experiences the child's current teacher thinks are crucial for this child in the next year.

In all classrooms, Author's Folders become an important source of information for children, teachers, and parents. At parent conferences they are a useful document for explaining the curriculum and for helping parents understand how they might support their child's growth in reading and writing, given the child's current level of progress.

Author's Folders, then, serve many functions. In them we record both reading and writing observations: the past, present, and future. It is not uncommon to find children looking through their current folder or asking to see all their folders to reread or to show them off to visitors who come to see them in their room. Often children return to their folders while in the midst of a new piece to check how they did something that is now giving them problems. Sometimes, in this process, they identify something they forgot they did, decide they really did like it, and decide to carry it forward to publication. Sometimes they laugh at things they used to do when they "were littler." They also refer to their list of possible writing topics that is kept in their folders. These ideas are initially a brainstormed list of experiences or topics that they feel they could write about. Later they add to the list as new ideas occur to them from teacher invitations to write, from books they are reading, from their own or other children's writing, or from their current experiences in school and at home.

In addition, the drafts in their folders are a source of possible publications. Twice a month authors are asked to look through their current folder to find things they wish to publish, that is, to take to an Authors' Circle to get responses and to move the rough draft to a publishable form.

Authors' Circle

As students move the drafts of their interviews through the authoring cycle, we introduce them to its various components. The next part of the cycle, Authors' Circle, is introduced as soon as three or four students have a complete rough draft that they are ready to think more about with other writers. Often these are drafts that students are considering taking to a published form. In Authors' Circle, authors read their pieces to the group for their reactions. The focus is always on responding to the meaning of the piece, not to the spelling, punctuation, or neatness.

Authors' Circles play a crucial role in helping authors develop the sense of audience that is so essential to becoming a writer who can successfully communicate with others. As authors read their pieces to the group and hear the group's responses, they develop a reader's perspective on their writing. Because the intent of writing is to communicate a message to others, every author needs to develop the perspective of a reader. The author needs an awareness of what the audience does and does not know in relation to the piece of writing to communicate effectively to that audience. Authors' Circles give children access to readers they know and trust and provide one important way that authors can gain a sense of audience by taking on the perspective of a reader.

The first criterion for coming to Authors' Circle is that everyone who comes—including the teacher—must have a draft of writing. Often this is a draft that the author is considering publishing. The second criterion is that the author likes the piece but wants to think more about it with others. Authors' Circle is different than Authors' Chair. At Authors' Chair, authors come to share. At Authors' Circle, authors come to receive help from other authors on what is and is not working in their piece and what, if anything, they might consider doing next. Participants at Authors' Circle are there for the expressed purpose of supporting their own and each other's authorship. If a child has a piece the child likes as is, we recommend that the child share it at Authors' Chair. Authors' Circle is for items the author likes but wants to continue to think more about. When this criterion is not insisted on, Authors' Circle becomes something quite different than what it is envisioned to be.

To facilitate these intents, Authors' Circle is under the direction of whichever author is presenting a piece. The presenting author shares the piece of writing, tells what he or she particularly likes about it, asks if it is clear, and identifies sections that are weak and that require the group's suggestions for improvement. The other authors receive the piece and offer supportive criticism. By what they say they demonstrate that they have listened to and heard the author.

Although authors generally find it difficult to hear criticism of their work, they nonetheless find such criticism helpful. The strategy, from the presenting author's perspective, is to try not to get defensive, but rather to take notes and later decide what to do with the information gathered. Because the author is the owner of the piece, the final decision about what changes will or will not be made rests with the author. The strategy, from the collaborative author's perspective, is to be helpful, take cues from the presenting author, and never challenge the ownership of the piece.

We typically introduce the Authors' Circle by

1. Sharing with children a piece we have been writing, such as a professional article or a children's story
2. Discussing how we got other authors to read and react to it, including the kinds of criticisms we found helpful, the kinds of questions we asked, and the specific kinds of help we requested
3. Detailing what we did with this information (tried to be accepting and took notes)
4. Showing how the new version incorporates or fails to incorporate the result of this experience

Throughout our introduction we stress both ownership and the kinds of comments we found supportive and not so supportive. We also point out that too much good advice can overwhelm the author, making the task of revision appear unmanageable. The criterion for a successful Authors' Circle is that the authors leave feeling they had a chance to think about their writing in a new way and with some ideas about what to do next with that piece. If teachers do not have a revised piece of their own writing to share, we suggest that they share a rough draft and a revised piece written by a previous student. Another option would be for teachers to share their own rough draft, have students ask questions, and then write and share a revised draft with students, telling them the kinds of questions that were helpful and how decisions about what to revise were made.

After setting a frame, we begin our first Authors' Circle by reading our interview aloud to the group. To demonstrate how Authors' Circle works we ask the participants at the circle to receive the piece by saying what they heard in the piece and whether it made sense. For this purpose we typically ask, "Well? What do you think? What did you hear? Was everything clear? What questions do you want to ask me?" We assume the author already likes the piece because the author selected it to bring to the circle, and so we inform children that telling an author merely that they like a piece is not particularly helpful. The children are asked to be specific in telling what they heard and what kinds of questions they have for the author. When they ask questions or identify areas not clearly written, the author simply takes notes on the rough draft itself to refer to later. We tell students that taking notes does not mean the changes will be made, but only that we will have the information to consider later. The other authors in turn read their pieces, and the listeners tell them what they heard in the pieces and whether the pieces were clear to them.

The format of the first circles, then, consists of the authors reading aloud, followed by the other authors telling what they heard and asking questions about the piece. Having the children first state what they heard in the piece creates a positive atmosphere in which the author feels that the piece has been listened to and that it has some merit. If the children move immediately to asking questions, it makes the author feel more defensive about the piece. The author needs to know *both* what is and is not working in a piece of writing. The questions and comments about unclear areas, however, are what really push the author to reconsider a piece in a new way. As Amy, a third-grade writer, told us, "When they tell me what they like, that doesn't really help me, but when they ask me questions, that really makes me think." During this part of the circle, children ask questions or comment on things they either didn't understand or want to know more about. They also make suggestions on how the author could improve the piece.

Teachers should demonstrate to students how to write a revised section on a new sheet of paper and to insert it into the text by cutting and pasting or by drawing arrows to another part of the paper where the insert is written. We also suggest that rough drafts be written on only one side of the paper and that students skip every other line on the paper when writing to make revision easier. Students are often reluctant to consider revisions because they believe that they will need to recopy their entire piece, and so these techniques for quick revisions affect their willingness to rethink and revise their writing.

In doing Authors' Circles with the interviews children have written about each other, it is best not to have both the interviewer and the interviewee in the same circle. Although having both does set up the need for revision in that one can tell the other what is missing in the report, this often puts the ownership of the piece in jeopardy. Instead, we encourage children to talk informally with the person they interviewed if questions come up as they write their rough draft or right before they go to an Authors' Circle.

Students need to be walked through their first Authors' Circle in a fairly thorough and systematic fashion. Teachers will find that after the first Authors' Circle less and less discussion of how to conduct the circle has to take place. Despite this, it is important that everyone has a good experience and that misconceptions are caught before they cause problems that undermine the very function that Authors' Circle is designed to serve.

It takes a while for children to understand how to receive and give constructive criticism. Initially many students will respond with "I like it," "It was fine," or "Make it longer." They are inexperienced in receiving and reacting to another author's writing, and so it takes time for them to learn how to respond in a specific and constructive manner.

During the first circles, teachers provide important demonstrations for the kinds of comments and questions that authors can use to support each other. As students gain experience in how to conduct an Authors' Circle, teachers will find that they need not—and, in fact, should not—be present at every circle. As authors prepare subsequent texts for publication, teachers should join one or two circles that they feel could particularly benefit from their presence.

The first circles may seem unproductive, but, given the chance, children will gradually discover the power of consulting with their fellow authors. We have found that many children need to participate in the entire authoring cycle before they begin to understand the purpose of Authors' Circle. Once their pieces are edited by an outside editor and then published and shared with the class, they begin to realize how helpful it is to receive input from other authors. This need to experience the entire authoring cycle is why we begin with a writing activity such as Getting to Know You that will quickly lead to a publication.

Although we have often used Getting to Know You or Family Stories to introduce students to the entire authoring cycle, any other strategy lesson that allows a publication to be quickly produced in a classroom can be used. In Gloria Kauffman's first-grade classroom, the children produced a Group Composed Book that went through the authoring cycle. During the second week of school, Gloria read the book *Ten Little Bears* (Ruwe 1971) to the children and then had them brainstorm ideas about other activities the bears might do. The children were then handed a piece of paper on which Gloria had written the repeating part of the sentence with a space for the children to write whatever each one decided to have the bear do. Once the children had completed their pages, they were stapled together to make a Group Composed Book called *Eighteen Little Bears*.

The class wrote several Group Composed Books based on patterns from predictable books during the first two weeks of school. With Parents' Night coming up at the school, we suggested that they publish one of their books for their parents to take home. The children selected *Eighteen Little Bears* as their favorite, and we made photocopies of their original pages to take to Authors' Circle. The children met in Authors' Circles and then revised their pages. These were then typed, illustrated by each child, and reduced on a copy machine to produce a book that each family took home on Parents' Night.

As we read through the children's revisions of their pages, we were excited to see that *all* the children revised for meaning rather than for conventions (see Figure 2.7 for several examples of children's revisions). This experience provided us with evidence to answer people who argued that young children would not understand the function of Authors' Circles. These first-grade children understood the need to focus on meaning before having to attend to conventions and were able to use their classmates' comments to revise for meaning.

Just as there are different ways that the authoring cycle can be introduced to a group of children, there are several different procedures for Authors' Circle. The format we first introduce to students is fairly uncomplicated because it involves the student reading aloud to others who say what they heard and liked ("receiving" the piece) and ask questions and make suggestions about the meaning of the piece.

After authors have experience with the circles, teachers and students may want to try a second format in which the author takes a larger role in determining the direction of the group discussion. The author begins by reading the piece aloud and stating what he or she likes best about it. The author then tells the group what parts of the piece are troublesome or need others' reactions. The group discusses and explores the ideas while the author makes quick notes on the group's suggestions. For example, the author might say, "I don't really like my introduction. It's too boring. I want to make it more exciting so people will want to read my story." Fellow authors then make suggestions or offer alternatives for a better introduction.

After the author is satisfied with the discussion of the identified problem areas, the others have a chance to talk about parts of the piece they particularly liked and to raise questions about meaning. The process continues in the same manner with each participating author.

Sometimes authors first want to get a general response from the

Sheila (Grade 1)
Transcription (Original):

One little bear
went out to eat.

Then four little
bears were left.

Sheila (Grade 1)
Transcription (Revision):

One little bear
went out to eat
at McDonalds.

Then four little
bears were left.

Figure 2.7 Originals and Revisions of Pages in Group Composed Books (Short 1986).

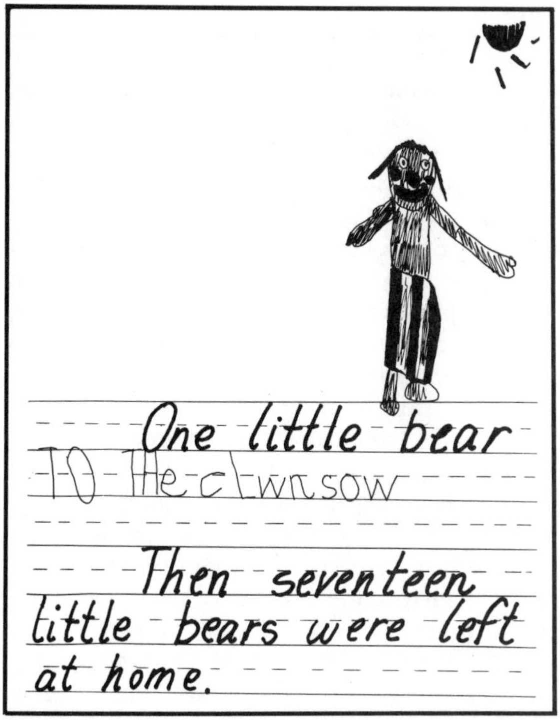

Stephanie (Grade 1)
Transcription (Original):

One little bear
to the clown show.

Then seventeen little
bears were left at home.

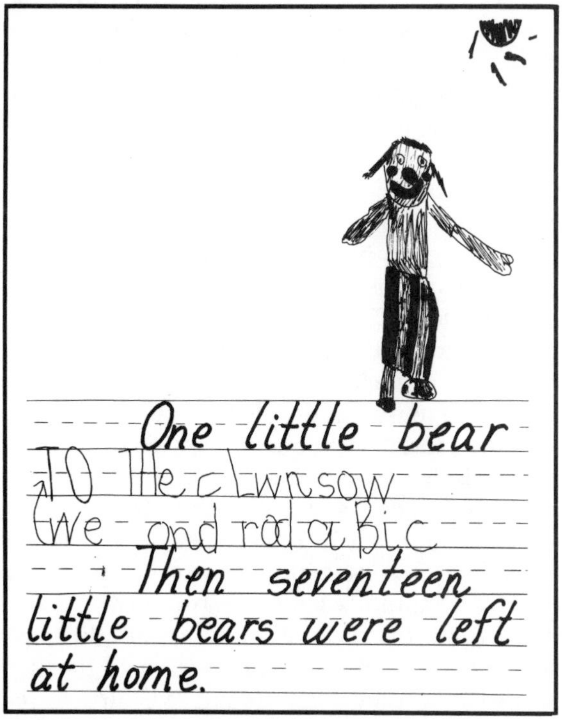

Stephanie (Grade 1)
Transcription (Revision):

One little bear
went to the clown show
and rode a bike.

Then seventeen little
bears were left at home.

Figure 2.7 *Continued*

group before identifying a specific part for discussion. In this case, the author reads the piece aloud and group members respond with statements about what was effective and what they had questions about. Following this discussion, the author may ask for responses to a specific section of the piece, if desired.

These last two formats are ones that we have found helpful in supporting authors as they revise for meaning and in allowing them to retain ownership of their pieces as they revise. We usually do not use these formats in the first circles because the presenting authors often have difficulty identifying specific areas for group response. They need the group discussion of their writing to help them identify an area. But once they have experience with an Authors' Circle, authors can identify specific parts of the text needing group response and suggestions. By having the author identify the area of difficulty before the listeners are allowed to ask questions, the author's agenda is given top priority. Our assumption is that the author's interest will largely determine what he or she learns from and uses in the revision process.

If authors come to an Authors' Circle without identifying what they want to think more about with the group, we remind them that Authors' Chair is for sharing; Authors' Circle is for seeking advice and thinking with others. Authors are responsible for deciding what to work on to improve their writing each time they come to a circle. Authors are never "done"; they just finally quit. The real issue for any author is not perfection but, rather, "Of all the things in need of improvement, what will I work on this time?" The teacher and other authors need to remember that the *author* makes these decisions, rather than others imposing on the author what they think is a good piece of writing. Some writers will choose to make no or few revisions in a current piece but will use the comments from Authors' Circle in their next piece of writing. Because the authors choose the focus of any revisions, they are able to retain ownership of their writing process and piece.

Reading their pieces aloud to the group allows authors to retain physical control of the draft, thereby maintaining ownership of the rough draft both in the circle and later as they decide whether to accept suggestions for changes. As listeners, the other authors are forced to focus on the meaning of the piece rather than on conventions such as spelling or punctuation.

If the listeners criticize the author's sentence structure or grammar, we simply remind them that before authors can edit (i.e., worry about grammar, spelling, and so on), they have to be sure they have included everything they want to say. We further remind them that often authors themselves realize they could have said something in a better way and that typically some of these changes will occur as they revise for meaning. At this point in the authoring cycle, authors are interested in whether they have included everything needed to communicate their story to others. The focus of Authors' Circle is on thinking about meaning. We will take care of spelling and grammar once we are sure our stories say what we want them to say. Editing for conventions is the function of Editors' Table. Thinking about meaning is the function of Authors' Circle.

Because sharing and discussing writing takes time, Authors' Circles should be kept small and discussion and turn-taking should be kept moving. Remind students who received help that it is their responsibility to give help when others want it. Even if they like the ending of someone's story but the author does not, they are obligated to offer other ways the author might explore for ending the piece. Although it does not hurt for them to say they like the ending the way it is, they should respond to the author's request for possible improvements.

Teachers should remember that the procedures for how to conduct an Authors' Circle should be adapted to fit the needs of the group and may change over time. Teachers need to be aware of how Authors' Circle supports an author and use this understanding in making adjustments so that these circles are productive for particular authors. We have found, for example, that sometimes authors have to read their pieces aloud twice when circles first begin because students have not yet learned how to listen and respond to another person's writing. Students need the first reading to get a frame for the story and the second reading to identify areas that are unclear.

When authors begin writing lengthy pieces, teachers may need to provide copies of their drafts for the receiving authors to look at because they cannot keep the entire story in their heads. This should be considered only after a tone has been set that focuses on content and not convention. We have also found that when pieces get longer, it is important to limit circles to three authors or authors begin to lose interest because of the length of time in the circle.

Sometimes authors run into difficulty in the middle of their piece and are unable to figure out a way to continue on with that piece of writing even after they have talked informally with others. The author can call a special Authors' Circle to brainstorm possible ways to deal with that section. The author might choose three or four students or ask for volunteers to meet briefly. The author first identifies what is causing difficulty and then reads that section of the piece aloud to the group. The group brainstorms suggestions with the author. In this type of Authors' Circle, the other group members do not also bring a piece of writing. The group meets only long enough to help the author think of some possible solutions to a difficulty and then disbands.

Because there is no one way to conduct an Authors' Circle, teachers should constantly evaluate these circles with their students so that they are effective for the particular group of authors in that classroom. Teachers need to examine whether these circles are helping students grow as authors.

Authors' Circles facilitate growth by capitalizing on the social nature of learning and authoring. Just the presence of listeners encourages the author to take a different perspective on the piece of writing. Authors shift to a reader's perspective as they read their pieces aloud to the group and receive comments about their pieces from other authors. As detailed in Chapter 1, Corey spontaneously edited his story about his smashed toe as he read it aloud to the rest of the group and then later made revisions in response to the group's comments. Authors are able to converse with a sample audience and to get a sense of what their story is like from that audience's point of view.

Authors' Circles also capitalize on the social nature of learning because authors see demonstrated a wide range of writing strategies. As the authors present their drafts, ask questions, and answer questions in an Authors' Circle, each author begins to see how other authors handle suggestions, solve problems, and revise their pieces. Authors' Circles provide a good opportunity to discuss writing strategies explicitly with other authors. Authors gradually begin to use these strategies in their own writing and to ask themselves the questions they predict other authors will ask in Authors' Circle as they work through their early drafts.

It is important that the teacher have the same role as other authors in Authors' Circle. When teachers want to participate in an Authors' Circle, they need to come as an author with a piece of writing. This allows teachers to participate with other authors, both receiving and giving suggestions, without imposing their judgments on students' work. Because the teacher is a participant, students feel freer to collaborate with the teacher and to reject suggestions that the teacher makes for revision instead of feeling that "I have to change it because the teacher said so." When teachers participate in the circles, they can demonstrate to students the strategies that a more experienced writer uses. Students come to see that all writers, including adults, produce drafts that need revision. This can be a revelation to students who think that adults produce perfect drafts the first time through. They begin to realize that revision is a natural part of authoring for everyone and so begin to value the process of conferring with others and revising for meaning.

Once students understand and value the role that other authors play in the revision process, they will begin taking charge of these circles themselves. Before long students who have pieces they want to revise will wait until one of their favorite authors also has something ready so they can be in the same group. These author friendship groups should be encouraged. All authors have fellow authors to whom they prefer to read their rough draft efforts, in part because they have proven trustworthy and in part because they intuitively seem to know each other and what is the most helpful thing to say at a certain point.

While Authors' Circle is the major form of conferring with other authors, this can occur in other classroom settings. These include student-to-student conferences that are more intimate and that begin to occur spontaneously because of the influence of Authors' Circles. Students may also quickly gather an informal group of authors to respond to something they have written rather than waiting for a formal Authors' Circle. Another setting is a student-teacher conference that gives the student a chance to interact with an author who has more experience with writing. This type of conference also gives the teacher a chance to do an instructional strategy lesson based on an immediate and felt need of the student.

Another variation of Authors' Circle is an activity called Writing in the Round. When authors suspect that they have a "hot piece" that they want to publish, a blank sheet of paper can be attached to the end of the draft and the draft left at the Writing-Reading Center. Those who read the piece (classmates, teachers, parents, visitors) are asked to write their comments and recommendations for revision on the attached sheet, dating and signing their comments. Authors are encouraged to make the first entry on the blank sheet telling their readers what they particularly like about the piece and what areas they see as still problematic (e.g., "I don't like my ending but I can't think of anything else").

These variations do not replace Authors' Circles but augment them. Any strategy used in this part of the authoring cycle functions to give authors feedback from their readership for the purpose of reconsidering their writing. As Atwell (1987) points out, the goal of conferences is not to get students to revise but to help them grow to independence as writers.

Through conferring with others, authors learn how to explore meaning with an audience and how to think critically about their writing. They become part of a thought collective in their classroom that expands their world as they hear others' ideas and perspectives and so leads them to outgrow their current understandings. Authors' Circles grow out of a real need for authors to communicate with others, to understand readers' perspectives, and to expand and clarify the ideas they want to express through writing. These same needs are present when students author meaning in other sign systems, such as art, drama, movement, mathematics, and music. Authors' Circle allows authors of all different kinds of meaning to think about and explore their ideas with others. Decisions about how to respond to the suggestions and comments of others, however, are made later in private.

Semantic Revision and Self-Editing

When authors leave an Authors' Circle, they often decide to do some semantic revision and self-editing of their rough draft and then submit it to the Editors' Table. Authors may occasionally decide that they no longer want to revise and publish a piece after meeting in Authors' Circle and return the piece to their Author's Folder. Most authors, however, make semantic revisions of their writing based on the suggestions made during Authors' Circle and then edit for conventions such as spelling that they have noticed as they read their piece to themselves and others.

Authors wait to revise their pieces until after Authors' Circle so they can consider in private the comments and suggestions that were made during the circle and not feel forced to make changes. They need not follow advice of other authors but instead can choose to make revisions based on their "vision" of what the piece should say and on the issues they feel ready to deal with in their writing. Although excellent suggestions may have been given in Authors' Circle, the author may not yet know how to deal with some issues that were raised or may have another agenda that is more important on that particular piece. Authors may also decide to act on suggestions in their next piece of writing instead of revising the current piece. The right to make decisions about semantic revision is imperative for authors to retain ownership of their writing.

We have observed teachers whose students turn out wonderful writing, but that writing is the teacher's rather than the student's. The teacher wants students' writing to be the best possible and so pushes students to make many revisions instead of allowing them to focus on the revisions they are most interested in and feel capable of handling. Teachers need to be sensitive to what the author is interested in exploring because those are the areas in which growth and learning are most likely. If the author wants to explore how better to end the story, this will be a productive area to explore even though the teacher can identify other parts of the story that could also be improved. Although the teacher or other students may mention some of these other areas in the circle, authors will find comments on the area they want to improve most helpful and will probably use only those suggestions during semantic revision. No author can work on improving all aspects of writing at one time, and so when teachers try to get authors to make many different kinds of revisions, they end up taking over the writing of the piece from the author.

That authors must have ownership of their pieces and make decisions on revisions does not mean that teachers no longer have a role in students' growth as authors. Teachers influence the growth of the authors in their classrooms just by establishing the authoring cycle structure because that structure promotes literacy. Teachers also influence authors by the invitations and suggestions they offer in informal conferences and Authors' Circles. The teacher uses what the author is exploring to make suggestions and invitations and so connects with that author instead of imposing the teacher's agenda and taking control of the piece and the writing process. Because the teacher is offering suggestions and invitations, the author still makes the final decision about semantic revision.

As authors read and reread their pieces to themselves and others, they also begin to self-edit their writing. Self-editing involves cleaning up conventional aspects such as spelling, grammar, punctuation, and capitalization. Once authors serve as outside editors for other authors, they often begin to do more self-editing of their own work before submitting it to Editors' Table. Although the major responsibility for editing occurs at Editors' Table, authors are encouraged to clean up any conventions they notice before submitting their writing to be edited by outside readers.

Authors are not required to copy over their work before submitting it to be edited. Instead, as they revise, they are asked to insert, cut and paste, and mark over their text so that all changes can be followed by the editors and typist. Only on the rare occasion when it is impossible to follow a revised copy is an author ever asked to recopy anything. If the revised draft is difficult to read, we usually have authors read their piece to the editor or typist rather than recopy it. Making authors recopy their writing can quickly kill their interest in making revisions. Young children who use few conventions in their writing generally read their pieces to the typist.

Sometimes, after extensive revision, authors will want to take their piece through Authors' Circle a second time, as Corey decided to do with his "smashed toe" story. This is encouraged and is evidence that Authors' Circle is becoming a natural part of the authoring process. Once authors are satisfied with their revised drafts, these drafts are submitted to Editors' Table.

Editors' Table

Because the purpose of written language is to communicate a message, authors focus on getting their meaning down during the early parts of the authoring cycle. When authors decide to take their pieces to publication, they edit them for convention to show their regard for readers. It needs to be stressed, however, that editing does not begin at those points labeled Self-Editing and Editors' Table on the authoring cycle. As students reread their in-process rough drafts or share their stories at Authors' Chair or Authors' Circle, they commonly correct many surface features of their texts. This is natural. Writers need to keep their mind on text, or the construction of meaning, as they write. Grammar and spelling miscues are a function of a mind-hand span—the mind is one place, the hand is another. Reading in the writing process serves a self-corrective function. "The first editor a writer faces," Margaret Atwell (1980, 90) says, "is him or herself."

The areas of the cycle labeled Self-Editing and Editors' Table represent points that highlight editing for purposes of moving a draft document to publication. The issue is thus not one of convention or meaning but rather a shift in focus. Authors use conventions all the time, but their focus is not always on those conventions. During the writing of the rough draft, when authors are focusing on constructing meaning, they intuitively use conventions and operate with their best current control of conventions. If they are required to focus on conventions during these early stages, the communicative aspects of writing suffer.

An example of the effect of this shift in focus from meaning to convention occurred in Gloria Kauffman's first-grade classroom.

Amy had finished writing a story about leaves in the fall and was waiting for an Authors' Circle to meet. Gloria was interested in what kinds of changes would result when an author changed focus from meaning to convention, and so she suggested that Amy go back through her story and make corrections in spelling. Figure 2.8 shows the self-editing Amy did five minutes after she finished writing her story. Amy obviously had more knowledge

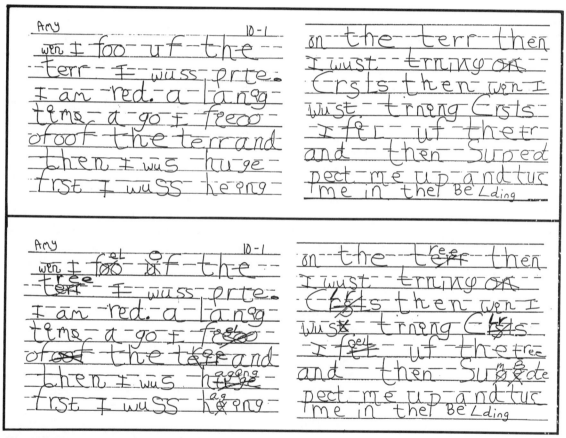

Transcription:

When I fell off the tree I was pretty. I am red. A long time ago I fell off the tree and then I was hanging. First I was hanging on the tree then I was turning colors. Then when I was turning colors I fell off the tree. And then somebody picked me up and took me in the building.

Figure 2.8   Amy's Original and Revised Leaf Stories (Amy, Grade 1).

about spelling than she was able to use when she was focusing on meaning. Once she got that meaning down, however, she shifted her focus to convention and used that knowledge.

During editing, the focus shifts to the use of conventions to support the reader. Conventions exist to support outside readers as they construct meaning through reading. The author already knows what the piece says, and so misspelled words or other conventional miscues do not interfere with the author's reading of the piece. Adults as well as children find it more difficult to proofread their own work versus proofreading the work of someone else. Although both revising and editing help authors develop the perspective of a reader, editing involves an *outside* reader who edits for meaning and conventions. During revision the author reads the piece to others, but during editing an outside reader is reading the piece and so conventions become more important. Editing is needed only when something is going to be published for an audience. The informal writing that authors do is not edited, only the few pieces that are being published for an outside audience to read.

When authors serve as editors of others' writing or have editors talk to them about their own work, they begin to understand the importance of conventions for reading. This shift in perspective from author to reader to editor produces a learning situation in which authors discover new conventions. Marvin, another first grader in Gloria Kauffman's classroom, was also writing a story about leaves when Gloria stopped by his desk for an informal conference. Gloria noticed from his draft that he was exploring the concept of the location of spaces and so commented to him, "You know, it would really help me as a reader if you would leave your spaces between the words." Marvin looked at her and said, "Oh, okay," and went back to his writing. As his draft in Figure 2.9 indicates, Marvin immediately began leaving spaces between his words. Although this was not a formal editing conference, this experience demonstrates that a shift in perspective from author to reader allows an author to discover new conventions.

Marvin's ability immediately to begin using spaces between words occurred because he was already exploring spacing. An author begins using conventions when they do not take the author's attention away from getting meaning down. This was obviously true for Marvin as he continued his story. The convention of putting spaces between words did not cost him a great deal of mental energy. He realized that it would support the reading of his story by other people, and so this convention entered naturally into his writing.

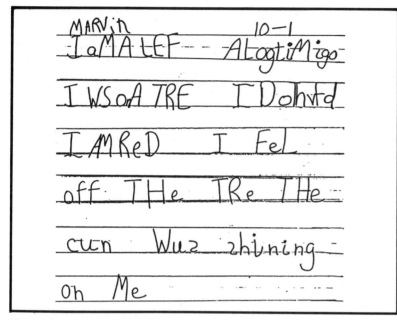

I am a leaf. A long time ago I was on a tree. I
don't have food. I am red. I fell off the tree.
The sun was shining on me.

Figure 2.9   Story Writing (Marvin, Grade 1).

Marvin's exploration of spacing demonstrates that authors need
the chance to explore alternatives to conventions and to use their
best current knowledge. This exploration of alternatives makes authors more receptive to learning the convention, as was evident
in Marvin's immediate response to Gloria's comment. Giving authors the chance to explore alternatives is not an attempt to put
off the learning of conventions but rather is a necessary part of
learning the convention. Although authors use their best current
knowledge of conventions as they write, through editing they are
able to go beyond their current understandings.

Editing is a social event and a natural part of authoring. All authors need outside editors. No writer singlehandedly controls the
authoring process. This is one misconception that past approaches
to reading and writing have perpetuated. The result is guilt, when
the simple fact of the matter is that almost every piece ever published has had the benefit of outside editing by others. Some authors dictate their books to secretaries who handle all the spelling
and typing. Being a writer is different from being a secretary. Stu-

dents need to understand that while not everyone is a secretary, everyone is an author.

In our classrooms, once a student has revised and self-edited a piece, it is put into the editors' box to be taken to Editors' Table. In most classrooms, the editors work with the handwritten revised rough draft. In some classrooms where a computer is available, volunteers or the students themselves type the text on the computer exactly as written and print it out triple-spaced. In one school there is a permanent computer and printer available in the classroom, while in another school the computer laboratory is scheduled for class use. This typed copy is given back to the author for one final proofing because "things often look and sound different to authors when typed" and "secretaries often make mistakes that need catching." Once the author has proofed the text after typing, it is placed in the in box at Editors' Table.

Editors' Table is a physically identifiable area in the classroom. In our classrooms, it includes a typewriter or computer, a set of basic reference books (thesaurus, spelling dictionary, regular dictionary, English stylebook, etc.), visor hats or buttons for the editors to wear, a "ready for typing box," an in box, a managing editor box, pens, pencils, colored markers, a sign reading "Quiet! Editors at Work," a poster of various editing marks, a chart of what this week's editors have decided specifically to look for when editing, and so on.

The physical presence of the area is important. Essentially Editors' Table needs to signal to the students more than "Editing is important." The center should physically and functionally signal "editing" at the same time it psychologically signals "authoring." Its presence should be a sign to students just beginning to draft a piece that it is all right to take risks, that their concerns for spelling and grammar are important, that this classroom is a safe environment that supports authors, and that when and if they decide to "go public," their "mechanical" concerns will be handled. Understanding the function and place of editing in the authoring cycle is important. The very presence of an Editors' Table allows real authoring to start.

Usually students volunteer to serve as outside editors for one week, although the length of time can vary with the type and frequency of publication. We select three to five students to serve as editors for a week. They are easily identifiable, because they inevitably wear their editor's visor or button from morning to evening.

Everyone, from the best and most proficient writer to the least proficient writer, gets a turn. Sometimes teachers think that only the better writers will be able to handle the demands of editing. We have found, however, that although the less proficient writers find fewer editorial changes than the proficient writers, they tend to benefit more from the experience. The less proficient writers use conventions the least and so benefit from focusing on conventions and looking at conventions in someone else's work.

During the week that students serve as editors, they have limited opportunities to work on their own materials. Keeping authors away from their own writing may conceptually bother a conscientious teacher. This change in perspective—from writer to editor, from user to critic—often is quite beneficial as well as motivating. After a week's hiatus students are often quite anxious to get on with their writing. They have new ideas as well as new perspectives on the process. The best learning situation to discover new conventions is to approach someone else's document, because conventions exist for the reader rather than the writer. It is easier to attend to conventions in another person's text where the reader does not already know the message than in one's own text where one already knows the meaning.

Editing involves both semantic editing and editing for convention. The first task of the outside editor is semantic editing—reading the piece to make sure it makes sense. Editors do not have the right to make meaning changes in the texts they read because editors do not own text; authors do. If something does not make sense, it is up to the editor to find the author, explain the problem, and let the author decide right then whether to change the text. Minor changes in text that do not change the intended meaning of the piece can be made by the editor without consultation. If editors have to ask if the change they are about to make is minor or major, we invariably suggest they consult the author.

We usually suggest that editors not bring more than three questions regarding meaning to the author so that the author does not feel overwhelmed with changes to consider. Some teachers initially have each piece read by two editors. Each editor initials the upper right-hand corner of the draft after reading it for any semantic changes. Once editors have read the piece for sense and consulted with the author, the piece is ready to edit for conventions.

Editing for conventions includes both grammatical editing and spelling editing. During grammatical editing, editors reread each piece several times, paying particular attention to the things they as a group have decided to worry about—run-on sentences, capitals and periods, quotation marks, commas, paragraphing, and so on. It is too overwhelming, especially in the initial stages of editing, for editors to have to look for all kinds of grammatical and spelling conventions, so the group of editors decides on one or two aspects to focus on as they edit. Standard editing marks or marks the editors have agreed on are used.

A final editing concerns spelling. We suggest that the editor read through the piece and highlight in Magic Marker any word or words that look questionable; that editors work together, consult each other on spellings, and look up words in the resource materials provided if they are unsure. One strategy that we have suggested to editors is that they write the word several times, trying out different spellings, and then choose the one they think looks correct. If a highlighted word turns out to be spelled correctly, the typist knows to ignore the highlighting. If a highlighted word is found to be spelled incorrectly, a new spelling is included above it and the typist uses this new spelling in the final document. In the initial stages of editing, teachers may want to tell editors that they only need to identify and check three words for spelling so that the spelling editing is not overwhelming and the author's paper does not have so many markings on it.

After a document goes through semantic editing and editing for conventions, including both grammatical editing and editing for spellings, it is ready to be sent to the managing editor. This is typically the classroom teacher or the person doing the final draft typing. If the rough draft was earlier typed into the computer, the corrections can be made on the computer without retyping the entire document. If errors in grammar or spelling remain, the managing editor can make these changes without consulting the author, just as a secretary will make corrections in convention during typing. Despite this managing editor's prerogative, it is important not to make any more changes in the final form than are necessary and never to make changes that affect the meaning of the piece.

In studying the process of editing as a function of student involvement in the authoring cycle during Mary Lynn Woods's summer program, we found that editors during the first week were aware of approximately 65 percent of conventional changes, a statistic that would please any English teacher. By the end of the third week, editors were aware of 89 percent of the conventional changes needed in a given text. This observation was interesting enough. The real finding, however, was that over time the function of the editor changed. As the program progressed, authors gained experience with the strategies used in the authoring cycle and during editing. As they gained experience, knowledge, and confidence, they began to assume more responsibility for self-editing, both for content and convention. Thus, outside editors needed to make fewer conventional changes, and in turn found the quality of the changes to be increasingly complex, calling for an even finer discrimination and understanding of English syntax.

We have found that some teachers hesitate to start Editors' Table when first trying to initiate the authoring cycle in their classrooms. They feel that editing is beyond the capabilities of their students, that the focus on editing will inhibit the students as they write, or that they do not have time to spend with both Authors' Circles and Editors' Table. As argued earlier, however, the presence of Editors' Table reassures students that they do not need to worry about conventions early in writing because their concerns will be dealt with later in the cycle. Even if students use many invented spellings in their writing, editing is beneficial for both more and less proficient writers in helping them take a reader's perspective and in gaining control over conventions. Teachers simply make adjustments in the amount and type of conventions students are expected to look for as they edit rather than taking over the process of editing themselves. Teachers should not expect or wait until students can do the same quality of editing that the teacher is able to do. Students should begin editing right away at whatever level they can handle. Just as we do not expect young children immediately to produce adult language as they learn to talk, we should not expect students immediately to meet adult standards for conventions in written language. They need time to explore and discover these conventions gradually instead of having to operate right away at the teacher's level of proficiency.

Finally, teachers should not need to be present at both Authors' Circles and Editors' Table. Once these groups are functioning, teachers should only occasionally join the groups. If the teacher is always present at each group, this is an indication that the teacher is controlling too much of the process and making students depend on teacher input rather than allowing the students to take over the process themselves. Students who need more support can initially edit with a partner rather than with the teacher.

Gloria Kauffman discovered the important function that editing plays when she held off beginning Editors' Table with her first-grade students, feeling they were not ready to handle it. She noted late in the year that few of the children were using punctuation in their writing. As we talked together we realized that the children did not understand the importance of conventions such as punctuation because she or another adult always served as the editor. Gloria already had heard the author read the piece and so did not need to ask the author about invented spellings or punctuation. If the students had served as outside editors of each other's pieces, they would have been faced with trying to read someone else's piece or with having an editor coming to talk to them about parts that were difficult to read. As argued earlier, conventions are important to readers, not authors, who need them to construct meaning. When Editors' Table is omitted from the authoring cycle, authors do not fully realize the function of conventions.

In introducing Editors' Table, we walk the first group through the process. We begin by sharing documents with the group similar to what the class is going to publish (e.g., books or newspapers) and talking about what an editor of this publication needs to do. We have also used the filmstrip *How a Picture Book Is Made* (Kellogg & Blantz 1976) to introduce authors to editing in the professional world of book publishing. In this filmstrip, Steven Kellogg describes how he came up with the idea for *Island of the Skog* (1973) and shows viewers the rough drafts he wrote and sketched and the dummy book he created to take to his editor. The filmstrip includes his visit to New York to consult with his editor and a discussion about the changes he made based on this conference. It ends with the book being run off on the presses to be sold in bookstores. The filmstrip gives authors a good overview of the publishing process and the role of editing in that process. Another resource on the process of publishing books is found in the children's book *How a Book Is Made* (Aliki 1986).

After listing some responsibilities of an editor, the group is presented with individual photocopies of the same rough draft, and they discuss to whom this draft belongs to stress the author's ownership. The teacher puts a copy of the rough draft on an overhead transparency. The group uses this draft to decide on the editorial markings that they will use for semantic editing and for the different kinds of editing for conventions. These rules are written on a blackboard or chart, and the editors then begin their first round of editing. At the end of this first round, the editors suggest changes in their rules.

The second group of editors the following week proceeds from the list that the first group has generated and makes any changes they consider important. For the most part, little consultation with the first group is needed, because by the time the first set of editors complete their week, authors have been consulted and reconsulted so often that everyone knows what one does at Editors' Table.

Depending on the type of publication, editors may have other responsibilities beyond editing texts. Especially if the publication is a newspaper, editors can be involved in deciding on layout, organization, assembly, and distribution of the publication. As described in Chapter 1, we have also found it exciting to invite readers to write letters to the editors giving their suggestions on how to improve a publication. When we were involved in producing a newspaper in a summer reading program in Indianapolis, readers wrote letters suggesting the addition of cartoons, jokes, page numbers, and different kinds of articles. They also wrote letters complaining about typing mistakes that had changed their articles. The editors printed these letters with their answers in future publications and made changes in the newspaper based on these suggestions. Everyone became more interested and involved in the newspaper because of these letters to the editors.

We want to stress that not every piece of writing that is written or even published needs to be edited. Students should be involved in many informal writing experiences (journals, pen pal letters, stories, etc.) that never go to publication. Only pieces that have been selected for formal publication need to go through editing. Editing may not be necessary for all pieces in a publication, such as letters to the editors or personal ads, or for more informal publications.

As with Authors' Circle, teachers need to remain flexible in how they adapt Editors' Table to meet the needs of their students. Initially this often means limiting the amount and types of editing that the editors are expected to do or having students edit in pairs so that editing is not too overwhelming. Later on, as students become familiar with the editing process, they will begin to do more self-editing and to edit informally with other authors; teachers will then need to work with students in changing the function of Editors' Table.

From Editors' Table, the manuscript goes to final typing, back to the editors for layout if it is going into a newspaper or magazine or to the author if it is going into a book, and then finally to publication and the celebration of authors and authorship. For authors who are producing a book, the process of illustrating their book is a significant part of the publication process as they author by constructing meaning through drawings rather than through writing. They often spend time consulting with published books and conferencing with favorite illustrators from the room as they work on getting their book to look just right. Once they complete their book, they celebrate their authorship of both writing and art as they present their book to the class.

Publishing/Celebrating Authorship

Although there are many forms of celebrating authorship, publication is clearly one of the most important. In fact, we would go so far as to say that to establish an authoring cycle in the classroom, the first thing that is needed is a publishing program. Publishing creates a real purpose for authors to move documents through the entire authoring cycle.

Several criteria define a published document. First, there must be a real audience for the document and a recognized need for publication. Second, there should be a continuing use of that publication to keep it alive and functional in the classroom. If a document is read only once and then disappears from view, why publish it? In our classrooms, published books, for example, become part of the classroom library and are read over and over so that students see a real purpose for publication.

Publication can be both informal and formal and can include group and individual books, newspapers, class magazines, displays in classrooms and hallways, posters, games, invitations, and announcements. The kind of publication, informal or formal, that occurs in a classroom is determined by the projected audience. In addition to classroom publications, students can submit their work to the school paper, the local newspaper, trade magazines that publish student writing, or writing contests.

Displays of student work on bulletin boards in the classroom and hallway are an informal form of publication that should be used and exploited. These displays can be made attractive by having students create posters or large murals on which student writing has been cut into interesting shapes and displayed in a visually attractive manner. During Author Sharing Times students may be invited to write a page of text building from another author's style or language patterns. The result of this invitation can be shared, displayed on a bulletin board, or put together in a Group Composed Book that is then available in the class library or at the Writing-Reading Center for others to read. Because this is an informal publication, no formal editing need be done. Instead, students' first draft efforts are used.

These informal publications work well in the secure environment of the classroom. Depending on the type of school the classroom is in, displaying such student work in the hallway may or may not be wise. This decision rests with the teacher, but the guideline to follow is that the teacher is there to support the students' use and exploration of writing, not to embarrass them when they engage in such exploration. If either the teacher or the students will be judged negatively by the work displayed in the hall, or if parents and administrators do not understand the program, then we recommend that teachers not display first drafts outside the low-risk environment of the classroom.

We use the same rule in deciding whether first draft work will go home. We generally do not send any rough drafts home until we have had a chance to talk with parents. At Parents' Day we explain the program and recommend that the home environment be a low-risk environment so that children can feel free to share first drafts. If, later on, parents come in wondering when their child is going to attend to spelling and grammar, we remind them that what they are reacting to are first drafts, and show them some of the child's writing that has been published.

As student work moves further and further from the supportive environment of the classroom, a more formal publishing program is needed. To create such a need we recommend that teachers set up a class magazine or newspaper and a book publishing program in addition to any more formal student publications that exist at the school or district level. These publications need not be fancy. The class magazine or newspaper can be run off on blue ditto or photocopied if such facilities are available.

Myriam Revel-Wood produces a class magazine that is blue ditto inside with a piece of construction paper outside. Mary Lynn Woods produces *The Write Type,* a hybrid newspaper/magazine that is typed, photocopied, collated, and stapled. Sue Robinson produces a class newspaper in blue ditto. Other teachers have each student produce an individual magazine as a semester-long project. Gloria Kauffman produces several photocopied newspapers a year on special topics that grow out of class units or field trips. In addition, her students publish many individual books, including both fiction stories and information books.

Although there are many ways to make books, we like Vera Milz's procedure best. Most of the teachers we have been working with find it relatively inexpensive and easy. Her procedure involves the creation of a cover from cereal boxes and a piece of contact paper or prepasted wallpaper. Pages are added by sewing down the middle of sheets of typing paper and then gluing the outside sheet to the cover. Self-adhesive, blank name labels can be used to put the title and author's name on the front cover. See *Bookmaking* in Section Two for diagrams and further information on how to make these books.

There is nothing particularly sacrosanct about these books, except that they are colorful and hold up well with handling. Students respond to these hardcover books more positively than to paper covers because they more closely resemble professional publications. The hardcovers signal "you are an author" to students.

We make a standard size using six sheets of paper. When the children publish shorter stories, the additional pages are removed. When children begin to write chapter books, several sets of sewn six-sheet book pages are combined by hand sewing them together before they are glued in the cover. For the most part, six-sheet book page sets work quite well and do not damage the average sewing maching.

This procedure is easy and makes a nice publication. Although there are many, many other ways to make books, most involve the teacher. Ours doesn't; it involves the parent!

Once the children have published their first book, the parents and children are invited in for Parents' Day. One of the activities is, of course, the children's sharing their publications with their parents. Then we announce that we would like to do a lot more writing of books during the year but the parents' help is needed. Parents need not come to school to help. Reams of typing paper can be sent home. Parents sew them in sets of six and return them with the child. Parents are asked to save cereal boxes and, once they have a collection (broken down so they can be folded and stacked), to send them to school with the child. When several boxes have been received, they are sent home to another parent who has volunteered to cut the boxes to book-cover size. We have also had good luck in asking parents to send in rolls of contact paper or prepasted wallpaper they find on sale or have available in the home. Other parents are sent rolls of the contact paper or prepasted wallpaper to cut to size and return with their child. Still other parents are sent rubber cement and sets of book pages, cardboard, and contact paper for final assembly. Many working parents like this program because they need not feel guilty that they cannot help out in their child's classroom during the school day. The procedure works extremely well, as there are always at least 70 blank books for use at the Writing-Reading Center at any given time.

Often one parent will coordinate the entire bookmaking process. Once Bookmaking is set up, be certain that, come the end of the year, there are at least 30 blank books for use next year.

If organizationally this procedure doesn't appeal, try a bookmaking party and invite everyone in for an evening of making books. Parents with portable sewing machines can bring them. Others can continue to provide cereal box-type cardboard and rolls of contact paper.

We've taken some time to describe Bookmaking because having blank books available as a publishing option is crucial. A publishing program must be in operation in the classroom to make the authoring cycle seem purposeful to children.

With few exceptions, final copies of books and articles in the class newspaper and magazine should be typed. Students should not be required to recopy unless they personally request to do so because of the nature of the piece. If students are routinely asked to recopy their drafts to final form, the publishing program is rapidly destroyed. "Copying it over in ink" feeds the students' already dysfunctional notions of revision. Professional writers rarely recopy their drafts. Typically they are typed by a secretary, revised by the author, and then retyped by someone else.

Ideally each classroom should have a word processing program, computer, and printer available for use. We have a parent who comes in and types materials for publication into the computer. Once this task is done, a rough draft is run for use in editing. Once the piece has been through Editors' Table it goes back to the computer, the text is updated, the print button is pushed, and the final copy comes out.

If a computer and printer are not available in the classroom, a parent who has these facilities or who can type can be asked to do final typing. This task does not need to be overwhelming. Average expectations will be about 60 relatively short stories or articles each month (two articles per child).

Materials for books made with 8 1/2" × 11" paper need to be run off using a 4 1/2" width. Typically, final copy stories that are to go in books are typed double spaced with triple spacing between paragraphs. When the final copy comes back, the author has to decide how to break the story to lay it out in the book. Once this decision is made, the text can be cut apart and rubber-cemented into the book at the locations selected. Illustrations, too, can be done on another sheet of paper and then rubber-cemented into the book. In this way, if the child doesn't like the outcome, only a single page need be redone.

Publishing a class newspaper or magazine involves formatting so that it fits the column width of the newspaper. Parents can be asked to type articles in final form in 3" columns so students can lay out the magazine or newspaper. Stencils can be made from a photocopy of the layout, and assembly can be a group process. If a computer and printer are available, a stencil can be slipped into a printer set to doublestrike, and a final typed stencil will result. Computer software programs, like *Newsroom* (1984), greatly facilitate layout and publication of a class newspaper. Many schools now have photocopiers available for general use so that stencils are not needed, and the entire publication is simply photocopied.

If running a publishing program sounds like too much work, remember we define publishing generously and are talking about one or two stories or articles per student each month. We think it's important to keep the publishing process going. We announce that although everyone will be writing on a daily basis, only two rough drafts each month for each student will be moved to publication. The authors decide where to publish their materials, either in book form or in the class newspaper or magazine. If students wish to publish more they may do so, but on their own time and with their own materials. We take this firm stand because we do not want publishing to be the entire language arts program. Although it is crucial that students have an outlet for their work and a ready audience, not everything written merits publication. We want children to have time to write daily, to explore using writing as a vehicle for learning, to experience the generative nature of the writing process, to learn how to support themselves and others in the process, to read like writers, and to use reading and writing as vehicles for exploring and expanding their world. Publishing is a central feature of the authoring process, but it is only one feature, and it cannot and should not overshadow everything else that is going on.

Many school districts publish a newspaper or a magazine at the district level. Sometimes a local newspaper will volunteer to publish at least three pieces of children's writing each week. Such programs, although they are excellent and should be encouraged, do not take the place of the classroom publishing program. If such opportunities are available, children working at the Editors' Table should be made responsible for identifying selections that they believe merit wider distribution. We usually ask the editors to select more articles than will actually be sent. The final decision of which materials to send is up to the managing editor, which means the classroom teacher or some adult charged with this responsibility. The managing editor exercises control to ensure that whatever is published will not embarrass the author or other class members. In this regard, the responsibility of the managing editor is the same here as it is for all class materials going public or being moved to a wider audience through publication. If the editors have not caught all the things wrong with a piece, the managing editor has the right to make last-minute changes, though these should be kept to a minimum.

To keep the publishing program going, we regularly announce when the next issue of the class magazine or newspaper will be coming out. Students are reminded that, if they haven't done so, they need to look through their Author's Folders and identify rough draft efforts that they want to be published. Students should be encouraged to take one piece of writing through the authoring cycle to publication about once every two weeks. Given the number of invitations to write, the problem never is having something to publish, but rather deciding which of all the things drafted are worth the extra investment of time and energy to take them to final publication.

Once a newspaper or book is published, we take time in the classroom to celebrate the authorship of that document. The publication of a newspaper is greeted with fanfare in the classroom, and everything stops while students take their newspapers and scatter around the room to read and enjoy them with one another. These newspapers are then taken home and shared with parents and other family members. Letters to the editors about the newspaper give authors and editors suggestions on how to improve their next newspaper and keep it going.

When a book is published, the author goes to the Authors' Chair and reads the entire book to the class or to a small group. Once the author has read the book, the listeners receive the book by telling what they heard, talking about what they liked about the book, and asking the author questions about the writing of the book. The questions and comments of the listeners differ from those in Authors' Circle in that the purpose is not to help authors think about or revise their stories but to celebrate their authorship. Authors are in their glory as they proudly share their publications with their friends. These books are taken home to share with family members and then brought back to school and placed in the classroom library until the end of the year. We have found that these books are often the most read materials in the classroom.

Other ways that teachers have involved authors in celebrating their authorship include having authors go to other classrooms to share a published book and having authors' teas. In one school, a third-grade and a sixth-grade classroom have paired up, and students from these grades take their published books to the other classroom to read to any interested students. Authors' teas can involve inviting other students, the principal, or parents to celebrate authorship. It is better if these occur several times during the year, rather than at the end of the year, because they motivate students to want to continue to write and publish. Usually the tea begins with authors briefly describing the authoring cycle. Then small groups form so that authors can read their entire books. These groups are made up of several authors plus their guests. The guests also have time to walk around and look at the various publications in the room and to enjoy refreshments made by the authors.

Young Authors Conferences provide a formal way for students, parents, and teachers to celebrate authorship. These conferences are usually organized by a county reading association or by a school system, and they occur on a Saturday morning. Children register for the conference and bring with them a book they wrote. The conference usually consists of listening to a professional children's author in a large group session and meeting in small groups with other children. Parent sessions are held to give parents ideas on how they can encourage their children in reading and writing.

If the authoring cycle has been operating, students should have many books from which to choose a book to take to the conference. In school systems where students write one book a year (the book they take to Young Authors Conference), this conference becomes a negative experience for many students. The conference should include small group sessions of six to ten children so that authors have an opportunity to celebrate their authorship by sharing their books with each other. All authors should be invited to attend the conference. When only several authors from a school are selected to attend, this reinforces the notion that writing is a special gift for only a few select people. When organized to include all authors and to give them a chance to celebrate their own authorship as well as listen to others, Young Authors Conferences can play a vital role in communicating the importance of authorship to students, parents, and the community.

Publication and celebration of authorship give students the chance to present their documents to other class members and to feel the satisfaction of successfully communicating with an audience. The thrill that authors experience as they present their work to others encourages them to continue writing and moving through the authoring cycle. Celebrating authorship is also essential in providing demonstrations to other authors of new ideas and strategies that they might use in their own writing, and this, in turn, encourages other authors to move through the authoring cycle. We have found that as soon as a few authors get their work published and celebrated, there is a sudden surge of rough drafts being written and taken to Authors' Circle by authors who had been relatively unproductive. The entire cycle finally fits together for them. Some students need to go through the whole cycle several times before they become fully engaged in it. The celebration of authorship brings both an end and a new beginning to the cycle as it offers new invitations to others to engage in the cycle anew.

Language Strategy Instruction/Invitations

A missing component in many process reading and writing classrooms is the strategy lesson. Strategy lessons are instructional activities designed to highlight some aspect of literacy that the teacher or student sees as important in relation to their current knowledge of how to use reading and writing to learn. Strategy lessons include both the psychological and sociological strategies employed by learners as they are involved in authoring. Students become aware of how to support their own learning as well as the learning of other students. Learners are invited to distance themselves from the immediate experience for purposes of offering new opportunities for growth to both themselves and others.

Watson (1982) defines a strategy lesson as an instructional episode or event in which all appropriate cueing systems of language and life are used to strengthen the language user's ability to process written language. We would like to add that a strategy lesson is an attempt to make the educational experience in which students have engaged generative. In this sense, strategy instruction represents that point in curriculum where both students and teachers are given the opportunity to be reflective. Students and teachers ask themselves: "What do I want to do differently next time?" "What did I learn from this experience that I can use in future engagements?" Strategy lessons are a time to explore options; to make unconscious strategies conscious for purposes of control and empowerment. Strategy lessons can be generated by students as well as by the teacher. Strategy lessons are self-correcting invitations to growth, self-evaluation, and curricular planning.

Observing and evaluating what students are doing in light of what is currently known, the teacher designs a classroom activity to highlight some aspect of literacy seen as important. Language activities are settings that call for students to use a variety of language strategies. Strategy lessons are language activities that have a more limited focus. Typically, strategy lessons highlight one particular cognitive or social activity that a language user might do in the name of literacy. Things are not taught because they are true, in part because our language truths may already be known, but because they appear to be useful, given our knowledge of the language users and how they operate in the class. The teacher does not follow a preordained curriculum but chooses strategy lessons that meet the current needs and explorations of specific learners in the classroom.

One of the benefits of being the managing editor is the opportunity to identify recurring patterns of strengths and problems that the students in the classroom seem to have. Selection and implementation of strategy lessons become a form of building curriculum using the child as the informant. In some instances strategy lessons support; in most instances they extend. Most importantly, they always build directly off of observations of a specific child. Our observations of Corey in Chapter 1 indicated that strategy lessons on expanding written pieces, quotation marks, and question marks would have been appropriate based on what he was currently attending to and exploring. We could then choose one of these to develop further in a strategy lesson or to involve Corey in an experience such as being an editor that would facilitate his explorations.

Strategy lessons can highlight learning language (new forms, new purposes, new genres), learning about language (new techniques, new markings) or learning through language (new ways of using language to learn). No strategy lesson includes just one or the other of these dimensions; rather, all are available, but one is simply highlighted in a particular lesson.

Strategy lessons have three parts (Goodman, Burke & Sherman 1980; Smith, Goodman & Meredith 1978; Goodman, Smith, Meredith & Goodman 1987):

1. Perceiving, a natural language setting in which the aspect of interest is highlighted
2. Ideating, an opportunity for children to discuss and make connections to what it is they currently know
3. Presenting, an opportunity to apply their new insight

Strategy instruction begins with the opportunity to engage in real reading and writing. If we decide that student stories are lacking in detail, we might bring in a book that has many details in its storyline. After discussion, we would invite students to try writing their next piece with more detail or to go to their Author's Folder and find a selection they believe would be improved if more details were added. At Author Sharing Time, we would ask students to reflect on how adding more detail helped or failed to help make their writing better. We would also discuss what strategies students used for deciding what kind of detail to add as well as where to add it.

Our intent here is to make children strategic rather than rote learners. With conscious awareness comes choice, and with choice comes empowerment. Unlike direct instruction, insights and discussion evolve from language in use. Strategies are not given as formulas or rules to be applied, but rather as options that can be used to construct meaning. For a strategy to be useful, students must understand at an intuitive level how the strategy relates to what proficient readers and writers do, as well as the conditions under which its use is appropriate.

Selection and implementation of strategy lessons focus on key strategies that successful readers and writers use or have used. The lessons should relate to what learners do as they engage in reading and writing processes and should include psychological strategies (e.g., self-correction, monitoring for meaning during reading), and sociological strategies (e.g., talking with a neighbor during writing, reading drafts aloud to someone else, getting someone to brainstorm initial thinking). Selection of strategy lessons builds on patterns observed in the student's reading and writing, but opens new worlds by inviting children to extend their knowing.

Synonym Substitution, described in *Strategies in Reading* (Goodman, Burke & Sherman 1980), is a strategy highlighting learning language that readers can use when they encounter something unknown in print. *Schema Stories,* a strategy lesson found in this manual, highlights language about language, in this instance how various types of print genre are organized. It helps language users understand that they already have information that they can access and use in reading materials in a genre they probably felt they didn't know anything about. *Cloning an Author,* another strategy lesson found in this manual, highlights learning through language, introducing a strategy readers might use to create a unified meaning from a text they have just read. *Generating Written Discourse* is an equivalent strategy in writing.

These strategy lessons have been teacher generated, but it must be remembered that students can and do generate their own strategy lessons. This often occurs through sharing. "Did you notice what Lisa did when she came to an unknown word? The next time we read a difficult text, why don't we try it. That's what good readers do when they read."

Amy wrote a story involving a new adventure with Peter Rabbit.

During sharing she commented, "What I learned was that you can take an idea from another author and change it to write your own story." We followed by saying, "Great. Good authors learn to live off the land." During the next several months students used Amy's strategy for beginning their own stories.

These strategy lessons are used to introduce students to options they *may* use as they process written language rather than as something they *must* do. They occur at the end of the cycle because they build off of the specific experiences of students with language. Students must first have experiences using language before they can consciously reflect on that use. Strategy lessons help make students consciously aware of their strategies; this awareness makes choice possible and allows learners to be strategic. Strategic behavior involves some element of conscious awareness so that learners can think about their options when they run into trouble. Just experiencing strategies may not be enough as learners fail to transfer that strategy to other new situations. Carolyn Burke reminds us, however, that "a little goes a long way" (1985b).

Conclusion

As a curricular frame, the authoring cycle does what a curriculum should do; it puts things into perspective. Olga Scibior, an ethnographer from Mount Saint Vincent University in Halifax, Canada, spent a year in Myriam Revel-Wood's room studying the effect of the authoring cycle over time (Scibior 1986). At the end of the year, she asked, "How did your writing change as a result of having been in this room?" "From the start of the year to now, what did you learn about reading that you didn't know before?"

About writing, Boyd, a fourth grader, responded, "Well, it was crazy, you know, at the start of the year, I just wrote, and I never thought about doing it better. Now we just know more, I guess. Now I want to revise. I want to make my writing better. I know other kids can help."

About reading, Boyd said, "I just read differently. First I get to pick out the books I read and that makes it different. I used to read thinking what does the teacher want. Now, I read what I want. It's just different."

Olga also reported that strategies introduced in instruction, such as Say Something, Cloning an Author, Generating Written Discourse, Authors' Circle, and Editors' Table, become natural strategies for children to use. As children experienced writers' block or had difficulty understanding what they were reading, they naturally moved to Say Something and then back to writing or reading. Early overconcern for spelling and grammar that blocked their involvement in the process gave way. By the end of the year such concerns were almost nonexistent during early phases of writing.

Students bring into a classroom instructional histories that can block a teacher's early attempts to involve them in the authoring cycle. Our major advice to teachers is "Be patient. Don't give up." The first Authors' Circles may flop, and students may be reluctant to write or to revise their writing. Teachers we have worked with have found that gradually students begin to take ownership in the cycle as the cycle becomes purposeful to them as language users and learners. When this happens, both students and teachers become excited about the learning that is occurring as students move through the authoring cycle.

Olga Scibior's report suggests that the strategies of instruction become the strategies of use. Her report also suggests that what were, for instructional purposes, distinct steps in an authoring cycle became, over time, a general process framework that children used to guide their own learning. It is at the point of having created an authoring cycle in the classroom that the teacher must address how it may be maintained and kept going. These topics are the subject of the next two chapters in this volume.

Reading as a Process of Authorship

Kathy G. Short / Gloria Kauffman

Introduction

Many educators are now calling for teachers to use process-
and meaning-centered approaches to curriculum. Even though as
teachers we agreed with these calls for more meaning-centered approaches, we faced many struggles and questions when we tried
to implement such an approach in the classroom. If we were no
longer simply taking textbook curriculum and imposing it onto
students, where did we get the curriculum? We found that as we
moved away from "scope and sequence" charts, we tended to put
together a collection of "neat" activities without a framework that
tied these activities together. We needed a framework that was
both theoretical and practical and that would allow us to generate and evaluate curricular experiences. As we worked together,
the curricular framework that formed the basis of our learning
environment gradually became the authoring cycle.

The Authoring Cycle as a Curricular Framework

Initially we saw the authoring cycle only as a framework for the
writing curriculum, and when Jerry Harste and Carolyn Burke suggested to us that the authoring cycle was a framework for curricu-

lum in general, we rejected their suggestion. As we continued to work with the authoring cycle and with curriculum development, however, the responses of the first-grade children with whom we were working forced us to see that this cycle was the general framework for which we were searching. Instead of seeing authoring only as a process of constructing meaning through writing, we realized that authoring is a general process of constructing meaning in many different communication systems (writing, reading, art, music, drama, movement, etc.) and fields of study. The authoring cycle emphasized for us that curriculum must always build from and connect with children's life experiences as they author. This happens through the children engaging in uninterrupted experiences with meaning, exploring some meanings more intensively with others, revising their meanings, presenting and sharing their meanings more publicly with others, reflecting on their learning, and accepting new learning invitations.

Using this understanding of authoring and the authoring cycle, we examined what we were doing in other communication systems and fields of study. We began by looking at the types of reading experiences we were providing. We realized right away that our curriculum did not fully support the children in moving through this cycle as authors of their reading. We were giving the children many choices in their reading materials and were involving them in many uninterrupted reading experiences. They had at least 30 minutes a day to read books they chose either with a partner or alone. We read to them several times a day and had listening centers where they could listen to tape recordings of books. We read many predictable books and used Big Books in Shared Reading experiences. We introduced children to books and authors and set up many different displays of literature. We had done a good job of involving children in reading widely. The room was filled with books, and children read constantly.

Something was missing, however, and when we looked at the reading experiences in our curriculum using the framework of the authoring cycle, we realized what was wrong. What was missing was a way for children to explore intensively the meanings they were constructing during reading with other readers and to present these meanings publicly to others. They often exchanged a few comments as they partner-read or when we talked together as a large group about the class read-aloud book, but the more intensive exploration of meaning that occurred in Authors' Circle was missing. We began looking for curricular strategies that would involve children in really expanding and exploring their thinking about what they were reading. We wanted to deepen their understandings about literature, and our experiences with Authors' Circle made us see that when learners talk together for a purpose, they really begin to explore and reflect on their authoring. About this time we met Karen Smith, a sixth-grade teacher from Arizona, and her discussions of the literature groups she used in her classroom gave us some ideas about how we could begin to work at authoring circles in reading in our classroom.

From the first day that we used Literature Circles in the classroom, it was evident that these circles gave readers the opportunity they needed to explore half-formed ideas with others and to revise their understandings of a piece of literature through hearing other readers' interpretations. The books they discussed in Literature Circles became significant parts of their life experiences and were the books they returned to in making connections in later reading and writing experiences. The children's thinking about literature became more complex and generative and moved them through the authoring cycle. The discussions helped them revise their understandings about literature, which they shared with other children through some type of *Literature Response Activity*. The children also changed in their ability to reflect on their own reading processes, on *how* they read as well as on *what* they read.

Our first experiences with Literature Circles were with first-grade students during a year-long collaborative study in which we worked closely on a daily basis and shared teaching and research responsibilities (Short 1986). Our discussion of Literature Circles here will draw from our experiences with these first-grade students as well as with the third-grade students that Gloria now teaches and the sixth-grade students of another teacher at the same school, Kaylene Yoder.

Although this article focuses on Literature Circles, we want to stress that children need to be involved in many extensive reading experiences and not just in Literature Circles. Kaylene found that her sixth-grade students were very hesitant to read for enjoyment because of their past experiences with books. She involved them in many uninterrupted experiences with books and brought in different kinds of reading materials, including newspapers and magazines, to get them involved in reading widely. We wanted our students to be flexible readers who had strategies for reading a wide variety of materials, not just literature. We have also found that language activities such as Say Something, Readers' Theatre, and *Sketch to Stretch* are excellent in creating an atmosphere in which children are more willing to discuss books with each other. This type of atmosphere is essential for Literature Circles to be successful.

Literature Circles in the Classroom

Preparing for Literature Circles

We begin Literature Circles by selecting the literature for the groups. The teacher, in consultation with the students, selects good literature of interest to the students and with enough depth for discussion. Enough choices are provided so that only four or five children will be in each group. The literature is then introduced to the class, and students individually decide which group they want to join. To help them make their choices, we generally give a short talk on each book or selection and then put the items on display for the children to look at and read. Some children read each choice, while others browse through the books.

With kindergarten and first-grade children, we read the choices aloud during class read-aloud times. We want books that have enough depth for good discussions, and because most of the predictable books these children are able to read on their own do not have that depth, we choose picture books and read them to the class. We also put out books with tapes so children can listen to them. The majority of children are able to read these books independently by the end of their Literature Circle.

At the end of a week, children decide which piece of literature they want to discuss the following week. They either sign up on a chart under the book title or write their top two choices on a piece of paper and hand it in to the teacher, who then assigns the children to groups, making sure everyone gets one of the choices. Several groups may be formed to discuss a popular book, or the book may be repeated in later weeks. We do *not* attempt to divide the children according to ability in these groups. Even if we feel a book might be difficult for a particular child, children are allowed to choose. Because the book was their choice and because they wanted to be with a particular group of children, we find that they are generally able to read the book. If not, they may read with a partner or listen to the story on a tape recording.

When the books being used in Literature Circles are longer chapter books, children sign up a full week ahead of time and read the books during their free reading time in school or as homework. When children come to a Literature Circle, we usually want them to have already read the book all the way through, even though they often reread parts during the week as they discuss the selection. Prior reading facilitates the discussion and avoids problems with children being at different points in the reading.

However, we do sometimes have students read the book as they are discussing it. The group meets each day to discuss what they read the previous day and to agree on how much they will read for the next meeting. These discussions are brief so that students have enough time to read the book each day. When they finish the book, the group takes several days for longer, more in-depth discussions. We used this variation when we first started reading chapter books with groups that needed more support and encouragement.

Participating in Literature Circles

We usually begin Literature Circles with a broad question such as "What was this story about?" to get the children to share their reactions to the book and to learn what they find most interesting in the book. The direction of the discussion over the next several days depends on the children's interests and the strengths of the particular book. If the book has particularly strong characterizations, we ask open-ended questions to get children to explore this aspect of the book. If children are interested in a particular event, character, or theme, we explore this in more depth. During the discussions, we also ask questions to help the children connect the literature they are reading to their own past experiences and to other pieces of literature that they have read or written earlier.

The children are encouraged to expand and support their comments and to build off of what other children have said. Different potential meanings for a story are explored and accepted, as long as the reader can support that interpretation. Pat's interpretation that in the familiar folktale of Hansel and Gretel, the witch was really the stepmother in disguise (see Chapter 1) is an example of participants accepting and supporting alternative meanings. Pat's idea allowed the other children and the teacher to see this familiar folktale from a new perspective.

We constantly challenge the children—and they challenge each other and us—to support the statements made in Literature Circles. Many "why" questions are raised. Some teachers think that these discussions involve just accepting whatever a child says, but we find instead that it means both accepting and challenging each other. Teachers are participants in the discussions along with the children, and so our interpretations are just one possible interpretation, not "the" interpretation.

The way children build off of their past experiences and each other in exploring a story is demonstrated in the following discussion that Kathy had with a group of first graders on the story *Rosie's Walk* (Hutchins 1968). The group began by discussing favorite parts of the story and by talking about what might have happened to the fox after the story ended. As the children re-turned to talking about Rosie walking with the fox behind her, a question that started an interesting debate occurred to Kathy:

> "I wonder why Rosie never turned around. Did she know that the fox was behind her?" Kathy asks the group. The children find this interesting and begin talking about it. "She looks like she knows—the expression on her face," says Erin. "I thought she would run," says Amy. Sherri says, "If she knew the fox was following her, then she wouldn't have looked back so he wouldn't know that she knew." Sheila asks, "Couldn't she hear all that stuff coming down behind her like the flour, the splash, and the wheelbarrow?" "Maybe she's deaf," comment both Amy and Michael. "She might have had an earache," explains Jessica. "I had one once and I couldn't hear," contributes Billie Jo. "She doesn't look like she has any ears," says Sheila. Kathy asks if any of them know if hens have ears and Michael explains, "They have ears behind their heads. You can't see them in the pictures" (Short 1986, 311-312).

After this debate, the discussion continued on a range of issues, including comparing this fox to the fox in *Henny Penny* as well as to other folktales involving animals chasing and eating each other, and discussing the techniques used in the illustrations. In this discussion the children are obviously exploring hypotheses or half-formed ideas about the story rather than deciding on only one right interpretation and are involved in making a variety of connections to other experiences. Because Literature Circles involve exploring half-formed ideas, children need time to explore and then to accept, modify, or reject their hypotheses rather than having the teacher immediately step in to correct any misinterpretations.

The Role of the Teacher in Literature Circles

In the initial Literature Circles, the teacher often plays the role of the leader, asking open-ended questions to get a discussion going. This provides children with a demonstration of the kinds of questions and discussion behaviors involved in a Literature Circle. More than with Authors' Circles, children bring with them a past history that says there is just one right interpretation of a story, and the teacher has it. They do not know how to really talk about a story and to explore meanings with each other, and they don't expect to be given the chance to do so.

Literature Circles were immediately successful for us the first year because we had already established a supportive classroom atmosphere. Both Gloria and Kaylene found, however, that with third graders and sixth graders the going was rough at first because the students were so concerned about getting the "right" answer.

We found that it helps if the teacher begins by just asking the students to talk about the story and what they liked, and then uses their comments to direct the discussion. After the children have shared their responses to the book on the first day, the children and the teacher summarize the discussion. They list possible topics to discuss, and then the students choose the first topic they want to pursue. The teacher facilitates the discussion process but is careful not to take over the discussion. We continuously had to discipline ourselves as teachers not to fill every silence but to wait and to participate with an occasional comment or question. However, because this kind of open-ended exploration of literature was so unfamiliar to our students, we came to expect the first several groups not to go well.

Students expect the teacher to be the "question-asker" in the group. When we joined in the discussion with comments about what we thought rather than only asking questions, this signaled to the students that the teacher was a participant rather than an evaluator. We made sure that our comments were not "Here's the right answer" but "This is what I thought. What did you think?" The teacher must not dominate the discussion with either comments or questions.

If Authors' Circles are operating in the classroom, these discussions of writing help children in their discussions of reading. Teachers can also demonstrate the kinds of issues and questions students can pursue about literature in whole-class discussions after class read-aloud time and by involving students in language activities such as Say Something. Gradually students begin opening up and debating and exploring their interpretations of literature with each other.

The circles can be structured to be run without the teacher's constant presence. The teacher can initially give the children several open-ended questions to use as a basis for discussion or provide a broad focus or problem such as "Talk about the relationships between people in this story" to explore on their own. Students can be encouraged to develop their own questions to ask each other in Literature Circles. Students can run the circles by deciding on their own focus and going ahead with the discussion. We found that the third- and sixth-grade students adopted the technique we had earlier demonstrated of spending the first day talking about their favorite parts and sharing general impressions, and then making a list of issues and topics they might want to discuss during the next several days. Students used their list to help them decide what to talk about each day, although the list was never strictly adhered to. Teachers do not need to be always present in these groups once they get going but should join groups they think could benefit from their presence.

Literature Logs can also be used to facilitate discussion. As children read their books, they are asked at certain points to make entries in their logs about their responses to what they have read. These entries are not summaries of the reading but notes about what they liked or didn't like, predictions, meanings they thought about, and connections they made to other books or experiences as they read. The logs are helpful in several ways. The process of writing helps students organize their thinking and think more deeply about the literature. In addition, the logs can be used to begin discussions in Literature Circles. At the beginning of the circle, students can share from their logs, and the discussion continues from this sharing. Literature Logs are helpful in early Literature Circles and in discussing a complex or difficult piece of literature. At other times, we usually give students the option of whether they write in their logs.

At the end of each Literature Circle, children decide what they will explore in the book the next time they meet. This gives them something to think about and to reread or search for before the group meets again. Because the children have this time to think, the next discussion gets off to a better start. Students may also write notes about the issue or question in their Literature Logs before the next discussion. Children may need a day off to reread and to explore before their group is ready to meet again. These reengagements with a book are important and need to be encouraged.

Presenting the Literature to the Class

Literature Circle discussions can last anywhere from two or three days to a week or two depending on the length of the book and how the discussion is going. At the end of the discussion, the group sometimes plans a presentation to the class about their piece of literature. Students do Readers' Theatre or dramas, create murals or dioramas, write a new ending or version of the story, or find some other way to share their book with the class. These presentations are not just "cute" activities based on a book but must in some way reflect what the group talked about or felt they learned as a result of their discussion. The students brainstorm a list of possible responses and decide on a response that they feel will best reflect their understanding of the book. Although students do not make presentations at the end of every Literature Circle, at least some of the circles lead to presentations as a way to celebrate authorship in reading. When Literature Circles do not move to presentations, students often share briefly in Author Sharing Time. These presentations, in turn, serve as invitations for other readers to books they might want to read or to response activities they might want to use.

Sometimes only half the class meets in various Literature Circles at one time. The rest of the class is extensively reading books of their choice or working on response activities. This way, both extensive and intensive reading continue in the classroom and neither becomes boring for students. For example, if the circles last for a week, half the class meets in Literature Circles and the rest read books of their own choice or work on projects. The next week they switch places. Fridays are often a sharing day, with groups presenting their interpretations of the book they read to the other children. Other times, the whole class has Literature Circles for several weeks and then takes a week off to read extensively.

Using Literature with Depth and Variety

Literature used in Literature Circles should have enough depth to support good discussions. Choices should also reflect a variety of types of literature at all grade levels. We use picture books, poetry, short stories, and chapter books and cover all different genres from folktales to information books. Many good picture books can be used with older students as well as with younger students.

One problem is obtaining multiple copies of books for everyone in the group to read. Our solution varies with the type of literature being used. Because picture books are short, one or two copies can be shared among the members of the group. Poetry and short stories can also be shared, although we often make extra photocopies of these for children. We put together *Text Sets,* sets of books that are related by theme or topic. For example, six different books on friendship might be placed in a Text Set that will be read and compared at Literature Circles. Only one copy of each book is needed to complete these sets. Chapter books are a more difficult problem, because each student needs a copy.

We borrow books from the library, from other teachers, and from the children themselves. We hunt in closets and check with Chapter 1 teachers and other resource teachers for sets of books that they might have. We use the bonus points offered when children buy from paperback clubs to purchase sets of books for the classroom. We talk to the parents' organization about providing money to buy some sets of books and to the school about letting us use workbook money to buy books instead of workbooks.

We also look through both old and new basals for good pieces of literature that we might use in these groups, because we have basals in multiple copies. However, we prefer to stay away from the basal in the first circles because of the past history that children bring with them regarding these basal stories. The children bring negative attitudes and expect the discussion to involve a series of closed questions (questions with only one right answer) about the story. This is frustrating when we are trying to get children to open up and explore meaning with each other. We find it better to begin with other kinds of literature; once discussions are going well, particular basal stories can then be used occasionally. We have also learned to check these stories to see if language has been changed and simplified in the basal version or if the basal has faithfully rendered the original piece of literature. If we use a basal story, we always bring in the actual original story.

The literature being discussed in Literature Circles should not just emerge from nowhere but should be connected to other parts of the curriculum. The literature can be related to units of study going on in the classroom, to a particular type of literature that is being explored, or to writing that children are doing. Or the literature may simply be a familiar story. The depth of discussion in Literature Circles depends on a rich history of stories to which the literature can be connected.

Variations of Literature Circles

Many different variations of Literature Circles are possible. We first began circles that focused on discussing one book. Later we had circles where we used Text Sets—sets of individual books that are related to each other in some way. These Text Sets include books or poetry by the same author; different versions of the same fairy tale; books on the same theme; books on the same topic, such as survival or friendship; books that are the same story but are illustrated by different people; books of the same genre, such as mysteries or folktales; books with similar story structures, such as the same type of cumulative pattern; books with the same characters; and books from the same culture or country. Sometimes everyone in the group reads the whole set of books, and other times each person reads only one or two books in the set. Both variations produce good discussions.

Whenever possible, we create sets that include a wide variety of reading materials. Our Text Set on pigs, for example, includes a book of poetry, an information book, familiar folktales, picture books, and chapter books, as well as farm magazine articles, photographs, diagrams, and brochures on pork. This range of types of materials and genres helps students explore a topic from many different angles and supports their development of more flexible reading strategies.

Text Set discussions usually begin with students telling each other about the different books they read and then beginning to make comparisons and contrasts across the books in the set. Although these discussions rarely go into great depth on any one book such as occurs in circles that discuss a single book, they highlight the process of making connections between books. We have also found Text Sets helpful with groups who were not talking with each other. Because students have each read a different but related book, they each have information the others do not have that has to be shared.

We also have had circles that focused on a local author whom we then invited to visit the classroom. One of the more exciting variations was to have circles on literature written by authors from the classroom. The group would discuss the book and then invite the author to join their group. Sometimes children from different classrooms or grade levels have formed groups for several days to discuss literature. These variations keep Literature Circles interesting and fresh and invite different kinds of insights and discussions. Circles can play many different functions in the curriculum. They can focus attention on the reading process and strategies, on literary concepts and genres, or on concepts related to certain topics or content areas. It is also important to occasionally have reflective Literature Circles where readers meet to critique the circles themselves and to comment on what is and is not going well in their discussions.

Conclusion

Literature Circles and other Literature Response Activities involve learners in extending and revising the meanings they have constructed from reading and in presenting these meanings to other classmates to celebrate their authorship as readers. The extensive reading in which children are involved gives them a wide range of experiences from which to draw and expand on in later experiences. If we want our students to be truly literate individuals, we must also provide intensive reading experiences through which their understandings about reading are deepened and extended. As students engage in reading widely and deeply, they are encouraged to be critical thinkers who see reading as well as writing as processes of authorship.

CHAPTER 3

Creating
a Classroom
for Authors
and Authorship

Introduction

The language activities presented in this chapter center on creating a conducive and a supportive classroom environment for
authors and authorship. A conducive context for learning must
be a low-risk (as opposed to a no-risk or high-risk) environment
in which children are given uninterrupted time to engage in, see
demonstrated, and come to value reading and writing as vehicles
for exploring and expanding their world. A supportive context
for learning acknowledges the social nature of language use and
learning.

The language activities discussed in this chapter are more or less
permanent features in our classrooms. From a language arts perspective, our first goal is to create a self-maintaining environment
for authors and authorship by providing time, functional reading
and writing activities, and opportunities for children to meet, learn
from, and come to see themselves and their classmates as authors.
A second goal is to juxtapose reading and writing so that the sense
of authorship students acquire in writing is a basis for taking ownership of reading and vice versa. A third goal is to litter the environment with print so that children are provided with numerous
reading and writing invitations. The avoidance of literacy encounters is not an issue in a classroom set up around the authoring cy-

117

cle; rather, children are asked to sample activities and then choose which option among several they will pursue.

This chapter, then, is structured around various organizational decisions we made as well as language activities we used to invite children to engage in, see demonstrated, and come to value the strategies of literacy. Conceptually, we see curriculum as made up of literacy events, and literacy events as made up of demonstrations and engagements. By *engagements,* we mean language activities that function as invitations for children to use reading and writing strategically to learn and to explore and expand their world. To be strategic, readers and writers must vary the strategies they use by both content and context. This means then that a good language arts curriculum is organized around the various contexts of literacy. The language activities we present include literature, journal writing, message boards, pen pal letters, newspapers, poetry, and more.

Within any literacy event multiple demonstrations are available. Frank Smith says:

> The first essential constituent of learning is the opportunity to see what can be done and how. Such opportunities may be termed demonstrations because they show a potential learner "This is how something is done." The world continually provides demonstrations, through people and through their products, by acts and artifacts (1981, 101).

Most of what we know about language and literacy has not been formally taught, but rather learned from our involvement in a variety of literacy events. For example, we not only learn "what to attend to" but "what to make of what is attended to," and often "why," as well as the consequences of attending or not attending to some demonstration from our involvement with others in literacy. As used by Smith and ourselves (Harste, Woodward & Burke 1984), the term *demonstrations* highlights the important role people play in expanding the learning potential of any situation. Deborah Rowe explains:

> When participants at the literacy centers author their own texts, talk about their work, or leave physical traces of these activities in the form of books, pictures, or songs, they provide demonstrations for their audience. These demonstrations add to the meanings which may potentially be constructed and to the learning which may potentially take place. Observing and talking with other authors has a powerful impact on learning precisely because the audience has the opportunity to see demonstrations of content information and process information linked in uses which are meaningful to both au-

dience and author. That is, in literacy events they are constructing together, the audience has the opportunity to see demonstrations of what authors might say/write/draw/play/etc. coupled with demonstrations of how it might be said/written/drawn/played/etc. as well as demonstrations of why or to what ends these engagements serve (1986, 102).

To be successful, language learners not only must learn the "what," or the content of literacy, but also the "how," or the interpretive procedures of literacy as they relate to specific intents, goals, or "whys." Growth in literacy entails not only identifying key demonstrations but also learning what to make of them. Having once sorted out the "how" and "what" demonstrations associated with certain features of a literacy event, given an explicit or assumed "why," other demonstrations can be attended to.

Curricularly this means that classrooms have to be natural language environments where children have opportunities to engage in and to see others engaged in using reading and writing to learn. Most adults in our society are victims of their own educational history. Because there is little evidence that the majority of citizens actively use reading and writing as tools and toys for learning, it is especially important that at school children see demonstrated the strategies of proficient learners. This is why teachers have to be learners in their classrooms and engage in the very reading and writing activities that children are invited to engage in. In fact, we argue, it is never hard to prove you are a *teacher*. The real trick and key to good literacy instruction from the standpoint of the teacher is to demonstrate that you are a *learner*. In providing these demonstrations, the most effective language arts instruction takes place.

From engagements and demonstrations comes learning. Through discussion and reflection on what worked or didn't work, children come to value the strategies of successful language use and learning. In addition to "engagements" and "demonstrations," this third curricular component, "coming to value," moves learning from intuition to consciousness. This move is central in literacy, as with consciousness comes choice and with choice comes empowerment.

In terms of curriculum, this means that there have to be opportunities to share, discuss, reflect, present, and make new plans. These opportunities cannot be just on a catch-as-catch-can basis. Opportunities must be planned and provided. Even in many good meaning-centered classrooms, children engage and connect but are not given the opportunities to reflect. This is a mistake. Some of the language activities we discuss in this section are designed to ensure that curricularly we have provided opportunities for reflection for all learners in the classroom.

Establishing a learning environment that encourages children to engage, see demonstrated, and come to value authoring involves organizational considerations as well as curricular considerations. In this chapter we will share important organizational decisions regarding the time, space, and content, as well as various language activities that help create an environment that encourages authoring. The authoring cycle shared in Chapter 2 assumes a supportive classroom environment. Authors' Circles and Literature Circles will fall flat if they are not part of a learning environment that values and supports authorship. The organizational and curricular considerations shared in this chapter are essential in creating a classroom for authors and authorship.

Work Time

Work Time is the official way that we put into practice having uninterrupted time for reading and writing each day in our classrooms. Too often organizational decisions cause us to fail to meet our goals in the language arts. Work Time is designed to send the message that we are here to learn by actively using reading, writing, and other sign systems as tools and toys for learning. As an organizational decision, Work Time supports the integration of the language arts and keeps the focus of everyone's attention on learning.

Work Time is the period during the morning when children are engaged in authoring through reading and writing—writing rough drafts, informally conferring with friends, meeting in Authors' Circles, reading books of their own choice either alone or with others, meeting in Literature Circles, working on Literature Response Activities, writing in Journals or Learning Logs, writing Pen Pal letters, editing another person's writing, illustrating a book for publication, meeting with the teacher for a strategy lesson, or writing a message for the Message Board. Obviously the list could go on and on. The major point is that during Work Time children engage in the experiences associated with the authoring cycle.

Essentially Work Time is a large chunk of time sandwiched between some type of group opening and closing each morning. Mary Lynn Woods begins each morning with Readers' Theatre and a short planning time and ends each morning with Author

Sharing Time. In between the children work at all kinds of reading and writing activities. Gloria Kauffman begins each morning with Journals and a planning meeting and ends with Literature Logs and Author Sharing Time. The time between is designated Work Time. Gloria has felt more comfortable breaking Work Time into a Reading Work Time and a Writing Work Time, which are back to back and which often begin gradually overlapping each other.

If an entire morning for Work Time seems lengthy, remember that once the cycle is started, children will be using reading and writing as vehicles for exploring and expanding their understanding of social studies, science, and math. Once the curriculum is functioning, it can be used as an organizational base in other curricular areas (see Chapter 4, "Keeping the Cycle Going").

Work Time is an organizational decision as well as an important issue. The curriculum must be set up so that children know they will have uninterrupted time for reading and writing each day. When children know they will be writing daily on their own topics, their approach to writing changes. They write before they start writing (see Graves 1985). When they are home or on the bus, when they read a book or go on an outing, they begin to plan. In short, they begin to engage in the behaviors we associate with proficient readers and writers. One of the most exciting things that will happen is that children will begin to read like writers—"If this is a true story, why did he start out with 'Once upon a time'? Can you do that?" "Oh, that's how you have different people talk in a story!" As they read, children get ideas about what they may write. What worked for other authors works for them. They also begin to write like readers as they use what they have discovered in their own writing through reading and as they recognize the importance of the audience in writing.

One preschooler in Heidi Mills's classroom in Grand Rapids, Michigan, came up to her on a field trip to the post office and announced, "I can hardly wait to get back to school to write about this in my journal!" We told Heidi that we may be carrying things too far if children can't enjoy firsthand experiences, but, upon further reflection, we see this as a mistaken notion. Real writers interact with the world, and their involvement in reading and writing helps them see and appreciate the world in new ways. Reading and writing are as much real experiences as are field trips and other real-life, lived-through adventures.

One simple but compelling justification for why the curriculum should not be compartmentalized is that there is no evidence supporting the notion that a special part of the brain handles

reading, another part handles writing, another spelling, another grammar, another art, another music, and so on. In fact, there is extensive evidence to the contrary. Reading clearly supports writing and vice versa. Watch two language users engaged in an event involving print—for example, buying something at a clothing store or purchasing a ticket at the local cinema. Take particular note of the modes of communication involved. In all likelihood there will be print, speech, gesture, and art. Language in use is a multimodal event involving reading, writing, speaking, listening, art, gesture, drama, and more. Never is there such a thing as a "pure" instance of writing. Writers read what they have written, talk to their neighbors, listen, draw sketches, and take even more mental journeys in the name of writing.

In setting up a conducive environment for literacy use and learning, the twin issues of time and compartmentalization need to be confronted. We're not talking about how to squeeze more in an already busy schedule. In other words, we do not—and we hope readers do not—see the authoring cycle as an additive curriculum, but rather one that replaces what currently is going on in the name of spelling, English, reading groups, creative writing, and penmanship. By combining all the time now consumed for these "stop-and-go activities" (Graves 1985), one rather large block of time can be retrieved. Teachers might begin by trying a language activity that looks manageable to them. From this base they can add another and slowly allow the curriculum to evolve. An excellent place to begin is by creating an uninterrupted time for reading and writing. Children can't engage in authoring unless they are given the chance to do so. Few organizational decisions will facilitate the goals of your language arts curriculum more.

Author Sharing Time

Authors need time to share with each other as they engage in various reading and writing activities. Our first response as adults when we read a good book is to tell other people about it. Children have the same need to share the excitement of authoring with others. Much of this sharing goes on informally during Work Time as children interact with each other during reading and writing, saying excitedly, "Look at this!" or "Listen to this!"

Although this spontaneous sharing is important, a planned group sharing time is also essential because it gives children a chance to share with a wider audience and to offer new demonstrations to other students. When children talk about books they've read and enjoyed during Author Sharing Time, there is a dramatic increase in the number of children who choose those specific books. When children share new techniques of illustrating or share new things they are doing in their writing, other children pick up on these demonstrations.

Author Sharing Time is a time when authors share with other authors, not for the purposes of critiquing but simply to share the excitement of discovery and authoring. There are many different kinds of Author Sharing Times. Readers' Theatre, for example, is a time when students share an author's book through reading. We use the term Author Sharing Time to refer to the time period when the class gathers as a whole group or in small groups for children to share what they have been working on as they engage in reading and writing experiences. In most classrooms, Author Sharing Time occurs at the end of the morning after Work Time.

Anyone who wants to is invited to share. Children share trade books by reading a key paragraph, a telling dialogue, or a favorite poem, or by retelling a favorite scene. Children share their writing by reading a section of a story or report, a journal entry, an especially good reply to a pen pal, a new poster or cartoon, a newly published edition of a story they have taken through the authoring cycle, or a letter they are writing. They share illustrations they are working on, a new way of putting their book together, or Literature Response Activities, such as a mural or a diorama.

Some classrooms have a sign-up sheet available, and a student volunteer is asked to organize the program so that it is interesting and no one abuses the time limits. Children do not share an entire book or story but instead only select a particular part that they most want the group to know about. We save the last five minutes of the Author Sharing Time to share what we have learned about reading and writing that day. Problems encountered in reading and writing and reports on how they were solved lead to new strategies that others are invited to record in their Learning Logs and test at their leisure.

Nanci Vargus, a first-grade teacher at Lynwood Elementary School in Indianapolis, Indiana, uses these discussions on what was learned each day to create a class language experience chart. She copies these on blue ditto at the end of the week and runs them off as a class newspaper that the children take home and read to their parents. This is a nice way to keep parents informed and a way of beginning a publishing program the very first week of first grade.

Hickman (1981), in her study of reader responses in three elementary classrooms, noted that the "impulse to share" was one of the most frequent responses that children made to literature. Hepler (1982) spent a year examining responses to literature in a fifth- and sixth-grade classroom and found that for a majority of readers, the single most influential factor in children's selection of books was the recommendation of another person. These recommendations primarily occurred during the group sharing time at the end of the morning. These studies plus our own experiences in classrooms lead us to value Author Sharing Time because of the essential role it plays in encouraging authors and in offering new demonstrations.

Authors' Chair

A special kind of author sharing occurs in Authors' Chair. At Authors' Chair students and teachers share an entire text with either a small group or the entire group. As Graves and Hansen (1983) point out, Authors' Chair is where the reader sits to share either a child-authored text or a professionally authored text. Children and teachers come to Authors' Chair to share texts they are writing or reading with a group through both reading that text aloud and discussing it with the group.

In several classrooms, teachers have two Authors' Chairs. One classroom uses two captain chairs; in another, two rocking chairs are used. What is important about Authors' Chair is not the specific chair but the need to share with other readers and writers. The children are invited to use these Authors' Chairs throughout Work Time or whenever they have something to share and can find an audience to listen. Unlike Author Sharing Time, at Authors' Chair children can read someone their whole text. Often children are invited at Author Sharing Time by other children to "do Authors' Chair tomorrow" because they would like to hear more of a text that has whetted their appetite.

Authors' Chair differs from Authors' Circle in that children come to Authors' Chair to share what they are reading or writing through reading the text and talking about it with others rather than for the specific intent of conferring to see what is and is not working in their texts. As argued earlier, Authors' Chair helps to preserve the function of Authors' Circles. If teachers are experiencing difficulties with children coming to Authors' Circles wanting to share rather than to think about or revise their piece, this may be occurring because no time is available for children just to share an entire text with others.

Authors' Chair encourages children to reread what they have written. Even though the focus is on sharing and not on rethinking their text, as they change perspectives from writer to reader, things in need of revision may be highlighted. It is not uncommon to see children stop while reading, change a spelling, add a word, or even shrug their shoulders when it appears that their thoughts have been too far ahead of their writing. Like all writers, children like to share their first draft efforts with others. We often read what we have written to a family member or an unsuspecting graduate student. Sometimes we are not so interested in feedback from our listener as we are in just finding out how it "sounds" and "reads." Children have these same needs. Authors' Chair meets those needs so that children will go to Authors' Circle for different purposes.

Children can indicate they want to share simply by walking over to Authors' Chair during Work Time. Anyone who wants to can go and join the author for sharing. Some teachers use a sign-up sheet where each morning children who want to share sign their name and what they want to share. Other children in the classroom can then decide whether they want to join a group during that morning. Children who are bringing their own writing to Authors' Chair may bring completed pieces as well as pieces they have partially written and need a chance to share with others to continue writing.

In addition to serving as a place for students to share with an audience during Work Time, Authors' Chair is also where teachers read aloud to the entire class. Although these Authors' Chairs may occur at different times throughout the day, the rule to follow is: *Read to your children every day.* This is not a reward—something you do if the kids are good—but an ongoing part of each classroom day. Teachers often begin the morning by reading a picture book aloud to the group and then reading from a chapter book right after lunch. Teachers also announce Authors' Chair as a flexible vehicle for pulling children together during Work Time when it appears that some redirection is needed.

Reading aloud to students is just as essential for older children as it is for young children. Through read-aloud times at Authors' Chair, children experience book language, the patterns of stories, and different types of literature. They develop an interest in books and are introduced to quality literature that might be beyond their reading ability but not their comprehension. Read-aloud time encourages children to grow as readers and broadens the types of literature they choose to read. Teachers can also use this time to demonstrate to children the types of questions and issues they can discuss in Literature Circles. Although fewer children can participate in whole-group discussions, these discussions help children become more independent in their ability to run their own Literature Circles because of the multiple demonstrations they offer.

Teachers can use this time to offer children invitations that will extend their experiences as writers as well as readers. Children can be invited to write the same type of story, such as a tall tale or a *Choose Your Own Adventure* (published by Bantam) story. Teachers can invite children to take a language pattern that the author has used and to write their own story using that language pattern (e.g., "Brown bear, Brown bear, What do you see?" [Martin 1970]). If the book is rich in descriptive language or dialogue, children can be invited to try this in their own pieces. Children start putting dedications and "curtains" (endpapers) in their books or using certain styles of illustration after noticing these in books shared at Authors' Chair. Since these are invitations, an author can decide whether to accept, ignore, or put on hold any invitation that is offered. No matter how an author responds, however, read-aloud times at Authors' Chair continually put new invitations and demonstrations on the floor so that students continue to grow and to be challenged in their authoring.

Although the teacher most often shares at Authors' Chair during group read-aloud times, children can also share a favorite book that they have practiced so that it is effectively presented to the group. A variety of literature needs to be shared during read-aloud times, including literature written by authors from the classroom as well as by professional authors. When teachers choose to read children's work to the class, they show that they value children's authorship. In choosing the work of professional authors, teachers should read picture books, poetry, chapter books, short stories, and information books to all age levels of children. Picture books, for example, are not just for young children. Many fine picture books are appropriate for older children and can provide them with a wider variety of reading experiences.

We suggest orally reading a book that is slightly above where most of the class is reading independently or that is a different type of book from what the majority of the class is reading. In first grade, for example, we introduce chapter books. If children are not reading historical fiction, we choose historical fiction to read to the group. Reading new materials aloud helps the children form a mental expectation for how such materials are organized and thus prepares them for reading such books on their own. One type of book that is often omitted during read-aloud times is nonfiction or fiction based on true events. These materials form the bulk of what students will be expected to read in high school and on the job and yet are rarely read aloud, and so students do not form mental sets for how to deal with these materials. If teachers need specific recommendations for titles, we recommend they consult Jim Trelease's *Read-Aloud Handbook* (1985).

When children find a book exciting, teachers should consider reading other books by the same author, thereby setting up an environment so that children can begin to recognize an author's work by his or her style (see *Authors Meeting Authors*). Teachers can also bring in other books that are the same type or have similar themes and either read them to students or give a short introduction to the books and put them into the classroom library corner.

The Curricular Components section of this book contains a list of poetry books (see *Poetry in Motion*), any combination of which, we think, all teachers should have on their desks. It is crucial that teachers share favorite poems with children on a regular basis. Although parents occasionally may read a newspaper item or a story with their children, poetry is almost never read. In part this is because many adults do not enjoy poetry or value it as an important literary form. In pursuing this issue with parents, we find that many parents (and teachers) do not know how to read poetry. Rather than following the allusions suggested by the rhythm and words of the poem, they read poetry as they would read an encyclopedia; namely, in terms of what facts the poem teaches. To ensure that children do not develop these faulty notions, the teacher might ask them to close their eyes and concentrate on the allusions that the poem creates. Sketch to Stretch, an activity discussed in the Curricular Components section, could also be used.

Children need to understand that reading strategies vary by context of situation and that they have a responsibility when reading poetry to discover the allusions, to use their past experiences as a working metaphor in comprehension, and to enjoy the lived-through experience. In other types of reading, the contract is different, but to enjoy poetry one cannot be textbound. Invite the children to find poetry they might like to share as well as to try their hand at writing poetry.

One side benefit of literacy is information. To understand this benefit, children must experience it. To this end, teachers need to read information books during Authors' Chair and to monitor the news to find items of interest to the children. Various newspapers in your area should be perused. Sometimes the only way you can find out what is happening in your town is by reading the local newspaper. In our town, if you want to know what is happening on campus, you must read the campus newspaper. It is important in sharing that you share not only the specific item, but also tell where such information is likely to be found. The majority of the content of news items you bring in should build naturally from what the children are studying in social studies, science, mathematics, music, and the like.

After the teacher brings in several newspaper clippings relevant to the topic and grade taught, children can be invited to bring in newspaper clippings to share with the class. In one fourth-grade class, this invitation led to a daily newscast. Three students each morning signed up to share items they found relevant to the topic. This school had a videotape camera and playback unit. As children presented their newscast (the class decided on a five-minute maximum program length) a videotape was cut that, after a replaying in the class, was made available to other classes in the school throughout the day. Written versions of these newscasts led to a mimeographed publication entitled "The Week in Review," which was distributed throughout the school. Many children in this class began reading the newspaper daily; all had a pretty good notion of what types of information were found in area newspapers as well as an understanding of what newspaper reporters could do that television newscasters could not.

Authors' Chair gives both teachers and students the chance to take the role of an author sharing a text with other authors. Although there are different reasons authors read aloud from their own or other's texts, Authors' Chair gives all authors the chance to share whole texts with others and to offer new demonstrations and insights to other authors through this sharing. The use of Authors' Chair by teachers to read aloud a variety of literature to the class is one activity that no class should ever be without because of the tremendous impact these read-aloud times have on children as writers and readers.

Classroom Library

An essential ingredient in a classroom where children are active readers and writers is a Classroom Library. When children have easy access to a variety of books, they more frequently read and refer to those books. We believe strongly in the principle of accessibility. The more accessible something is, the more likely it is to be used. We want to highlight the importance of literature in our classrooms, and so Classroom Libraries are a prominent and permanent feature.

Children need to be assured access to books by putting books easily within children's reach, by creating attractive displays of books related to a certain theme or author, and by providing time for children to browse and read the books. All this occurs in the Classroom Library. In focusing on the importance of having a library in the classroom, we are not trying to deemphasize the importance of the school library. We have found that having an active Classroom Library increases children's use of the school library because they become more interested in books and more aware of what kinds of books are available and so go in search of them in the school library.

A Classroom Library is usually found in a corner of the room that has been comfortably arranged with a piece of carpet, some pillows, a rocking chair or other comfortable seating arrangements, and, most importantly, shelves of books. In one classroom, the teacher talked a local factory into supplying the materials for a reading loft and then had a Parents' Night to build and paint the loft. Another teacher got hold of several rows of old choir risers and put pillows on them so children could either lie or sit in various positions. Creating a comfortable corner for reading signals to children that reading books is valued in that classroom.

Fill the Classroom Library with all kinds of books, focusing on both the variety and the quality of the literature. With the tremendous amount of books available today for children, it is possible for children to read only substandard books and never read a significant piece of literature. Quality literature provides children with a "lived-through experience" and bears rereading and reflection. The library should be filled with quality literature that covers a wide range of genres, topics, themes, authors, and illustrators. Various types of fiction, nonfiction, and poetry should be available in the library. Teachers can also collect Text Sets, sets of books that are related in some way, so that children begin to build connections between literature. In addition, one section of the library should be used to display books published by children in the classroom. These books are often the most frequently chosen reading materials.

We have found that the books in a Classroom Library at all grades should range from picture books to chapter books and from highly predictable books that provide easy reading experiences to more difficult and challenging books. Teachers need to look closely at their students and provide the kinds of books they need to support their current levels of reading proficiency. We found out how important having supportive reading materials was several years ago in Gloria Kauffman's first-grade classroom. Early in the year, many predictable books had been brought into the classroom and the children were soon active readers who constantly had books in their hands. In January, we returned most of the predictable book sets to the library from which we had borrowed them. The children were left with the existing Classroom Library, which contained few predictable books. To our amazement, the same group of children who had been reading anything in sight almost stopped reading. We quickly started bringing back 10-20 predictable books a week from the library and started checking out more books from the school library for the room. The children soon returned to being avid readers.

We learned several lessons from this experience. One is that if children are not choosing to read, it may be that the reading materials being provided are not supportive for them. For young children, this means having many predictable books available. For older children, this means having picture books and short stories available, as well as chapter books. Older children respond better to "soft" materials such as paperbacks, magazines, and newspapers because these books look so different from the hardback textbooks they have grown to dislike and to associate with boring reading.

Another lesson we learned was that children need to have some really easy books and old favorites available in the Classroom Library as well as new, more challenging books. The children constantly moved back and forth between easy and challenging books and between old favorites and new books. Having both available allowed them to meet their needs of fluency and challenge. Teachers sometimes feel that letting children read a book below their reading level is cheating. What we found is that children used these books to "take a break" after they had finished a particularly difficult book and to build fluency in their reading.

A major issue that teachers face is how to get the books needed to build a good Classroom Library. Obviously this does not happen overnight. We have used a variety of sources. Paperback book clubs provide teachers with free books when students buy books. If teachers choose book clubs that offer quality literature, such as the Scholastic and Trumpet Book Clubs, they can quickly begin building a quality library. The parent-teacher organization can be a source of money for classroom libraries. Many teachers have their own personal collections that they share with children. Finally, books should be continuously rotated through the classroom from the school library. We have been known to wheel a whole cartload of books from the library to take to the classroom for several weeks and then to exchange those books for another cartload.

The books in the library area should be organized so that students know where to find and return books to the shelves. Teachers often categorize books by the author's last name or by the type of literature (historical fiction, poetry, picture book, etc.). Children can be assigned the task of coming up with their own categorization systems, which often results in unusual and fun categories for the books. We use magazine holders to hold sets of books related in some way, such as having the same topic or author. In addition, most of our Classroom Libraries have some sort of book display unit that highlights certain books each week.

Making books available, putting books on display, and providing time for children to browse and read increases the amount of time children spend reading those books. Teachers can further increase the chances children will read the books available in the classroom by reading them aloud to the class and by giving short introductions to books on display. Try a little experiment sometime and introduce some of the books on display and not others and see which books the children interact with the most.

The easy access to books that a Classroom Library provides is important not only in encouraging children to read more widely but also in facilitating Literature Response Activities. Janet Hickman (1981) found that the direct accessibility of a book was of primary importance to children's willingness to express any response to that book. They needed to be able to return to the remembered books as they wrote, created artwork, or discussed literature with others. Some children were not willing even to talk about a book unless they were able to touch the book as they talked. Hickman also found that the books that generated the most responses were the books the teacher had introduced or read to the class and the books organized around a theme or in some way related to one another. These related books, or Text Sets, got children involved in making comparisons among books and helped them see similarities and connections.

Classroom Libraries play an essential role in supporting and encouraging authoring in the classroom. Without an active Classroom Library, teachers will find it difficult to create a classroom for authors and authorship.

Writing-Reading Center

Another important area in the classroom is the Writing-Reading Center, a place where the materials children need to explore writing and reading are kept. Caroline Mattson, a primary-level teacher from Alaska, developed a Writing-Reading Center in her classroom as a way to encourage her students to engage in reading and writing experiences.

The Writing-Reading Center in Caroline Mattson's room was a combination table, bookshelf, post office, and writing supply area in the very center of the classroom. The predictable books that Mrs. Mattson introduced to the children during Author Sharing Time or Authors' Chair were kept and made available here (see the language activity entitled Shared Reading in Section Two). Here children put the books they had drafted and written, after having shared some portion during Author Sharing Time. Here children found writing materials, invitations, and a variety of paper, pens, and other writing instruments for their every writing need. Here children were given time simply to explore books, paper, and pen.

One day during Author Sharing Time, Mrs. Mattson invited the children in her kindergarten classroom to write their own stories to the wordless books she had introduced. Kammi elected to write a story about a group of children finding and burying a dead bird.

To prepare for this experience, Caroline Mattson had made photocopies of the book's pages so that children had room to write their text on the pages themselves (see Wordless Picture Books in Section Two). She had already stapled these and had multiple sets available at the Writing-Reading Center. With longer books, pages can be left unstapled and children can be invited to select the pages they want to make a "mini-story." This makes manageable what appears an overwhelming task to some children.

Kammi began her story, "Once upon a time there was a dead bird," spelling it, WANS APNATIM THAIR WAS A DED BRD. The next pages read, " 'That bird is dead,' said Tommy" (THAT BRDA IS DED, SED TOMMY). " 'Oh, what a poor bird' " (OH WAT A POR BIRD). "The girl is crying" (THE GIRY IS CRING). "They're walking to the forest" (THAIR WOKING TO THE FORIST). "They're burying the bird" (THAIR BAIRING THE BIRD). "They are bringing flowers" (THEY R BRINGING FLOWRS). "They are sad" (THEY R SAD). "Tommy looked up at the sky" (TOMMY LOOKT UP AT THE SCI). "They are playing ball" (THEYR PLAIN BLL). Thus drafted, Kammi's story was added to the Writing-Reading Center.

Almost a week to the day after Kammi had contributed her book to the Writing-Reading Center, one of Kammi's classmates, Stephanie, read Kammi's book. When she got done she commented, "Oh, Kammi, I like your book."

"Oh," reflected Kammi, "I don't think I much care for it anymore."

Overhearing the conversation, Caroline Mattson remarked, "And why is that?"

"Oh, I made a mistake. I shouldn't have just described the pictures. I should have written about what they [the characters in the pictures] were thinking."

"Well, there are more copies of the book at the Writing-Reading Center. You might like to redo your story now that you've got a better idea. Most writers, I know, have to rewrite things several times to get them the way they want."

Kammi accepted the invitation. Her second version read: "Once upon a time there was a dead bird" (WANS A PON ATIME THAIR WAS A DEAD BRID). "Tommy said, 'Look at the poor bird'" (TOMMY SEID LOOK AT THT POR BRID). "'I wonder how that bird got killed'" (I WUNDER HOW THAT BIRD GOT KILD). "'Let's bury the bird,' said Tory" (LETS BARE THE BIRD, SAID TORY). "So Tory, Kammi, Tommy, and Dick all set out to bury the bird" (SO TORY KAMMI TOMMY AND DICK ALL SET OUT TO BARE THE BIRD). "So Tommy put the bird on the maple leaf so that they didn't have to carry him" (SO TOMMY PUT THE BIRD ON THE MAPLE LEFE SO THAT THEY DIDT HAF TO KAIRY HIM). "Kammi's bringing lots of flowers" (KAMMI'S BRINGING LOTS OF FLOWRS). "They scratched a sign on a rock" (THAY SCRATCHT A SINE NO A ROCK). "They all looked up at the sky to see how the bird got killed" (THEY ALL LOOKT UP AT THE SKY TO SEE HOW THE BIRD GOT KILD). "They were glad that they had buried the bird" (THEY WERE GLAD THAT THEY BAIRED THE BIRD).

What is impressive about Kammi's revision is that she not only follows through by speculating on what the characters were thinking about, but she explicates several key causal relationships, semantically elaborates all the elements of her story structure, reduces semantic redundancy by combining several sentences, cleans up many of her misspellings, and develops a clear voice in her writing. Even before the revision, Kammi's involvement in the authoring cycle permitted her to test her growing understanding of storiness, of how one keeps ideas apart in writing, of how the sounds of language are mapped onto written letters, of how one uses writing to mean, and more. Revision gave her an additional opportunity to orchestrate what she already knew by permitting her to take the stance of a reader as well as a writer.

The Writing-Reading Center evolved from our research with young children (Harste, Woodward & Burke 1984), which suggested that in homes where reading and writing materials were available, children engaged in many more literacy events than in homes where these things were absent or less accessible. Therefore, we developed the motto *litter the environment with print* as we attempted to apply this research finding to curricular practice. In a preschool in which we were working, we recorded how selected children used the room as well as what activities they engaged in. After getting this baseline data, we followed our motto and pulled the reading area out of the corner and into the middle of the room. We then added a notepad by the telephone in the play area, had children sign in as an alternative to taking attendance, and generally took every opportunity we could think of to "litter the environment with print." The result was that children spent up to ten times more time engaged in literacy events. Since then we have applied this finding to other groups. The results—regardless of age—are always the same.

The trick is to place the Writing-Reading Center so that it is in a direct path to the door coming into the classroom. When placed in this fashion, the center signs to visitors that something different is happening in this classroom. As children enter, opportunities for reading and writing litter their path.

The Writing-Reading Center that we created in one classroom consisted of a table, a boxlike structure with shelves that held a variety of paper (constructed by the husband of the teacher involved), and a bookshelf in which children could place rough drafts of stories they wanted to share (see Figure 3.1). The shelf was also used to make available the books we had read during Authors' Chair or introduced during Author Sharing Time.

Blank books to be used for final editions of books, rubber cement, and other supplies for publishing were also kept there. Books children published in the classroom were kept on the bookshelf. The rule established in this classroom was that each book published had to be left for at least one month for others to enjoy. From there the book went to the school library for yet another month for other children in the school to enjoy. Only after this period did children take the book home. Other teachers have the books remain in the classroom until the end of the year. Many

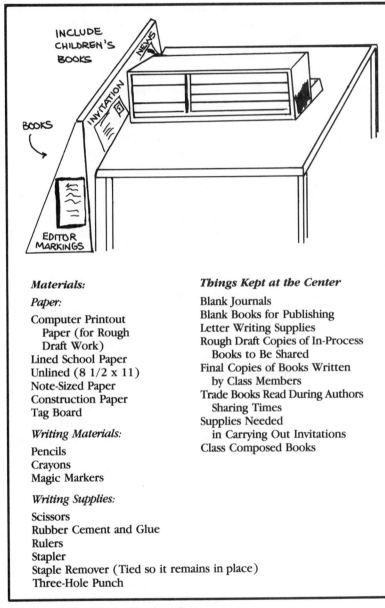

Materials:

Paper:

Computer Printout
  Paper (for Rough
  Draft Work)
Lined School Paper
Unlined (8 1/2 x 11)
Note-Sized Paper
Construction Paper
Tag Board

Writing Materials:

Pencils
Crayons
Magic Markers

Writing Supplies:

Scissors
Rubber Cement and Glue
Rulers
Stapler
Staple Remover (Tied so it remains in place)
Three-Hole Punch

Things Kept at the Center

Blank Journals
Blank Books for Publishing
Letter Writing Supplies
Rough Draft Copies of In-Process
  Books to Be Shared
Final Copies of Books Written
  by Class Members
Trade Books Read During Authors
  Sharing Times
Supplies Needed
  in Carrying Out Invitations
Class Composed Books

Figure 3.1   The Writing-Reading Center.

children made themselves a second copy of their book to take home, and they were invited to do this. Another option was for the book to be donated to the classroom library. This has resulted in a fine collection of children's stories over the years.

Mary Lynn Woods has the children in her room organize their books so that there are several blank pages in the back of the book. The book is placed in the Writing-Reading Center for other children to write and sign comments to the author on these blank pages. Parents and other adults who read the book are also invited to write notes to the author. The result is often more than a nice touch, as these notes frequently encourage sequels and second and third editions.

The back of the bookshelf was used to post invitations made for writing throughout the day. In the upper grades, this was often just a listing of ideas. In the lower grades, the written invitation was more elaborate. If, for example, we had read a predictable book like *It Didn't Frighten Me!* (Goss & Harste [1981] 1985) and had invited the children to do their own page of things that frighten them, this invitation would be accompanied by a sheet of paper with at least part of the text written. For very young children, this may have meant providing all the text except for the animal's name and a place for the children to draw a picture. A box was set aside to collect the children's efforts, and once several completed pages were received, they were bound into a Group Composed Book. This book was then read at Authors' Chair and added to the Writing-Reading Center for the children's reading enjoyment.

The Writing-Reading Center provides teachers and students with the supplies they need to support the wide variety of reading and writing experiences going on in the classroom. Both time and ideas are lost when teachers have not provided an organized center for materials.

Readers' Theatre

In addition to the organizational decisions we have already discussed, we believe that a number of key curricular activities should be part of a classroom that supports authorship. One of these is Readers' Theatre. Although there are many ways officially to begin and end the school day, predictability is important. Mary Lynn Woods started each morning with Readers' Theatre. Other teachers begin the morning with Journals and have Readers' Theatre occasionally during Author Sharing Time or Authors' Chair.

To conduct Readers' Theatre, multiple copies or a set of transparencies of the book to be shared are needed. Because making overheads or duplicating multiple copies of stories can be a problem if budgets are tight, in one classroom we use basal reader stories for Readers' Theatre. We ask children to look through the basal and find a story for the next day. Stories are read in the order children select them. No attempt is made to read all the stories, only those the children have self-identified as "good." Because many basals contain children's literature, and because sets of basals are available in as many as 85 percent of the classrooms in the United States, this is a practical—if not totally ideal—option for many teachers. When made a part of Readers' Theatre, the basal is used, at least, without risk of its taking over or becoming the reading program.

In another setting we held a summer workshop preparing materials for Readers' Theatre. In this instance, the school had multiple copies of old basals that were about to be thrown away. We looked through these basals, found what we wanted, ripped the pages out, and stapled them between pieces of construction paper. If and when the students selected these stories, they were invited to illustrate the cover. The result was a unique set of Readers' Theatre selections that children in subsequent years found attractive to use and explore.

Some stories, of course, work better than others for Readers' Theatre. Look for stories with dialogue and stories to which sound effects can be added. Poetry works well. Sometimes background music can be added to set the stage for reading, music is especially effective with folktales, poems, and some of the African and Australian texts that are now available. We have created an audiocassette tape with four-minute segments of ten different styles of music ranging from classical to country-Western. As we read various stories, we use these segments as background music and discuss how they either contributed or failed to contribute to the meaning of the selection.

Once the selection is made, the various reading parts are marked with different color highlighter pens to indicate those to be read by individuals and those to be read by groups. Before actually starting, individual children are asked to read key roles and given a moment to look through the text. After the group is called together the readers take their position in front. In one classroom a theatre area with bar stools on which the children sat as they read their assigned character parts provided an ideal setting. There are no costumes, and if props are used they are kept simple and are initiated by the children themselves. When the character speaks, the rest of the group listens. The narration in the story is read by the entire group or by one or several narrators. With this simple preparation, oral reading begins. After the first time through, the children discuss how the story may have been broken up differently, make new decisions, and begin again. Once students understand how the parts are assigned in a Readers' Theatre, they are able to read from stories that have not been highlighted.

One student, who had difficulty deciding when to read and when to be quiet, asked, "How did everyone know when to stop reading?" This led to a discussion of quotation marks and the response, "Oh, that's what those things do, huh?" We never try to second-guess problems. Sometimes such emergent problems set up the best learning situations one could hope for. What we found particularly interesting was that after this "aha experience," this child's written stories were full of dialogue. His latest language discovery was what he was most interested in exploring. As adults, we experience this same natural phenomenon when we continually try to insert a newly learned term into almost every conversation.

Theoretically, Readers' Theatre allows stories to come to life. Many written texts need to be read orally to be appreciated. The sound of the language adds a new dimension of meaning. Further, interpretation is highlighted in Readers' Theatre. Inevitably, discussions ensue as to how the group might have read something differently. Once this begins, it's time to invite the children to try it again and to follow up by discussing how various readings create different meanings. Children need the teacher to confirm the fact that a good text allows multiple interpretations; that language is open; that interpretation is what distinguishes a good reader from a poor reader; that reading is an active process of composition; that although all interpretations are good, some are more powerful than others. Readers' Theatre has all of the advantages of choral reading. Individual children are not put on the spot, less capable readers find support in reading along with the group, meaning, rather than sounding out words, is the focus, and because key characters see their parts ahead of time, they can practice and perform as well as anyone else when it comes time for them to read. Readers' Theatre presentations do not require costumes or long hours of rehearsal but instead can be quickly prepared for sharing in the classroom. Interpretation centers on the expressiveness of the voice.

Often Readers' Theatre becomes a source of useful reading strategy demonstrations. If foreign works or translations are read, many proper names will be unfamiliar. We don't introduce these words to children beforehand. As children encounter such words in oral reading they must decide how to handle them. After a moment's hesitation, someone makes a decision and the rest of the group follows along. After the story is finished these decisions often become the focus of some part of the discussion. Other alternatives that proficient readers use are presented. They might put in a more familiar name, substitute a more pronounceable nickname, or even use the character's initials. Children are invited to try these or other alternatives as the occasion arises.

Once children have had the experience of Readers' Theatre, it is time to give them invitations to further authorship. If, for example, the story was one that appealed to the group, children can be invited to try their hand at writing a similar kind of text. If the story was a folktale, children are invited to play ethnographer by interviewing their parents, grandparents, and others in search of stories they might record. Don't worry if few children take the invitation initially. Once someone writes a folktale and shares it at Author Sharing Time, other folktales will magically appear.

After the teacher has selected a few stories, it's time to invite someone in the class to choose and prepare the next story for Readers' Theatre. The students, rather than the teacher, need to "own" this activity if it is to be successful. We've done this as early as the first day of the school year if the story we initially selected was good and enthusiasm high. After discussing the story, the teacher can ask who would like to bring in a favorite story or find one for the group to read the next day. The requirements are that the student look through the story, assign roles by highlighting various parts, and make sure that multiple copies of the story are available or that overheads have been made. A sign-up sheet in the Readers' Theatre area will allow others to volunteer either as individuals or in pairs.

Stories that the children write should also be among the selections used at Readers' Theatre. To get the right to select a story for Readers' Theatre, the teacher signs up just like the rest of the class. It's important for teachers to exercise this right and use it to demonstrate that the stories the students write are as much "good literature" as the other materials they have been using. If the only materials that teachers ever select are from published trade books, children soon discover that while teachers say one thing, they do another: Child-authored stories are second-class. Already prepared Readers' Theatre scripts are also available commercially.

Children need to understand that basal stories are only one of their many options as they look for a good selection for Readers' Theatre. Choice is central to literacy. Literacy learning is best served when children feel free to select from what's available, bring something in from home, interview librarians to find good materials, and do any of a number of other things in fulfilling their role. If you ask, "Where did you find that wonderful story?" the strategies that the child used in locating and selecting good materials will be made available for tryout by other children. True engagement and commitment comes when children are given choice in deciding what to read as well as what not to read. These decisions must then be honored by teacher and students. We have found that having stories that work as well as stories that don't work only adds to the richness of the Readers' Theatre experience. As Readers' Theatre becomes a familiar part of classroom life, we see children spontaneously using it during their Work Time as a way to do Shared Reading. They simply gather as many people as they need to read the story and have their own Readers' Theatre off in a corner. Many times these are not shared with the rest of the class but are done simply to enjoy reading the story together.

Shared Reading

A learning environment needs to be organized to provide maximum support for reading. Shared Reading is a curricular activity that provides this support by involving language users in sharing with each other in the reading of meaningful, predictable texts. Reading and rereading familiar and predictable stories with others provides successful and enjoyable reading experiences that can then lead to other kinds of Literature Response Activities that cut across communication systems. Less proficient readers especially benefit from this activity because it supports their initial reading experiences and encourages them to take risks and to make predictions based on meaning and structure as they read.

Shared Reading can involve whole-group experiences where the teacher and class read together, either in unison or in choral reading, from books that are highly predictable for that group of children. Shared Reading also refers to several children who decide to read together during Work Time. Although Shared Reading can take place in many different ways, the essential criterion for Shared Reading is that the reading experience is set up so that readers support and share with each other using a predictable text setting.

The books used in Shared Reading provide highly predictable text settings through the use of both reader experiences and the text organization. Some books are predictable because they reflect life experiences about which readers have a great deal of knowledge. A child who has grown up on a farm will find a story about farms more predictable than a story about the city. Margaret Atwell (1985) points out that this is also true for older readers who find books about topics such as growing up and getting along with family members and their peers predictable because they involve experiences with which they are currently concerned.

Readers find books predictable if they have heard them before or if they are books that they have frequently experienced. Books that children have had read to them at home or at school are predictable, especially if children have heard them over and over, because the children already know the plot, language, and characters from the book. Children who have seen television shows and movies based on children's books, especially chapter books such as *Charlotte's Web* (White 1952), may find the books predictable.

Children also find books predictable that are a type with which they have had many reading experiences. Books by the same author, in the same genre, or in a particular series become predictable for readers because of common structural elements. Children who read or have read to them many fairy tales are able to make easy predictions about the story structure for new fairy tales. Older children often read a whole series of books such as lots of science fiction or all the Nancy Drew (Keene 1930-) or Hardy Boys (Dixon 1933-) books. After reading several Nancy Drew stories, the reader can predict the plot of the next Nancy Drew story because all the books follow a similar format. *Choose Your Own Adventure* books, a series published by Bantam that is often read by upper elementary children, is another example of a predictable format.

Lynn Rhodes (1981) points out that elements such as repetitive patterns or refrains, the match between the text and the illustrations, the rhythm of the language, familiar sequences, rhymes, and cumulative patterns help to make books more predictable for readers. Stories such as *The Very Hungry Caterpillar* (Carle 1969), *Brown Bear, Brown Bear, What Do You See?* (Martin 1970), and *The Great Big Enormous Turnip* (Tolstoy 1971) are examples of books that use these organizational devices. Although many teachers tend to think of predictable books only as books for young children that have these organizational elements, the previous discussion should make it obvious that predictability can be a characteristic of books for all age levels and is based on a combination of both reader factors and text factors. What is predictable thus varies according to the particular age and experience level of the specific children in a classroom.

One type of Shared Reading experience occurs when the teacher or another child reads a predictable book to the entire class and invites them to join in the reading. We usually begin a Shared Reading experience by reading the title of the book and having the students predict what the story might be about based on the title and the cover illustration. We then read the story to the children, inviting them to join in on any repeating phrases or parts of the story whenever they feel ready. We often stop at certain points and have the students predict what the next word or phrase will be or what will happen next. Depending on the predictability of the text, most students will be reading the most predictable parts of the text along with us by the end of the book.

If students have responded enthusiastically to the story, we ask them if they want to read it again. On the second reading, many more students usually join in on reading the text, and the teacher's voice can be phased out so that the children are actually doing the reading. Multiple rereadings of books help children gain control over the content, language, and organization of the story. After the first or second reading, students can share their feelings about the story, confirm their predictions, and talk about parts of the story they especially liked.

Sometimes students request a third reading of the story; other times the story is put away to be brought out another day. The number of times we reread a story depends on whether the students enjoy it and request it and on how well they are able to join in on reading the story. Sometimes it takes several rereadings before students can join in the reading, and other times the students join in reading the first time through. If students do not enjoy a story or it is apparent that the story is too difficult, we may read it only once or twice and then no longer use it during Shared Reading.

These whole-group Shared Reading experiences often involve the use of Big Books (Holdaway 1979)—books with enlarged print so that all the children can see the print as well as the illustrations. These books can be purchased commercially but can also be made by having the children do the illustrations and an adult write the text. When a Big Book is used, we run our hand under the print so the children know what we are reading. Songs and poems can be put on large charts so that all the children can see. An alternative to Big Books is to put the story on overheads.

We follow Holdaway's (1979) recommendation in making our Shared Reading a time of sharing old favorites as well as a time of introducing new poems, songs, and stories. We begin with some old favorites, taking requests from the students as well as using our own choices, and then move on to a new story, song, or poem. The unison rereading provides support for readers at different levels of proficiency—ranging from children who have no difficulty reading the print to children who are following the group's lead but are unable to read the print on their own. Children are not made to feel embarrassed or inadequate, but everyone joins in as able. As the story is reread, more and more children are able to read it with the rest of the group. During these rereadings, children become familiar with the language and story structure of the book, gain fluency in their oral reading, and begin to notice certain visual features. Each rereading allows children to attend to new demonstrations. The old favorites that are read repeatedly become the stories children draw from in their writing and in Literature Response Activities.

Following rereading, the book is placed in the Classroom Library or the Writing-Reading Center so that students can continue to get independent practice reading the book. Sometimes the book is placed in a listening center for students who need continued practice hearing the story. Shared Reading is based on the model of lap or bedtime-story reading (Doake 1986; Holdaway 1979). This model was developed from noting that young children naturally learned to read books when their parents read and reread the same stories to them and that the children then independently explored these same books during play. In Shared Reading, therefore, we give equal emphasis to the group reading and rereading and the independent exploration times in helping children gain control of a particular story.

Other types of Shared Reading occur during Work Time as students read with a partner or with a small group. During Work

Time we allow children to choose whether they will read alone or with other children. If they decide to do Shared Reading with another child, the two children must then decide how they will share the reading. The most common ways of sharing the reading are to take turns reading pages or parts of the story or to each read a different story to the other person. Sometimes readers decide to read in unison.

If one reader is more proficient than the other, the more proficient reader may read the less predictable parts and the less proficient reader the repeating refrains, or the more proficient reader may read the first part of the story and the less proficient reader may read the second part. Either strategy provides support for the less proficient reader, because having the proficient reader read first introduces the characters, author's style, and story schema. Classrooms with listening centers of books and taped readings provide another way that children can read along with someone else.

Harmony, a first-grade child who was experiencing difficulty in reading, taught us another strategy when she often approached more proficient readers and asked them to read her a book one or two times before she attempted to read it herself. Children in Harmony's classroom began approaching each other asking, "Do you want to learn to read my book?" or "Will you teach me to read your book?" They read both trade books and books they had published to each other.

Another type of Shared Reading, called *Popcorn Reading,* is done with a small group of children. Each child has a copy of the text being read. One person starts reading aloud and then stops at any point. Whoever jumps in first continues on reading until he or she decides to stop reading, and someone else quickly jumps in and begins reading. No one is forced to read, and there is no order for how readers will take over. Readers' Theatre can also be a form of Shared Reading that children use during Work Time.

One final variation consists of children sitting together at a table or on a rug and all reading silently from the same text for a period of time. The group then stops and shares their reading with one another. This variation of Shared Reading is called Reading Round Table and is often used with informational books or textbooks.

All these variations of Shared Reading build on the social nature of the learning process and allow children to support each other as they gain proficiency in reading. Although Shared Reading tends to be associated with young children, the many variations described support Shared Reading as a curricular strategy that is also useful with older children.

Because Shared Reading involves rereading predictable books, these books are a natural choice for a variety of response activities including drama, art, music, and writing. Students often choose to use the language or structural patterns of these books in their own writing. These books are also a natural choice for Group Composed Books.

Group Composed Books can be written by offering an invitation for each child to write one page using the pattern and then gathering the pages together into one book. Another option, however, is to make the writing of the book truly a group process. Those interested in writing a story gather together, and either the teacher or another child serves as a scribe to write down the story on the blackboard as the group develops it together. Although each child still decides what his or her page will say, that child does so knowing what the other pages will say and with the support of the rest of the group. Once the group has finished the story, each child copies his or her own page from the board and illustrates it for the group book. This activity of shared writing offers an excellent opportunity for children to observe and discuss the composing process as they work together to create a Group Composed Book. Both Group Composed Books and Shared Reading thus provide learning environments that highlight the support that language users can provide for each other in reading and writing with predictable text materials.

Authors Meeting Authors

A curriculum based on authoring should be a curriculum that introduces children to authors as people. Authors Meeting Authors is a strategy that focuses on introducing authors to children so that children realize that the books they read and enjoy are written by real people who work hard at their authoring rather than by a machine that impersonally puts out books. They develop a warm, personal feeling for authors to whom they have been introduced and search for their work in the library. As they learn about authors' lives and their thoughts about the authoring process, children become more aware of their own authoring processes and of options they may not have considered before in their authoring.

When children are introduced to a series of books by the same author or illustrator, they begin to recognize an author's work by his or her style. In one study (Harste 1986) we attempted to identify those strategies used by proficient readers to comprehend texts and found that author recognition played a significant role. Once readers had identified the authorship of a selection, comprehension was greatly facilitated. When readers were unable to identify the author, they puzzled and speculated about possible authorship throughout their reading.

We usually devote one of our daily class read-aloud times to focus on an author or illustrator. On the first day of a particular author focus, after setting up a display of that person's books, we spend some time just talking about the person and giving a little bit of background and any interesting stories we have been able to learn about that person. We then briefly introduce the books on the display. On the following days, we read to the class from that author's books. If the author writes chapter books, we choose one to read to the class and briefly introduce the others or read excerpts from them. As we read, we tell any additional stories we know about the author or quote what the author has said about the particular book or about his or her work.

The best source of information about children's authors is a set of encyclopedias called *Something About the Author* (Commire 1984). New volumes come out each year. The articles are comprehensive and give additional sources of information on each person. Lee Bennett Hopkins's interviews with children's authors are compiled in *Books Are by People* (1969) and *More Books by More People* (1974). If an author or illustrator has won a Caldecott or Newbery Medal, the August issue of *Horn Book* magazine will carry a copy of the acceptance speech and a biography. *Horn Book* also carries articles written by authors and illustrators about their work. The periodical *Language Arts* often carries a profile on a particular author. There are many individual as well as collective biographies on authors. Check local libraries to see what is available. In addition to information on the authors, these sources often include comments by the authors on their writing processes. Such comments provide students with new demonstrations of strategies they can use in their writing.

Sometimes a particular author focus involves just introducing and reading that author's works, but other times the focus leads to additional activities. Drama, art, and writing projects related to that author's books may be developed. Films and filmstrips about the authors or their books may be shown to the class. Weston Woods and Random House both produce filmstrips and films in which authors and illustrators discuss their writing and illustrating processes. Children can create an "I recommend" file for their Classroom Library. Alphabetized by author, the file consists of cards that children write to recommend a particular author's book for others to read. We have found that if we tell parents whom we are focusing on, they may help their child find that author's books at the public library.

Another common activity is to have children write to the author. Beverly Cleary, in her children's book *Dear Mr. Henshaw* (1983), pointed out that having children write simply for the sake of writing, as an imposed assignment, is not beneficial to either the child or the author. Letters to authors should grow out of a child's desire to communicate with that person rather than to complete an assignment. As we discuss an author's work and children ask questions about that person or talk about how much they like that author's work, we encourage them to write to that author. Once several children receive responses, other children become interested in writing to an author they particularly like. Vera Milz concludes an author study by having one or two children volunteer to create a card and write a message and then the other children sign their names. Her children also send cards to their favorite authors on the authors' birthdays or on holidays. It is best to send correspondence to authors in care of whichever publisher is currently publishing their hardback books. Bernice Cullinan (1981) has a listing of the birthdays of many children's authors.

One year, all of Tomie de Paola's books were read in Vera Milz's first- and second-grade classroom in Bloomfield Hills, Michigan. On a large sheet of paper, children were invited to list their favorite selection and give the reason for their choice. A class mural was thus created and sent to the author. This activity had an additional benefit. Jennifer decided to do a series of *Talking Egg Books*. By the end of the year, her series included titles such as *The Talking Egg Takes Up Jogging, The Talking Egg Goes Camping, The Talking Egg Tries a Cigarette,* and *The Talking Egg Eats a Peanut Butter Sandwich.* When the children were interviewed at the end of the year, many children selected Jennifer as their favorite author of children's books.

This focus on authors should not be limited only to the authoring process of writing. People who author in other communication systems should be featured in our classrooms for the same reasons authors of children's books need to be featured. A focus on illustrators, musicians, artists, mathematicians, and others should be considered an essential part of Authors Meeting Authors.

It is particularly exciting if classrooms can have an author actually visit their classroom or school. The author can be a community person publishing through a local press or a more well-known author. A retired teacher who had published a book of poetry at a small press visited Gloria Kauffman's first-grade classroom. The children prepared for her visit by reading her poetry and discussing it in Literature Circles. They brainstormed questions they wanted to ask her, and each child wrote down several questions to remember what they wanted to ask. When the author visited the classroom, she brought in her rough drafts and talked about her writing process, showed the different stages the book went through in the publication process, and answered the children's questions. The children then moved into their writing Work Time. They had each put their own favorite published work out on their desks. As they worked, the author walked around, and each child author briefly shared a piece of his or her own work with the visiting author. Several children listed this experience as the highlight of the year for them. It validated for them that they were involved in the same process of authoring that adult authors went through.

The elementary schools around Columbus, Ohio, benefit from the many authors who visit The Ohio State University. They arrange for those authors to come a day early and visit their schools as well, thus keeping the cost of the visit down. One of the authors of this book, Kathy Short, visited Highland Park Elementary School as they prepared for a visit from children's author Eve Merriam. For several weeks before she came, the entire school was involved in units developed around her poetry. Individual classrooms carried out projects related to her work, and copies of her books were available for student purchase. Many classrooms were involved in poetry units in which children read poetry, wrote their own poetry, and did other kinds of Literature Response Activities such as murals, dioramas, giant books, and displays. Teachers also worked with students in helping them generate questions they wanted to ask Eve Merriam during her visit.

In addition to the individual classroom projects, there were a number of projects building off of particular poems that cut across the school. The front lobby of the school was converted into a museum where displays were set up related to a particular poem; the school faculty put on a play for the children from one of the books; a school poetry reading assembly was held; and a poem on pizza led to making giant pizzas that were wheeled around the school with each classroom adding something to them.

One morning mini-courses focused on activities related to Eve Merriam's poems were offered by each adult in the school. The children signed up so that one or two children from each class attended a particular workshop. When the children returned to their classrooms after the morning workshops, they shared what they had done, providing new ideas for Literature Response Activities for the other children. The mini-courses included making T-shirts, paper pizzas, mobiles, stuffed objects, kites, pocket poems, thumbprints, sea shells, pancakes, windchimes, monster masks, taking field trips to a pizza shop, and working on a drama.

On the day Eve Merriam came to visit, the entire school was filled with murals, posters, dioramas, books, and displays related to her work. Her day at the school began with a tour of each room. Each class had fifteen minutes to share some of their responses to her work and to ask several questions. She then had lunch with a group of children (one child had been chosen from each room) followed by lunch with the teachers. After lunch, she met with small groups of children who had been chosen to share some particularly special projects with her. An assembly was then called, where she read from her poetry and talked about her writing.

The day ended with an autograph session in the gymnasium. Booths had been set up all around the perimeter of the gym with activities to do as the children waited in the long autograph line. It was an exciting day for both Eve Merriam and the children.

Although getting a major author to visit your school is expensive, there are ways to offset the costs. Check with the publisher to see if the author will be near your area for another engagement so that you would not have to bear all the transportation costs. See if you can split the costs with another group, such as a local college or your area's Young Authors Conference. Publishers are often willing to pay the costs for new authors whom they are trying to promote. Some schools have fundraisers to get the money they need for these visits. Finally, do not forget the authors who may live near your area. We were surprised when we began doing some research on authors who lived in or near Indiana. In addition, many authors today are willing to do telephone conference calls. These can usually be arranged through the author's publisher.

Authors Meeting Authors focuses on authors from outside the classroom so that children realize that the authoring processes they are engaged in are processes that authors in the "real" world also use. Although this activity emphasizes outside authors, we encourage this same focus for authors within the classroom. Some classrooms have an Author of the Week. The writing of that author is displayed and read during the week, and children interview the author about the writing process. Classroom-authored books can be used in Literature Circles and then the author can be invited to join the group so the group can ask questions. It is important that children feel that we value their work and that they can learn from each other as well as from the work of outside authors.

The teacher is another classroom author who can demonstrate valuable strategies that proficient language users engage in. Teachers need to share their writing and discuss their writing processes with children. They are the most accessible and constant demonstration of an adult author for children. When teachers serve as demonstrating authors, they allow children to see them as learners who are continuing to grow and learn rather than as adults who have everything learned and who have "perfect" use of language.

Authors Meeting Authors is a curricular activity that provides children with many demonstrations about authoring through looking at outside authors as well as authors from within the classroom. These demonstrations help them come to value authoring as a central process of bringing meaning to their lives.

Literature Response Activities

As children read and construct meanings from the literature, they also need to be involved in deepening and extending their understandings of that literature through Literature Response Activities. These activities allow them to return to a piece of literature from a new perspective. Readers have time to reflect and to savor and absorb books so that those books become a significant part of their lives. Readers need to be involved both in reading extensively (reading a wide variety of literature without taking that reading on to response activities) and in reading intensively (reading some books with deeper responses through Literature Response Activities). These activities are called response activities because they deepen and extend the responses of understanding that a reader has about a particular piece of literature.

Literature Response Activities can be used at many different points in the curriculum. Readers may be asked to respond in some way to the class read-aloud book, to the literature they have been discussing in Literature Circles, or to a favorite piece of literature they have read independently during Work Time. The responses can be individual or small-group projects that children work on during Work Time. We usually have children choose from a variety of kinds of responses, although there are times when the whole group may be involved in a response activity such as Say Something, especially when that activity is first introduced. We often have Friday's Author Sharing Time reserved as a time for students to share their Literature Response Activities with each other.

One type of Literature Response Activity that should be part of every classroom is giving readers extended and repeated opportunities to talk about what they have read. Important cognitive and interpretive thinking strategies are developed as children talk about and debate their understandings of literature with one another. Readers discuss their differing interpretations, draw in other experiences and pieces of literature that are related to the literature being discussed, make various kinds of comparisons, and build a critical framework for how to talk and think about literature. These discussions need to be open-ended discussions rather than teacher-directed quizzes to see if students have the "right" answers for what a book means.

Some curricular activities that build on the need to talk about literature with others include Literature Circles, Say Something, *Save the Last Word for Me,* and Cloning an Author. All these activities are based on the belief that there is no one "right" answer to a book's meaning. Different interpretations are accepted as long as readers can support that interpretation by referring to the book and to their experiences. Although teachers should be present at some of these discussions to demonstrate how one talks about literature, their presence affects the dynamics of the group because of their greater knowledge and experience. Children also need to be given many opportunities to talk with each other without the teacher's presence. Although much of this talk initially may appear pointless and rambling, the students need time to explore half-formed ideas and hypotheses to develop more complex understandings.

Literature Response Activities involve many other communication systems besides language. In fact, we have found that nonverbal response activities are especially important in getting children to think about literature from a different perspective and to get beyond their concerns that there is one "right" interpretation. An activity such as Sketch to Stretch, which has students draw the meaning of a piece of literature, requires the readers to take a meaning they constructed through language and figure out how to construct that meaning in a different communication system—art. In taking meaning from one system to another, in this case from reading to art, readers reflect on that literature in a different way to discover ways to express meaning through drawing.

Literature Response Activities involve responding through discussion, writing, drama, music, art, movement, and any other communication system that will deepen and extend their understanding of literature. In Gloria Kauffman's first-grade classroom, the children were involved in reading fairy tales over a six-week period. During that time, they responded to those fairy tales through Literature Circles and other informal discussions, through acting out their favorite tales as well as their own versions of these tales, through writing stories using the story structure of fairy tales, and through creating dioramas, murals, and illustrations. The children's understandings of fairy tales and their ability to make connections to fairy tales in later experiences were complex because of the many different experiences they had with reading and responding to these fairy tales.

We often have children brainstorm a list of possible ways they could respond to a piece of literature so that they have a range of options to choose from in making their response. The Writing-Reading Center can include a list of these brainstormed ideas and the materials students need for these activities. The activities that the children at Highland Park School were involved in when they prepared for Eve Merriam's visit is a good example of the tremendous variety of response activities that children can use.

Over a period of time, students may be involved in several different ways of responding to the same piece of literature as they talk about the book, write about it in a Literature Log or use the literature in some way in their own writing, and draw or in some other way represent the book in art. Each response deepens their understanding of that literature. Janet Hickman (1981) observed how children responded to literature in three elementary classrooms and identified the following categories of response:

1. Listening behaviors (body stances, laughter and applause, exclamations, joining in refrains)
2. Contact with books (browsing, showing intense attention, keeping books at hand)

3. Acting on impulse to share (reading together, sharing discoveries)

4. Oral responses (retelling, storytelling, discussion statements, free comments)

5. Actions and drama (echoing the action, demonstrating meaning, dramatic play, child-initiated drama, teacher-initiated drama)

6. Making things (pictures and related artwork, three-dimensional art and construction, miscellaneous products such as games, displays, collections, cookery, etc.)

7. Writing (restating and summarizing, writing about literature, using literary models deliberately, using unrecognized models and sources)

Although these response activities are not the only possibilities, they show the range of responses in which children can be involved. The absence of communication systems such as music from the list indicates that these are areas that teachers and students need to explore more fully as possible response activities. Literature Response Activities give readers the chance to extend their responses and to revisit past readings in a new light so that each response is more complex and more reflective.

Journals

Writing plays many different functions in our lives, and writing in schools should reflect that range of functions. Journals meet an informal, personal function that is often not present in schools. Although we used to think we knew how Journals should be used in a classroom, we've had that confidence shattered through experience. Our notion was that the teacher made Journals available and invited children to use them as a personal diary, with the sole stipulation that entries be made daily; sharing of entries was left to student discretion.

We saw Journals as a contrast to other writing done in the classroom; their function was to create a very low-risk, informal means for children to explore, among other things, the recording function of language. They also served as a personal record that could be consulted as needed to refresh children's memories not only when reviewing the week, month, or year, but also when attempting something in writing (such as a response to a pen pal).

Because the content of a journal was open, each child decided what function and purpose the personal journal would serve.

Few teachers we have ever worked with have used Journals in exactly this way. Myriam Revel-Wood introduces Journals by giving children a list of the kinds of things they might like to consider recording—for example, something that happened at home, what you did today in school, how you are feeling about something. Rather than allowing the function of the journal just to evolve, she channels it, arguing that the children need such direction.

Although we began with different premises, we ended up at the same place. In part this is due to Myriam's acceptance of the children's work. As individuals and groups of children move their journal in certain directions, she graciously accepts and encourages this—one group of boys turned their journals into a daily comic strip; one girl saw her journal as a potential historical document from which "future people" might piece together classroom life in the 1980s; two girls from Saudi Arabia used their journals to practice their English (initially they wrote in Arabic and then together worked out an English translation); many used their journals for emotional release, recording in them their likes, dislikes, and ever-changing feelings; others turned their journal pages into letters to the teacher. They were not above demanding a response.

In Myriam's classroom, blank journals are prepared by one child's mother, using 8 1/2" × 11" pieces of typing paper sewn down the center. Construction paper covers are decorated by the children. Each journal has 32 blank pages (8 pieces of paper folded in half and sewn). Initially it was assumed that a journal would last about one month. Although this planning seemed sound, it didn't work; some children used two pages each day, others three. Whenever the child finishes a journal, Myriam asks to see it. Pages that children do not want her to read are marked VP (very private), or simply folded over. Some children develop another code, VVP (very, very private). After Myriam looks through the journal, she returns it to the child and leaves a personal note on the Message Board about something she really liked in the journal.

When we interviewed children at the end of the year about all the writing they had done in the classroom and which form was their favorite, "Personal Journals" won the popularity contest. Children in Myriam's classroom typically complete eight journals each year. We have yet to meet a child willing to allow us to keep one of their journals for use in preservice and inservice education. Reasons run from "Oh, no, it's got some of my favorite cartoons in it" to "It's personal stuff" to "Just because." Fortunately, the daughter of one of the authors was in Myriam's class, and so we often show off her journal. However, she insists that we read only selected entries. On an occasion when we were discussing this, she said, "Oh, I suppose you better read one of my VVP pages, too, or they won't understand why we like Journals so much."

Mary Lynn Woods, a teacher from the Indianapolis area, uses Journals in a different way. Initially we were sure her plan was the perfect way to destroy everything that Journals were supposed to be, though now we think we like her approach as well as the others. Clearly, Journals in Mary Lynn's room are quite different commodities than they are in Myriam's room.

Mary Lynn makes her journals by running off a colored paper cover with the class logo on it and staples in 20 or so pieces of lined 8 1/2" × 11" paper. The first page of the journal contains a set of directions. Children are told to write about things that interest them, that sometimes topics will be assigned, that all entries are public, and that they are to make at least three Journal entries each week.

Children do not write Journals during school time in Mary Lynn's room. They are homework. During Author Sharing Time, children discuss possible topics that they might all write about in their journals. These are then discussed and ranked, and a decision is arrived at concerning the topic to be chosen. Children are invited to write about the class choice (e.g., what they will do once vacation starts, a moment that meant a lot to them, their pets), but are always told that it is their choice and that they may select a different topic if the one the group has selected doesn't appeal.

As children come into the classroom in the morning, they place their journal on a special table. During Work Time each child in the class is expected to go over to the journal table, read at least two other people's entries, write a written response to each at the end of the entry, and sign their reaction. Written reactions are intended to tell the author if the content is meaningful. For example, margin feedback might read, "I can tell by your enthusiastic words that you really had a great vacation!" or "I can tell that you were really scared when you fell into the corn bin. You wrote it so well, you scared me, too!"

Children are told that they have a responsibility to make sure that everyone's journal has been read by at least two people and that they are to make their selection of what journal to read on the basis of how many written reactions are already in the journal at the time of their arrival at the table. The second reader is asked to react to the original journal entry as well as to the written reaction of the first reader. Mary Lynn makes sure that she, too, gets to the table during Work Time and reads and reacts to at least two journals. Often both she and the children read many more entries than just two. This is both permitted and encouraged. Her journal, which she writes at home, is added to the table like everyone else's. At Author Sharing Time, some children elect to share parts of a journal entry; all discuss potential new topics, agree on a choice, and then pick up their journals to take home.

Sue Robinson has used a variation of Mary Lynn's Journals. She has the children write their journal entries first thing each morning on any topic they choose. Sue and the children then put their journals out on a table to be responded to by at least one person sometime during that day. Children can choose to keep their journal private by closing it rather than keeping it open for response.

Journals in Mary Lynn's room are therefore more like Dialogue Journals than Personal Journals. By combining what one normally thinks of as a journal with a variation on Writing in the Round (see Say Something), a unique and highly motivating writing program is started.

Mary Lynn's use of Journals has a number of effects that don't emerge in Myriam's room. Because of the nature of the entries, many rough draft journal entries in Mary Lynn's class end up being selected to take to published form. Rarely do journal entries result in a published document in Myriam's room.

A side benefit of Mary Lynn's use of Journals is that parents see children writing at home, not once but three times each week! By catching the interest of parents, typically Mary Lynn gets from 85 to 95 percent of her parents to come on Parents' Day. Many announce as they enter the classroom, "I just wanted to see what was going on. Steve hated reading and writing last year, but now he just seems to be writing all of the time." One summer Parents' Day was held from 8:30 to 11:30 one Friday morning, not a particularly good time to attract many parents. To our surprise, not only was every family represented by at least one parent or grandparent, but 85 percent of the fathers showed up! Many parents had taken time off work, and although they couldn't stay the entire morning, either their child's enthusiasm or their own curiosity had gotten the best of them.

Despite the fact that Journals are a lot like other kinds of invitations to write in Mary Lynn's class, they do serve some valuable purposes in addition to those we normally associate with Journals. Our own feeling is that her use of Journals, with its entree to parents, makes the approach worth closer examination by other teachers. Also, the dialogue that takes place in writing is invaluable. It encourages reading, helps children understand how authors support one another, and naturally sets up the authoring cycle.

Gloria Kauffman has worked to preserve the more personal function of Journals in both her first-grade and her third-grade classrooms. In first grade, Journals were introduced as diaries in which the children could write about events and feelings related to school or home. A diary written by a grandparent was shared with them, as were several books, such as *Dear Mr. Henshaw* (Cleary 1983), that used diary entries. Initially children had a difficult time understanding this personal function. We realized that writing for oneself to explore feelings and to record what is happening to oneself is a function that is not used to its potential in our society and so was one that many children had not seen other adults use. They were more familiar with writing to communicate to someone else.

Many of the children's early journal entries consisted of drawings with a few words, "I love" messages, and an occasional sentence about something that had happened. Gloria was frustrated because many of the children did not enjoy Journal time or use it to explore personal meaning. She persisted, however, in having a Journal time and in accepting whatever children chose to write. She did not respond to their journals but did usually read through them about once a week just to see what children were doing. Near the end of November, Journals finally clicked, and children who had persisted in drawing pictures suddenly began writing long entries in their journals about things that were happening to them. Children no longer complained about writing in their journals but complained if, for some reason, there was no time to write in their journals.

In January, Gloria introduced the option of Dialogue Journals. She did this because a number of children were indicating a need for more attention and interaction with her. She felt comfortable introducing this option in January because she knew that the children understood and valued the personal function of Journals and so could really make a choice. Each day when children wrote in their journals, they could choose either to leave the journals open for her response or to leave them closed. The majority of children chose to continue using the journal as a personal journal and only occasionally used the journal as a dialogue journal. Mondays tended to be a day when more children wanted Gloria to read and respond to their descriptions of their weekends. A few children switched to using their journals almost entirely as dialogue journals and having Gloria respond each day.

Later, when Gloria taught third grade, she again introduced Journals as a diary in which children could write about things happening to them and about their feelings. She immediately introduced the option of leaving the journals open for her response or closing them if they did not want her to respond. She found, however, that nearly all the children wanted responses and that Journals became a way to send her messages and to complain about other children rather than a place to explore the personal function of writing. Gloria felt that this occurred for two reasons: (1) the option of Dialogue Journals was introduced before the children had a chance to explore the personal function of Journals, and (2) the children's past experiences with Journals in other classrooms had been limited to Dialogue Journals in first and second grade, and so to them Journals were a way to send messages, not to explore personal meaning.

Gloria now uses only Personal Journals. The children write their journal entries each morning as they arrive and then put their journals away. Once in a while Gloria reads through their journals, except for the pages the children have indicated that she is not to read, but she does not respond. Initially the children found this difficult, but Gloria knew from her previous experiences that if she gave them enough time really to explore the personal function of Journals they would discover the potential of Personal Journals. She did not give them specific topics to write on or a certain amount to write. During the first several weeks, she did have a Journal time that lasted for ten minutes when everyone had to be writing in the journals. She also occasionally asked if anyone wanted to share something they had written in their journals so that other children could get some ideas of things they might want to write about. The specified period of time and the sharing were used to get Journals going and then eliminated. By October, Journals were valued highly by the children and were an integral part of their day.

Gloria found that having the children use spiral notebooks made the journals seem like "real" journals to them. One year she used paper stapled between wallpaper covers, but she quickly found that the children did not respond as well, and so she returned to having each child bring in a spiral notebook for the journal.

Probably what is needed are several kinds of Journals going on in the classrooms at one time. Kittye Copeland, a teacher in a multi-age (K-6) classroom in Columbia, Missouri, has children in her classroom keep a Learning Log. The Learning Log (see the Curricular Components section for a description of the various Journals mentioned here) is a kind of journal in which children record what they learn each day. This journal encourages children to be reflective and to bring to conscious awareness things that they experience throughout the day.

Both Myriam Revel-Wood and Tim O'Keefe, a second-grade teacher at Lynwood Elementary School in Indianapolis, use Science Logs in their classrooms. These are a kind of personal journal in which children record observations they make relative to a self-selected topic within a science unit they are studying. Community or Class Logs work well, too. These logs are placed next to an area where students can observe a plant or animal. Anyone from the class can make entries in the log each day. In one first-grade classroom, Community Logs were permanently placed outside the terrarium and gerbil cage. Children were invited to record, date, and sign their names to entries indicating what they observed as they spent time in these centers throughout the day. These logs were later used as the basis of a class discussion.

Another type of log that is frequently used is the Literature Log. Gloria Kauffman's third-grade class uses Literature Logs to write about their reactions to books they are reading independently or to the chapter book that she is reading aloud to the class. Sometimes she assigns a particular topic to write about, and other times children write anything they want about a book they want to share with her. The children make several entries a week in their logs, and Gloria responds to their entries. Her responses are not evaluative—"That's good"—but instead she discusses and extends what the child has written. She sees these logs as a place where she can have conversations with the children about what they are reading.

Kaylene Yoder, a sixth-grade teacher at the same school where Gloria Kauffman teaches, uses Nancie Atwell's idea of Literature Logs as letters (Atwell 1984). Her students write an entry each week that is a letter to Kaylene about the book they are reading independently. She feels that having them write to her about a book they are reading on their own rather than a book that the class or a small group is reading together gives them a real purpose for making the entry. The children enjoy using the log as a letter to her.

Both Gloria and Kaylene have also used Literature Logs in combination with Literature Circles. The logs have been used at several different points during the circles. Sometimes students make entries at the end of each day while they are reading the book. When the group meets to discuss the book, they share some of their entries as a way to begin discussion and to determine major issues or areas of interest they want to discuss. Other times, students make entries during the time they are discussing the book. At the end of each day's discussion, the group decides what they want to focus on during their next meeting. Each group member thinks about that area of focus and makes an entry in the Literature Log. These entries are shared at the beginning of the next circle.

We have used Journals not only in elementary classrooms but also in workshops and college classes. They give participants a more functional view of both writing and reading processes. The issue is not which of these many Journals to try, but rather how to get many started to meet the needs of your classroom learning environment.

Pen Pals

Although Journals focus on using writing as a personal learning tool, Pen Pals focuses on informal writing to communicate with others. Before you say, "I tried that once, and it didn't work, kids lost interest," let us discuss why this might have happened, how to solve the problem, and why Pen Pals is worth a second try.

First, if the class pen pals are in Hawaii, Australia, California, or some other exotic spot, no matter how rapidly teachers move on setting up a pen pal exchange in September (and this assumes the teacher has made contact with some other teacher over the summer), it is often mid-November or December before the class actually gets responses. If this is the child's first experience with Pen Pals, there are no fond memories of past pen pal experiences to fall back on. Under these conditions only the most tenacious maintain interest. What one ends up with is a hit-and-miss pen pal program. Some children have a great experience; most, however, do not. Under these conditions it's hard to think of the pen pal program as a serious and integral part of your language arts curriculum.

But this need not be the scenario. There are alternatives. Keep the infrequent long-distance pen pals, but also have pen pals who live nearby. We have found, for example, that having pen pals in the same town solves the problem of turnaround time without seriously detracting from the notion of Pen Pals. We identify a willing teacher in the same city but in a different school who lives nearby. Once the program is under way, we stop at the other teacher's house or school each Friday on the way home from work to deliver students' letters, and pick up the letters to members of our class. On Monday we distribute the letters and announce that they have until Friday to write a response and place it in the mail bag. Students who don't get their letters in on time miss out and have lots to explain to their pen pal next time. On Friday, whether all the letters are in or not, the exchange is made once again. Come Monday, another letter is awaiting the pen pal.

In one fourth-grade classroom we had three sets of pen pals going concurrently. One set was with children in a fourth-grade class in a neighboring school, another set was with a first-grade class across town, and a third set was with college students in a reading and language arts methods class at the university. We made carbon paper available to encourage children to keep a copy of the letters they sent their pen pals. Students kept both their own letters and the letters from their pen pals in a pocket folder in their desks. Later in the year they were invited to contrast the letters written to the fourth graders with those to the first graders, and both of these with the letters to the college students. This led to a discussion about similarity and differences between the various sets of letters in terms of length, topics discussed, language used, handwriting changes, and such features as the use of art. This discussion led to insights into how successful language users vary language by the circumstances of use, a discussion on language variation within the community, a dialect dictionary project, and a general sensitivity and understanding of culture and language diversity.

The university students, by the way, used the pen pal letters they had written and received to conduct their own child-as-informant language studies. Everyone benefited intellectually. Interestingly, the university students found it more awkward to write their initial letters than did the children in our class. On several occasions we held Meet Your Pen Pal parties. The university students were as excited and anxious about meeting their pen pals as were the children in meeting them. Getting the pen pals together added to the success of the program. Sometimes these pen pal meetings have been author teas to which both pen pals brought pieces they had written to share with each other or the two pen pals had a writing session to co-author a story.

In another classroom a pen pal program was set up with residents in a nursing home that happened to be located between the teacher's home and school. This proved as beneficial an experience as writing to the university students.

One day, Maura, a fourth grader in Myriam Revel-Wood's classroom, excitedly commented, as she finished reading her pen pal's letter, "I can hardly wait to tell her." Having overheard her enthusiasm, we were surprised when seconds later she put the letter in her notebook and began working on something else. Never willing to leave well enough alone, we asked, "Well, if you're so excited, why aren't you writing her back immediately?" To this, Maura said, "I don't want to right now. I don't have any stationery. I'll get some at home and write her tomorrow." We had never thought about the fact that the children, like the adults with whom they were corresponding, would like special stationery, and we hastily decided to self-correct. We handed her a blue ditto and asked, "Would you like to design some stationery that we all might use this week? We're sure others feel like you do and would like some stationery, too." Maura took up the offer. From then on not only was there designer-named stationery in the classroom (children took turns), but, by taking apart an envelope and drawing its outline on another blue stencil, envelopes could be designed to match the stationery (children had to cut and glue it together to use). Multiple copies of "This Week's Designer Stationery and Envelopes" were made available at the Writing-Reading Center. By the end of the year we had a wide variety of stationery to choose from, and probably one of the most unusual and interesting sets any writer could hope to use.

Nanci Vargus (1982) formally studied how letter writing changes in a first-grade classroom over the course of a semester. Jenny's first and ninth letters are illustrative (see Figure 3.2).

The letters got longer, the variety of topics expanded, and shifts in responsibility occurred. By the ninth letter, children no longer took refuge in ritualistic form and the answering of questions posed by their correspondent, but took ownership and responsibility for generating and communicating new information. With time—that is, with more and more opportunities to write letters—children began to explore the potential of this literary

I Like you mrs vargus
I wish I could write
to you all the time.

Love Jenny Haggard

I love you

Dear Mrs Vargus

my dad is warking at
us air line's naw. and we get
leoft over tickets. I do not no
wear we air going yet but
hear are sum name's of sum
placees we might go.

kuntuke. florda. texes.

my grandma and
grandpa have a
house in
kentuke

my ocean
house

Figure 3.2 First and Ninth Pen Pal Letters from Jenny.

genre. By the ninth letter exchange, letter writing was quite a different experience than it had been the first time these children engaged in it. If ever one needs evidence of the value of letter writing in the classroom, Nanci Vargus's study provides it.

Message Board

Note passing is a communicative function of writing that many students already use undercover in classrooms. Message Board legitimizes the passing of messages between class members. Although some teachers use individual mailboxes, we prefer a bulletin board in a central location. Students and teachers use this board to post messages for each other as well as the whole class.

In Myriam Revel-Wood's room, children make their own mail pocket out of two pieces of tagboard (one 6" × 6", one 6" × 4", which they tape together along the three overlapping sides). They write their names in bold print on their mail pockets and decorate them to their personal liking. The pockets are put in two or three rows on a bulletin board entitled Message Board. Messages are placed in the respective pockets by the person sending the message. Myriam makes herself a pocket, too, as do others who are in the classroom on a regular or semiregular basis.

Sue Robinson is short on bulletin board space in her inner-city classroom. Her Message Board is a 4' × 6' mobile bulletin board that she places in the chalk tray of the blackboard near the entrance to her classroom. Students mail messages back and forth by writing the recipient's name on a folded flap of their 4" × 6" message paper and simply tacking it anywhere on the bulletin board. Unlike Myriam's classroom where children can see whether there are messages in their pocket from across the classroom, in Sue's room they must read. Because messages can be located anywhere on the Message Board, students must physically come up and look over the messages to find one that belongs to them.

Sue uses Message Board for both public and private messages. Public messages are just tacked up with the print side showing. Private messages are folded with the recipient's name on the outside. Teachers and students can create both kinds of messages. The only rule Sue has is: *No message may hurt anyone else's feelings.* One year students used the board to exchange jokes and riddles. A student would put the joke or riddle on the board, and others would put their answers below it. After several days, the answer would be posted by the first student.

Another strong aspect of Sue's Message Board is how she uses it in relation to the publication program in her classroom. Class newspapers are produced and distributed to students in her room and other students in the building. In the class newspaper, readers are informed that writers like to hear from their readers. If readers have questions about what they read, or want to make a comment, they are told to stop by the room and leave a note to the author on the Message Board. As a result, after the first edition of the class newspaper, students in Sue's class receive notes from other children in the building. Sometimes these are just brief messages such as "I liked your story. Tom." Others, however, ask for clarification, suggest the author do a sequel next month, or even tell how the story reminded them of something that happened to them. On several occasions these notes led to second editions of the original text.

Mary Lynn Woods brings in a large piece of cardboard that the children design and color to use as the Message Board. The summer we were working in her classroom the children made a huge apple tree. This was taped to the wall near the entrance so that everyone had ready access. Mary Lynn put a small desk-sized table off to the side of the Message Board where she placed stacks of blank notepaper, tied two pencils, and placed a box of tacks. Just as in Sue's room, notes were placed at random on the Message Board. A particularly nice feature of Mary Lynn's Message Board was that it provided children with a place to write if the message they received called for a response.

Regardless of the physical appearance, the Message Board is a popular area in each classroom. Myriam initially thought that she didn't need a Message Board as she had so many other kinds of informal writing going on. Whenever the need arose to compliment a child on something he or she did (like supporting another reader or writer or taking a risk in writing that he or she had not been able to do before), we would remind Myriam how nice a Message Board would be. She finally gave in. At the end of the year, as we were discussing what things she had tried and how she felt about them, the Message Board was mentioned as "a nice touch." When we asked her why, she said, "It's great. When you write a message about something you either like or don't like, it is so much more effective than when you just talk to the kids or casually say something." She also brought out several messages sent to her by the children that she had saved. Her favorite was, "Thanks for starting the message center. I like it because now I can sort of talk to you whenever I want. I don't have to wait. Love, Ariel."

Conclusion

From a curricular perspective, celebrating authors and authorship has as its focus the setting up of a conducive classroom environment for language use and learning. To that end we have suggested organizational decisions such as Work Time, Author Sharing Time, Authors' Chair, Classroom Library, and Writing-Reading Center, as well as curricular activities such as Readers' Theatre, Shared Reading, Authors Meeting Authors, Journals, Pen Pals, and Message Board as vehicles that might be explored. These activities, however, are meant to be suggestions rather than an exhaustive list.

In addition to the basic set of activities described in this section, all the teachers we know use additional activities. For example, Myriam Revel-Wood regularly schedules *Book Sales* (see Literature Response Activities in Section Two). Kittye Copeland, a first-grade teacher from Columbia, Missouri, uses Sustained Silent Reading and Sustained Silent Writing. Gloria Kauffman uses Say Something and Sketch to Stretch on a regular basis.

The key is to set up an environment where there are many invitations to read and write, where reading and writing are juxtaposed and used for a variety of purposes, and where children have opportunities to meet and come to see themselves as authors. The environment should also be one where they see their teacher as an author and a learner. Each curricular component suggested in this section provides children with invitations to engage, see demonstrated, and come to value the strategies involved in authoring. Each curricular component suggested provides a basis from which the authoring cycle can begin anew. How this can happen is shown in Chapter 1, where a letter to the editor about the need for illustrations in the class newspaper led to a new round of authoring and learning.

Each activity described in this chapter became a more or less permanent feature of classroom life in the classrooms in which we worked. They ensured that reading and writing invitations were always present, that various contexts of literacy were being addressed, and that the language arts curriculum was more than just a "needs curriculum." Children were given the opportunity to try things on for size, to grow, to discover, and to experience, see demonstrated, and come to value the potential of literacy in its multiple forms.

In introducing any of these activities to a class, we recommend that teachers begin by suggesting that for the next several months the class will be having Message Board, Journals, or whatever the activity is that has been selected. Everyone will be expected to participate during this trial period, after which time the teacher and students will see whether the entire group or only selected individuals will elect to continue. By introducing the language activities in this fashion, choice is maintained, reflexivity is encouraged, and ownership of the language arts curriculum is made possible.

When the right classroom context has been set, the teacher does not spend evenings grading papers, but rather writing notes for distribution in the morning, keeping up with a journal, reading like a practicing writer, answering pen pal letters, and planning new invitations based on observations and suggestions received from the co-authors of the curriculum.

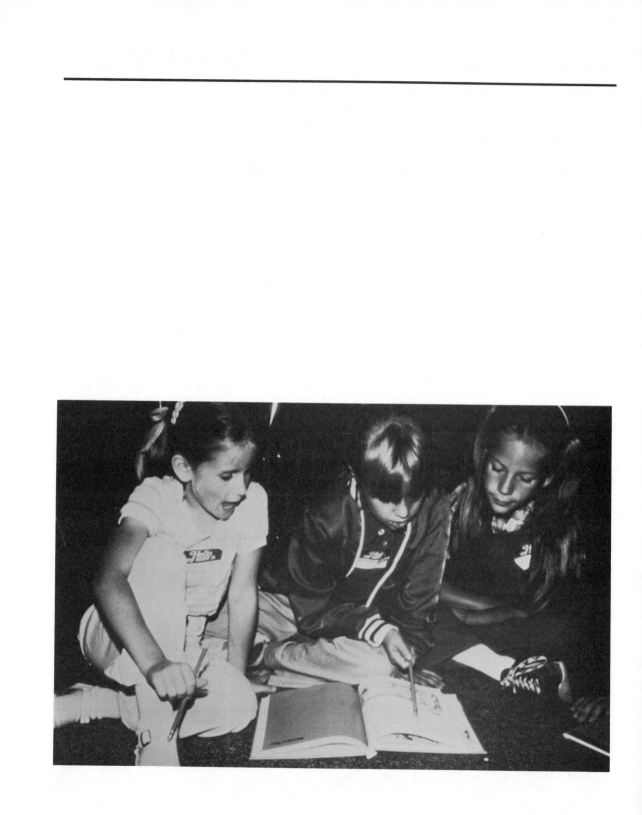

Invitations to Read, to Write, to Learn

Myriam Revel-Wood

Introduction

A classroom for authors and authorship provides children with lots of invitations to write, to read, and to learn. Such a classroom works to create a learning community where all learners, including the teacher, can grow as human beings. The teacher is a kid-watcher who joins students as they explore and discover language together, engages them through demonstrations of learning, and creates a warm and supportive atmosphere that encourages change.

A classroom for authors and authorship is a lush environment that surrounds students with all kinds of print media; science materials to manipulate and investigate; maps, globes and atlases; art and writing materials; and challenging units of study. Educational experiences are based on a plan that integrates reading and writing across the curriculum. Such a plan is necessary to provide students with a multitude of invitations to read and write and to allow them the freedom and control they must have to develop as learners.

Harste, Woodward, and Burke (1984) suggest that the most valuable gift we can give language learners is to litter their environment with enticing language opportunities and guarantee them the freedom to experiment with them. In this article, I would like

169

to describe some ways that such ideals are put into practice in my fourth-grade classroom.

Invitations to Read

One of the first steps in creating a lush environment in which students are surrounded by, or immersed in, print media is to make a multitude of materials available and highly accessible to them. These materials include hundreds of paperbacks, library books, field guides, encyclopedias, atlases, brochures, magazines, pictures and posters, newspapers, good texts, and the students' own writing.

Students read when attractive and interesting books are all around them and the pleasure of getting lost in a book is demonstrated to them. Because I want students to have easy access to all kinds of books, my fourth-grade classroom has accumulated over one thousand paperbacks on a variety of subjects such as earth science, biology, history, mythology, folktales, sports, historical fiction, biographies, mysteries, fantasy, and science fiction. The books range in reading level from second through ninth or tenth grade and even include some adult works.

The books that we own only one copy of make up the Paperback Library. Students are free to check out these books at any time, to read at school or to take home.

To encourage reluctant readers to explore books and to celebrate published authors, we hold weekly or monthly Book Sales. Students who have finished a book and want to "sell it"—persuade someone else to read it—stand before the class and tell about the book. Readers may choose to explain the main points of the book, or they may tell about the author, the characters, the setting, or some interesting parts; they may also give their personal reactions to the book, somewhat like a testimonial. Students interested in reading the book being sold have the next turn checking it out of the library.

We have also acquired multiple copies of many paperbacks. Some Text Sets are related to science units such as The Geological Development of Monroe County, The Energy Cycle, and Classification of Living Things. Other sets support units on First Americans, Colonial History, Pioneers and the Settlement of Indiana, Black Americans, Famous Scientists, and Folktales of the World. Other titles, some of which are the focus of literature study, include *The Big Wave* (Buck 1986); *The Chronicles of Narnia* (Lewis 1950); *The Prydain Chronicles* (Alexander 1968); *Bridge to Terabithia* (Paterson 1977); *The Indian in the Cupboard* (Banks 1981); *The Old Man and the Sea* (Hemingway 1952); and *Bury My Heart at Wounded Knee* (Brown [1971] 1984). These books are used for reading instruction that I handle through Literature Circles. They may be chosen because they relate to a content area unit, because students suggested them, or because they are marvelous literature. A variety of strategies such as Say Something, Sketch to Stretch, and Save the Last Word for Me help make these books meaningful and accessible to students.

Other reading materials available to students include two sets of wildlife encyclopedias and *Junior Britannica;* the *Audubon* (published by Doubleday), *Peterson* (Houghton Mifflin) and *Golden Book* (Western) *Field Guides;* comprehensive resource books published by the National Geographic Society, National Wildlife Federation, Audubon, the American Museum of Natural History, and others; old science and social studies texts with material that is still accurate and relevant; and magazines such as *Ranger Rick, International Wildlife, National Wildlife, Natural History, National Geographic, Smithsonian, Newsweek, Arizona Highways,* and *Outdoor Indiana.*

We have torn articles and pictures out of many old magazines and books to collect materials related to themes studied throughout the year. Articles on science and social studies topics are also cut out of newspapers. Some of the most frequently used articles have been laminated and are kept in a larger binder, but most articles and hundreds of pictures are filed in shirt boxes. Children use them as reference materials or to illustrate research reports and stories.

Our classroom also provides "tools" or "special places" for investigating, sharing, writing, losing oneself in a book, and discussing ideas. The special places include a writing corner, a geography corner, a science area, a computer center, a Message Board, and reading areas with rugs and pillows. At the Writing-Reading Center are found materials such as an inexhaustible supply of note and doodle paper (usually computer printouts), construction, plain and lined paper; teacher-made journals; blank books for stories and poems; classroom newspapers and magazines; student-authored storybooks; scissors and crayons; as well as specific invitations to read and write based on ongoing classroom activities.

Invitations to Write

In a classroom for authors and authorship there are countless invitations and opportunities to write. In our classroom we write for different purposes and to different audiences.

One of my main concerns is with students' self-concept as writers. I want them to feel they can write. Producing many stories for the first three or four weeks of school seems the best way to help students want to write, to loosen up as writers, and to believe they are authors.

Teacher-made journals are handed out the first day of school. Students are told: "Like many other people, such as Benjamin Franklin, Thomas Jefferson, and Leigh Books (of recent *Dear Mr. Henshaw* [Cleary 1983] fame), we are going to keep journals. We will write everyday about anything we want. This is our own private writing, only for us to read or to choose who may read it. We can write about what we do, what we think, how we feel, about our wishes and our moods. We will get the most enjoyment from rereading our journals in years to come if our entries are more than just a record of our activities." I then give some concrete examples from journals of famous people, former students, or my own.

Personal Journals can be kept in different ways. The first two

Figure FA3.1   Journal Entry.

years I used them, students were told that when they finished a journal they should give it to me and I would glance through it and give it right back. It was decided that entries that students did not want anyone to read should be prefaced by the letters VP, for "very private."

When students start keeping journals, their entries are full of surprises. One of my favorites is shown in Figure FA3.1.

Personal Journals often become Dialogue Journals. Lucy, for example, started each entry with "Dear Diary," but then began with a directive—"Mrs. Wood"—to which I was to respond. Susie, another fourth grader, usually ended her entries by asking me to comment on something. She wrote a question followed by a line and the words, "Mrs. Wood, write here." Mudhi used a similar technique, as shown in Figure FA3.2.

Students' sense of ownership regarding Personal Journals is a key to their effectiveness. When fourth graders were asked why they liked keeping journals, their responses included:

"I like journals because you're your own boss and can tell yourself what to write, how long to write, and stuff like that."

"Every day I look back and see what I wrote before."

"I like journals because I can write my thoughts, dreams or news in them, and read my last entries and keep track of activities. I sometimes write stories, poems, and book reviews to reread."

"When you're lonely it's like having company."

"Journals help me to express my private parts of my life."

"It will listen."

A Message Board provides countless opportunities for informal writing among students and between teacher and students. Notes to the teacher are full of surprises. They are pleasant, funny, sad, touching, informative and helpful (see Figure FA3.3). I soon found out that the more notes I wrote, the more responses I got.

Writing is more than a means of self-expression and a way to communicate with others. It helps learners seek and build knowledge. Writing is a medium through which content learning occurs and thinking develops. It includes planning investigations and keeping records of observations; making predictions and venturing hypotheses; analyzing information; making inferences, interpreting data, and drawing conclusions; identifying key ideas; explaining a topic; taking meaningful notes; and writing research reports.

11/7

Do you like to go to school? Well in the night I can't wait to go to school. But in the morning I don't feel like going to school. Now you tell me.

It is the same with me. I don't like to get up so early in the morning, when it's still dark.

Mrs. W.

Figure FA3.2   Dialogue Journal Entry.

Mrs. Wood,

Stephanie wrote a cuss word on my writing book she will probably erase it but I think you should talk to her.

Sincerely,
Ben

Mrs. Wood,   4/1ª/25

Something is wrong with the pencil sharpener. I found that out at, 2:43 during Archeology.

Anne

Mrs. Wood
do you want a small frog about this big?

Saul

Figure FA3.3   Notes (Message Board).

Invitations to Use Reading and Writing to Learn

I like to begin the school year by getting children involved in original research. Rather than confront reading and writing head on, students begin these units by using other strategies they have for learning. I want students to know that reading and writing are but two ways of knowing. Although the unit often begins from some base other than reading or writing, it rapidly incorporates these.

Class field trips can become springboards for original research. Early one fall we went to Fish Creek, a forest in the uplands of South Central Indiana. Students hiked in small groups, each with an adult leader, armed with field guides, binoculars, clue charts and pencils, digging tools, collecting jars, nets, and buckets. They observed, took notes, collected specimens when possible, and talked about Fish Creek as a place for wildlife.

Back in the classroom, students were asked to write about Fish Creek as a habitat for birds, mammals, reptiles and amphibians, wildflowers and fungi, according to what each group had chosen to observe. Children used the Generating Written Discourse strategy to explore main ideas and to find supporting little ideas; they wrote discovery drafts; shared them with classmates and teacher; revised them; took them through editing; and produced a polished draft. There are no books or articles about Fish Creek from which students could get their ideas; they had to draw conclusions about the basic needs of the organisms in question based on their own observations and their reading.

The same fall we began a Living Indiana History Unit. Early in November, my fourth graders wrote to their grandparents, great-grandparents, and older relatives asking how they celebrated Thanksgiving when they were little. As had been the case when we used this activity in previous years, students were amazed by their grandparents' obvious pleasure upon receiving a letter and by the amount of information they wrote back. As a class we decided to put together what we learned from our research in a booklet entitled *History We Learned from Our Elders.* Students took pages from their relatives' letters, wrote brief explanations of their source, and illustrated them (see Figure FA3.4). The booklet was divided in three sections: "Thanksgiving Feasts," "Food Preparation in the Early 1900s," and "Transportation at the Turn of the Century."

"I have been thinking about what Thanksgiving was like when I was a girl your age.
If my memory serves me right at our house it was what was known as 'Hog Killing Day'.
Usually the weather was cool or cold enough to keep the meat from spoiling."

Told by my Great Aunt Myrtle

Emily Connell

Figure FA3.4   Page from Booklet *History We Learned from Our Elders*.

A third way I help students use reading and writing to learn is to introduce them to some form of Semantic Mapping. When a group of third graders read a book about Abraham Lincoln, there was much discussion about this man who played such an important role in our nation's history and yet had a rather simple life as a country boy and youth. I asked students to identify the experiences that they believed prepared Abraham Lincoln to become president. I explained that we would use Semantic Mapping to express what we had learned about this topic. I presented the activity by walking with the students through an example on the chalkboard. I mapped "Experiences That Helped Abraham Lincoln When He Became President." Students selected some of Lincoln's most worthwhile pre-presidency experiences, and we mapped them on the board.

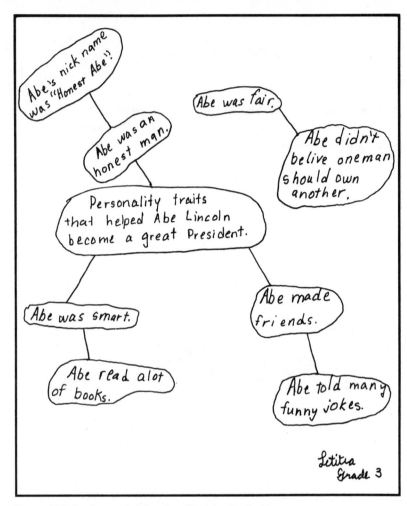

Figure FA3.5   Semantic Mapping (Letitia, Grade 3).

An invitation followed. As they read the next several chapters, students were invited to use their Literature Logs to map what they identified as "Personality Traits That Helped Abraham Lincoln Become a Great President." From here, students were invited to use mapping as a general tool for helping them better understand what they had read as well as to organize their thoughts before writing. Figure FA3.5 shows Letitia's map of what she believes are significant personality traits that Abraham Lincoln possessed.

Conclusion

In a classroom for authors and authorship a basic function of the teacher is to design a program of study that is challenging, useful, and attractive. These requirements are best met by an integrative curriculum that unifies all aspects of learning. This curriculum is organized around broad themes from the content areas.

Teachers need to find out what "turns their kids on" to learning; but they should also design units on challenging topics, or disciplines, of which their students might not even be aware. Teachers must be mind stretchers, forever holding in front of their students the carrot of human knowledge; they do this when they demonstrate their own curiosity and excitement about new topics, and when they are eager to study alongside their students. Social science and science books, magazine articles, commercially available programs, or even required textbooks can be the springboard for creating intellectually stimulating units.

Aware of studies that expand their students' horizons, and sensitive to their preferences, teachers can design a rich curriculum that is also challenging and useful. I view such challenging and useful learning as a combination of knowledge, or cultural literacy, and the natural experiences that provide students the opportunities to learn language, learn about language, and learn through language (Halliday 1985).

If learning is indeed to be a catalyst of personal growth, it must be more than acquiring basic skills and accumulating information; it must help students develop reasoning and valuing abilities. The acquisition of knowledge by itself is not sufficient for critical thinking and decision making, but neither do students gain expertise and judgment as generic abilities independent of content. An integrative curriculum surrounds the members of our learning community with occasions to read, talk, listen, question, and write to get something done, to accomplish our objectives; in so doing, we gain the wisdom and judgment needed to decide how to act. In a classroom for authors and authorship, students soak up the collaborative skills successful authors use. As children learn to see reading and writing as tools for learning, both you and they grow as human beings.

CHAPTER 4

Keeping the Cycle Going

Introduction

Curriculum is communication. How something is taught all too often determines what is learned. If we want children to see the use of reading and writing as well as art, music, drama, mathematics, science, and social studies as forms of literacy, then how we teach makes a difference.

As a curricular frame, the authoring cycle constitutes an attempt to orchestrate the how and what of teaching. By organizing curriculum around a learning cycle, participants experience, see demonstrated, and come to value how they might use literacy strategically to learn. From this perspective, authoring is a metaphor for learning, while learning is what literacy is all about. Orchestrating the how and what of our teaching helps us clarify for ourselves what we are about, helps children develop more functional notions of what it means to be literate, and, in the same fashion, communicates to others what instruction in the language arts is and is not.

To these ends we want to describe what the authoring cycle looks like as it is used as a frame for organizing instruction for ourselves as well as for parents and children. In this chapter, the reader will be walked through units in both social studies and science conceptually organized around the authoring cycle. Readers will see how the authoring cycle can be used to highlight alternate forms of literacy, as well as how Parents' Day and Young Authors Conferences are variations, yet extensions, of the cycle.

This chapter, then, demonstrates several applications of the authoring cycle. By using the authoring cycle as an organizational frame for social studies, science, math, and so on, reading and writing become vehicles for learning rather than objects of study in their own right. Although the slogan *Every teacher a reading and writing specialist* may be overly optimistic, it is not too much to expect teachers of all ilk, including content area specialists, not to violate what we know about the processes of reading and writing when teaching in the content areas. Multimedia Blitz and Science and Social Studies Clubs, described in the ensuing sections of this chapter, are but two ways to begin.

Language is one way of knowing. To be truly literate, one needs to know more than just how to use reading and writing to learn. Music, art, mathematics, and the like are other forms of knowing. Helping students understand the multimodal nature of literacy and how the authoring cycle capitalizes on as well as relates to other ways of knowing is what we describe in this chapter in the language activities entitled *Environmental Print Walks, Books, and Recipes,* and *Teachers and Students as Resident Artists.*

Literacy is everybody's business. If we do not help others understand recent insights into literacy and learning for the purpose of establishing new goals for the language arts, we can hardly be surprised when the criteria they use to judge the effectiveness of our language arts curriculum are based on outdated and dysfunctional notions. It is in the profession's interest to be as concerned about the community's growth in literacy as it is about the children's growth. Without community growth, professional growth is often stifled.

The business of education is learning, and learning, like literacy, is everyone's business. Rather than packaging our curricula and shutting our classroom doors, we must learn to open our doors and think communication.

To keep the cycle going, in this sense, means moving outside the four walls of the classroom. It means talking with administrators, parents, and the community. Two vehicles we use for these purposes will be explained—Parents' Day and Young Authors Conference. It also means using the authoring cycle ourselves as an organizational frame to grow. The section entitled "Units of Study: The Teacher as Learner" demonstrates how one teacher grew in her understanding of curriculum as a function of her involvement and use of the authoring cycle in her classroom.

As the authoring cycle is extended, the relationship between reading, writing, and reasoning is demonstrated, experienced, and finally understood for what it is—a learning cycle. By orchestrating the how and what of our teaching, curriculum and its relationship to reading, writing, and learning is clarified. In the same way that the authoring cycle has been used to communicate this message to students, so, too, it communicates to us and others what instruction in the language arts is and potentially can be.

None of the activities we describe is sacrosanct. Each has a potential for good and a potential for misuse. Rather than being seen as a formula for how to set up a meaning-centered reading and writing program, each is best seen as a single version of a potentially limitless number of versions of the authoring cycle, encouraging you and the children you teach to discover and explore.

Multimedia Blitz

Sue Robinson begins her multi-age summer program by announcing that in science the class will be studying different units, the first of which is nature. Students are told that they can select any topic within this unit that interests them, that the topic they select is important because they will become the resident "expert" in this area, and that the result of their study will be a published research report made available to the other students in the room and displayed at the School Learning Fair.

She begins by using a strategy that she calls Multimedia Blitz. Essentially, Multimedia Blitz is a set of learning centers that she has set up around the room. At each center are books, filmstrips, posters, pamphlets, buttons, artifacts, and other materials on selected topics—lizards, trees, animals, and so on. Students are told that they will become experts in an area of their choice and are invited to explore the various centers in the next two days. Students are encouraged to think about several topics, discuss them with friends, and finally choose one. Sue also encourages them to consider topics not presented in class by talking with parents, naturalists, and others who might have good ideas.

To help students get started researching their topics, Sue uses several techniques. She asks them to write down everything they currently know about the topic they've chosen on 3" × 5" cards and then helps them locate information in their initial visits to the library. Library research continues during Work Time on subsequent days, with students working on their reports, getting library passes, and spending the morning in the library rather than in the classroom. Sue checks to see how students are doing, pulls groups together when information on a topic is difficult to find, and explores where, besides books, the children might go to get information. Children are encouraged to call naturalists, interview college professors, visit "known" good farmers, talk to veterinarians, and seek out tree specialists in their neighborhood and community, all the time recording new pieces of information on $3" \times 5"$ cards or slips of paper. Students are also reminded that they might like to clip and save any pictures they run across in magazines, or make copies of charts or graphs that they think are really helpful. They may later decide to add these to their reports.

Status reports are given on a daily basis at Author Sharing Time. After the project has been under way for a week or more, Sue calls the group together to get them thinking about how they might organize the information they have gathered. Students are asked to consider the range of subtopics within their projects, to produce tentative arrangements of their ideas using their cards, and to "talk their way through" this organization with an interested neighbor before beginning to write (see Generating Written Discourse in Section Two). Once children have a complete draft of the various subsections of the first major section of their report, Sue suggests that they take it to Authors' Circle, get feedback, and revise this section before going on.

By repeating this cycle, the result is a complete report or, if not finished, as completed as the child is willing or able to go at that point in time. More often than not, in the process of drafting one major section or another, students find out that they really do not have as much information in an area as they thought and so are thrown back into doing basic library or field research. Rather than spread their energies too thin, children are encouraged to get everything they can as quickly as possible and get on with their drafting. Late-breaking news can be added later. Students are informed that their problem is not uncommon to other researchers. If researchers waited until they had a topic completely researched, no research reports would ever be written. To a large extent this is true because the research process, as a particular form of the learning process from which it springs, guarantees that the researcher is constantly learning.

By the end of the fifth week of the unit of study, the complete report is reread, revised, and submitted to Editors' Table for proofing and final typing. Galley proofs are given to the author to lay out in a report format of his or her choosing. Pictures, charts, graphs, and other illustrations are added. An attractive cover is made. Publishing is both a celebration and, if the student desires, a release from the topic. While serving as a stopping point, publishing is an important way to document what has been accomplished, as well as to reflect on where one has come from. Final products are shared in the class at Authors' Chair and with the community at the School Learning Fair, and portions are published in the class newspaper.

This walk through the cycle misses many things. Not discussed are the moments when children consult the "class expert" on trees, or salamanders, or lizards long after the unit is over. Not discussed is the arrival of children at school with stacks of books from home or other libraries because they might be helpful to a classmate. Not discussed are the pictures: the picture of David surrounded by at least ten open documents, working on his report on PCBs (a radioactive substance dumped randomly throughout the state of Indiana); the picture of Sarah bringing in a limb of a pin oak tree with a colony of web worms living on it; or the picture of Jason's indignation when he found out that the Department of Natural Resources in Indiana did not have guidelines that companies might use in an effort to control acid rain. Through these responses, Sue begins to see the real success of the authoring cycle.

Of course, children start the authoring cycle at different places. Although some reports produced in Sue's room were so insightful it would have been hard for any adult not to be impressed, not all reports were equally expert. However, with knowledge of the individual authors, even these reports were often impressive accomplishments. One advantage of the authoring cycle when used in the content areas is that it allows children to get in at their own level and go as far as they are willing and able to go. Although the authoring cycle is clearly a curriculum in which the gifted and talented can grow, it is also a supportive curriculum in which the least proficient reader and writer can achieve. Danny was one such student in Sue Robinson's multi-age summer program. His response to the science project provides a nice illustration of the success of the authoring cycle as a learning cycle as well as why all children must be given the same invitations to think as those given to their more academically talented peers. If teachers provide certain children with a disabled curriculum, these children's "disability" may be more a reflection of the curriculum provided than a true assessment of abilities.

Danny's cumulative record showed him to be reading two years below grade level and three years below in usage and mechanics of English. In this unit Danny chose to study lizards, one of the Multimedia Blitz center topics that Sue had selected and set up in her room. For the most part Danny did not do much library or field research; rather, he obtained most of his information from the books and science magazines in Sue's room by looking at the pictures and reading small sections or asking others to read to him. For the first section of his report he had, at the time he started drafting, five 3" × 5" cards, having discarded all the cards on which he had recorded things he personally knew about different types of lizards before the start of his research. The cards he was left with read:

(1) A BASCLISK CAN RUN ON TWO FEET;
(2) THE HORNED LIZARD CAN SQRNT BLOOD FROM HIS EYE LIDS;
(3) CHAMELEONS CAN CHAGES CULRS;
(4) THE FLYING LIZARDS LIVES IN SOUTH ASIA;
(5) THE KOMODO DRAGON CAN GET 10 FEET LONG THREE HUNDRED POUNDS.

These Danny organized around a card he entitled "Lizards," which he elected to use later as the title of this section of his report. After talking his report through with a neighbor, he used the remaining cards as the basis of his first draft for this section of his report. His first draft was entitled "Lizards" and read:

THE BASCLISH CAN RUN ON TWO FEET LIKE A HUMANBEING. THE HORNED LIZARD CAN SQRUNT BLOOK FROM HIS EYE LIDS TO SKCRAWAY HIS ENMES THE FLYING LIZARDS CAN RELLY FLY IT LIVES IN SOUTH ASIA. THE CHANELEONS CAN CHAGES CULRS IT ALSO CAN MOVE THAR EYE IN DEFERENT PLCES AT ONE TIME THE KOMODO DRAGON ANT RELLY A DRAGON I DONT THINK IT IS JUST A LIZARD BUT IT CAN GROW 10 FEET LONG AND CAN WHIE THREE HUNDRED POUNDS. DANNY.

With this draft in hand, Danny went to Authors' Circle, received feedback, made minimal revisions, sent this and other sections of his report to Editors' Table, and finally ended up with a publication that he illustrated using pictures he had gathered from various sources. The significant thing about this experience for Danny was the pride he felt in his achievement and the ownership of his text he exhibited. On Parents' Day, Danny's mother was the first mother in the room; her first stop was Danny's science report. She was rightfully impressed. This was the first text that she had seen or known Danny to have ever written. It was the first time she had ever seen Danny seek out materials to read at home. Danny, too, said it was his first "real report."

Still, we might note that Danny does not take the initiative very often in his report. He is willing to drop his ideas for those he finds in books. For the most part, there is a very close correspondence between the cards he made from his readings and the sentences he has in his final report. Yet he does make analogies ("like a human being"), infers cause and effect ("to scare away his enemies"), and makes evaluative statements ("ain't really a dragon I don't think"). There is much we could have done with Danny to get him to improve this piece further; yet, given where Danny started from (including the history of literacy he brought to this setting), he has come a long way via this single trip through the authoring cycle.

There is a perfect ending to this story. Guess what Danny wants to be when he grows up? A naturalist. Guess who was the first person to enroll the following year in Sue Robinson's summer reading and writing program for young authors? Danny. When we observe students responding by independently choosing to immerse themselves in the process of authoring and by taking pride and ownership of their learning, our evaluation is that the curriculum is providing the meaningful experiences and demonstrations of authoring that have led them to value it in such a personal way.

Sue's unit on nature took six weeks. During the regular school year, Sue and the other teachers we worked with use a similar format by dividing the year into six- and nine-week units. During each of these periods, students explore various aspects of science.

In a unit, for example, that the students in Myriam Revel-Wood's fourth-grade classroom did on "the experimental method," the publication was a tagboard chart complete with graphs and illustrations. This chart summarized what the student saw as his or her major question, hypotheses or predictions, procedures, observations, results, and conclusions. Students could choose any topic they wished to explore. Some ran training programs for their pets with or without the presence of food, others did public surveys to confirm or disconfirm claims made by advertisers, and still others tested which of several recommendations in their science book was best for displaying the workings of a volcano. Children displayed the results of their unit of study at the School Learning Fair and were available to answer visitors' questions.

Science and Social Studies Clubs

Although Myriam handles science somewhat differently than Sue, the open and invitational nature of her curriculum is similar. Myriam understands that children do not need to engage in the same activity to have an equivalent experience. Rather than be concerned with the surface structure of lessons—whether the students are studying birds, animals, magnets, and so on—she is worried about the deep structure—whether the students are experiencing and coming to value the process of learning using the perspective of whatever discipline they are studying.

At the beginning of the year, she talked with the children about all the various units of study that—given the textbooks adopted by the school system—fourth graders are expected to deal with in science. To this end, students are given some time to explore the various areas fourth-grade science is supposed to cover and with this information form themselves into Science Clubs. The only requirement that Myriam sets is that each club have at least two members. Because Myriam believes both language and learning are social events, this requirement is understandable. The actual clubs formed are of the children's choosing, but have included The Birds Club, The Fungi Club, The Using Metric Club, The Batteries Club, The Toads, Frogs, and Salamanders Club, The Useful Insects Club, and so on. Club members meet regularly, and work with Myriam in formulating questions, selecting topics of study, conducting investigations, and reporting back to the class on new projects and findings.

At the beginning of the year, Myriam meets with each club to explore student interests and suggest possible directions. She helps students set goals, lay out plans, and conduct programs of study. Often she brings in articles that she knows will be of particular interest to club members. Together she and students plan how long projects will take and what must be accomplished on a week by week basis. Although some clubs run the entire year, others last only a semester.

Students in Myriam's room have begun a wildlife area in between the various buildings making up the complex of their elementary school. Over the years, this area has been planted with bushes and shrubs that attract various birds and wild animals. Students in clubs concerned with nature (e.g., The Birds Club) write reports on topics of interest to them. These reports include such things as *The Golden Finch, How Birds Winter,* or *The Misunderstood English Sparrow.* Children also use the wildlife area to make observations in their Science Logs and take ownership of the wildlife area by adding a plant that will attract new wildlife or by adopting a plant or animal that they see as endangered.

Myriam Revel-Wood also uses the authoring cycle as a conceptual frame for organizing her social studies program. Students in fourth grade in Indiana must study Indiana history. Within this broad frame, students are invited to explore any topic of interest by forming themselves into Social Studies Clubs. Myriam uses much the same approach as Sue does in science, permitting each child to begin in terms of personal interest and life experience and extending this base via topic exploration, discussion, and interviews. Students then move from these experiences to field and library research. To support students drafting their reports she introduces Generating Written Discourse, and from the first draft children move to Authors' Circle, Editors' Table, and finally to publication and the celebration of authorship. To help children organize their time over the eight-week period of her typical social studies unit, she runs copies of a checklist for each child to keep in the front of his or her social studies folder. The checklist reads:

Week of _____ Select topic
Interview parents
Look for sources of information
Read and take notes
Keep a bibliography

Week of _____ Continue reading
Interview community members
Look for other sources of information
Continue taking notes

Week of _____ Continue reading and taking notes
Look through your cards
Identify central ideas
Share your central ideas with at least
   two other classmates
Get feedback on your ideas
Revise central ideas if needed

Week of _____ Continue reading & taking notes
Look through your cards to find
   information that goes with your
   central ideas
Share the notes that go with a central
   idea with a classmate
Get feedback
Begin drafting this section of your
   report

Etc. . . . . .

Myriam's role during this unit of study is one of a resource person, often helping children to find materials to read, suggesting resource people to contact or other places they might find useful information on their topic, and occasionally (given her insights into the needs of her students) offering strategy lessons that highlight key aspects of language arts or science. Rather than imparting information, she is a ready collaborator on the topic under study. Children retain ownership of their topic and become real experts, by anyone's definition of the term. She rightfully defers to them when issues are raised relative to their areas of expertise. Social studies reports in Myriam Revel-Wood's room have included: *The History of the Indianapolis 500, Covered Bridges in Indiana,* and *A Historical Guide to the State Parks of Southern Indiana.*

A visitor in Myriam Revel-Wood's room may well have difficulty knowing what phase of the authoring cycle children are in or when the reading and writing period has occurred. What they see is children reading and writing as they actively explore a topic. The authoring cycle is not perceived as something endemic to language arts, but as a general learning cycle. Children begin with what they know (life experiences), talk, sketch, read, write, listen, rethink, revise, edit, synthesize, and present. Although this is the authoring process, it is also the learning cycle. During the course of a unit of study, this cycle is engaged in over and over again. Sometimes the publication or synthesis is oral; at other times, written or visual. Although the result typically is a formal, edited, written document, this document does not represent a single step-by-step trip through the cycle, but rather multiple trips. Components of the authoring cycle (Life Experiences, Uninterrupted Reading and Writing, Author's Folder, Authors' Circle, Self-Editing, Editors' Table, Publication/Celebrating Authorship, Invitations/Strategy Lessons) blend and become blurred as the strategies these points in the cycle represent become a natural part of the learning process. When the authoring cycle is seen as a learning cycle, and the learning cycle is used as a framework for guiding and self-monitoring action, then teachers and pupils have moved from authoring to curriculum.

Environmental Print
Walks, Books, and Recipes

In our studies of what preschool children know about literacy before coming to school (Harste, Woodward & Burke 1981, 1983,

1984), we showed children various pieces of environmental print and asked them what it said (a cup from McDonald's with the word "McDonald's" on it, a photograph of a stop sign, an empty carton of Crest toothpaste, etc.) One of the things we found was that children as young as three years of age expected print to be meaningful. They never said "Crest," "toothpaste," or "brush teeth" when shown the cup from McDonald's, or said "McDonald's," "Ronald McDonald," or "eat it" when shown the Crest toothpaste carton. When shown the red, white, and blue logo of U.S. mail they responded "mail," "U.S. Army," and "American picture sign." All the responses children made, in other words, fell within a "semantic ballpark" of meaningfulness. If children couldn't think of a context with which they were familiar and in which what we had shown them made sense, they either did not respond or responded "I don't know." However, once they had identified a context in which what we had shown them made sense, they began to make predictions that made sense. Over time, their responses became more finely orchestrated so that what they said matched the amount of print shown as well as the print itself. All of the children could read "stop" and "McDonald's." No child was unable to read, although when print was abstracted away from its natural environment ("McDonald's" typed on a $3'' \times 5''$ card) this was less true. What children could read depended on the quality of print environment we provided as well as the quality of experiences they had had with the print setting itself. Some preschoolers read "Please put litter in its place" on the McDonald's cup as well as the word "McDonald's." One five-year-old read "with fluoride" on the Crest carton in addition to "Crest."

In thinking about how to use these findings in a beginning program of literacy, we struck upon the idea of an environmental print unit. Vera Milz, a first/second-grade teacher from Bloomfield Hills, Michigan, had successfully used environmental print to initiate her reading program, and so we decided to adopt her procedures. At the time we were working in a first-grade classroom.

We began the first day of class by discussing with the children what they wanted to learn to do in first grade. Many children responded "Learn to read." We told the children that they were already readers and that we had found that many three-year-olds could already read. To prove this point we took an Environmental Print Walk. As we paraded in twos through the school building and around the school grounds, we asked children to find something they could read. When we returned to the classroom, children were given a blank sheet of paper and asked to draw a picture of what they could read and—"doing the best you can"—write what it said. Children who said they could not write were told to "pretend you can write" using whatever markings they wished so long as the markings would help them remember what they had written. The children's environmental print pictures were collected, put in a Group Composed Book, and shared with the class on the next day with each child reading the page he or she had contributed.

During Author Sharing Time, children were invited to go home and look through their cupboards to find things that they could read. They were asked to bring in as many labels as they could read off the items.

At school the next day, the children each received a blank book (see Bookmaking) and were invited to trim their labels, glue one per page, and write—again "doing the best you can"—whatever they wished under each. Because many labels on cans and boxes, for example, have two usable sides, children who did not bring in labels were invited to look through the extras that other children had brought in to find some they could use.

At Author Sharing Time, each child shared one page of the book and read what he or she had written. Children who did what some call "scribble writing" were treated just the same as children who wrote more conventionally. Children were asked to invite other children to Authors' Chair to hear their entire book if they so desired. Figure 4.1 shows several pages of Alison's environmental print book. Environmental print books were not sent home, but were used to kick off sharing at Parents' Day.

Logos from labels not used were put on 3″ × 5″ cards for use by children as a shopping list before they went to the classroom

Figure 4.1   Pages from Environmental Print Book (Alison, Grade 1).

grocery store. The classroom grocery store consisted of empty food cans and boxes brought in by children and displayed on shelves in one corner of the room. At the checkout counter, the checker determined whether the shopper had purchased all the items on the list by matching the 3″ × 5″ cards with products in the toy shopping cart. Other logos were kept and used for environmental print jingles and environmental print recipes.

Because children knew several environmental print jingles that went with their labels (Micky D's is some kind of place/They serve you rattlesnakes/French fries between your toes/And don't forget those good old shakes/Made from polluted lakes/Micky D's is some kind of place"), they were invited to collect these and/or write a commercial for a product of their choice. A compilation of commercials and environmental print jingles were collected and became a second Group Composed Book.

Some children collected jump rope jingles instead of environmental print jingles. This error quite naturally led to the creation of a jump rope book in which children dictated and illustrated the jump rope jingles that they knew or overheard on the playground. Since many of these were extremely predictable ("Teddy bear, Teddy bear, turn around/Teddy bear, Teddy bear, touch the ground") it rapidly became a favorite book in the class and led to the creation of several books in which children recorded their favorite songs in invented spellings and illustrated them (e.g., Old McDonald Had a Farm, Little Red Caboose, Itsy Bitsy Spider).

At the same time that the unit of study on environmental print was taking place in the first-grade classroom, the senior author and his wife were working one morning each week with three-year-olds in the area of cooking. What they learned from that involvement in cooking with three-year-olds was placed in practice in the first grade.

One of the things they learned, for example, was that when family-sized recipes were used, children often participated only in a portion of rather than the entire cooking experience. To give everyone a chance to participate, individual students only participated in one small part of the cooking experience, and no student followed the recipe from start to finish. As a result of prolonged experiences of this sort, they learned that fourth graders often had no better idea about cooking than did preschool children.

This finding led us to experiment with creating individual-sized recipes, and while some were simple, such as play dough, and bugs on a log with celery, peanut butter, and raisins, others were more involved, like apple pie for two. In this way each child or a pair of children could involve themselves in the entire process of getting ingredients, making the entire recipe, and cleaning up their mess.

Through experimentation, we found that it was preferable to arrange the cooking area in three "stops," or areas. At the first stop in the center, we had a tagboard listing each utensil that was needed, using the utensil's name and a drawing. Beneath this tagboard was a table with many more utensils than were needed. The first task of the cook was to take all the utensils that were not needed and put them out of the way on the floor under the table or on a shelf.

At the second stop in the cooking center, we had a tagboard listing each needed ingredient. Each ingredient was drawn and the actual logo from the product glued in place. Beneath this tagboard

Figure 4.2 Environmental Print Recipe.

was a table with many more ingredients on it than needed. Again, the task of the cook was to eliminate all ingredients that were not needed.

At the third stop in the cooking center, we had a tagboard with the recipe written out as it might be found in a cookbook devoid of pictures. By looking across the "Utensils," "Ingredients," and "Recipe" tagboards, children were required to read the recipe as they completed each step. For example, "1 teaspoon alum" necessitated the cook to read and locate the "1 teaspoon" from the utensils tagboard and the "alum" from the ingredients tagboard to perform the necessary action. The write-up of each recipe ended with instructions to enjoy what they had fixed, to clean up the center, and to remember that before they left, the center was to look as they had found it, complete with all the utensils and ingredients back on their respective tables. In this way, once the cooking center was set up, it ran relatively independently throughout the year. Figure 4.2 contains an example of an environmental print recipe and its various components.

Figure 4.2   *Continued*

Because the senior author and his wife also had learned that in classrooms that claimed to do a lot of cooking, invitations were offered only three or four times a semester, we set up our center so that children cooked each week. The cooking center led to several discussions and the class composition of *Our Favorite Recipes*. After an invitation to parents, some children brought in their favorite recipe in individual-sized portions, and thus this center, too, became the impetus for creating and re-creating the authoring cycle in the classroom.

Students need to read from a variety of materials. Literature is only one source of reading materials. Environmental print materials involve students in reading the print that constantly surrounds them as they go about their daily lives. Recently several relevant publications have come on the market, such as *I Read Signs* (Hoban 1983), *I Walk and Read* (Hoban 1984), *Signs* (Goor 1983), and *The Tale of Thomas Mead* (Hutchins 1980). Teachers interested in using environmental print might explore these resources.

Teachers and Students as Resident Artists

Randy Beard, a lead singer and guitarist for a local band, was an undergraduate student in our methods of teaching reading and writing course at Indiana University. When we found out that he could compose music as well as sing, his special talents offered new possibilities for supporting children in reading and writing.

For his undergraduate project, Randy went to several elementary schools in the area. After sharing his music he invited the students to write their own. In each instance Randy emphasized that it was not necessary that the lines in their songs rhymed. Once children individually or in pairs had composed a piece, Randy would sing it in several beats (rock and roll, blues, country-western) and permit the authors to elect which one they preferred. After the songs were put on overhead acetate sheets or chart paper so that the whole class could see, they were shared and sung by the class.

Randy made several points in the write-up of his project. First, children who were thought of as nonreaders by their teachers could read and follow along once they had heard a particular song. Second, children were highly motivated to write once they saw some of their friends' work being written and sung. Third, slow readers read more fluently during the choral reading of songs than they did when reading independently.

As a result of Randy's success (several newspapers in the area ran stories of his visits to classrooms), we invited Randy to School 39 at Indianapolis. Randy began by singing a song he had written and sharing with his audience how it had evolved and the revisions that had been made to get the piece to its current form. He invited children to work in groups to write a song that he would put to music.

Because the children in Sue Robinson's classrooms had each authored several books and, in fact, thought of themselves as authors, our impression was that they would rapidly transfer this knowledge to songwriting. You can imagine how surprised we were when even the best writers in class had difficulty. We reminded them that their pieces need not rhyme, though this did not seem to help. Seeing failure on the horizon, we offered to take dictation. "What are you thinking?" we asked. "Shoot," someone said. We wrote it down. "Sick of school," someone else said. We wrote it down. After working in this fashion, we asked students if they wanted to move around any of the lines they had composed. Surprisingly they did, after which time we gave it to Randy to put it to music. He asked the principal author, "What kind of music did you have in mind?" The child responded, "Sad. Sort of tired." Randy tried one version and then elected a blues rhythm as an alternative. The author and his classmates were delighted with the result. "Bad to the Bone" became an instant hit. (Readers may wish to view videotape 7, "Celebrating Authors & Authorship," in the videotape series *The Authoring Cycle: Read Better, Write Better, Reason Better* [Harste & Jurewicz 1985], to get a feel for the success of this moment.)

Shortly after this it was lunchtime. When we came back from lunch, seven different children who just moments before had no ideas now composed songs. During the singing of these, one child suggested, "We ought to make a songbook." This comment was well received by the group as well as by the music teacher at the school. In subsequent days, songs were drafted and taken through Authors' Circle, self-editing, outside editing, and finally publication. By the end of the year, the sixth graders in School 39 had released two *Innercity Songbooks* replete with musical notations for the songs they had written. These notations were transcribed by the school music teacher.

What we find particularly fascinating about this experience is that here were children who had been writing all year. Yet, when we asked them to think of themselves as songwriters rather than as authors of books, they couldn't. Once one child and Randy Beard demonstrated what was possible so as to give them a notion of the meaning potential that was available to them through this medium, they quickly explored the challenge.

An excellent society has excellent songs as well as books. To be truly literate is to use sign systems to mean as well as to explore and expand the world. A good language arts program opens communication potential rather than shuts it down. In one preschool classroom in our city, children are provided staff paper and encouraged to compose songs at the piano that might be shared with the class, much as they are invited to write at the writing table (see Clyde 1986; Rowe 1986). They "invent" the musical notations just as they invent spelling. If they decide to publish their songs, they play it for the teacher who puts it in conventional musical notations. Other teachers who have a flair for art begin there. Many good books have begun with a picture, and many famous works of art are the result of several trips through an authoring cycle. When authorship in alternate communication systems is offered as an invitation, teachers and children can use, rather than ignore, their talents to support literacy instruction and learning.

Parents' Day

We have no evidence that the learning process is different for adults than it is for children. To this end, we recommend that teachers introduce the authoring cycle to parents in the same way it was introduced to the children—by experiencing it. Parents' Day should take place after the children have had considerable experience with the authoring process. Some teachers plan Parents' Day to coincide with the presentation of a class publication. Parents or guardians are not necessarily the only visitors who could be included on this day. The principal, superintendent, school board members, curriculum coordinator, remedial reading teacher, education reporter for the local newspaper, and language arts and reading professors from the local college are others who might wish to participate in this celebration of authorship.

Parents' Day is a special occasion. It is a half-day program (a full morning, afternoon, or evening)—two or three hours that are planned by the children to introduce their parents and other visitors to their learning environment. Parents' Day is also an opportunity for the teacher to talk with parents and visitors about the theoretical basis for the program, to walk them through the authoring cycle, and to demonstrate for them the instructional activities the teacher feels are related to quality literacy learning. Providing parents and visitors with this background will prove essential in gathering the support needed for the program.

To plan Parents' Day, Mary Lynn Woods asked children in her room to think about all the activities they had experienced and to select those that they thought their parents would enjoy. Students wrote invitations, divided responsibilities, and then walked their way through each lesson. In past years, students in her program have selected Readers' Theatre, Written Conversation, Journals, Think-Me-a-Poem, and Peanut Butter Fudge (see Schema Stories in Section Two) as favorite classroom activities.

As parents and visitors arrived, children invited them on a tour of the classroom and then sat down and had a Written Conversation about various things they had seen, or merely something they wished to discuss. Some children elected to do a shared writing in their journals with their visitors. Once most of the adults had arrived, the children took charge of the program by inviting everyone to participate in Readers' Theatre. To begin, they discussed the rules, assigned parts, and, with the parents actively participating, shared some of their favorite Readers' Theatre stories.

At the close of Readers' Theatre, one of the children invited the parents to participate in Think-Me-a-Poem, an activity designed to generate a group-written poem. In this case, *Our Children* was chosen as the topic of the poem. The group was told that the parents would work together—collaborate—to write a poem about children, and then, later, the children would collaborate to write a poem about parents.

All parents were given a piece of scratch paper and asked to jot down candid thoughts about the topic. Volunteers were then asked to share their thoughts with the group while another volunteer was asked to jot these thoughts down on the blackboard or an overhead projector transparency. After all thoughts were expressed, the group talked about the thoughts, arranged and rearranged the ideas, and changed and added new ideas as they collaboratively decided on the poem's message. After discussion of the content was finished, the group was asked if they wanted to make any further changes before the poem was submitted for publication. Parents then discussed conventional concerns such as capitalization and punctuation. A volunteer was asked to copy the poem from the board, to request help from a final outside editor who could go over the poem for any final changes, and then to submit it to Mary Lynn for publication. Children witnessed their parents traveling through the same authoring cycle that they had experienced themselves many times before. They saw firsthand how their parents generated the content of a text, edited it for the sake of content and convention, sought reader feedback, and finally submitted it for publication. The students were then invited to go through the same process, preparing a poem for their parents with the assistance of a volunteer aide or parent.

As the children did this, Mary Lynn invited the parents to come into another room where she talked to them about the theory behind a writing and reading instructional plan and described in further detail the instructional activities used with their children.

During this portion of Parents' Day, Mary Lynn began by telling parents about some things researchers have been learning about reading and writing and its relationship to learning. "One of the things we've been finding out," she explained, "is that we have been giving children very dysfunctional notions about reading and writing. Too many children think that reading is sounding out words, and that writing is something one does perfectly on the first go-round. What I want to say to you is that educators can design curriculum where students learn that reading and writing are process-oriented events, requiring the thoughtful nurturing of ideas. Reading is not reading until comprehension of the author's message is attained; writing is not writing until the author has reworked the ideas into a clear, meaningful message intended for interpretation by a reader. The type of curriculum in which your child has been participating in this course is one designed to provide meaningful learning experiences so that your child will begin to view literacy in a more functional way."

When talking about the authoring cycle, Mary Lynn used overhead transparencies of student work to illustrate her views as she informally discussed recent insights into reading and writing. The curriculum model of the authoring cycle was presented and discussed. In addition to talking about the cycle, she carefully described how the Parents' Day activities fit into the cycle.

From this base, she talked about the various components of the curriculum and made specific recommendations about supporting literacy learning in the home. She explained the need for parental involvement and support, asking for volunteers to sew book pages and collect cereal boxes for book covers, requesting information about their areas of expertise, and inviting them to visit the classroom often. After passing out a short article or two supporting the notion of quality literacy instruction, she fielded questions and then returned the parents to the classroom to participate in the making of Peanut Butter Fudge with their children. This activity, a group cooking experience, asks parents and children to use their background knowledge, reading experience, and decision-making ability to create a tasty recipe.

Once the peanut butter fudge was done, parents and children gathered, some sitting on the floor, some in chairs. The highlight of the day had arrived—the reading of the class publication! In each course, students publish a collection of stories, character sketches, interviews, or a newspaper. Now parents and children were invited to share in the celebration of authorship by participating in a shared reading of the class publication. Students were told they could read aloud from their own text, or they could ask another to read their text aloud to the group. Parents were also invited to volunteer to read texts aloud. Inevitably, after each reading, the listeners showed their pride with spontaneous applause. The final reading, which is a course tradition, was the group-written poems entitled *Our Children* and *Our Parents*.

Thus Parents' Day ended. Good-byes were said as parents and students left the room carrying with them the class publication, the parent/children poems, the written recipe for peanut butter fudge, the peanut butter fudge (of course), and, best of all, the joy of celebrating authorship.

Janice Harste was hired by the Monroe County Community School Corporation in Bloomington, Indiana, to work with "bright second-grade children" who were not doing well in the school's basal reading program. The children she worked with decided to call themselves The Write Group. She conceptualized reading and writing experiences using the authoring cycle as a curricular frame. Students read trade books that highlighted various components of good literature. The first Text Set she used in Literature Circle highlighted story characters. Students read, discussed, developed, and then described and drew their own story characters. The second Text Set she used highlighted story settings. Students read, discussed, and then developed a setting for the story characters they had developed. With these two pieces taken through the authoring cycle, students began to think about and draft an adventure for their characters in the setting they had described. Parents' Day focused on students presenting to parents their setting, characters, the process by which each piece had moved from rough draft to final form, and the tentative beginnings of their new adventure piece. After these introductions, parents were invited to work with their children in Authors' Circles. Results of parent-student work groups were shared as a culminating activity for Parents' Day.

We mention this option because we see it as a particularly nice way to give parents a sense of what the authoring cycle as a curricular frame is all about. Rather than talk about components of the curriculum, parents in Janice Harste's classroom walked away with a sense of the total curriculum as well as how they might more effectively support their own child's literacy learning at home.

Young Authors Conferences provide a more formal way for students, parents, and teachers to celebrate authorship. Typically, a noted children's author is invited to speak to children and parents. Children bring a book they have written to share. If the authoring cycle has been operating, children will have lots of books to choose from in making their selection to take to the conference. Parents are invited to attend a session on how they might continue to support their child's reading and writing activities at home.

Young Authors Conferences are an important extension of the authoring cycle. Gala events such as these demand press coverage and heighten everyone's awareness of literacy. In our community, the local council of the International Reading Association sponsors a read-a-thon in the local shopping mall, bookmaking sessions at the local library, and poster and young author book displays at the library and shopping mall. The council also contacts bookstore owners and encourages them to feature the books by the author who spoke at the Young Authors Conference in their displays. The messages communicated are that authors are special people, that the children are real authors, that schools and teachers are taking literacy seriously and doing positive things to support growth, that their child's school is a special place, that public education is good education, and that literacy is everyone's business.

Units of Study: The Teacher as Learner

As we worked with various teachers in implementing curriculum based on the authoring cycle, we realized that these teachers began taking a different perspective toward curriculum development and toward their role as teachers. They began to construct curriculum *with* children, rather than to impose a mandated curriculum onto children, and to recognize themselves as learners. The realization that the classroom is a community of learners who are all exploring and learning together and that the teacher is one of those learners has many ramifications for how teachers view their role in the classroom. Hierarchial distinctions begin to fall away, and students and teachers learn to work together and to value what each can offer to that learning environment.

An experience we had with Gloria Kauffman and her first-grade students helped us further explore the concept of teachers as learners. One of the authors, Kathy Short, spent a year in Gloria's classroom working collaboratively with her as a researcher teacher, while the other author, Jerry Harste, was a long-distance collaborator. Gloria worked with us in exploring over a period of time the changes that occurred within the classroom as she began building a curriculum based on the authoring cycle.

In previous years, Gloria had used a unit approach to social studies and science in which the class would focus on a particular topic over several weeks. These units involved children reading, writing, and doing a variety of creative activities related to that topic. Although these units had been successful, they had also been teacher-directed, as Gloria dictated what the activities would be and required everyone to participate in each activity. She wanted to change this approach to units but was not sure how to make them more open-ended.

Gloria wanted the units to be based on children's interests, but she struggled with how to develop units from their interests without feeling that she had lost control of the situation. One idea she began working on was having each child ask a question that he or she had always wanted to know about and then using that question to go off on individual or small group units. She had the children generate the questions, but then she felt uncomfortable at the thought of having all the children go in different directions and so moved no further with that idea.

Finally Gloria decided to return to the unit structure that she had used in previous years and chose a unit on the ocean that had always been one of her most successful units. She set up an attractive display of shells and sea specimens, as well as displays of books related to the ocean. She began reading the children information books on the ocean and showing them filmstrips about ocean life. Each child drew and colored an imaginary fish to make a large mural. Each child also made a watercolor wash on ocean life. She even had a father bring a scuba diving outfit into the classroom. The children simply did not respond. Very few went over to the display of shells, and although they did not openly rebel, their response was that this unit was "ho-hum." After trying for several weeks to get the unit going, Gloria gave up and got involved in fall holiday activities.

This was a frustrating experience for Gloria because this unit had always been successful with other groups of children. As we talked about this experience, Gloria realized that she had established a different kind of learning environment with these students than in previous years. These children had already been making many choices in the reading and writing curriculum and so had come to expect a voice in the learning environment. They therefore did not respond to a unit that was so teacher-directed and that left them few options. We decided to try a different approach to units after the holidays that would build more directly from children's interests and yet provide some structure.

Throughout the fall a small group of children had been reading and talking on their own about dinosaurs and had often requested more books on dinosaurs. Gloria decided to do something about their constant requests for information. She gathered books, filmstrips, records, and other pieces of information and put them out for anyone who was interested. After the materials had been out for several days, she called a meeting for anyone who was interested in doing a study on dinosaurs. About half of the class came to this meeting and talked about the kinds of topics they wanted to explore on dinosaurs. The group then brainstormed a list of possible projects they could use to explore and expand on what they were learning about dinosaurs.

During the next several weeks, members of this group pursued many of these projects. Several children worked together to create a mural, others built milk carton dinosaurs, several made dioramas, some wrote and illustrated flip books, wordless books, or fiction and nonfiction books about dinosaurs, one child wrote a song, and all the children read and listened to stories and songs about dinosaurs. These experiences cut across the entire day, with children choosing to read and write about dinosaurs during the morning Work Time as well as working on various projects in the afternoon when they focused on units of study.

Gloria was kept busy during these two weeks supplying whatever resources the children needed for their various projects. She was kept so busy fulfilling these requests that she did not have time to work with the rest of the children and so told them that they needed to decide what topics they wanted to explore. Instead of pursuing individual topics, they decided collectively that they wanted to explore puppets. Because Gloria was so involved with the dinosaur group, she left the puppet group to work on their own. She did get them some books on puppets and paper bags and scraps, but that was the only direct support she provided. For several days it looked as if this group was not going to go anywhere. Then one afternoon the group sat down and on their own brainstormed a list of ideas for puppets similar to the one that Gloria had brainstormed with the dinosaur group. With this organization, they were able to proceed with their unit. Their unit also cut across the entire day as they wrote puppet plays and read about making puppets during morning Work Time and worked on constructing puppets and practicing their puppet plays in the afternoon.

The children's involvement and excitement during these two units was in marked contrast to what had occurred in the ocean unit. We talked about this with Gloria and puzzled over what the differences between the two units had been for the children. We could see that the dinosaur and puppet units had built off of their interests and that they had more control of their learning than in the ocean unit, but we felt that there were still other factors that we were not fully understanding. Finally, several months after these units occurred, we sat down with the children to ask them how these units had been different for them.

We told the children that we had been talking about these two experiences and the different ways they had responded, but that we had never really figured out what made the two experiences so different for them. As we talked together, the children first discussed the content of the two experiences and why they thought that dinosaurs and puppets were more interesting and exciting than the ocean.

The discussion then moved to other reasons, and the children raised three major points. One was the element of choice. A number of children mentioned getting to choose and to make decisions about the content and about how they responded to the content in the second experience. Stephanie said, "We got together to decide what we were going to do with puppets." Richard commented, "Miss Kauffman told us some ideas for dinosaurs and then we chose." The second was the importance of being able to form groups to work together on projects of their own choice during the second experience. As Kristine said, "During the fish, we all worked at our desks, but during dinosaurs, we worked in groups." An example of Kristine's point was the difference in the construction of the mural in the two experiences. During the ocean unit, the children were each assigned to design and color an imaginary fish at their desks at the same time to put up on the mural. The dinosaur mural resulted from three or four children deciding to make a mural as part of their study of dinosaurs and going off to the back table to work on it together.

The third point the children raised was, as Pat said, "We got to do artist's work," or, as Jessica said, "We made things." As we explored this further with them, it became obvious that the ocean unit had primarily involved the children using reading and writing with a few art projects thrown in. During the dinosaur and puppet units, the children were active doers who constructed meaning in a variety of sign systems, including art, music, drama, and language.

We were extremely excited by this discussion and by the insights the children offered about their own learning processes and about curriculum. They had helped Gloria and us see three major features of curriculum through their reflections on their learning: the importance of choice and ownership, the social nature of learning, and the need to be active doers who construct meaning through multiple sign systems.

This experience helped Gloria see how she could collaborate and work with children in constructing curriculum instead of either imposing curriculum onto them or letting them just take over. The children had been involved through the choices and decisions they made and because the units built off of their interests and needs, as well as through their later reflections on this experience. Gloria was also involved through the way she structured the learning environment to make resources and ideas available for them so they could keep their units going without her taking control of the unit away from them.

Gloria later involved the children in units on the family, fairy tales, and zoo animals, during which everyone was involved in studying the same topic, but she used her experiences with the earlier units so that these were collaborative experiences. These three units did not appear out of nowhere as the ocean unit had but were carefully based on the children's interests and earlier classroom experiences. The children were involved as collaborators in planning the units and in making decisions about what specific topics within a unit they were going to explore, as well as which books they were going to read and what kinds of response activities they completed. They also reflected on what they were learning and how they were learning during these units. In between these three units, children explored individual topics so that both group units and individual units were part of the curriculum (see *Theme Cycles* in Section Two for a further discussion of working collaboratively with students in developing units of study).

One of the most important results of this experience was that both Gloria and the children recognized that Gloria was a learner along with them. She did not have all the answers but instead needed to observe, try out her ideas, and reflect on the experiences with others—the same learning process that she was involving the children in as they moved through the authoring cycle. She was learning from them, just as they were learning from her. The classroom was committed to a process of facilitating each other's growth as learners. This did not negate Gloria's responsibilities as a teacher or her greater experience and knowledge, but acknowledged that learning is a process that never stops and that she could learn from the children as well as help them learn.

When teachers recognize that they are learners, this realization has a dramatic impact on the classroom. Teachers become flexible in their ability to learn from children and to use these insights in constructing curriculum. There is a greater sense of teachers and students working together rather than against each other and a recognition that each person has something to offer, rather than that only the teacher can offer anything to students. When teachers recognize themselves as learners, they can continue to grow beyond their current selves and to develop new curricular ideas and concepts. They take ownership of their own learning and become their own change agents rather than stagnating and depending on "experts" to feed them new ideas. Because they are continually growing and changing, the classroom remains an exciting place for teachers and their students.

Conclusion

As educators, we must act come Monday morning. We cannot wait until all the facts are in. In many ways, we are like sailors at high sea. Rather than abandoning ship, what we need to do is examine all planks in the hull and replace them one at a time as we charge full steam ahead. This volume is our attempt to build a new ship. Although we don't know all there is to know, what we currently know can be used to improve instruction.

This volume gives teachers a framework—an authoring cycle—around which they can plan curricular experiences and gain a perspective on literacy and the teaching of literacy. Similarly, students benefit in that, as a result of their participation in reading and writing programs conceptually organized to highlight the authoring cycle, they experience, see demonstrated, and come to value the psycholinguistic and sociolinguistic strategies involved in literacy use and learning.

At the beginning of this volume, we stated that curriculum was that place where theory and practice transact. A theory of instruction is necessarily larger than a theory of reading, writing, or literacy because it involves a theory of learning, a theory of curriculum, a theory of child growth and development, and more. Despite this, a theory of instruction ought not violate a theory of literacy, but rather extend it. This volume moves from theory to practice but stresses practical theory. It stresses the development of a theory of language arts instruction from observation of language in use in classrooms. It calls for teachers to test their best instructional hypotheses and, on the basis of the anomalies they naturally face, reflectively to revise their evolving theory of instruction.

If, however, this call is to be more than mere rhetoric, it behooves each of us to be reflective, to examine presuppositions, and to put these to the test. In reflecting on the curriculum presented, we have made a great number of assumptions. We not only need to be cognizant of these assumptions, but also need to work actively to uncover the flaws in what we currently know.

Several new tenets characterize the comprehension-centered reading and writing program we have presented in this volume. It is upon this base that we build.

1. It focuses on process, defining the language arts curriculum in terms of psycholinguistic and sociolinguistic strategies, and suggests that the content of instruction be the strategies of successful language use and learning. Convention, while important, is not the content of instruction. The difference between a skill and a strategy still needs further clarification.

2. It views reading and writing as a disciplined creative activity that can be analyzed, described, and taught by creating supportive contexts in which the strategies of successful language use and learning can be experienced, demonstrated, and valued. The difference between intervention and support needs further clarification.

3. It emphasizes that reading and writing are ways of learning and developing as well as communicating what has already been learned. In so doing, it establishes new goals for the language arts at the very point when most of the profession is involved in discussing more effective techniques for reaching old goals. It calls for basic research on the further clarification and identification of successful psychological and sociological strategies involved in reading and writing.

4. It identifies cognitive universals across all language users regardless of age and posits experience rather than developmental stage as the key variable in the evolution of literacy. The same language environment that is good for adults is seen as good for children.

5. It suggests that in terms of what the mind does, reading and writing share much in common. It questions much of the curricular fragmentation that currently exists.

6. It suggests that current approaches to the evaluation of a process curriculum have failed. Needed is a focus on strategies and cognitive universals (i.e., the assumption of significance, the search for a unified meaning, etc.) rather than on correctness of form.

7. It suggests that literacy is relative, an open potential, dependent on context of situation. The language arts curriculum should help students both understand and expand the history of literacy they and their society bring to the process.

8. It is holistic, viewing reading and writing as multimodal events and one of several systems of knowing. It stresses that a good language arts program expands communication potential, not just the potential to mean via language. It sees reading and writing as a process of signification having much to gain from interdisciplinary study and application. It sees education as synthesis and the role of educator as synthesizer.

9. It highlights the functional nature of literacy both psychologically and sociologically. In so doing, it stresses the generative nature of reading and writing as a vehicle for growth at both a personal and a societal level. Qualities of a natural language environment, as well as what advantages the school environment has over and above such an environment, need to be identified.

10. It teaches strategies whereby students can solve problems and learn how to learn using reading and writing as tools for learning. Although reading and writing are seen as objects worthy of study in their own right, it stresses language in use and sees learning language, learning about language, and learning through language as natural components of every literacy event.

11. It stresses the inherently social nature of language and language learning. It sees knowledge as socially constituted and

calls into question psychological models of learning that fail to capitalize on the social nature of classrooms.

12. It stresses the principle that reading and writing teachers should be people who read and write with children to provide demonstrations of the strategies involved in successful written language use and learning. Teachers are encouraged to use children and themselves as curricular informants.

13. It sees research and curriculum development as formal forms of learning and calls for a collaborative pedagogy dedicated to the development of practical theory. In this process, teaching and researching join hands, change places, and, like reading and writing, come to be seen as two names for the same process.

14. It sees learning as continuous and the function of curriculum as setting up the learning cycle. It suggests that teaching children the strategies involved in how to learn are the real strategies of literacy. It posits anomalies rather than cognitive dissonance as the key construct in learning. Anomalies are transactions that occur as a function of both environmental and cognitive phenomenon and include unsuspected harmonies as well as surprises. It suggests that teachers as well as children are learners and that humility and reflectivity are the hallmarks of literacy in process.

15. It sees the past and future of literacy and curriculum as potentials rather than problems. Both are opportunities to debug the system by engaging in the authoring cycle and in the process to create rather than just live out our future. To fail to rise to the challenge is to fail to understand what real literacy as it relates to learning is all about.

Our work continues. We have started a new videotape project. As we visit some of the best process reading and process writing classrooms, we find that teachers are continuing to struggle with the challenge of how to move beyond learning environments that still involve more action than reflection, more separate activities than integrated curriculum, more applications of the authoring cycle to reading and writing than to other forms of knowing, more focus on implementing a reading-to-mean model than a reading-to-learn model, more teacher-planned units of study than negotiated curricula, and more assignments than invitations. The challenge remains for all of us to continue working to develop classroom environments that actually demonstrate reading and writing as tools for learning.

This volume argues that we need to "think curriculum." If new insights, no matter how brilliant, are not the basis of instruction, then classroom practice will continue to play second fiddle to the business of research and theory. Operationalized, but unstated, in this volume is our firm belief that new advances in literacy will have to be collaboratively built and firmly grounded in a theory of language in use in classrooms. The authoring cycle as explicated in this volume is our attempt to author curricular change and to begin to build a new theory of literacy and literacy instruction, given what is currently known. We believe this agenda will benefit from wide participation. We close this section by simply inviting you and your students to join us in the collaborative efforts of authoring curricular change and of celebrating literacy learning.

THE AUTHORING CYCLE: CURRICULAR COMPONENTS

Anomalies

Introduction

We learn from the things that cause us tension. It is the "yet to be understood" that fascinates us and that serves our natural desire to learn. When we are faced with an anomaly, an unexpected occurrence or surprise, our attention turns to generating hypotheses to explain that anomaly. Once we reach a working solution, our attention turns elsewhere. This tension in learning reminds us that knowledge is always tentative. The next anomaly could cause us to make major changes in our beliefs about how the world works. This tension keeps us alert, monitoring our experiences for ambiguities, stretching ourselves and our capabilities. Only when outside forces act coercively on learners do learners begin disregarding or refusing to deal with anomalies because the price of pursuing them is too costly.

Materials/Procedures

* Multiple copies of a reading selection
* Four 3" × 5" cards or slips of paper per reader

1. Readers are asked to read the same selection. The selection chosen should be a text that contains issues that are potentially controversial or new for the particular students involved.

2. Students are asked to write one quotation from the selection on each of four 3" × 5" cards, either during or after reading. The quotations selected should be items that were new and exciting or that caused them problems as they read. They can also be points at which readers found themselves stopping and rethinking or rereading.

215

3. As readers finish reading and writing the four cards, they rank order their four cards from most anomalous or surprising to least anomalous.

4. The readers come back together in a group; each person reads his or her top anomaly to the group and shares why that item was surprising.

5. After sharing, discussion turns to why certain tensions experienced were similar or different across the people in the group.

Teacher's Role

The teacher's major role is to establish a learning environment that encourages students to take the risk of pursuing tensions rather than only looking for further support for beliefs they already hold. Depending on students' past instructional histories, they may hesitate to pursue anomalies and instead search for the "right" answer that they believe the teacher will ask them to provide. The teacher may need to involve students in this activity several times to demonstrate that it really is okay to search for and think about the things that puzzle *them*.

Follow-Up

1. Instead of students copying quotations that they find anomalous, they can record on the cards the questions and issues that trouble them as they read the selection (see Figures CC1.1 and CC1.2).

2. This activity can also be used with a presentation or lecture, a piece of art, a musical composition, a dramatic presentation, or other form of communication. As students listen or observe, they write down the anomalies they feel as learners.

3. Students can record the anomalies they experienced on a worksheet (see Figure CC1.3), rather than on the cards.

4. Students can be asked to write about an experience that "caused them to think." This invitation gives writers the space to formulate as well as to resolve a problem. When students share these pieces of writing, others will be able to follow the mental processes of the writers to see how they resolved the tensions they felt through problem solving.

Figure CC1.1   List of Anomalies by Amy (Grade 3) for *The Flunking of Joshua T. Bates* (Shreve 1984).

Figure CC1.2   Anomalies by an Adult for *What's Whole in Whole Language?* (Goodman 1986).

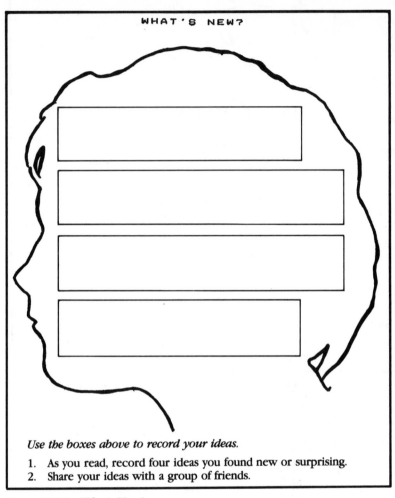

WHAT'S NEW?

Use the boxes above to record your ideas.
1. As you read, record four ideas you found new or surprising.
2. Share your ideas with a group of friends.

Figure CC1.3   What's New?

Reference

This strategy lesson was developed by Jerome Harste as a result of studying what adult readers did in learning from complex text. See:

Harste, J. C. 1986. What it means to be strategic: Good readers as informants. Paper presented at the National Reading Conference, Austin, Texas.

Authors' Chair

Introduction

When learners finish reading or writing a book, they often feel the need to share that book with others. Authors' Chair provides a way for students to share with each other the excitement of a particular moment in relation to a book. Readers may want to share all or parts of a particularly well-written or exciting book. Writers often need to hear their texts read aloud to discover how they sound. By providing a way for students to share with others, Authors' Chair helps reserve Authors' Circle and Literature Circle for students who want to explore and rethink their interpretations of a text in more depth. Even though Authors' Chair highlights sharing and not revising, students often discover what needs to be revised as they read a text aloud to a group, and this gives them specific areas to explore when they go to Authors' Circle.

Reading aloud to students allows them to experience book language, the patterns of stories, and different types of literature. They develop an interest in books and are introduced to quality literature that goes beyond what they are currently reading. Students of all ages benefit from having frequent read-aloud times in their classrooms.

Materials/Procedures

* A chair

1. The chair designated the Authors' Chair should be placed in a corner where a group of students can gather to hear a story.
2. During Work Time when students are reading and writing, students who want to share a particular text can use the Authors' Chair to read to a small group. This can be handled in several ways:

219

   a. Students who want to share can sign their names and in-
      dicate what they want to share on a sign-up sheet each
      morning before Work Time. Other students can then de-
      cide whether they will go to any of these Authors' Chairs.
   b. During Work Time, any student who wants to share a
      book can simply walk over to the Authors' Chair and
      announce what will be shared. Anyone who wants to join
      that student goes over to listen.

3. Authors' Chair is also used for whole-group reading times
   when the teacher or a student reads aloud to the whole class.

4. Following the reading of a text, the group receives the book
   by commenting on parts of the text they liked and by discussing the book with the reader.

Teacher's Role

The teacher needs to establish clear procedures for Authors' Chair;
a specific chair should be designated only for Authors' Chair so
students know what the chair symbolizes and how to use it. The
teacher may initially need to demonstrate how to receive a text.
Teachers also need to ensure that some of the literature being
read at Authors' Chair pushes students beyond what they are
currently reading and exposes them to a wide variety of literature,
including poetry and information books as well as fiction. Teachers
should read the published work of classroom students as well as
professionally published books.

Follow-Up

Students may want to read aloud from their writing or from
literature with students at other grade levels.

References

Graves, D., & Hansen, J. 1983. The authors' chair. *Language Arts*
    60(2):176-183.
Taylor, D., & Strickland, D. 1986. *Family storybook reading*. Portsmouth,
    NH: Heinemann.
Trelease, J. 1985. *The read-aloud handbook*. rev. ed. New York: Penguin.

Authors' Circle

Introduction

Authors' Circle demonstrates to writers that their first concern is with the meaning of what they want to say, not with the conventions of writing. It helps them see that writing is an ongoing process that may require revision to clarify meaning. Authors' Circle demonstrates the social nature of writing and helps develop a sense of audience as writers read what they have written to an audience, and the audience responds to it. This process gives authors the opportunity to shift from the perspective of writer to reader to critic and so to take a new look at their compositions.

Because only meaning-related questions are asked of the writer, risk taking is facilitated. Authors' Circle helps less proficient writers clarify what they have written based on the audience's questions and responses. Authors receive help on what is and is not working in their writing and what, if anything, they might consider doing next. It forces writers to consider the reactions of others, although they are not obligated to modify what they have written because of the questions asked.

Because every student's writing progresses at a different rate, not all students will be ready to attend an Authors' Circle at the same time. The Authors' Circle is made up of three to four authors who have a piece they would like to think more about with others. This means that the piece has been self-revised and deemed worthy, in the author's eyes, of possibly moving to publication in some form. Each participant in the Authors' Circle—including the teacher—must bring a piece.

Usually only pieces that are going through some type of publication cycle go to Authors' Circle. Not all writing should be for publication. The writer should also be involved in informal writing, such as keeping journals and writing pen pal letters, and in many other kinds of uninterrupted writing experiences from which writers can choose pieces they want to publish.

When Authors' Circle meets, authors read their pieces aloud to the group rather than presenting them in written form so that the group will focus on meaning rather than on conventions such as spelling. The content deserves attention first, and only after authors have said all they want to say are they ready to focus on convention. This focus occurs during Editors' Table.

Authors do not revise during the circle but afterward consider privately the recommendations made and arrive at their own decisions regarding any changes in their writing. It is essential that this decision making remain the author's responsibility so that the student maintains ownership of the piece. After leaving the Authors' Circle and making decisions on revisions, authors may choose to return with the piece to another Authors' Circle, to take their piece to Editors' Table, or to put the piece back into their Authors' Folder and not publish it at that time.

Authors' Circle is different from Authors' Chair. At Authors' Chair, students come together just to share their writing. At Authors' Circle, students bring rough drafts that they want to think more about before publication. Authors should be helped to understand that the function of Authors' Circle is to help them become better writers and that, as members of Authors' Circle, their role is to support the further development of themselves and each other as writers. If Authors' Circle becomes just another Author Sharing Time, its curricular impact will be lost.

Materials/Procedures

* Sign-up sheets for Authors' Circle or a revision box for rough drafts ready to go to Authors' Circle
* Small round table or desks formed into a circle

Small groups of three to four writers who have a piece they want to revise and possibly publish in some way (newspaper, book, report, etc.) attend an Authors' Circle. Several different variations of Authors' Circle are presented here. All these variations focus on supporting authors in exploring and thinking more about their pieces of writing but differ according to the experience of the authors in Authors' Circles and their needs as authors.

Procedure A (often used in beginning circles)

1. The first author reads the piece aloud to the other authors in the Authors' Circle.

2. The listeners receive the piece by telling what they heard in the piece, especially focusing on what they found most effective.

3. The listeners then have the opportunity to raise questions about parts that were unclear to them or areas where they felt additional information was needed, or to make any other comments about the meaning of the piece. The author can take notes to remember comments.

4. The next author reads a piece and the process continues until each author has been heard and responded to.

5. The authors then leave the circle to consider the suggestions that were made and to arrive at their own decisions.

Procedure B (often used once students have experience with circles)

1. The first author reads the piece aloud to the authors attending Authors' Circle, then states what he or she likes best about the piece, identifies troublesome parts, or asks for group responses about certain areas.

2. The group discusses and explores ideas on how to deal with the author's concerns. The author makes notes on the listeners' recommendations.

3. Once the group has discussed the identified areas to the author's satisfaction, they discuss parts of the piece they particularly liked and raise questions about meaning.

4. The next author continues the process in the same manner until all participants have had a chance to get a response to their writing. The authors then consider revisions in private.

5. Sometimes authors do not want to have the group immediately respond to specific parts of a piece. Instead, they want to get the group's general response. In this case, the author reads the piece to the group, which responds with statements about what they found effective and what they had questions about. Following this discussion, the author may ask for help with specific areas if desired.

Procedure C (used when authors need help with a specific problem)

1. During writing, authors sometimes encounter difficulty with a particular part of the text and are unable to figure out how to deal with it, even after talking informally with other writers. The author may call a special Authors' Circle to deal with a specific problem.

2. The author calls together a group of students to help brainstorm possible ways to deal with the difficult part. Sometimes the author chooses three or four particular students the author feels will be able to help think through the difficulty. Other times the author asks for volunteers.

3. The author identifies the problem area and then reads the piece aloud to the group.

4. The group and the author brainstorm possible ways of handling the problem.

5. The group disbands when the author feels that he or she has enough suggestions to consider in revising that section. This is one type of Authors' Circle in which only one author brings a piece of writing, and the group meets just long enough to satisfy that author's need.

Teacher's Role

Like other participants at Authors' Circle, teachers are free to make suggestions, but their recommendations bear no more weight than anyone else's. The teacher must develop a relationship with the students that allows them to feel free to reject a teacher's recommendation. Although teachers do not need to participate in every Authors' Circle, they should stagger the scheduling of Authors' Circles initially so they can walk students through the process the first time. Teachers also need to be aware of the authors' needs and experiences in developing procedures for Authors' Circle that support authors in thinking about their writing with other authors. Although Authors' Circle has a structure to support authors as they think with one another, this structure should not become so routinized that authors ask automatic questions of one another without really listening or thinking with others.

When Authors' Circles first begin, the teacher plays the essential role of setting the tone for the type of exchange that will occur. The goal is to create a supportive environment for authors. Students will initially be unsure of the types of questions to ask or how really to listen to someone else's piece. It may even be necessary at first for authors to read their pieces through twice so that listeners get a frame for the piece and then are really able to listen for meaning the second time. Comments that are non-supportive or that deal with aspects other than meaning are not allowed. Similarly, comments that deal with portions of the story that the author did not identify as problematic should play only a minor role in the discussion. The goal is to give the author ideas but to permit the author to take the lead, and to limit the majority of suggestions to what the author wishes to address.

Once students understand how to conduct Authors' Circles, the teacher does not need to be present in every circle. Students may form and meet in Authors' Circles by themselves, with the teacher joining the groups only occasionally or briefly.

Remember that Authors' Circles are part of a larger authoring cycle that consists of students' life experiences, uninterrupted reading and writing, the selection of pieces to be published from each student's Author's Folder, Authors' Circle, self-revision, outside editing, publishing/celebrating authorship, and invitations/language strategy instruction.

Follow-Up

1. Once the Authors' Circle pattern has been established, students may be encouraged to gather a few classmates informally to listen and respond to a piece. Even one or two listeners may be sufficient to meet an author's needs. In many instances, the authors will select students whose opinions they value on the topic of concern to them.

2. As authors' pieces become lengthier, it may be necessary to provide copies of the drafts for each listener. This should be considered only after a tone has been set that focuses on content and not on convention.

3. Paul Crowley of Columbia, Missouri, introduces revision by having students share their writing in small groups. Students exchange papers with one another and write one question they believe the author should answer to improve the draft. After each member of the small group has read each paper and written a question, the author gets the piece back and decides which, if any, of the questions will be answered in a second draft.

4. Students can use drama to help them think through their stories, especially if their stories involve action or dialogue. The author watches as other students either read through the story as a Readers' Theatre or act out the story as a drama. Drama can be used during writing to help the author get past a difficult section, or after the story is finished if the author is considering possible revisions.

References

This strategy was originally developed by Carolyn Burke and Chrystine Bouffler. Other references include:

Calkins, L. M. 1983. *Lessons from a child.* Portsmouth, NH: Heinemann.
——— . 1986. *The art of teaching writing.* Portsmouth, NH: Heinemann.
Graves, D. 1983. *Writing: Teachers and children at work.* Portsmouth, NH: Heinemann.

Author's Folder

Introduction

Writing is an ongoing process that involves constant decision making by the author on how to communicate a written message. Authors need a learning environment that provides a structure that supports them in focusing on meaning, taking risks, making choices, and keeping track of ideas and pieces of writing. Authors also need varying amounts of time to be able to develop their pieces. They should not feel pressured to complete writing in one day's time.

Author's Folders provide the organizational support that authors need for writing over time. Authors keep both current and past drafts of writing in their folders, along with lists of ideas for writing. They can thus continue to work on pieces of writing that are currently in progress and to revisit earlier drafts as they write. These folders highlight and support the role of the author as a decision maker in choosing what to write, how to write, and how long to write.

Monitoring growth as a writer is central to an author's continued development. Author's Folders give both students and teachers a way to monitor and evaluate growth over time and to focus on process as well as mechanics. The folders provide a cumulative record of an author's pieces of writing. Authors can use the folders to remember and revisit the past, to work in the present, and to plan the future.

Students use the pieces of writing in their Author's Folders to choose what writing will be published. Once they have written three or four pieces, they can choose one to take to Authors' Circle and Editors' Table to move that piece to publication.

Materials/Procedures

* One or two strong manila file folders for each student
* Cardboard box for storing the file folders
* Date stamp and inkpad

1. As soon as students begin writing, they are given a file folder to collect their writing over the course of the year. The writing kept in the folders consists of the stories and articles that students perceive as publishable rather than such informal writing as pen pal letters and messages. Pieces of writing in the folder are in various stages of revision, and include jottings of ideas, pieces that are currently being written or revised, partial or completed pieces that the author has abandoned or decided not to publish, and pieces that have already been published.

2. Students date each piece of writing, staple all draft copies of a single piece together, and file the writing in the folder from oldest to newest. A list of all of the pieces is kept on one side of the folder with asterisks next to the titles of published pieces.

3. The folders are stored in a cardboard box in a set location in the classroom so that when students are going to write, they can easily get their folders. Folders are returned to the box when writing is completed for the day.

4. A brainstormed list of ideas or topics to write about is usually kept in the folder, to be changed as the author adds or uses ideas from the list. When ideas occur to students as they are involved in writing, reading, and other kinds of experiences or as they interact with other children in the classroom, they quickly jot these ideas down on their lists for future reference.

5. An evaluation form is stapled to the inside cover of the folder. This form is divided into three sections that are labeled "Mechanics," "Strategies," and "Insights." Observations about a student's growth are written under the appropriate section and dated according to the date on the student's draft. Students as well as teachers can write comments on the evaluation form. New forms are stapled on top whenever a form is filled.

    a. In the "Mechanics" section, student and teacher record any growth in writing mechanics, including spelling, punctuation, capitalization, and grammar. Everything the student knows about mechanics is not recorded, but instead surprises or new areas of growth in relation to mechanics are recorded.

b. The "Strategies" section is used to record new writing process strategies, including both the strategies students use during writing and revising their own work and the strategies they use in supporting other authors in the classroom. These process observations are based on both the writing in the folder and observations of the student. Observations made during the course of the day can be recorded on self-adhesive mailing labels that are later peeled off and placed on the evaluation form. Students also write their own comments about their writing process.

c. The "Insights" section is used to record three kinds of insights: the "aha experiences" the student has had, insights the teacher has about what the student knows, and strategies or connections the teacher or student believes the student is ready to make based on observations of the student.

6. Three pieces of writing are chosen each year by the student and the teacher to be placed in a cumulative folder that is forwarded to the student's next teacher. This process gradually builds a record of the student's growth throughout elementary school for referral. The rest of the writing is sent home with the student at the end of the year.

Teacher's Role

The teacher's primary function is to create an organizational structure that facilitates writing as an ongoing process of creating meaning. Author's Folders are an essential part of the structure that teachers need to provide for authors. The teacher needs to establish a location and a procedure for using the writing folders. The teacher also works at developing an evaluation system that allows the teacher and the author, as well as parents and administrators, to use the Author's Folder to monitor a student's growth as an author over time.

Author's Folders are an important self-evaluation tool because authors can see their growth by looking back through their writing and can use the evaluation form to monitor growth in particular areas. These folders provide a way for students to be reflective about their writing, because they can look at their writing from various perspectives over time.

Teachers use the folders and the evaluation system to plan appropriate learning experiences for authors. Teachers need to develop a system that allows them regularly to read through students' folders and make comments. Many teachers find it helpful to look through five or six folders each day or evening rather than trying to look at all the folders at one time.

Follow-Up

1. Authors will often need more than one folder as their writing piles up during the year. Teachers can establish two different sets of folders for authors. The first set contains folders in which students keep work that is currently in progress as well as their evaluation sheets and lists of topics. The second set is for folders of past work that students either abandoned or completed. It is important that students be able to return to past work to see how they handled problems in an earlier draft and to be able to look at their growth throughout the year. Students may also decide to reactivate an earlier piece and either continue writing a piece that had been partially completed or write a new draft of a completed piece.

2. Large three-ring binders can be used instead of folders for students' writing from year to year. At the end of each year, the student and teacher decide which pieces will go into the binder. At the end of elementary school, the student is given the collection of writing as a graduation present.

3. Cumulative writing folders or binders can be used to demonstrate growth to curriculum coordinators and administrators and to develop handouts to orient parents to the kinds of growth they can expect in their children as a result of the process writing program. Teachers should always have these folders available for referral during parent-teacher conferences.

4. Teachers can keep a folder of their own writing to share with students. This type of file has been used by Paul Crowley to demonstrate the value of revision, to illustrate why certain attitudes are problematic to the growth of a writer, and to point out and invite students to develop their own writing styles and idiosyncrasies.

References

Calkins, L. M. 1986. *The art of teaching writing*. Portsmouth, NH: Heinemann.

Graves, D. 1983. *Writing: Teachers and children at work*. Portsmouth, NH: Heinemann.

Mills, H. A. 1986. Evaluating literacy: A transactional process. Ph.D. diss., Indiana University, Bloomington.

Newkirk, T., & Atwell, N., eds. 1988. *Understanding writing: Ways of observing, learning, and teaching*. 2d ed. Portsmouth, NH: Heinemann.

CURRICULAR COMPONENT

Authors Meeting Authors

Introduction

Students' recognition of themselves as authors is facilitated when they have the chance to meet professionally published authors or when they hear and read about the lives and the writing of professional authors. They begin to see professional authors as real people who have to work hard at their writing and who encounter difficulties in their writing, just as students do. Learning about and meeting authors demystifies the authoring process and opens students up to exploring different strategies in their own writing. Students also develop a personal feeling for authors whom they have met or learned about, and so they search for that person's work at the library. They begin to recognize an individual author's or illustrator's style. As they become familiar with certain authors, they are able to make better predictions as they read that person's work, and this, in turn, facilitates their comprehension.

Materials/Procedures

* Biographical information on an author
* Display of the author's books

There are two sets of procedures for this strategy lesson, depending on whether the author will actually visit the classroom.

Procedure A: Author and Illustrator Introductions

1. The teacher sets up a display of the author's work in the classroom and briefly introduces the books to the class.

232

2. The teacher compiles biographical information on the author or illustrator and adds this to the display.

3. On the first day, the teacher or a student introduces the author or illustrator to the class by telling briefly about the person's background and sharing any personal life stories or comments the person has made about his or her work. If a film or filmstrip on the person is available, it is shown to the class (Weston Woods and Random House are the best sources of films and filmstrips).

4. On the following days, books written or illustrated by that person are shared with the class through giving short book introductions, reading excerpts, or reading the entire books. Students are also encouraged to choose that person's work for their own reading.

5. Once students have had a chance to explore the person's work and to learn more about the author or illustrator as a person, they should be given an opportunity to respond in some way. This response might simply be group sharing times or Literature Circles in which students talk with each other about that person's work, or the response might be whole-class, small-group, or individual projects. Students might create a drama based on a book, do various kinds of art projects related to a book, perform a Readers' Theatre from one or several books, create a display based on a book, or write their own stories using characters from the books or copying the author's style. Students often write to the author asking questions that grow out of their study of the person and the person's work.

Procedure B: Interviewing an Author or Illustrator

1. The teacher should look through the person's published writings or drawings and review available biographical information. The class then spends time exploring that person's life and reading their work.

2. Students should make a list of information they already know about the author or illustrator.

3. Students working in small groups should list questions they would like the author or illustrator to answer. The teacher should ask them, "What else do you want to know about

this author?" Before the groups are brought back together, they should check their questions against the chart of known information and eliminate unneeded questions.

4. After the students are brought back together, they should compile their questions into one list. (More than one list may be needed if several interviews will be taking place.)

5. The teacher should invite the author or illustrator to visit the class, asking that person to share some writings or drawings, samples of rough drafts, and a brief personal history. As the person shares, students should be listening for answers to their questions and crossing off those that have already been addressed.

   If an actual visit is not possible, communication can occur through writing or through a telephone conference call.

6. After this sharing session, the teacher should open up the floor to discussion and questions from the students. They will undoubtedly think of new questions to ask in addition to those on their lists. Students can also share with the author or illustrator any special projects they completed that were based on that person's work.

Teacher's Role

The teacher's major role is as an organizer and resource person. The teacher needs to locate an available local author or illustrator, make arrangements for a visit, and clearly communicate what kinds of items the person should bring and what should be shared. The teacher also serves as a resource in locating published writings and information on the person. Students should be involved in this search for information and writings as much as possible. Several good reference books that give biographical information are listed at the end of this strategy lesson.

It is important that the students have really had time to explore and think about an author's or illustrator's work before that person visits, or the visit will not be productive. The students should have a good understanding of the person and the person's work so that their questions have real depth. Students also need to understand the importance of listening to the person and to each other's questions so they don't repeat questions or ask questions that have already been answered.

Follow-Up

1. Small groups or a single group may be assigned to compile the information learned about the person and to write a biographical sketch or interview for the class newspaper. If two or more groups work independently, the two different pieces can be used as the basis for a revision session as students compile the drafts into a single piece. These written interviews can be compiled into a class guest book.

2. Students should write thank-you notes to the guest, including comments about what new information they have learned about the author and the authoring process. The class could also work on a Group Composed Book that is personalized to the person.

3. An "I Recommend" file can be created from author and illustrator studies. After a particular study, students write "I Recommend" cards for a favorite book by that author or illustrator. These are placed in a classroom library card file alphabetized by author; students can use the file to locate a recommended book to read.

4. Writing letters to authors is a favorite follow-up activity to classroom units on authors (see Figure CC5.1). These letters should not be written as assignments but should only be written when children really want to communicate with a particular author. Students can also write cards to the author on holidays or on the author's birthday. Such correspondence should be sent to the publisher who is currently publishing that author's hardback books. These publishers usually have biographical information sheets on authors that they will send free on request.

5. This activity should highlight authors from within the classroom, both students and the teacher, as well as outside authors. An "Author of the Week" may be designated—a particular author's work is displayed and read during the week. The author can be interviewed about the writing process and one of the author's published pieces can be used as a choice for a Literature Circle.

6. Parents should be informed about which authors or illustrators are being featured in the classroom and encouraged to look for that person's work when they take their children to the library.

April 2, 1985

Dear Dr. Harste,
    Thank for coming to the class room
You wright good books. I liked the book
it didn't frighten me becuase I am afrad
of the dark. I think there are monsters
under my bed and I hare to have a light
on in the house. I think there are warew
olves, mummyes, Frankenstines and these
little deformed cild thateats raw meat,

I liked My Iky Picky Sister
because my little cousin is a
brat and she all was bothers my
ather cousin and me. I am going to
tall Bissy my cousin all about your
books,   by.
                        Your friend,
                        Kim

Figure CC5.1   Letter to an Author (Kim, Grade 2).

7. Students can do individual author and illustrator studies using the same pattern as the group studies, looking for books written by that person and reading biographical information. These studies can be presented to the class through displays, artwork, drama, and so on.

References

Many good sources provide information on authors and illustrators. You may want to read Beverly Cleary's book *Dear Mr. Henshaw*

(1983), a children's book that includes a child's letters to an author, in addition to the following sources:

Commire, A. 1971-   . *Something about the author* (series). Detroit: Gale. (An excellent set of encyclopedias on children's authors that adds new volumes every year.)

Hopkins, L. B. 1969. *Books are by people.* New York: Citation.

——. 1974. *More books by more people.* New York: Citation.

H. W. Wilson Co. 1940-78. *Junior book of authors.* (Four editions are currently available.)

Kingman, L. 1968, 1977. *Illustrators of children's books.* Boston: Horn Book.

Wintle, J., & Fisher, E. 1974. *The pied pipers: Interviews with the influential creators of children's literature.* New York: Paddington.

In addition, periodicals such as *Horn Book* and *Language Arts* carry features on authors and illustrators.

The following articles discuss visits to classrooms by authors:

Parker, M. 1981. An author is coming to school: Madeleine L'Engle. *The Web,* Spring, 24-26.

——. 1981. A visit from a poet. *Language Arts,* 58(4):448-451.

Bookmaking

Introduction

Celebrating authorship is an important component of an authoring cycle. Although there are many different ways to celebrate authorship, some type of publication program is clearly an important way that authors can present their authorship publicly. Publication allows authors to share and celebrate their authorship with others and gives them a real reason for moving some of their writing through the entire authoring cycle. From their writings, authors choose documents to revise and edit for publication for a wider audience.

A published document should have a real audience that goes beyond the author and the teacher, and should have some type of continuing use that keeps it alive and functional within the classroom setting. One type of formal publication involves making books that can be added to the classroom library for students to read on an ongoing basis. When a ready supply of blank books is available for student use, authorship is encouraged and involvement in the authoring cycle is seen as a functional activity. Bookmaking introduces students and teachers to an easy procedure for making durable and attractive blank books for classroom use. To emphasize that student-authored works are "real" books, this procedure focuses on making hardcover books that resemble professionally published books.

Materials/Procedures

* Rolls of contact paper or prepasted wallpaper; fabric can also be used, but it must be glued down
* Cardboard (posterboard or cereal boxes)

* Regular-sized white typing or ditto paper
* Sewing machine
* Rubber cement
* Scissors

1. A stack of six to ten pieces of typing or ditto paper is folded in half and stitched down the center, using a sewing machine on the widest stitch possible. About 1″ should be left before each end of the paper (see Figure CC6.1).

Figure CC6.1

2. Two 6″ × 9″ pieces of cardboard cut from the front and back of a cereal box or from a large sheet of posterboard will form the cover.

3. A piece of contact paper or wallpaper should be cut to measure 12″ × 15″. Backing on the contact paper is removed, or prepasted wallpaper is moistened.

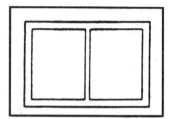

Figure CC6.2

4. The two cardboard pieces should be centered on the sticky side of the contact paper or wallpaper, leaving 1/8″ to 1/4″ between the two pieces of cardboard so the book will close (see Figure CC6.2). Corners are mitered by cutting off each of the four corners of the contact paper or wallpaper. All four sides of the paper are folded in over the edges of the cardboard to complete the book cover (see Figure CC6.3). The corners that were cut off can then be pasted over the inside corners to reinforce them.

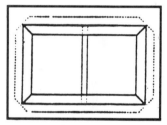

Figure CC6.3

5. The entire backs of the outside book pages are covered with rubber cement.

6. The book pages are glued to the inside of the finished cardboard cover by placing the book pages so that the stitching runs between the two cardboard pieces (see Figure CC6.4).

7. Students' manuscripts are typed and then cut apart and glued onto the pages of the book. Illustrations can be drawn directly into the book or drawn on pieces of paper that are then glued onto the desired page.

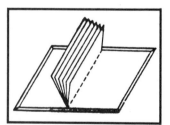

Teacher's Role

Figure CC6.4

Many teachers have a Parents' Night when parents are invited to make blank books for the classroom. Stacks of finished covers and sewed pages are then put into the Writing-Reading Center. When students have a typed manuscript, they glue the book pages into the cover and then cut out and glue their manuscript into the book.

Teachers should demonstrate how to make decisions on how to cut apart a story and decide what goes on each page before they ask students to do so.

Once students have finished making the book, teachers need to provide a time for sharing and celebrating that book with others. Either the teacher or the author should share the book during Author Sharing Time or at Authors' Chair. Teachers need to treat student-authored books as real literature by providing time for these works to be read aloud and by placing student books into the class library to be read by other students. Authors often want to take the books home first to share with family members, but these books should then be placed in the classroom library for class members to read. The books are returned to the authors to take home at the end of the year.

Follow-Up

1. Different-sized books can be made by keeping the following measurements in mind. The cardboard covers should each be cut 1/2″ larger than the pages that have been cut and sewn. The material used to cover the cardboard should be 2″ larger than the cardboard.

2. Students often take several of their writings to a published form each month. They may publish their work either in a book or in the classroom newspaper or magazine.

3. If the school system has a Young Authors Conference, students can look through all the books they have written to choose one to take to the conference. The chosen book can be taken as originally published, or the author may decide to rework the text or illustrations and publish a revised version for the conference.

4. Students should be invited to make two copies of several of their books during the year. One copy is theirs to keep, and the other copy is added to the permanent collection of the classroom or school library.

5. This same Bookmaking process can be used to make various kinds of Group Composed Books including birthday books, messages to a favorite author, thank-yous to a special guest, group composed stories, a collection of reports or short stories on the same theme, and stories based on a certain structural pattern from a predictable book.

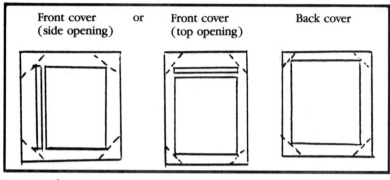

Front cover (side opening) or Front cover (top opening) Back cover

Figure CC6.5

6. Group Composed Books are often too thick to be folded down the middle and sewn. The following procedure allows the pages to be stapled together in a way that still allows the cover to fold back easily.

   a. Two covers of the same size are cut out from the cardboard. A 1/4″ strip is cut off the cardboard that will serve as the book's front cover. The strip is cut from the side if the book opens on the side or from the top if the cover is to lift up (see Figure CC6.5).

   b. Each cover is covered separately with either contact paper or wallpaper. The cardboard for the front cover is placed onto the contact paper or wallpaper, leaving a small space between the strip and the rest of the cover. The contact paper or wallpaper should completely cover over the strip to connect it with the the rest of the front cover.

   c. The individual pages are then placed between the two covers and stapled on the strip with a heavy-duty stapler. The small space that was left between the strip and the rest of the front cover allows the front cover to bend back easily.

7. Other types of publications include class newspapers or magazines, gameboards, bulletin board displays, posters, and so on.

References

This particular version of Bookmaking was adapted from Vera Milz. See:

Milz, V. 1980. The comprehension-centered classroom: Setting it up and making it work. In D. Strickler & B. Farr, eds. *Handbook, Reading comprehension videotape series.* Portsmouth, NH: Heinemann.

Weiss, H. 1974. *How to make your own books.* New York: Crowell.

For blank books, ideas, and kits that teachers and parents can make with children, contact N. O. Steffel and S. L. Griffin, Parents Nurturing Literacy, P.O. Box 90216, Indianapolis, IN 46290-0216.

Choose Your Own Story

Introduction

Often students in basal programs have learned to be cautious and to take no risks as they read. For the authoring cycle to work, however, a different response is needed. As they read, students must risk making predictions, a process that involves students in actively making choices. Choice is an integral part of literacy learning. The realization that we have choices, that alternatives are open to us as learners, allows us to develop a sense of ownership and responsibility about learning. When we make choices, we have to think critically about those choices as we sift through and weigh a variety of information.

Choose Your Own Story highlights choice through involving students in reading and writing multiple storyline books, such as the *Choose Your Own Adventure* series published by Bantam. Multiple storyline books focus on the decision-making process as the learner becomes actively involved in making many different choices. The reader creates the plot by choosing story options at decision points throughout the book. The role of the reader as a storyteller is thus highlighted through active involvement in the creation of story.

Materials/Procedures

* Multiple storyline books
* Large sheets of paper

1. A display of multiple storyline books should be set up in the classroom.
2. The teacher introduces the books by reading part of one

of them to the group, going through several different pages where choices must be made so that students understand how the books work and begin to explore the consequences of the different kinds of decisions.

3. Students are invited to read the books alone or in pairs.

4. After students have had time to read through the books, they should discuss how the books are written, whether there are patterns in how the books are set up, and whether certain kinds of choices lead to certain consequences.

5. Interested students may write their own Choose Your Own Story adventures. Writers will need to think through the type of story, the main character, the setting, the central theme, the plot, and the choices. Because of the complexity of the different subplots and endings, it is helpful to create an outline or a flow chart to map out all the adventures of the story. The outline should show the order of the storyline and a brief description of each adventure. Writing this type of story works well as a collaborative writing strategy for partners or small groups.

Teacher's Role

Although multiple storyline books are not high-quality literature, they provide students with an enjoyable reading experience. They are especially good books for students who feel overwhelmed by chapter books. Students read only a page or two before making a choice and can follow one plot through the book in a relatively short time. Once readers have read several of these books, the books become predictable because they follow a certain standard plot structure. After students have explored multiple storyline books, teachers can introduce them to mysteries and adventure stories to lead them to other kinds of literature.

Follow-Up

1. Students can create gameboards based on one of the books. It is best to include only two or three adventures from the same book on the game. The students draw cards that tell them where to go and to determine what happens to them as they go around the board.

2. Multiple storyline dramas can be performed. As students act out the different parts of the story, they pause and let the audience vote on which choice they should make in continuing the story. The audience can be given choices at several points in the drama or just for the ending.

3. Students can make a timeline, map, or flow chart of the various adventures in one of the books.

References

Susan Robinson initially developed this strategy. Bantam Books, publisher of the *Choose Your Own Adventure* series, has a booklet for students on how to write multiple storyline books; other available brochures give ideas on further uses of these books in classrooms. These materials are available by writing to Bantam Books, 666 Fifth Avenue, New York, NY 10103.

Classroom Newspaper

Introduction

A publication program is essential to making the authoring cycle work in a classroom. Publication encourages authorship and makes involvement in the authoring cycle a functional activity. The essential criteria of a publication program is that the published document have both a real audience and a continuing use that keeps it alive and functional in the classroom or to a wider audience. One type of published document that students have usually seen read by adults outside school is the newspaper. Publishing a classroom newspaper to be read by class members as well as by other students in the school and by family members involves students in an ongoing publication.

Publishing a newspaper involves students in many different roles, including reporters, editors, cartoonists, artists, typists, and layout designers.

Materials/Procedures

* Various kinds of articles and artwork
* Scissors and tape
* Typewriter or computer

1. The first decision that must be made is the type of newspaper to publish. Here are some options:
   a. Students can create a newspaper containing a range of articles and topics such as found in local newspapers. Students first examine local papers and brainstorm a list of possible topics and types of articles they want to have in their newspaper. These could include news reports,

messages, announcements, cartoons, puzzles, want ads, movie and book reviews, letters to the editors, and so on.

b. Themes related to classroom study can be used in constructing a newspaper. For example, a newspaper can publish various reports on a class field trip and on class projects and studies relating to that trip. If the class is involved in a specific unit of study, articles and stories related to that unit can be used to produce a theme newspaper, for example on space or other science or social studies topics.

c. If class members have been involved in a special writing experience, such as Getting to Know You or Family Stories, these can be collected and published in a newspaper.

d. The newspaper can be used to report to parents about school occurrences. Reports on school activities, messages to parents, future plans, and information such as school menus can be included in the newspaper.

e. The newspaper can be a literary magazine that consists of a collection of student writing drawn from Author's Folders or published books.

f. Two or more types of newspapers can be combined in any way to create the classroom newspaper.

2. Once the type of newspaper has been decided, calls for writing to be submitted to the newspaper should be made. A box in a specific location should be designated for students' submissions. A sign-up sheet or chart can be created for students to sign up for articles or other work they intend to submit.

3. Positions that need to be filled are also announced. Sign-up sheets for editors, assistant editors, cartoonists, reporters, and typists can be posted on the Message Board, or students can fill out applications for particular positions. These jobs should rotate among students for each issue of the paper.

4. The class should decide on a name for the newspaper. A local newspaper may be willing to provide a typeset copy of the class newspaper's masthead, especially if you will be reusing it many times. Or, you could create the masthead yourself using rub-down lettering.

5. Once the copy for the paper has been collected, either from already existing writing or from writing done especially for the newspaper, outside editors edit the pieces. The articles

are then given to the managing editor (usually a teacher or parent) for typing. If articles are already typed, they can be used as they are or retyped using a standard column width.

6. The layout designers cut and arrange the typed copy and artwork onto master sheets.

7. The newspaper is then duplicated and assembled by students for distribution to the class, family members, or other students in the school.

8. The newspaper should include an invitation for readers to respond with letters to the editors, suggesting improvements for the next issue and responding to the content of the current issue. These letters to the editors open the way for changes and improvements in subsequent issues and help students to be more aware of their audience. A box or Message Board should be designated for these letters. Subsequent issues of the paper should publish both the letters and the editors' responses.

9. The next issue of the newspaper should be announced so that students can begin to identify and write pieces for it.

Teacher's Role

The teacher first needs to decide with students what kind of paper the class will produce and to show examples of that type of newspaper so students can generate ideas about their own paper. Once a decision has been made on the type of newspaper, the teacher's role is to provide organizational support in getting students assigned to and working in various roles and in making sure that writing is being submitted. Although teachers may feel that it is easier to carry out the publication of the newspaper themselves, it is important that students, as much as possible, carry out the responsibilities and assigned roles in publishing the paper. Problems and mistakes in the first publication of a newspaper are learning situations that students can deal with in subsequent issues.

The elaborateness and frequency of a classroom newspaper will vary greatly from classroom to classroom. Some teachers publish a weekly or biweekly classroom news sheet that is brief and quickly put together, while other teachers publish more elaborate newspapers several times a year. Teachers need to look at their publishing program as a whole and the needs of students to determine what kind of publishing program will best fit the students in a particular classroom. Some classrooms with extensive book publishing programs only publish several newspapers a year. Others put their focus on newspaper or magazine publishing and publish fewer books.

The same type of newspaper does not need to be published throughout the year. The class may do a newsletter one time, a topic-centered newspaper another time, and a standard newspaper format another time. However, staying with the same type of newspaper over several issues better allows students to use what they have learned from one issue to the next.

Teachers need to participate along with students in submitting work to be published in the newspaper.

Follow-Up

1. A variation on a newspaper is a classroom magazine. Literary magazines are the most common type of magazine published, but other types can be used as well. The format and types of articles included vary from those used for a newspaper. If students decide to publish a magazine, they should spend time browsing through magazines to see what kinds of things they want to include in their magazine.

2. Some teachers have each student produce an individual magazine as a semester-long or year-long project. Each magazine contains samples of the various types of writing that the student has taken through the authoring cycle. Students make enough copies of their magazine so that everyone in the class gets a copy of everyone else's magazine.

3. Individual students or small groups of students may decide to publish a newspaper focused on their particular interests. For example, a small group of fourth-grade boys decided to publish a newspaper of jokes once a month because of their interest in collecting jokes and riddles. They handled the entire process of writing and publishing on their own and then distributed copies to class members.

4. Newspapers can be made more participatory by leaving blank spaces where readers can write or draw their own responses to articles or drawings in the newspaper. For example, if the newspaper includes a picture, a blank space can be provided below it for readers to draw their own picture (see Figure CC8.1).

How To Get To Lauren's House

　　　Go straight.　Take a left
turn that way.　Go up Sayre Road.
Go straight again and then you
turn this way.　When you go up the
hill you need to turn this way.　Then
you turn in wherever there's a guest
spot.

LAYREA

Draw your house here!

How To Get To Jocelyn's House

　　　First you go this way.　Then
we go that way.　Then they have to go
this pointy way.　Then they have to
turn left, and then we get there.
Whenever you see inside my house, you
are there.

Figure CC8.1　Page from Preschool Newspaper (Clyde 1987).

5. Newspapers created by preschool children can include both the child's original writing for child audiences and below that a conventional version of the child's writing for adult audiences.

6. Students can create a video "newspaper" by taping news reports in which they read news articles that they wrote themselves about local or national news. These news reports are then made available for viewing in other classes at school.

7. Teachers may want to create a special bulletin board or sharing time for students to bring in articles of interest from the local newspaper for sharing and critiquing. Teachers may also want to have a newspaper delivered to the school for students to read; many newspapers are willing to provide free newspapers to classrooms for students' use. Students may want to rewrite newspaper items they bring in and publish their own news magazine for other students to read and critique.

8. Parents and other people in the school or community can be invited to submit articles, ads, and other items to the newspaper.

9. The teacher should check other newspapers and magazines that publish students' work. Some school districts publish a newspaper or magazine at the district level. Sometimes local newspapers include some writing by children in a weekly section or in a special section during "Newspaper in Education Week" (usually held nationwide the first week in March). *Stone Soup,* a national periodical for children, consists of artwork and stories by children. (Send pieces to Stone Soup, Children's Art Foundation, 915 Cedar Street, Santa Cruz, CA 95060.)

10. See Bookmaking for further discussion of other ways to publish.

References

Many people have worked with Classroom Newspapers. The basic strategy lesson shared here grew out of work by Carolyn Burke, Jerome Harste, and other Indiana University graduate students with Mary Lynn Woods in the Zionsville Schools and Susan Robinson in the Indianapolis school system. See also:

Clyde, J. A. 1986. A collaborative venture: Exploring the socio-psycholinguistic nature of literacy. Ph.D. diss., Indiana University, Bloomington.

Perl, S., & Wilson, N. 1986. *Through Teachers' Eyes.* Portsmouth, NH: Heinemann.

Several computer software programs are available to help in preparing Classroom Newspapers. See:

Newsroom. 1984. Minneapolis, MN: Springboard Software.

Cloning an Author

Introduction

Successful reading and writing involve the creation of a text world in which meaning is organized and unified. Although each language user must take ownership of this process, teachers can support the process.

Successful comprehension involves synthesizing what is read into a set of key ideas or generalizations. Readers must be actively involved in this process, assuming responsibility both to themselves and to the author. Good readers understand that key ideas are a function of the text, the context, and the purpose for reading.

This activity focuses on creating a unified meaning for each reader rather than on replicating the author's unified meaning. Participants "clone" the activities of an author, hence the title of the activity is Cloning an Author (the reader), not Cloning the Author (the writer).

Materials/Procedures

* Multiple copies of a selection to read
* Stack of eight 3" × 5" cards for each student (or students may create eight cards from a single sheet of paper)

1. Students are given a stack of eight cards and a copy of the article to be read. When used as an ongoing activity, different color cards should be used for each selection read or the ends of each set of cards marked with a different color marker (see Follow-Up).

2. Students are asked to identify what they see as the eight key concepts in the selection and to put each concept on a

253

separate card. Students may complete these cards as they are reading or immediately after they finish reading the selection. Students need not write in complete sentences, but rather write just enough to remind them of the concept.

3. Once students have completed their cards, they select what they see as the five key concepts (see Figure CC9.1) and discard the remaining cards. (While this may initially seem cruel, we have found that throwing cards away encourages decision making and active reading.)

4. Having reduced their stack of cards to five, students identify the idea they see as most central to the selection they have

A humpback whale is the biggest jumping whale.

A humpedback is 17 meters or 55 feet.

when a father of a baby whale sense danger it make a sound that can be heard a hundred miles in the ocean.

every six months a humpback whale moves to a different home

A baby whale has two enemies which are a shark and a killer whale.

The big whales can gulp a million krill in one mouth full.

The biggest whale is over a hundred feet long.

The smallest whale is 10 feet long and that a Pigmy-Sperm whale.

A bull is a male whale.
A cow is a female whale.
A calf is a young whale.

Humpback whales eat little fish, shrimp called krill.

A

B

Figure CC9.1   Two Sets of Cards for *Little Humpback Whale* (McGovern 1979) by Two Third Graders (A—Bill; B—Sam).

read. They place this card in the center of their desk or tabletop. If students cannot find such a card, they are invited to cross out one of their entries and write a card that they believe fills this function.

5. Once this center card has been selected, students place the remaining cards around it, reflecting how they see the concepts tied to the central concept and to each other.

6. Working in pairs, students take turns explaining to their partners their reasons for selecting the center card and for the placement of the other cards.

7. As a group, students discuss what commonalities as well as differences existed across readers and why such variation is an expected event in reading.

Teacher's Role

Teachers should participate in all phases of this activity by identifying what they see as key concepts, laying out their cards, and sharing their cards with a student. A whole-class discussion may be used as a follow-up.

If Cloning an Author is used as an ongoing reading activity, teachers must coordinate how various sets of cards will be identified and which color will be used with which selection.

Follow-Up

1. Student pairs may exchange stacks of cards and lay out what they believe to be the other's organization. The original author of the card stack listens to what the new student did with the cards and then shares his or her original organization scheme. Rather than insist that theirs is the "correct" organization, authors should be encouraged to explore the organizational possibilities demonstrated by their partner's decisions.

2. Different colored cards can be used by students for each related reading experience (white for Reading Experience 1, green for Reading Experience 2, etc.). Different sets of cards can be made for each chapter in a longer book or for different reading selections. Once each student has several sets of cards, these cards can be combined into one set

during this strategy lesson. For example, if two selections have been read, students can be asked to take their five white cards from Reading Experience 1 and their five green cards from Reading Experience 2, shuffle them, and select a new set (approximately seven cards) from which to create a map covering both selections read. Students share these new maps with their fellow students and discuss differences and similarities that occur. Using colored cards allows students to get back to their original sets after they have engaged in this activity.

3. Teachers are encouraged to engage participants in Cloning an Author after reading a variety of related selections in a unit of study. After all selections have been read, all cards are shuffled and participants select the five to seven key concepts they see as central in this unit of study. Results can either be shared orally or written in an uninterrupted writing session.

4. Students should be encouraged to use this strategy as a way of summarizing materials they have read. College students in our classes have found it to be an excellent device to prepare for class discussions and essay examinations.

5. With kindergarten and elementary school children, students can be encouraged to write down or draw pictures of what they want to remember as they read the story. Once they have done this they can put their cards in the order they wish and use them during Book Sales or Author Sharing Times. When we have used this activity in primary classrooms we have found that story retellings are not only much longer, but qualitatively much improved.

6. See Generating Written Discourse as an example of another card procedure that is used for writing reports.

Reference

Cloning an Author was initially developed by Jerome Harste.

Editors' Table

Introduction

Because the function of written language is to communicate a message, writers should focus on getting their meaning down during early stages of the writing process. When an author decides to take a manuscript to publication, however, it is edited for convention to show the author's regard for readers.

The editing process consists of both semantic editing and editing for convention. Semantic editing by outside readers focuses on the identification of unclear or confusing portions of the text. It extends the focus on meaning by encouraging authors to take another perspective on their writing. Editing for convention occurs after semantic editing to highlight the notion that control of conventions is not a prerequisite to production of meaningful messages. Instead, it is a final concern for manuscripts that the author chooses to make public. After editing, the text goes to the typist who serves as a final check on conventions. The typist serves the same function that a secretary would for an employer.

The editing process provides a demonstration of an effective strategy used by published authors for dealing with aspects of convention. Serving as editors of one another's texts helps students develop an appreciation of audience and the communicative commitment they make to their readers.

Editors' Table is helpful for any writers who are taking their pieces to publication. It allows them to attend to meaning rather than to be overly concerned with conventions early in the process. It also helps them develop a personal strategy for self-editing and editing of other's texts.

Materials/Procedures

* Table
* Box for writers' rough drafts
* Blackboard or paper on which to write editing rules
* Visors, armbands, buttons, and so on to identify editors
* Variety of regular and colored pencils or highlighter pens
* Scrap paper
* Dictionary, spelling dictionary, thesaurus, English stylebook, and other useful reference books
* Typewriter or computer
* Overhead projector
* Folders or boxes for texts in process of being edited or typed
* Tape, scissors, rubber cement, and blank paper for pasting up galleys
* Copies of publications similar to those being published

1. Before the editorial board is set up, it is important to establish a need for publication in the authoring cycle. Writers must have drafts that they have shared in Authors' Circles. Authors will choose only some of their pieces to go through the publication process.
2. The teacher should establish an editors' box in the classroom where students can place pieces that they want to have published that have gone through an Authors' Circle.
3. Volunteers can be asked to serve as editors for the first publication. Children should submit their names in a box or folder and then names can be drawn to determine who will serve as the first editors. It is helpful to include children of different ages and ability levels on the editorial board. This process will be repeated for subsequent publications so that others have an opportunity to serve as editors. Decisions regarding length of board membership should be based on frequency and type of publication.
4. An editorial board meeting should be called. Badges, visors, or armbands can be distributed to identify students during their terms as editors.
5. The editorial board should examine and discuss published documents similar to the ones that the class will publish (trade books, newspapers, etc.). The teacher should ask chil-

dren what an editor does and compile a list that reflects the dual responsibilities of editors: editing for meaning and editing for convention. During semantic editing, editors focus on meaning and are concerned that the text makes sense and that the meaning is clear. When they edit for convention, they are concerned with spelling, punctuation, and capitalization. Semantic editing should always precede editing for convention. This will require several readings of each manuscript. Text ownership should be discussed. Each editor should take a rough draft from the editors' box, then answer the question, "Whose paper is this?" The idea that it is the author's text and that no one except the author has the right to change the meaning or structure of the text should be clearly established.

6. The teacher may wish to prepare a student text in advance for use on the overhead projector to assist students in generating and applying editorial rules. It may be helpful if each editor has a copy of that student text. The editors should establish enough rules and symbols to enable them to begin the editing process. It is quite likely that other rules will evolve as the need arises. The list should be considered as a set of working guidelines that are subject to change with adequate justification by any subsequent editorial board. One of the participants acts as scribe, recording the suggestions (preferably on a chalkboard to emphasize the tentative nature of the decisions). Markings should be easily identifiable, yet small, so the author's manuscript is marked as little as possible. It is helpful if a rule is devised to identify what phase of editing a document is in and who is responsible, so that questions can be easily referred to the appropriate person.

7. These rules should be posted in the editors' corner and added to and changed when suggestions are made by the editorial board.

8. Editing may not be necessary for all pieces in a publication or for all types of informal publications. The teacher and/or editors may decide to exclude some pieces from the editing process and print them as submitted (e.g., letters to the editor, artwork, personal ads, and other pieces whose original form is an integral part of the message).

9. Once the editorial board has decided on the rules and symbols, they should begin the editing process with a rough draft.
   a. Semantic editing: The editors' primary focus is identifying

and marking with the agreed-on symbols any portions of a text that require additional information to be understood, that seem confused, or that need clarification. The teacher should stress the cardinal rule: No one has the right to alter the structure or meaning of a text except the author.

b. Semantic meeting: If questions regarding meaning arise, the editor must confer with the author. The editor should locate the author and ask questions based on the semantic editing. The author decides whether to make any changes and, if so, makes them during the conference.

c. Editing for conventions: Once all questions regarding meaning have been resolved with the author, the editor rereads the rough draft to edit for conventions such as spelling, punctuation, and capitalization. These changes are marked right in the text. Highlighter pens can be used to mark words that the editor feels are functionally spelled, and the conventional spelling of the word can be written above any misspelled word. If unsure of the conventional spelling, the editor might write out alternative spellings on a piece of paper, look up the word in the dictionary, or consult with other editors, including the teacher. If the editor is still unsure of the spelling, the word can be left highlighted for the managing editor or final typist (usually the teacher or a parent volunteer) to deal with.

d. Typing of manuscript: The rough draft is given to the typist, who may make final changes in spelling, punctuation, or capitalization if nonconventional forms would embarrass either the teacher, the child, or the school.

e. Editors' conference: At the end of the first editing session, it is important for editors to regroup and discuss problems and issues that have arisen. This is a good opportunity to revise and add to editorial rules and policies.

Teacher's Role

The teacher needs to walk students through Editors' Table, making sure they understand the limits of their roles and responsibilities. If the editing process is initially too overwhelming for students, teachers may want to limit the amount of editing that each editor is expected to do. For example, editors may look only for misspelled words or punctuation during editing for conventions instead of editing for all conventions. Teachers may serve as a spelling resource during editing for conventions.

The teacher is the managing editor, and in this role makes final decisions about whether something will be released for publication. To make sure that the goal of the reading and writing program does not become publishing, it is necessary for the teacher to establish the rule that only a given number of all pieces drafted will be taken through the authoring cycle; we recommend a maximum of two items per student per month. If students wish to publish more than this, they may do so on their own time at home.

Editors' Table is the one part of the authoring cycle that teachers often drop, feeling that students cannot handle editing or that there is not enough time for Editors' Table. But Editors' Table should always be part of the cycle, even for young children, because of its role in allowing students to explore conventions.

Follow-Up

1. When a second editorial board is established, procedures 1-5 may be repeated during the initial meeting. Because a set of editorial rules already exists, step 6 will involve the sharing of current working rules for the editing process, rather than the generation of a new list. Former editors may be enlisted to explain existing policies. The tentativeness of these guidelines should be emphasized so that editors will feel comfortable in suggesting changes and refining policies.

2. Editors may find readers' comments useful in shaping their next publication. Reexamining an assortment of published materials may provide editors with ideas for responding to a wide range of reader requests. For instance, newspaper editors may receive requests for new types of articles, or for the addition of illustrations and artwork to make the document more interesting and appealing to readers. If publishing books, editors may receive suggestions concerning such features as a dedication or a table of contents. As the editors make decisions about their responses to such suggestions, they may wish to make applications available for new staff positions designed to respond to these reader-identified problem areas (cartoonists, artists, etc.).

3. Editing texts for publication is only one responsibility of editors. They may also be involved in making decisions about

layout, organization of a collection of pieces, assembly and distribution of the publication, and types of future publications. As editors take responsibility for the entire publication process, it may be necessary to create specialized editorial positions to deal with these aspects of publication.

4. As the authoring cycle continues to operate over time and with various kinds of publications, the role taken by editors will change. The Editors' Table, as initially implemented, serves as a demonstration of editing to students. As they become familiar with the editing process, students gradually begin to self-edit and to edit informally with other authors.

5. More informal variations of the editing strategy may be used with different kinds of publications.

6. The role of the editor in publishing books is discussed in *How a Picture Book Is Made* (Kellogg & Blantz 1976), a filmstrip from Weston Woods, and *How a Book Is Made* (Aliki 1986).

References

Editors' Table was initially developed by Carolyn Burke and then further developed by Jean Anne Clyde, Deborah Rowe, and Kathy Short. Additional references include:

Calkins, L. M. 1986. *The art of teaching writing.* Portsmouth, NH: Heinemann.
Graves, D. 1983. *Writing: Teachers and children at work.* Portsmouth, NH: Heinemann.

Family Stories

Introduction

Learning is always a process of connecting our current experiences to our past stories. The more we know and explore our past stories, the more potential exists for making richer and more complex ties with our current experiences—which, in turn, enhances learning. One important source of past stories are stories that families tell over and over again about events that happened to family members. These stories are an insightful source of how families interpret their experiences and what they value.

Gathering Family Stories engages students in a process of research as they learn techniques of interviewing, note taking, oral storytelling, and writing a story from the data they collect. This is a good introduction to research because they care about the subject and already have a great deal of knowledge about it. This facilitates the research process and the use of primary sources for information, and so avoids the problem of students copying reports from encyclopedias. Family Stories combine content and a language strategy in an effective way and so create a context for involved learning in the classroom.

Materials/Procedures

* Paper for note taking and writing stories

1. The teacher should tell students that all of us carry important stories around inside us. Some of these stories are family stories or "remember when" stories that family members tell over and over again about things that happened a long time ago to them or to other people in their family. The children

are going to become researchers and collect these family stories over the next several weeks.

2. Students are asked to interview family members about these stories and to take notes on the stories so they can share them with the class.

3. During the next several weeks, each day students are asked to share orally any family stories they have collected.

4. Students are then asked to list the family stories they have collected and to decide which ones they want to write (see Figure CC11.1). These can then be published in individual books, class books, or a class newspaper. In one classroom, students each published individual collections and then chose their favorite story to put in a class newspaper that was sent home.

5. Students can discuss the various strategies they used for note taking, interviewing, sharing orally, and writing, and how they can use these strategies in other situations when they need to do research.

IFel owt of the truk
I Was olea 2 yir's old and
my Dad was olea 19 yir's old.
I was wiring a dipr and a srt
and me and my Dad was
kuming bak frum kolneline and.
we wr haf wa home and
I opind the dor and fel out,
of the truk and I wit kboum
on the rod. My dipr got tor up
to pecis The End.

Figure CC11.1   Family Story (Richard, Grade 1).

Transcription:

I fell out of the truck.
I was only 2 years old and
my Dad was only 19 years old.
I was wearing a diaper and a shirt
and me and my Dad was
coming back from Countyline and
we were halfway home and
I opened the door and fell out
of the truck and I went kaboom
on the road. My diaper got tore up
to pieces. The End.

Teacher's Role

Teachers need to engage in the same process of researching their own Family Stories to show students that these stories are important to all of us and to demonstrate the research process. Once students get to the point of writing their stories, it is helpful if the teacher chooses one of his or her own stories and actually goes through the process of writing the story from notes with the children watching. The teacher can do this either on an overhead or on the blackboard.

Teachers also need to allow class time for oral sharing of these stories. This is a crucial part of the process as children gain experience in how to tell these stories. Also, as they hear others' stories, they are reminded of additional stories in their own families and are motivated to do more interviewing. During this sharing, the class can explore similarities and differences that run across their stories. For example, many children will have "broken bone" and "hospital" stories to share.

As the children gather family stories, the teacher should share with children literature that involves family stories. See the list included at the end of this strategy lesson. Two books that have worked well are *Sarah Plain and Tall* (MacLachlan 1985) and *The Relatives Came* (Rylant 1986). Students can also be involved in studying and reading the work of authors, such as Pat Hutchins, who write books based on things that happened to their families. The teacher could choose to introduce Family Stories by sharing a piece of literature that is a family story. These books can be used as both read-aloud books and books for Literature Circles, so that students can explore how others have written family stories. The literature can be read both before and during the time students are telling and writing their own stories.

Follow-Up

1. Students can become involved in researching and writing community stories or tales of long ago from elderly people in the community.
2. Students can explore folktales, looking at both oral storytelling and what happens to these stories when they are written down.

3. Family Stories lead naturally to further exploration of other and more complex research strategies, including using observation and written references. One classroom of first graders built from this experience of researching Family Stories to researching zoo animals. They each chose a zoo animal they wanted to become an expert on and then talked to other people and read books on that animal. They also observed their animal during their annual trip to the zoo. A variation of Generating Written Discourse was introduced to the class as another way of taking notes and organizing them to write a report.

4. Students can become involved in researching issues of importance to themselves and their community. A bilingual teacher had her students interview various community members to find out how they felt about being bilingual and for what purpose and under what conditions they used various languages. Several other bilingual teachers had students in two different communities examine their community's murals and public pieces of art. Students took pictures of these works, discussed cultural, economic, and religious symbolism, and exchanged their insights in a newsletter with students from the other community. (For more information on these projects, see Moll & Diaz 1987.)

    Shirley Brice Heath involved students in researching what it meant to be literate in the community in which they lived. Students made observations and wrote up their findings about how various groups of people in the community used reading and writing.

5. Instead of always involving students in research to discover what we or others already know, teachers can involve them in original research. For example, students may research why a local creek has a particular name or write to grandparents to find out how they celebrated certain holidays. They can survey the community to identify possible places of historical significance and use this information to prepare a history book on the sites in their community.

6. Alternative ways to present research to others, including art and drama, can be explored instead of always relying on a written report. In addition, when the class becomes involved in writing expository reports, the teacher should introduce various kinds of nonfiction so that they are aware of some of the options that are available for writing nonfiction.

References

This strategy was developed by Jerome Harste, Kathy Short, and Gloria Kauffman. Additional sources of information are:

Moll, L., & Diaz, S. 1987. A socio-cultural approach to the study of Hispanic children. In A. Allen, ed., *Library services for Hispanic children*. Phoenix, AZ: Oryx Press.

Woolsey, D., & Burton, F. 1986. Blending literary and informational ways of knowing. *Language Arts* 63(3):273-280.

Appendix: Children's Literature with Family Stories

Baylor, B. 1983. *Best town in the world*. New York: Scribner.

Brink, C. R. 1935. *Caddie Woodlawn*. New York: Macmillan.

Cooney, B. 1982. *Miss Rumphius*. New York: Viking.

de Paola, T. 1978. *Nan upstairs, Nana downstairs*. New York: Penguin.

Hutchins, P. 1971. *Titch*. New York: Macmillan.

———. 1986. *The doorbell rang*. New York: Greenwillow.

Lasky, K. 1981. *The night journey*. New York: Penguin.

———. 1984. *A baby for Max*. New York: Macmillan.

Lawson, R. 1941. *They were strong and good*. New York: Viking.

Levinson, R. 1985. *Watch the stars come out*. New York: Dutton.

———. 1986. *I go with my family to grandma's*. New York: Dutton.

MacLachlan, P. 1985. *Sarah plain and tall*. New York: Harper & Row.

McCloskey, R. 1958. *Time of wonder*. New York: Viking.

Rylant, C. 1983. *Miss Maggie*. New York: Dutton.

———. 1983. *When I was young in the mountains*. New York: Dutton.

———. 1986. *The relatives came*. New York: Bradbury.

Taylor, M. 1987. *The gold cadillac*. New York: Dial.

Uchida, Y. 1971. *Journey to Topaz*. New York: Scribner.

Wilder, L. I. 1935. *Little house on the prairie*. New York: Harper.

Generating Written Discourse

Introduction

Writing is a decision-making process guided by the author's attempt to create an overall framework for meaning. The writer then uses this structure to add more specific pieces of information and to generate the text itself. Generating Written Discourse is an activity that supports writers in focusing on the more global aspects of constructing texts. This activity helps readers generate a global structure for their topic that is more flexible than structures generated by more traditional methods, such as using an outline.

The strategy of Generating Written Discourse focuses on supporting the writer in discovering, generating, and structuring major ideas. Writers develop and organize their ideas on cards before beginning to write. Because all the ideas and thoughts are on separate cards, writers can easily add and delete ideas and reorganize their meanings. They are not, however, rigidly tied to the ideas or structure as they write the text. A one-to-one correspondence between the text and the cards is not necessary, and writers are urged to generate more ideas during the writing process. The process of discovery and decision making is thus highlighted both before and during the writing process.

Generating Written Discourse demonstrates that writing is not a linear process. Writers do not start at the beginning and plow through to the end. The writing process involves being able to shift ideas around within an evolving text, juxtaposing parts to strengthen the organization of the whole.

Organizing the text is especially difficult for writers who are writing expository texts. There is no story plot for them to follow, as in narrative texts. Often their expository texts have no clear structure, but jump around from fact to fact. The need to move parts of the text around and to try various organizations therefore becomes especially important when authors are first trying to write expository texts.

Materials/Procedures

* Large pile of small file cards or pieces of paper
* Paper and pencils
* Large, clear surface on which to lay out the cards

1. Each student takes several small slips of paper or cards and writes one idea for a possible writing topic on each card. These ideas can be on any topic the student chooses, or the teacher may ask students to write down ideas related to a general topic the students have been studying.
2. As the students are thinking about and writing down their ideas, they informally share the topics with each other. This sharing allows for further exploration of possible writing topics.
3. Once students have had an adequate amount of time to generate and share their ideas with one another, they select the idea they most want to write about. The other idea cards are placed into their Author's Folders for future reference.
4. After choosing their topics, the writers think about all the major ideas related to their topic. These ideas are each written on separate cards and arranged below the topic idea. Students are told that they can add or delete cards as needed and can move the cards around. These major ideas will serve as headings for expansion of the topic. Students should be encouraged to write down as many related ideas as possible.
5. On other cards, the students write ideas they have for expanding their headings. They write as many specific ideas as they can think of for each of their major idea cards. These specific ideas are then arranged below each major idea.

   Only one idea is written per card, and the student decides how much to write. Some write entire sentences, while others write a phrase or a single word. The cards serve as placeholders for meanings students want to remember during the writing process, and so they must make their own decisions about what to write to jog their memory.
6. When students first use this strategy or when they are having difficulty with any of these steps, time can be spent sharing

with one another after each step. Students can share their topics, their major idea cards, and their specific idea cards. This sharing allows them to see demonstrations of how other students are developing each of these steps and gives them the opportunity to think of new ideas. Once students are familiar with the strategy, the sharing will occur informally whenever they feel the need for it.

7. When the cards are arranged in what the student feels is the best order, the student is ready to begin writing. Writers may rearrange and add or delete ideas as they wish during the writing process. The organized cards serve only as a guide for predicted text meanings (see Figure CC12.1).

Teacher's Role

The teacher should participate in the same process of listing topics, writing ideas on cards, and writing a story based on that organization along with the students. The teacher may first want to walk the students through the process by sharing an example of someone's piece of writing at each of the different stages. This piece of writing could be a piece written earlier by the teacher or by another student.

The major focus of this strategy is on helping students generate and structure a broad framework from which to write. Students may need help moving beyond just listing specific details on their cards to listing major ideas. Ownership of text is crucial, however, and ultimate decisions about meaning must remain the author's responsibility.

Follow-Up

1. Instead of the author immediately starting to write once the cards have first been organized, the ideas are shuffled together. The following day, the author takes out the ideas and tries out several different organizations. The author then selects a tentative structure, either the original or one of the alternate ones, and writes a rough draft.

   A variation of this shuffle strategy involves having another writer help the author explore alternate organizations. Each writer shuffles the cards and, in groups of twos, the writers exchange cards. Each author becomes the "reader" and

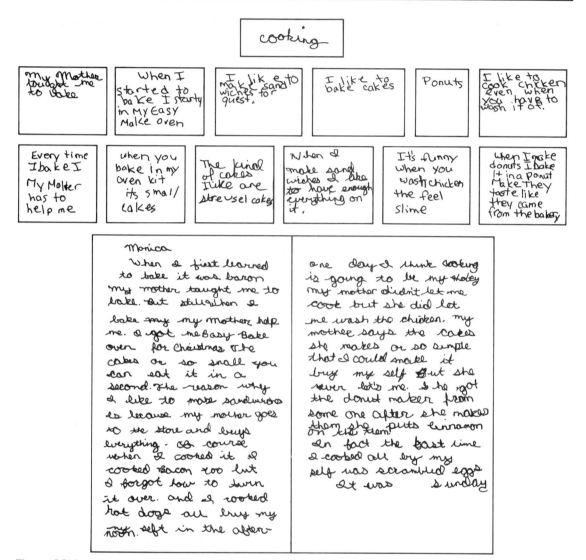

Figure CC12.1 Notes and Article Using Generating Written Discourse. See Kucer (1983).

attempts to put the other person's cards together in an order that makes sense. The reader explains the order to the author and gives reasons for that ordering. The author then puts the cards in the original order and explains that order to the reader. The students locate new partners and repeat the procedure. Before writing the first draft of their texts, the authors generate one alternate way in which their text might be structured. The author then chooses one structure, either the original, the alternate, or one of the options produced by the readers, and writes a rough draft.

Either of these variations is helpful for supporting language users who do not look for alternate ways in which to structure meaning or who resist new meanings because they require reorganization of the text.

2. Students are asked to select one or two parts of their text, or one or two of their major idea cards, that need to be more fully developed. Students are then asked to write down all the specific ideas they can think of for that major idea or section. In small groups, the students share their specific ideas with others who help the author think of specific ideas that could be added. The other students also discuss with the author which of the ideas should or should not be placed in the text. The authors then choose the specific ideas they want to use in their texts and place these cards in with the other cards in the order that they will be written about. If the text is already written, the sections for which the ideas were generated are revised.

3. Generating Written Discourse can be used as a research strategy as well as a strategy for generating an expository text. Students select the topic they want to research, and write on cards the major questions they will need to answer to write a report. They then write on separate cards any information they already have and place these under the corresponding question. Remaining questions are used to guide the student's research. Notes are taken on separate cards and placed under the appropriate question as the student researches the topic. New questions are written as students encounter new ideas they had not previously considered. The question and information cards are then organized and used to write the report.

4. Students can be formed into groups of three and each group provided with an envelope containing a set of idea cards. These idea cards created by the teacher are on a particular topic or theme and are related to one another in a variety of ways. The number of different idea cards used will vary according to the students and can be anywhere from 10 to 50 cards. Each group gets the entire set of cards. The students are first asked to read all the cards and to generate a list of

possible categories that they could sort their cards into. They are told to sort the cards into piles so that all the cards in a pile are related to one another in some way. As the groups finish sorting, they check with nearby groups to see how they sorted their cards. When all the groups are finished, each group shares their categories with the other groups.

5. This activity can be used to generate multiple-authored writing. Two or three authors work together in writing ideas on cards and then organizing them. The students could then each write their own sections or could work together as a group in writing each part.

6. Cloning an Author plays a similar role for readers in working at text organization as this activity plays for writers.

References

This strategy and its variations were developed by Stephen Kucer as part of his dissertation research. It has been extensively used and adapted by Myriam Revel-Wood. Further information on Generating Written Discourse can be found in:

Kucer, S. 1983. Using text comprehension as a metaphor for understanding text production: Building bridges between reading and writing. Ph.D. diss., Indiana University, Bloomington.

CURRICULAR COMPONENT

Getting to Know You

Introduction

Becoming an effective language user involves using language with other people for real purposes. Getting to Know You facilitates social interaction as each person learns something about another individual. Because the activity is informal, the language user's attention is focused on meaning. The reading and writing that occur are motivated by the need to record and convey meaning to others. In addition, this strategy focuses on the interrelationship of reading, writing, listening, and speaking.

Getting to Know You allows reluctant writers to see written language as a useful vehicle for helping them remember information. Because no one else reads their interview notes, the language users are encouraged to risk using functional spellings. This activity allows language users to discover the convenience of written language literacy as a vehicle in exploring their world. This strategy also effectively introduces students to the authoring cycle by quickly moving their writing from a rough draft to a publication in the classroom.

Materials/Procedures

* Paper and pencils

1. Students are told that they will be interviewing each other to produce a class newspaper or magazine that will introduce them to parents, visitors, or pen pals as well as to each other. There must be some real purpose for producing the newspaper.

2. The strategy is introduced by sharing an interview written by a student their age or by the teacher in a previous setting. The interview is read and then the notes and rough draft are shared to introduce students to the process they will be moving through in interviewing, taking notes, writing a rough draft, going to Authors' Circle, revising their draft, sending it to Editors' Table, and then publishing it in a newspaper or magazine.

3. The class can then either brainstorm some questions to ask during the interviews, or each student can think up individual questions.

4. Once students have some ideas of questions to ask, they pair up and conduct their interviews. They are encouraged to take notes during their interviews so they will be able to remember the information. They each make the decision, however, about how much and what to write down. The notes taken during interviewing can consist of drawings as well as words or phrases.

5. Students use their notes to write or dictate an article about the person they interviewed.

6. Once the students produce rough drafts, they take them to Authors' Circle to get suggestions for revision. It is better if the person who is the subject of the interview is not part of the Authors' Circle, because this tends to take ownership of the text away from the writer.

7. Following the Authors' Circle, the interview is revised and sent to the Editors' Table and then put into a publication that is shared with others.

Teacher's Role

The teacher should participate in these interviews along with the students and write an interview for publication. The teacher uses this strategy to introduce the authoring cycle so that students understand how a piece moves from the idea to a rough draft to a revised draft to an edited draft to a publication. As students complete their drafts, they begin writing other pieces for their Author's Folders.

Follow-Up

1. Intead of writing up the interviews, students can use their notes to introduce their partner orally to the rest of the group or to dictate their interview to the teacher for publication.

2. Extensions of this activity include interviews with community members on some local civic issue; interviews with authors, athletes, police officers, doctors, or others about their occupations; surveys of class members on specific topics; and collections of family stories.

3. "Shoebox" biographies can be used to introduce class members to each other. The teacher introduces the activity by bringing in five to ten personal items in a shoebox. These items are used to share a personal experience or interest. The students are then asked to interview each other and to use that interview to assemble items that reflect that person's interests into a shoebox biography of the person. Once the shoeboxes are assembled, the students use the shoeboxes to introduce the people they interviewed. Instead of shoeboxes, students could use a large bag or knapsack to make a "me bag."

4. Another way to introduce a person involves making a collage of words and pictures related to that person's life and interests.

Reference

Getting to Know You was originally developed by Carolyn Burke and Mary Lynn Woods.

Group Composed Books

Introduction

Writers are supported in the writing process when they share in writing texts with other writers. Through a shared writing process, writers are able to offer demonstrations to each other about strategies they use while composing. Less proficient writers are supported by the group process and feel less overwhelmed by the amount of writing they need to contribute to the book.

Materials/Procedures

* Paper and writing supplies

1. The content of a Group Composed Book should grow out of units of study or activities that are part of classroom life. The books may be initiated by the teacher or a student.
   a. Students can use the language pattern or plot structure of a favorite predictable book or a favorite author's book to create their own text. For example, they may use the pattern from *The Very Hungry Caterpillar* (Carle 1969) to write "The Very Hungry Tadpole" (change from tadpole to frog through eating each day) or "The Very Healthy Person" (change from unhealthy to healthy person through exercises each day). Figure CC14.1 is an example from a Group Composed Book based on *Rosie's Walk* (Hutchins 1968).
   b. Students can create an information book in which each page contains information about a topic the class has been studying ("What We Know About ——— ").
   c. Students can put together birthday books or thank-you

Figure CC14.1 Pages from First-Grade Group Book Based on *Rosie's Walk* (Hutchins 1968).

books that contain letters and messages for a child having a birthday or for a guest speaker.

d. Collections can include favorite nursery rhymes, songs, jump rope rhymes, environmental print, commercials, and so on.

2. Either the teacher or a student issues an invitation for class members to join a group to write a book on a particular topic.

3. The students who join the group discuss their ideas for what they want to write about. Time is spent raising ideas, exploring those ideas, and thinking about how to express those ideas.

4. The students in the group each write a page for the group book, and these are then gathered together. The process of writing can occur in two ways:

   a. After a group discussion about the topic of the book, each student individually writes and illustrates a page. These are then compiled and stapled into the book.

   b. After the group discusses what they might write about, one person, either the teacher or a student, acts as a scribe to write down the story on the blackboard as the group develops it together. Individual students may still compose a certain page but they do so knowing what the other pages say and with the support of the rest of the group. After the story is finished, each student is responsible for copying one page of the book from the blackboard and illustrating it. These pages are then assembled into a group book.

5. The finished book is read to the class with each student reading his or her contribution to the book, which is then placed into the classroom library.

Teacher's Role

In writing a Group Composed Book, a great deal of coordination and cooperation must occur among writers. The teacher needs to attend to the group dynamics and help students develop decision-making strategies as they struggle to reach consensus as a group, especially when the group works together to compose the book. In general, avoid taking a vote and having the majority rule and instead work to have the group reach a consensus that takes into consideration the differing perspectives of group members.

Journals

Introduction

Successful readers and writers have learned that the very process of writing produces growth and new understandings. Putting thoughts, feelings, and ideas into words is not a representation of what one knows, but an extension of that knowing. Language, like art and drama, is but one means of communication through which humans construct meaning and grow.

Writing plays many different functions in our lives; students should experience those different functions in the writing they do in the classroom. Journals can fulfill both an informal personal function and a recording function for the writer. In a journal, a writer makes a personal record of thoughts, feelings, happenings, plans, and problems. The content of a journal is thus open to each writer to decide. Journals allow students to explore writing for personal growth and reflection.

Journals can either be private or they can be informal dialogues with another person. Either way, they provide writers with an informal and safe situation in which they can focus on their own thoughts and feelings and on meaning and fluency, rather than on assigned topics or on conventions.

Materials/Procedures

* Pens, pencils, or other writing materials
* Spiral-bound notebooks or paper stapled into construction paper or wallpaper covers
* Date stamp

As the group works to write a Group Composed Book, encourage students to observe and discuss one another's composing strategies or to notice certain aspects of the written message. The group composing process can provide important demonstrations to writers. Be careful, however, of overdoing the talk about composing and thereby losing the focus on the story being developed.

Follow-Up

1. Instead of the whole class, small groups or pairs of students may decide to write a group book.
2. Group Composed Books may be performed as Readers' Theatres for other groups.
3. A traveling story can be created. One person begins to write a story and then passes the paper on to the next person, who adds to the story and then passes it on to another writer. This continues until the last person receives the story and writes an ending.
4. Teachers can take pictures of classroom events, either daily activities or special events. These pictures are then placed in Photo Group Composed Books and individual students either write or dictate a description or story about what they were doing in each picture.
5. See Shared Reading for the counterpart of this strategy in reading.

References

This particular version of Group Composed Books was written by Kathy Short and Jerome Harste. Parts of the strategy were adapted from Moira McKenzie's work at the London Centre for Language in Primary Education. For a description of Photo Group Composed Books, see:

Mills, H. A. 1986. Evaluating literacy: A transactional process. Ph.D. diss., Indiana University, Bloomington.

1. The teacher should introduce the journal to the class and describe the type of entry students will be writing. If the journals are private journals (see Figure CC15.1), bring in diaries or books that contain diary entries and share these with students. If the journals are dialogue journals (see Figure CC15.2), briefly share some examples of this type of journal in which two people write comments back and forth to each other.

2. Each day students get their journals, write or stamp the date at the top of the page, and write their entry. Entries can include drawings or sketches as well as writing.

3. Journals are returned to the box or space where they are

Corey 11-19-84

Monday I was
sike and I was
coffing to much
and it hrte win
I coffed and
teecher didit
like wen coffed
beckus it sowdid
Like I was
blowen my guts
out the end

10/4

Yesterday I went to Kings
Island. I went with lots
of girl scouts. We all
went by bus. It was
fun. I rode on almost
everything. From the
Beastie To the
Backward Racer

I like King's Island Too.
Its the only one with
really good rides. I think
its evin better than Walt
Disney World.
                Mrs. Wood

Figure CC15.1 Journal Entry (Corey, Grade 1).

Figure CC15.2 Dialogue Journal (Alison, Grade 4).

stored. If the journals are dialogue journals, they are placed at an agreed-on spot for response. If the student wants a particular person to respond to the journal, it could be placed on the person's desk.

4. Some type of system needs to be worked out for entries that the student does not want anyone to read. Such pages can be marked VP (very private), folded over, or stapled shut.

Teacher's Role

The teacher's first role is carefully to introduce the journals to the class. Especially if journals are private, it may take a while before students really begin to explore the function that private writing can play. This private function is often an unfamiliar one in their lives and in the lives of their family members, so initially they may not know what to write in their journals. Teachers should talk about the function that journals will play in the classroom and describe some of the things students might write in their journals. Actual diaries or books that contain diaries, such as *Dear Mr. Henshaw* (Cleary 1983) or *A Gathering of Days* (Blos 1979) could be read to students or used as a set in Literature Circles to introduce students to journals. Another source of examples are primary historical documents, such as the journals of historical figures like Benjamin Franklin or Paul Revere.

Private journals are not shared with others unless a student chooses to do so. The agreement teachers usually make with students on private journals is that the teacher will occasionally read through the journal, except for pages indicated private, but will not write or comment in the journal. Some teachers do not read the journals at all but simply do a quick check or page count to see that the student is writing entries.

Dialogue journals are shared with others, either the teacher or classmates. The reader writes a response to the journal's content in the journal. Dialogue journals become a written dialogue between the journal owner and a selected partner. They are an expanded Written Conversation. The teacher may first want to demonstrate the type of journal responses that are appropriate by writing the first several responses in journals before students respond to others' journals. It is important that responses deal with the feelings of the writer, not surface conventions. If dialogue journals are used, the teacher will need to set up a good system for the exchange of journals.

Providing a sufficient amount of time for journal writing on a regular basis is critical to the success of Journals. Students need to be able to predict when journal writing will occur so they can be thinking about what they want to write. Initially, it is important to have a special time set aside for journal writing. Later it can be one of the tasks that students perform during their Work Time. One time that seems to work well for journals is right away when students arrive at school.

Journals will play differing roles in the lives of students. Some students will write long, involved entries, while others will write brief entries or say they have nothing to write. Sometimes a student will have little to write in a journal for several weeks (or months) and then will suddenly write long entries. Teachers need to have patience and to support students having difficulty with journal writing, as well as to allow for individual variation in the role that journal writing plays for students. Sometimes, teachers ask all students to write in their journals for the first several months and then let students individually decide whether they will continue the journal.

Some teachers have found it helpful initially to have students brainstorm on topics they can write about in their journals or for the teacher to mention a few ideas that students could write about on a given day. Although this may be used to get journals going, journals are personal writing and therefore are not appropriate places for assigning topics. Assigning topics destroys the purpose for which journals exist.

Teachers should have their own journals and write in them when students write. If dialogue journals are being used, teachers should place their journals out for response just as the students do.

Follow-Up

1. The type of journal being used in the classroom, private or dialogue, can change according to the needs of the class. Teachers may begin with private journals and then switch to dialogue journals, or vice versa. Students can also be given an option of which type of journal entry they want to write. After they finish their journal entry, they can either put their

journal away if they want it to be private or take it to a partner for response.

2. A variation of dialogue journals used by Mary Lynn Woods is to have students write their journal entries as homework each evening. Students write about their own topics, or the class agrees on a particular topic that everyone will make an entry about. Each morning the students place their journals on a table. During the day, each student (and the teacher) responds to two other journals.

3. Some teachers use the journals as private journals, but set aside one day a week for a sharing session. Students always know on which day they will get together in small groups and share their entries, and so they write an entry that they feel comfortable making public. This variation allows students to use the journals for both personal and sharing purposes and demonstrates other possibilities for journal entries.

4. Walking Journals are a more public variation of dialogue journals. They are a public dialogue among various class members over issues of interest to the group. At various times students are invited to share their thinking about class projects, events, or problems. The Walking Journal is a class journal that is passed around from person to person; each person has the opportunity to write in the journal, sharing thoughts on the topic being discussed as well as responding to previous entries. The teacher takes a turn just like everyone else.

5. Students may keep Reflective Journals, in which they write what they are thinking about as they read a complex text. They can jot down notes as they read and later expand these notes into journal entries, explaining what they thought about as well as what in the text triggered their thinking.

6. See Written Conversation and Learning Logs for other variations.

References

Heine, D. In process. A collaborative study of school change. Ph.D. diss., Indiana University, Bloomington.

Staton, J.; Shuy, R.; Kreeft, J.; & Reed, L. 1986. *Interactive writing in dialogue journals.* Norwood, NJ: Ablex.

Appendix: Children's Books That Contain Diaries

Blos, J. 1979. *A gathering of days: A New England girl's journal, 1830–32.*
   New York: Scribner.
Cleary, B. 1983. *Dear Mr. Henshaw.* New York: Morrow.
Fitzhugh, L. 1964. *Harriet the spy.* New York: Harper & Row.
Frank, A. 1967. *Anne Frank: The diary of a young girl.* New York:
   Doubleday.
Harvey, B. 1986. *My prairie year: Based on the diary of Elenore Plaisted.*
   New York: Holiday House.

Learning Logs

Introduction

Learners not only need time to engage in many different reading and writing experiences, but they also need time to reflect on what they are learning and the processes they have used in that learning. When learners reflect, they come to value the strategies they are developing through engaging in reading and writing and through observing the demonstrations of other readers and writers around them. Learning Logs provide learners with the opportunity to reflect on both process and content in reading and writing, as well as in various units of study in fields such as math, science, social studies, and literature.

Learning Logs give teachers, parents, and students another source of information and evaluation on what students are learning. Students often fail to recognize the small steps they are making in learning. Learning Logs provide students with an opportunity to reflect on the day's activities and to ask themselves, "What have I learned today?" Because Learning Logs are informal and personal, the focus of students is on communicating ideas or problems with what they are learning rather than on correct spelling or grammar.

Materials/Procedures

* Pencils or pens
* Spiral notebooks or paper stapled into covers
* Date stamp

1. At the end of an activity, a morning, or an entire day, students take out their Learning Logs, stamp or write the date, and make an entry.

286

2. Students are asked to write about something new they learned that day at school. They can respond either to what they learned—content—or how they went about learning it—process (see Figure CC16.1).

If students have difficulty focusing on something new that was learned, the entries can be introduced as writing a reaction or response to the day or to a particular activity. Students should also be encouraged to make connections in their entries between the new learning and what they already knew (see Figure CC16.2).

Questions that can be used to help students think about their entries are: What did I understand about the work I did in class today? What didn't I understand? At what point did I get confused or did I begin to understand? What do I know now that I didn't know when I got to school today? What can I do better today than I could yesterday? What do I have questions about or wonder about?

It may sometimes be helpful to have a brief discussion of

10-2-86

I just got done reading the Westing Game. I liked it a lot. Saturday when I was reading The Westing Game I stoped to go to something else but I couldn't do anything but read on and on. Was it that way when you read it?

I don't know what my favorit part is. I guess I liked it all.

Now I'm reading Cousins at Camm Corners. I've just started the book but I can already tell that I'm not going to like this book as much as the Westing Game.

When you read a book that you realy like it's hard to go and read another book that is not as good as the one before.

The first chapter, beginning on page 7 makes great sense to me. I can "see" how we make language development hard by breaking it into parts.

I know from experience the difficulty even children in the "advanced" reading group can have with memorizing meanings for prefixes and suffixes. Yet, I am asked to teach and test that skill. I'm not sure I could pass the test. It doesn't make sense to me either.

What are we doing?

Figure CC16.1 Literature Log Entry (Andrea, Grade 6).

Figure CC16.2 Connections by an Adult to *What's Whole in Whole Language?* (Goodman 1986).

the day's events before students write to encourage them to select from the entire day rather than the most recent event.

3. After students have written for about ten minutes, they should be invited to share their entries with each other. This sharing is especially important when Learning Logs are first introduced. Later on, the sharing may occur only occasionally.

4. Teachers may choose to write a response to students' entries in their Learning Logs.

Teacher's Role

Before introducing the logs, the teacher may want to have several discussions with students about what they are learning. After a science activity or other special learning event, ask the students to talk about what they have learned that they didn't know before participating in the activity. Through the discussion, highlight the inevitable fact that different people chose to talk about different aspects of the activity and that what we learn depends on what we already know and find interesting. After several discussions, the Learning Logs can then be introduced.

Many students will initially find it difficult to know what to write about. Much of our learning remains at a tacit level, and they will need some time to begin recognizing what and how they are learning. Having a brief sharing time and writing a response to student entries are both methods of facilitating the responses of students in their logs. When these logs are used on a regular basis, students begin to search for the learning potential as they engage in activities.

Teachers can support the student who never seems to have something to write about by observing that student's activities during the day and making note of special accomplishments. The observations can be shared with the student or used to ask open-ended questions to help the student.

Learning Logs require a trusting atmosphere in which students feel free to explore their ideas and to talk about what they *don't* know as well as what they *do* know. If teachers are responding to the logs, they should refrain from making judgmental or evaluative comments. Teachers should also keep their own Learning Logs and write in them at the same time that the students write. A teacher Learning Log can sharpen observational skills and help the teacher gain confidence that some progress is being made in his or her own growth.

Teachers and students need to decide what type of Learning Logs will be used in the classroom. Several different kinds of logs can be used at the same time. These logs can be used at the end of the day, and students can respond to any instance of learning, or they can be used specifically in relation to a particular area of study. For example, at the end of a math lesson, the teacher might ask the students to spend five to ten minutes writing an entry about math in their Learning Logs. No matter what types of logs are used, teachers must make sure that students have a sufficient amount of time on a regular basis for writing in their logs.

Students will often find that language is not sufficient to record their learnings. Teachers should encourage students to move into art and other types of symbols, such as arrows, mathematical symbols, charts, and graphs, to present their ideas.

Follow-Up

1. Literature Logs are Learning Logs in which students write about their responses to a particular piece of literature. These logs can be used for students to write their responses to the literature they read independently, to the class read-aloud book, or to the literature they are reading for Literature Circles. Students should be encouraged to write their reactions and responses rather than a summary of the story (see Figure CC16.3).

   Nancie Atwell had her students write in their Literature Logs about books they were reading independently. Their entries took the form of a letter to her in which they discussed what they thought and felt about what they read, what they liked and didn't like, and what the book meant to them. In addition, they could ask her questions or ask for help and could respond to her written comments. The teacher writes letters back to the students responding both to the student's letter and to the book itself.

   Another type of Literature Log is made by stapling five or six bookmark-sized pieces of paper together. The students use the log as both a bookmark and a log on which to record their thoughts while reading.

2. Science Logs can be used by students to record their explorations and experiments during a science unit or in a science center. These entries can include their questions, the materials they used and the steps they went through in an ex-

The book read is called ⊙ The Basket Courts. I felt kind of sad for Mel because some of the other boys made fun of him. I thought it was good because at the end Mel helped one of the boys get out of cold water that he fell in when he was skating. After that they were pretty good friends. I liked how they beat about every game because that made Mel feel better. I didn't like when one of the boys fell in the cold water because I thought he was going to drown. It told me how you make friends if somebody gets hurt help them. It makes me think of when my brother fell in the water tank. I helped him out. Can you make some connections with ✏ what I wrote?

Boy Daryl -- You're really going to make me think. I'll go answer another person's journal while I'm thinking.

OK, I'm back. I think one connection I could make is when one of my best friends from college and I had some miscommunication and we didn't know what to say to each other for awhile and then when I helped her out at her house one day, we became friends again.

Also this reminds me of Jesse in Bridge to Terabithia. Jesse didn't really appreciate May Belle because he thought she was a tag along and a pest. Then at the end after Leslie had died May Belle followed Jess to Terabithia to cheer him up and she got caught in the middle of the bridge and was scared to go any further. Jess then needed to help her across. I think Jess realized how May Belle looked up to him and wanted to be his friend and help him out. Jess then became friends with May Belle.

Do you agree with my connections?

Ms Y

Figure CC16.3   Literature Log Entry (Daryl, Grade 6) and Teacher's Response.

periment, their predictions, their findings, and their ideas for future experiments or observations. These logs can be kept in the science center for other students to refer to as they do their own experiments.

3. A class observation log can be kept next to classroom animals or to a particular classroom experiment such as growing plants. Anyone can make an entry in the class log of observations about the animal or plants.

4. Other types of logs, such as math logs or logs on a particular social studies unit, can be used in the classroom (see Figure CC16.4).

5. A class Learning Log can be kept. At the end of each day, the class discusses significant events that occurred. The class can then either dictate an entry on a language experience chart or each day one student can be assigned to write an entry in the log for the class. The class entries can be bound into a class book or used in a weekly class newsletter to let parents know what is happening at school.

I leaned there are diffrent ways im math to do things.
I like the game we played.
I learned there are games you can make and it can have math in them. I am begening to like math.
I think we are learning som thing.
I want to learn how to carry and when you don't need to carry. I want to Learn how to divid and Maltoply.

Figure CC16.4   Math Journal Entry (Sherri, Grade 3).

6. Students can be asked to reflect on their understandings about a particular topic at a number of different points in time. Before the unit or topic is introduced to the class, they can write what they already know about it and what they predict the topic might involve. During the time they are involved with the topic, they can write their understandings and responses. Once the unit of study has ended, students can write a reflective entry looking back over the whole experience.

7. A related log is a project or research log that students keep as they work on individual research projects. In this log, they write what they already know about the topic, their questions, a list of sources they want to check for further information, and notes about their research.

   A variation of the research log is a log used by Nancy Shanklin in her college classes. She has her students do a "Learn Something New" project. They keep Learning Logs documenting all the reading, writing, speaking, and listening they do as they research their topic. At the end of the course, students use their logs to write a paper reflecting on their learning processes and how they used language to learn.

8. At the end of each grading period or at the end of the year, students can be asked to look back through their Learning Log entries and to write a self-evaluative entry about their learning during that time period.

References

Many different people have worked at developing the various types of Learning Logs. Below are listed several sources of further information on Learning Logs:

Atwell, N. 1984. Writing and reading literature from the inside out. *Language Arts* 61(3):240-252.

——— . 1987. *In the middle: Writing, reading, and learning with adolescents.* Portsmouth, NH: Boynton/Cook-Heinemann.

Pierce, K. M. 1986. Curriculum as collaboration: Toward practical theory. Ph.D. diss., Indiana University, Bloomington. (Includes examples of both Learning Logs and Science Logs.)

Literature Circles

Introduction

Readers need time to read both extensively for enjoyment and information and intensively to deepen and enrich a reading experience. When readers are given time to respond to a book, they make the ideas encountered in the literature personally meaningful and are able to extend those ideas in a variety of ways. Through talking about books with others, readers are given the time they need to absorb and savor a book so that the book becomes a significant part of their life experiences.

Talking about a piece of literature with others gives readers time to explore half-formed ideas, to expand their understandings of literature through hearing others' interpretations, and to become readers who think critically and deeply about what they read. Readers need to understand that a variety of interpretations exist for any piece of literature and that they can collaboratively explore their interpretations with one another to reach new understandings. Literature Circles help readers become literate.

Literature provides readers with an important way of learning about the world. Literature combines both knowing and feeling. Literature educates and entertains. It stretches the imagination, allowing readers to see their world in a new way and to imagine other possible worlds. The stories we create from our experiences allow us to bring meaning to those experiences and to understand how our world works. Literature, however, is just one kind of literacy that students need to become proficient readers. There are many different kinds of reading materials in addition to literature that students should be reading, such as magazines, newspapers, directions, maps, and so on.

Materials/Procedures

* Multiple copies of good literature that will support intensive discussion

1. Several pieces of literature should be selected by the teacher, the students, or both. These are introduced to the class by giving short book talks and then making the books available for the students to browse through. For young children, the teacher may read each choice aloud to the class.

2. Students must then decide whether they want to sign up for a Literature Circle and which one they want to join. This choice can be indicated either by signing up on a chart for a certain piece of literature or by having students mark their first and second choices on a piece of paper that they give to the teacher, who then forms the groups. These groups should have four or five members.

3. Students read the piece of literature and meet in Literature Circles to discuss the book. There are several variations depending on whether students read the book before beginning the discussion.

   a. Students must read the piece of literature before coming to the circle. Students reading longer chapter books can read these the preceding week, either as homework or during their extensive reading time. For young children who cannot read the literature independently, teachers can read the literature to them and then place the literature with a tape in the listening center.

   b. Students read the literature as they discuss it. Each day, the group meets to discuss briefly the part of the literature they read the previous day and to decide as a group what they will read for the next day. Once the book is finished, the group meets for more intensive discussion of the entire book.

4. Literature Circles usually last anywhere from two days to a week, depending on the length of the book and the depth of the discussion about the book. Often only half the class is involved in Literature Circles at any one time, and the others are doing extensive reading, Literature Response Activities, writing, and so on.

5. The Literature Circle discussions are open-ended, focusing on bringing the literature and the reader together. The fol-

lowing are some variations in how these discussions can be conducted:

a. The teacher begins the discussion on the first day by asking a broad question, such as "What was this story about?" or by asking students to "Talk about this book while I listen." From this initial discussion, the teacher gets an idea of which aspects of the book the students find the most interesting. The teacher participates as a member of the group, contributing comments and asking open-ended questions. The direction of the discussion in the Literature Circle and the types of questions asked depend on what the readers are most interested in and on which aspects of the book are most outstanding. For example, if the book is an excellent example of character development or description of setting, then this as well as the students' interests would influence the focus of discussion. Group members should be encouraged to make links between the book and their life experiences as well as other pieces of literature. This should be done in a way that deepens and extends their understanding of the literature without taking them away from the story.

b. The group can begin by discussing reactions to the book, sharing favorite parts, and raising questions about parts that they did not understand or that surprised them. The group then makes a list of issues or questions they want to discuss. They use this list to guide their discussion over the next few days.

6. At the end of each day's discussion, the group should decide on what they want to talk about the next time they meet. This gives students time to reread certain sections of the book and to think about the topic or question so they are more prepared to talk the next time. Some teachers give students the option of writing their ideas in Literature Logs. The Literature Circle then begins by having students share from their logs.

7. Although the teacher will often begin as the leader of Literature Circles, once the students understand how these groups operate, the teacher should not always be involved as a member or leader. The section on the teacher's role discusses a variety of ways to involve teachers and students in the circles.

8. At the conclusion of a Literature Circle, the members of that circle can be asked to present the book to the rest of the

class or to write personal responses to the book in Literature Logs.

Teacher's Role

For Literature Circles to be successful, there needs to be a classroom environment already established that supports risk taking and varied constructions of meaning from reading. If the students feel that they must reproduce what the teacher thinks is *the* meaning of a piece of literature, the Literature Circles will not be productive. Students who have a long literacy history of basal reading groups may initially treat Literature Circles as basal reader discussions and focus on the text to come up with the "right" interpretation. They will be used to sitting back and answering the teacher's questions and may not know how to talk and work collaboratively with other students. The teacher will need to provide other kinds of curricular strategies to establish a learning environment that supports Literature Circles and should not be discouraged if students say little when they first become involved in these discussions.

Some curricular strategies that will help establish a supportive learning atmosphere include Sketch to Stretch, Say Something, Save the Last Word for Me, Written Conversation, Literature Logs, Literature Response Activities, Readers' Theatre, Uninterrupted Reading and Writing, and so on. It is essential that students have time daily to read widely from many different kinds of reading materials. They also need to be authors who have published their own writing and participated in Authors' Circles. The discussions in Authors' Circles have a major impact on Literature Circles. The teacher should be reading aloud to the class and using the whole-class discussions after reading aloud to demonstrate the types of questions and topics that the students can focus on in Literature Circles. In addition, students should be involved in responding over time in a variety of ways to literature including art, music, drama, writing, and so on.

Literature Circles should be connected to other parts of the curriculum. If students are focusing on a study of families or different cultures, then literature can be chosen that deals with family situations or the clash of cultures. If students are reading a particular genre, such as folktales, they should be invited to try writing their own folktales; or if students are going to be writing some type of nonfiction report, Literature Circles can focus on nonfiction.

The depth of discussion in Literature Circles depends on the rich history of stories to which the pieces of literature being discussed are connected. There are various ways that this rich history can be built: use of familiar stories that students have heard over and over, multiple readings of the same story in the classroom, relating the book to other books read previously in the classroom through topic, genre, theme, author, and so on, or relating the literature to themes or topics being discussed in the classroom.

During the initial circles, the teacher should demonstrate the types of questions and discussion behaviors that are appropriate to establish a supportive context for sharing and constructing interpretations of literature. Varied interpretations are accepted as long as the reader can support them. Readers are asked to support and explain what they say, rather than simply making statements about their reading experience with a particular book. The teacher also encourages readers to explore each others' interpretations and collaboratively to build new understandings of the literature during the Literature Circle. Literature Circles are a time of exploration with one another, not a time to present a formal or final interpretation of a particular piece of literature. Readers need to listen to each other (that includes the teacher) and to build off of each others' comments. Both the students and the teacher should reply to one another rather than assess, to avoid cutting off discussion.

Literature Circles can be organized in a variety of ways so that teachers and students share in the control of these groups. Although the groups will probably begin with the teacher taking an active role as the group leader, the teacher needs to allow students to take over and direct the discussion. Because of the teacher's greater experience and knowledge, the teacher's presence in Literature Circles influences the dynamics of the group. Teachers can change their role from leader to member by waiting for student responses rather than dominating the discussion and by occasionally offering their own opinions about what is being discussed rather than asking questions. Teachers can offer differing amounts of support and share control with students by trying different variations of the circles in which they are sometimes present and at other times circulate from group to group, or not join the group at all. Instead of the teacher serving as the source of open-ended questions or of a broad focus for the discussion, students can come to the circle with their own questions or focus. These options ensure that the groups have a specific purpose or problem that is being discussed but vary who is establishing that purpose or problem: the teacher, the students, or teacher and students together.

The teacher needs to obtain multiple copies of books, especially if the books are chapter books. Picture books can be easily shared among the group members, but students need their own copies of the longer books. Check the libraries, other teachers, Chapter 1 and resource teacher collections, and closets. Use the bonus points from paperback book clubs to buy sets. See if the school will let you use some of your textbook or workbook money to buy sets (get several teachers to join together and share sets). See if you can get money to buy sets through the parent-teacher organization or a fundraiser. Short stories and poems can be photocopied. Remember that picture books are not just for young children but can be used productively with older readers. It is best to use a variety of literature, including fiction and nonfiction, poetry, short stories, picture books, and chapter books.

Follow-Up

1. Students may discuss one piece of literature that everyone has read.

2. Students may discuss a variety of texts that are related in some way (see Text Sets).

3. The circle may focus on literature by a particular author or poet.

4. Students may discuss literature by a local author who can then visit the group.

5. By discussing literature written by class members, Literature Circles may recognize the authorship of children within the room and can lead to interesting and insightful discussions. The group first meets and discusses the book without the author present and then invites the author to join the group.

6. Any of the discussions described can occur in groups that cut across grade levels.

7. Calkins (1986) describes literature groups in which the teacher had the entire class reading the same genre. Each day, the teacher had a secret question for the students to discuss. After discussing the question in small groups, the class then came together as a whole to discuss the question. Sometimes

the small groups had read the same book and, at other times, each child had read a different book. However, because the books came from the same genre (mystery stories), the students were able to discuss the questions productively with one another.

8. Karen Smith uses read-aloud time to help students listen and build their comments off of each other. After reading aloud, she steps outside the group and asks them to discuss the chapter while she takes notes. At the end of the discussion, she shares her observations with the students, particularly noting any comments that students made that built off of what someone else had said.

References

The concept of Literature Circles was developed by Kathy Short and Gloria Kauffman, based on Karen Smith's work with literature studies. Their initial exploration of this curricular strategy is discussed in:

Short, K. G. 1986. Literacy as a collaborative experience. Ph.D. diss., Indiana University, Bloomington.

Other references include:

Barnes, D. 1975. *From communication to curriculum*. New York: Penguin.
Calkins, L. M. 1986. *The art of teaching writing*, chapters 22-24. Portsmouth, NH: Heinemann.
Hepler, S. I. 1982. Patterns of response to literature: A one-year study of a fifth and sixth grade classroom. Ph.D. diss., Ohio State University, Columbus.
Huck, C. 1977. Literature as the content of reading. *Theory into Practice* 16(5):363-371.
Sloan, G. 1984. *The child as critic*. 2nd ed. New York: Teachers College Press.
Vandergrift, K. 1980. *Child and story*. New York: Neal-Schuman.

Appendix A: Examples of Open-Ended Questions

The following questions are taken from *The Child as Critic*, 2d ed., by Glenna Davis Sloan. New York: Teachers College Press, 1984.

1. Where and when does the story take place? How do you know? If the story took place somewhere else or in a different time, how would it be changed?

2. What incident, problem, conflict, or situation does the author use to get the story started?

3. What does the author do to create suspense, to make you want to read on to find out what happens?

4. Trace the main events of the story. Could you change their order or leave any of them out? Why or why not?

5. Think of a different ending to the story. How would the rest of the story have to be changed to fit the new ending?

6. Did the story end the way you expected it to? What clues did the author offer to prepare you to expect this ending? Did you recognize these clues as important to the story as you were first reading/hearing it?

7. Who is the main character of the story? What kind of person is the character? How do you know?

8. Are any characters changed during the story? If they are, how are they different? What changed them? Did it seem believable?

9. Some characters play small but important roles in a story. Name such a character. Why is this character necessary for the story?

10. Who is the teller of the story? How would the story change if someone else in the book or an outside narrator told the story?

11. Does the story as a whole create a certain mood or feeling? What is the mood? How is it created?

12. Did you have strong feelings as you read the story? What did the author do to make you feel strongly?

13. What are the main ideas behind the story? What makes you think of them as you read the story?

14. Is this story like any other story you have read or watched?

15. Think about the characters in the story. Are any of them the same type of character that you have met in other stories?

The following questions are taken from *Child and Story,* by Kay Vandergrift. New York: Neal-Schuman Publishers, 1980.

1. What idea or ideas does this story make you think about? How does the author get you to think about this?

2. Do any particular feelings come across in this story? Does the story actually make you feel in a certain way or does it make you think about what it's like to feel that way? How does the author do this?

3. Is there one character that you know more about than any of the others? Who is this character and what kind of person is he/she? How does the author reveal the character to you? What words would you use to describe the main character's feelings in this book?

4. Are there other characters important to the story? Who are they? Why are they important?

5. Is there anything that seems to make this particular author's work unique? If so, what?

6. Did you notice any particular patterns in the form of this book? If you are reading this book in more than one sitting, are there natural points at which to break off your reading? If so, what are these?

7. Were there any clues that the author built into the story that helped you to anticipate the outcome? If so, what were they? Did you think these clues were important when you read them?

8. Does the story language seem natural for the intent of the story and for the various speakers?

9. Every writer creates a make-believe work and peoples it with characters. Even where the world is far different from your own, how does the author make the story seem possible or probable?

10. What questions would you ask if the author were here? Which would be the most important question? How might the author answer it?

Appendix B: Literature to Explore

Picture Books

Aardema, V. 1975. *Why mosquitoes buzz in people's ears*. New York: Dial.
Anderson, H. C. 1979. *The ugly duckling*. New York: Harcourt Brace Jovanovich.
Bulla, R. 1955. *The poppy seeds*. New York: Crowell.
Carle, E. 1977. *The grouchy ladybug*. New York: Crowell.
Carrick, C. 1976. *The accident*. New York: Clarion.

Cooney, B. 1982. *Miss Rumphius*. New York: Viking.

de Paola, T. 1978. *The clown of God*. New York: Harcourt Brace Jovanovich.

Freschet, B. 1973. *Bear mouse*. New York: Scribner.

Galdone, P. 1970. *The three little pigs*. New York: Clarion.

Hazen, B. 1979. *Tight times*. New York: Viking.

Hodges, M. 1984. *Saint George and the dragon*. Boston: Little, Brown.

Innocenti, R. 1985. *Rose Blanche*. Mankato, MN: Creative Education.

Keats, E. J. 1967. *Peter's chair*. New York: Harper & Row.

———— . 1968. *A letter to Amy*. New York: Harper & Row.

Lionni, L. 1963. *Swimmy*. New York: Pantheon.

———— .1967. *Frederick*. New York: Pantheon.

Lobel, A. 1967. *Potatoes, potatoes*. New York: Harper & Row.

———— . 1972. *Frog and toad together*. New York: Harper & Row.

———— . 1982. *Ming Lo moves the mountain*. New York: Greenwillow.

Luenn, N. 1982. *The dragon kite*. New York: Harcourt Brace Jovanovich.

Maruki, T. 1980. *Hiroshima no pika*. New York: Lothrop, Lee, and Shepard.

Mayer, M. 1968. *There's a nightmare in my closet*. New York: Dial.

———— . 1976. *Everyone knows what a dragon looks like*. New York: Four Winds.

Miles, M. 1979. *Annie and the old one*. Boston: Little, Brown.

Ness, E. 1967. *Sam, bangs and moonshine*. New York: Holt, Rinehart & Winston.

Perrault, C. 1954. *Cinderella*. Illustrated by M. Brown. New York: Scribner.

Sendak, M. 1963. *Where the wild things are*. New York: Harper & Row.

———— . 1981. *Outside over there*. New York: Harper & Row.

Spier, P. 1977. *Noah's ark*. Garden City, NY: Doubleday.

Steig, W. 1977. *Caleb and Kate*. New York: Farrar Straus Giroux.

———— . 1979. *Sylvester and the magic pebble*. New York: Windmill.

Steptoe, J. 1969. *Stevie*. New York: Harper & Row.

———— . 1984. *The story of the jumping mouse*. New York: Lothrop, Lee, and Shepard.

Van Allsburg, C. 1981. *Jumanji*. Boston: Houghton Mifflin.

———— . 1984. *The mysteries of Harris Burdick*. Boston: Houghton Mifflin.

Waber, B. 1972. *Ira sleeps over*. Boston: Houghton Mifflin.

Ward, L. 1952. *The biggest bear*. Boston: Houghton Mifflin.

Wilde, O. 1984. *The selfish giant*. Natick, MA: Picture Book Studio.

Yashima, T. 1955. *Crow boy*. New York: Viking.

Yolen, J. 1977. *The seeing stick*. New York: Crowell.

Zolotow, C. 1972. *William wants a doll*. New York: Harper & Row.

Chapter Books

Alexander, L. 1965. *The black cauldron*. New York: Holt, Rinehart & Winston (Also other Prydain books).

———— . 1981. *Westmark*. New York: Dutton.

Armstrong, W. 1969. *Sounder.* New York: Harper & Row.

Babbit, N. 1975. *Tuck everlasting.* New York: Farrar Straus Giroux.

Banks, L. R. 1981. *The Indian in the cupboard.* Garden City, NY: Double-day.

Bishop, C. 1964. *Twenty and ten.* New York: Viking.

Burnett, F. [1910] 1962. *The secret garden.* New York: Lippincott.

Byars, B. 1970. *Summer of the swans.* New York: Viking.

——— . 1977. *The pinballs.* New York: Harper & Row.

Cleary, B. 1983. *Dear Mr. Henshaw.* New York: Morrow.

Collier, J., & Collier, C. 1974. *My brother Sam is dead.* New York: Four Winds.

Coerr, E. 1977. *Sadako and the thousand paper cranes.* New York: Putnam.

Estes, E. 1944. *The hundred dresses.* New York: Harcourt Brace World.

Fox, P. 1984. *One-eyed cat.* New York: Bradbury.

Fritz, J. 1982. *Homesick: My own story.* New York: Putnam.

George, J. 1972. *Julie of the wolves.* New York: Harper & Row.

Hunter, M. 1975. *A stranger came ashore.* New York: Harper & Row.

Juster, N. 1961. *The phantom tollbooth.* New York: Random House.

L'Engle, M. 1962. *Wrinkle in time.* New York: Farrar Straus Giroux.

——— . 1981. *Ring of endless light.* New York: Farrar Straus Giroux.

LeGuin, U. 1968. *Wizard of Earthsea.* Emeryville, CA: Parnassus.

Lewis, C. S. 1961. *The lion, the witch, and the wardrobe,* New York: Macmillan.

Lowry, L. 1977. *A summer to die.* Boston: Houghton Mifflin.

MacLachlan, P. 1985. *Sarah plain and tall.* New York: Harper & Row.

——— . *Seven kisses in a row.* New York: Harper & Row.

McKinley, R. 1978. *Beauty.* New York: Harper & Row.

——— . 1982. *The blue sword.* New York: Greenwillow.

O'Brien, R. 1971. *Mrs. Frisby and the rats of NIMH.* New York: Atheneum.

O'Dell, S. 1960. *Island of the blue dolphins.* Boston: Houghton Mifflin.

——— . 1970. *Sing down the moon.* Boston: Houghton Mifflin.

Paterson, K. 1977. *Bridge to Terabithia.* New York: Crowell.

——— . 1978. *The great Gilly Hopkins.* New York: Crowell.

——— . 1980. *Jacob have I loved.* New York: Crowell.

Raskin, E. 1978. *The Westing game.* New York: Dutton.

Rawls, W. 1961. *Where the red fern grows.* Garden City, NY: Doubleday.

Rylant, C. 1986. *Every living thing.* New York: Bradbury.

Smith, D. B. 1973. *A taste of blackberries.* New York: Crowell.

——— . 1975. *Kelly's creek.* New York: Crowell.

Smith, R. 1984. *The war with grandpa.* New York: Delacorte.

Speare, E. 1983. *Sign of the beaver.* Boston: Houghton Mifflin.

Taylor, M. 1976. *Roll of thunder, hear my cry.* New York: Dial.

——— . 1981. *Let the circle be unbroken.* New York: Dial.

——— . 1987. *The gold cadillac.* New York: Dial.

Taylor, T. 1969. *The cay.* Garden City, NY: Doubleday.

——— . 1981. *The trouble with Tuck.* Garden City, NY: Doubleday.

Voight, C. 1982. *Dicey's song.* New York: Atheneum.
—— . 1984. *Solitary blue.* New York: Atheneum.
—— . 1987. *Come a stranger.* New York: Atheneum.
Yolen, J. 1974. *The girl who cried flowers.* New York: Schocken.
—— . 1977. *The hundredth dove.* New York: Schocken.

Poetry

Greenfield, E. 1978. *Honey, I love.* New York: Crowell.
Livingston, M. 1958. *Whispers and other poems.* New York: Harcourt Brace World.
McCord, D. 1977. *One at a time.* Boston: Little, Brown.
Merriam, E. 1984. *Jamboree.* New York: Dell.
—— . 1986. *A sky full of poems.* New York: Dell.
Prelutsky, J. 1984. *The new kid on the block.* New York: Greenwillow.

See Text Sets (pages 358-365) for examples of the following sets of literature:

1. Variations of the same folktale
2. Versions of the same folktale
3. Books by one author or illustrator
4. Books on a certain theme or topic
5. Books in the same genre
6. The same text with different illustrators
7. Books with similar structures
8. Books with the same characters
9. Books written from the same culture

Literature Response Activities

Introduction

Readers deepen and extend their interpretations of literature when they respond to that literature in a variety of ways. Involving readers in response activities allows language users to savor and absorb books and gives them time for reflection. Both verbal and nonverbal responses should be encouraged. When readers move from reading to writing or from reading to art or drama, they take a new perspective on the piece of literature. In the process of trying to express their interpretation of the literature through various sign systems, they discover new meanings and expand their understandings of what they had earlier read. Students need the chance to respond to literature in a variety of ways over time. Their responses become more complex and reflective when response is not seen as a one-shot affair.

Materials/Procedures

* Literature
* Supplies needed for responses through talking, writing, art, drama, movement, music, and so on

1. A piece of literature should be read individually, in small groups, or as a whole class.
2. Students should have time to share their responses to a particular book informally with one another.
3. The teacher should invite students to explore the variety of ways in which they can respond to a piece of literature. Supplies for the various kinds of responses should be located in a center for easy access by students. A brainstormed list

305

of possible ways to respond to a book should also be in the center.

The following is a list of some types of response activities:

a. Book Sales involve students in creating a commercial to sell a favorite book to the class.

b. Students can create murals, dioramas, roller TV shows, pictures, paintings, papier-mâché, collage, sculpture, mobiles, and posters.

c. Students can perform dramatized versions of the literature or create a puppet show.

d. Writing or dramatizing a story can involve students in building off of the literature. For example, children can create a new ending, write a different story with the same theme or characters, or tell the story from a different character's point of view.

e. Journals or letters can be written from the point of view of characters in the book, or students can create a newspaper based on the time period and events in the book.

f. Students may write about their responses to the literature in Literature Logs.

g. Readers may meet to discuss and explore their interpretations of literature in Literature Circles.

h. Children may use Sketch to Stretch, in which readers sketch the meaning of the story and share their sketches with each other.

i. A Readers' Theatre may be developed from the literature.

j. A game from the book for others to play can be created. Games can be board games or be based on TV game shows.

k. Displays or learning centers related to the literature may be set up.

l. Cooking experiences may be used to extend learning.

m. Informal Author Sharing Times allow students to talk with one another about the literature they are reading.

n. Students may interview one another about their response to the book or simulate an interview with the author.

o. Students may research the setting of the book or the life of the author.

p. Comparison charts or webs of related books or topics may be developed.

q. Children may participate in a book party, dressing up as book characters.

r. Children may create a tableau, a living picture of an action or scene frozen in time, arranged on stage.

4. Students need the opportunity to respond to literature in a variety of ways over a period of time.

5. Students should be encouraged to share their responses with one another as well as with other audiences when appropriate. These Literature Response Activities should be received by the group just as pieces of writing are received. The audience tells what they liked about the response and has a chance to ask questions.

Teacher's Role

At the beginning of the year, the teacher needs to spend some time with students exploring the variety of ways in which they can respond to literature. This exploration can take the form of brainstorming as well as the actual involvement of students in a variety of types of responses. The teacher can create a center that lists the types of responses students can make and contains the supplies they are most likely to need for these responses. The teacher can also offer specific invitations of ways students can respond to books read aloud to the class.

Follow-Up

1. Related activities include Literature Circles, Say Something, Learning Log, Sketch to Stretch, Cloning an Author, and Save the Last Word for Me.

2. Instead of asking students to retell a story, the teacher can ask them to talk about how they have changed as a result of reading the book or what they know now that they didn't know before.

References

The following books contain suggestions for Literature Response Activities:

Coody, B. 1983. *Using literature with young children.* 3d ed. Dubuque, IA: William C. Brown.

Cullinan, B., ed. 1987. *Children's literature in the reading program.* Newark, DE: International Reading Association.

Moss, J. 1984. *Focus units in literature.* Urbana, IL: National Council of Teachers of English.

Somers, A., & Worthington, J. 1979. *Response guides for teaching children's books.* Urbana, IL: National Council of Teachers of English.

Whitehead, R. 1968. *Children's literature: Strategies of teaching.* Englewood Cliffs, NJ: Prentice-Hall.

Message Board

Introduction

Readers and writers of all ages and levels of experience should engage in literacy activities that are both meaningful and functional. Message Board provides such opportunities. Through the process of sending and receiving messages, readers and writers, particularly young or inexperienced ones, come to understand that literacy is a multimodal communicative process. It helps learners understand that written language as well as oral language involves social interaction.

Materials/Procedures

* Bulletin board in a central location
* Ample supply of various sizes of paper and envelopes
* Writing instruments
* Thumbtacks

1. To initiate the Message Board, the teacher may write a message to the entire class or a message to a particular student and place it on the board.
2. When the students discover the message, they are invited to write messages to one another and to the teacher. The only restriction is that messages must be signed. Each message may be hung publicly or sealed in an envelope.
3. A trip to the grocery store or other local businesses may provide useful examples of ways adults use bulletin boards to advertise goods and services for sale and to post lost-and-found notices.

309

A

> ♡
> Good Morning!
> ♡
>   Donna

Figure CC19.1 Message Board
(A—Donna, Grade 4;
B—Gidget, Grade 2;
C—Marvin, Grade 3).

B

> Room6
> Hi you had
> a good stories
> I want to
> Know how old
> he is and wat
> grade is he in Room5
> Gidget

C

> Dear Kathy,
> Here is a poem for you.
>   I like to play in the snow
> and watch a movie/show.
> when I want to eat,
> I make a popcorn treat.
> To make your day better
> Just write me a Letter.
> I'll write one to you,
> If you'll write one, too
>   Marvin

4. A variety of types of messages can be posted on the Message Board by teachers, students, and parents, including personal messages, announcements, records of class assignments, invitations, jokes or riddles for class members to respond to, items to sell, current events, sign-up sheets for classroom activities such as songs, drama, or sharing stories—anything that needs to be communicated with others. Messages can also be exchanged between classrooms (see Figure CC19.1).

Teacher's Role

Message Boards often seem to go through cycles of use by the students. When the teacher sees that students' use of the board is dying down, the teacher can encourage new types of uses. Teachers can continuously demonstrate and encourage use of the board by the messages they send on it. One particularly effective use of the board by teachers is to send notes complimenting children on their use of new reading or writing strategies.

Students may also use art to communicate meaning. The teacher should support this use of an alternate communication system and help students understand that print is only one of the vehicles for conveying meaning.

Because young children's knowledge of conventional representations is sometimes limited, functional spelling may dominate, and some children may have difficulty reading the messages from their classmates. The teacher can encourage the reader to predict "indecipherable" portions of the message from the portions that have been read. If the functional spelling is particularly difficult to understand, the reader may be encouraged to see the author of the message for clarification. Here, common sense rules—what would *you* do if you wanted to read the message and couldn't quite make it out? These inevitable events may lead the children to seek editing help in relation to the Message Board.

Follow-Up

1. Students may be asked to date their entries on the Message Board to keep the board current. As the Message Board gets crowded, students may wish to divide the board into categories based on the general types of messages being posted.

2. A diary of class events may be collected by keeping samples from the Message Board in a class scrapbook. This provides opportunities for reading and rereading messages and for discussing events that took place in the past. It emphasizes the shared history of that classroom.

3. A variation on Message Board includes posters. For example, students may be invited to make political campaign posters for their favorite candidates and display them in the classroom. Issue campaigns, such as smoking, drugs, alcohol, pollution, and safety, or upcoming school or community events can also provide opportunities for posters to be created and displayed. Planning sketches, creating rough drafts, and editing can all play a role in the production of these posters.

4. In one classroom of young children, the teacher used Message Board in conjunction with sharing time. Children who had something they wanted to share with the rest of the class during the class sharing time wrote their message on a piece of paper and posted it on the Message Board. At the end of the day, everyone came together for sharing time, and the children who had earlier put messages on the board read them to the class. Only children with written messages were allowed to share. Because each child read his or her own message, it did not matter if the message was written conventionally.

5. Several teachers have used a special Message Board to manage their classroom newspaper or magazine. Sign-up sheets for

different positions on the newspaper, notices and requests for certain kinds of articles, and articles for the newspaper were all posted on the Message Board.

6. One classroom decided to use their Message Board during the second half of the year to send messages to their "Students of the Week." Each week, several students' names were drawn from a hat, and each person in the class wrote messages to the selected students and posted them on the board. At the end of the week, the messages were taken down and given to the Students of the Week.

7. Message Board provides a functional way to handle some of the mundane business of school. Other tasks, such as handling lunch money and taking attendance, can also become functional language activities that involve the students. In one preschool, the children learn to write their names through signing in each morning as a way to take attendance. The board can also be used by students to post messages to the teacher instead of interrupting the teacher during class time.

8. Exchanging letters with pen pals is another informal way of communicating with others. Several different kinds of pen pal exchanges may be set up. Long-distance pen pals allow students to communicate with someone from a different community and culture, but usually the exchanges occur infrequently. Teachers will also want to have a pen pal exchange with another class from a nearby school so that letters can be exchanged frequently on a regular basis. Choose a teacher who lives on or near the route you follow between home and school each day so that the letters can be easily exchanged. If there is a nearby college, an exchange can be set up with undergraduate students in a language arts methods class.

Reference

This activity was originally developed by Carolyn Burke.

Mine, Yours, and Ours

Introduction

None of us has direct access to knowing about the world. To make sense of our world, we create stories about our experiences that include both the experience and our interpretation of it. These stories can be constructed only by making connections between something in our current experience to stories we had already constructed from earlier experiences. Our views of the world become a web of interconnected stories that continue to change and grow in complexity. This web of stories that each of us constructs is the perspective from which we interpret our further learning. We all view the world from a different perspective based on our web of stories.

Because we are social beings living in a social world, our understandings of that world both influence and are influenced by others' understandings of the world. It is as social beings that our world becomes multidimensional. We borrow others' perspectives to extend our ability to make sense of the world, and to enable us mentally to stand both inside and outside an event at the same time. The realization that we can be in two places at once forms the basis for reflection and reflexivity. As we become aware of and reflect on the logic of others, we become more aware of the variety of interpretations and solutions available to any one situation or text. We also are encouraged to reflexively explore the potential that our current knowledge has for solving problems other than one that we have been immediately investigating. We begin to seek more generalized knowledge and understanding.

Mine, Yours, and Ours encourages learners to take different perspectives on knowing. Learners need to know their position, as well as others' positions, and to find out where the tensions lie between these positions. Learners learn to live with the tensions that exist between their world views and others' world views, as well as to interconnect their knowing with others. Learning, then, for all of us, is a process of connected knowing and storying.

Materials/Procedures

* Paper and pencils

1. Students participate in a common experience, such as a lecture or a field trip.
2. Following the experience, students write a story summarizing what they perceive to be the most significant aspects of that experience (see Figure CC20.1).
3. Students pair off to compare stories to see what the connections are between them. They discuss where they agree and disagree and what kinds of meanings are in one story but not in the other.
4. The two students explore the connections between their stories to discover the underlying assumptions, beliefs, and values of each story.
5. Once the pairs of students have discussed their stories, the group comes back together to share their insights about why their stories did and did not connect.

Teacher's Role

The teacher needs to participate with students in this experience by writing a story and comparing that story with another person's story. The teacher's story has no more weight than any of the students' stories and should be examined along with the other stories.

Follow-Up

1. Students can each read the same text, write a story that highlights the important features of that text, and then compare and explore their stories in pairs.
2. This same activity can be used to compare meaning created

The Overnight was really fun! We had spaghetti dinner, strawberry shortcake, and Kool-aid! We also got to sleep outside! But I finally went back inside. Outside was cold!! Later on, by looking at the clock, I found out that it 4:00 in the morning! I went right to sleep, but at first, I wasn't very sleepy. The next day, I woke up, and had a breakfast of donuts! I really had fun! I got to have dinner, an overnight, and breakfast all!

A

My favorite part of the year was the overnight. Mom had to go back to my house because I forgot my sleeping bag. I was in the observation booth with Jason W. Me and Jason didn't get any sleep instead we talked the whole night. People kept on peeking in to our booth because everyone wanted to be in a booth. The next morning me and Jason got 10 more doughnuts than we were supposed to have. we started to get hungry so we kept getting more doughnuts. when we were done we were both stuffed.

B

Figure CC20.1 Two Narratives of an Overnight Experience (A—Brad, Age 10; B—Joey, Age 6). From Pierce (1986).

in other sign systems. Students can watch the same drama or dance, listen to the same piece of music, or look at the same piece of art, and then write and compare their stories about these events.

3. Instead of students *writing* stories, they can create stories through art, drama, music, movement, or other modes and then compare these stories. For example, Sketch to Stretch involves students in drawing a sketch of the meaning of a reading selection. They can then compare their sketches with each other to see what kinds of connections exist.

4. A variation used by David Bleich in literature classes involves students in first writing a written response to two different novels of their choice. The students share their responses and look for patterns of similarity and differences within and among their responses and those of their classmates. Students individually and together write a paper exploring and explaining what differences they found and why they believe they tend to respond in the manner in which they do. When students are asked to read a third novel, they are told to take a new stance by selecting some other classmate as a model and to respond to the novel as they believe he or she would.

5. This activity can be used as a research technique. Research participants watch the same event on videotape, and then each writes an interpretation of the event. These interpretations are compared, and differences in underlying assumptions are discussed.

6. Students can read books that present the same story from different people's perspectives. A list of children's literature that presents a story from various perspectives is included at the end of this strategy lesson.

7. Students can take a piece of their own writing or a piece of literature and retell the story from the perspective of one of the characters in the story. This perspective should not be the one from which the story was originally told.

8. In social studies projects, students can be asked to think of themselves as characters in various historical periods. Students become characters from that period and work together to write and produce plays that make history come alive. Students can also write stories, journals, or letters from their characters' viewpoints and experiences.

References

This activity was adapted by Jerome Harste and Kathy Short. For basic references, see:

Erikson, F. 1984. School literacy, reasoning, and civility: An anthropologist's perspective. *Review of Educational Research* 54(4):525-546.

Pierce, K. M. 1986. Curriculum as collaboration: Toward practical theory. Ph.D. diss., Indiana University, Bloomington.

Rosen, H. 1984. *Stories and meanings.* London: National Association for the Teaching of English.

Short, K. G. 1986. Literacy as a collaborative experience. Ph.D. diss., Indiana University, Bloomington.

Wells, G. 1986. *The meaning makers: Children learning language and using language to learn.* Portsmouth, NH: Heinemann.

Appendix: Children's Literature That Compares Perspectives

Aardema, V. 1975. *Why mosquitoes buzz in people's ears.* New York: Dial.

Ahlberg, A. & J. 1986. *Jolly postman.* Boston: Little, Brown.

Blume, J. 1984. *The pain and the great one.* New York: Bradbury.

Botell, M. 1973. *That ugly Cinderella.* New York: Heath.

Childress, A. 1973. *A hero ain't nothin' but a sandwich.* New York: Coward.

———. 1981. *Rainbow Jordan.* New York: Coward.

Lionni, L. 1970. *Fish is fish.* New York: Pantheon.

Stolz, M. 1960. *A boy on Barkham Street.* New York: Harper & Row.

———. 1963. *The bully of Barkham Street.* New York: Harper & Row.

Turkle, B. 1976. *Deep in the forest.* New York: Dutton.

Viorst, J. 1974. *Rosie and Michael.* New York: Atheneum.

Yolen, J. 1985. Happy dens, or A day in the old wolves home. In *Dragonfield and other stories.* New York: Ace Fantasy Books, Berkley.

CURRICULAR COMPONENT

Picture Setting

Introduction

Picture Setting helps students identify a topic of personal interest to write about. By choosing a picture of a setting that reminds them of events that have occurred in their lives, participants begin considering experiences to write about that they might not have considered initially as possible topics. Asking students to go home and invest some time looking through magazines for a Picture Setting they might use permits them to be actively involved in authoring; that is, "writing" before they actually start writing. By beginning with an alternate communication system (pictures), participants get in touch with their feelings and what the experience meant to them.

As students engage in this activity, the different components of a story (setting, character, plot, and theme) are each highlighted for them to think about as they gradually build their stories. Students become more familiar with the story structure of narratives and with how to select and organize information in generating a written text. The time spent choosing the setting, drawing the characters, and sharing their thinking with others gives participants an opportunity to think through their story, to plan, and to engage in strategies that proficient writers find supportive of the writing process.

Materials/Procedures

* Wide selection of pictures without people or animals for settings
* Construction paper, both 8 1/2″ × 11″ and 3″ × 3″
* Stapler or tape

* Paper, pencils, and crayons
* Scissors

1. Students are asked to go home and look through magazines to identify a picture of a setting that reminds them of an important moment or event in their lives. They should focus on events they see as significant and disregard whether they believe others would see it as significant. If students forget to bring a picture, they should look through and select a picture from a pile the teacher has provided. This picture becomes the setting for their story.

2. The teacher calls a group of six to eight students together for Picture Setting. Other students should be engaged in reading or in working on other pieces of writing.

3. Using small ($3'' \times 3''$) pieces of construction paper, students at Picture Setting are asked to draw and color the characters (people and animals) involved in the story they want to write. Thinking about the color of the clothes that various persons were wearing is an important part of the experience that often helps put writers in touch with their feelings and emotions.

4. Students cut out their characters so they can physically move the characters around as they orally share with the group what they are thinking about writing.

5. After everyone has had an opportunity to share what they are thinking about writing, uninterrupted time for writing is scheduled. (An example of a completed story is shown in Figure CC21.1.)

6. After an extended period of writing, or after some students have finished writing, everyone can be asked to share what they have written up to that point and how they plan to finish their pieces.

7. Students who have not finished drafting their stories are given time to do so. Others should be permitted to move on to other activities.

Teacher's Role

Teachers first need to identify two or three pictures of settings that personally remind them of important moments in their lives. These pictures are shown to the students to introduce them to the

The neighborhoo___ ___

The Graveyard 1

One day in a nice neighbor hood there was a big house and only a woman and boy lived there. The Womans name was Mary and the boys name was Bryan; his father had died when he was 7 months old and he lives with his mother; Mary Bryan liked to ride bicycles a lot But one day he was thinking how his father looked when he was alive. Then after a while he got off his bed and

2

asked his mother, "what's my father's name"? Then his mother said John That afternoon Bryan went on his bicycle to the graveyard and looked for the name John Mcfee. After two hours he found his father's grave and then he heard a voice say you are not suppose to be here; It was a gentle voice after Bryan heard that voice he ran as fast as he can till he got back home; Then his mother asked

3

have you been Bryan? Then Bryan said playing with the other boys; we were racing With the bicycles and that took a long time. Then him mother said how come your wheels are muddy. Then his mother said again The truth, The truth Bryan and then Bryan said to the

4

Graveyard. Then his mother said to the what to the Graveyard Bryan said again. Then his mother said do you want to hear a tape of your fathers voice Then Bryan said, "Yeeees", And when he heard the voice it was the same and he told his mothe and the went to that grave-yard Every Day.

Figure CC21.1   Picture Setting Story (Mudhi, Grade 4).

activity. Teachers discuss what each picture reminds them of and what they would write about if a specific picture was selected. Students are then asked to select pictures that are background settings only, devoid of characters. Only experiences that can be publicly shared should be identified.

As students bring in their Picture Settings, these are trimmed and stapled on pieces of 8 1/2" × 11" construction paper. The teacher actively engages in all drawing, writing, and sharing activities that occur during Picture Setting at the same time that the students are engaged in these activities. At sharing times, the teacher receives all student pieces and demonstrates how to be supportive by asking authors open-ended questions about where they see their piece going. All student responses are accepted with few or no extensions. Once students complete their rough drafts, the character pictures can be stapled or taped to the picture so they are not lost.

Some students will elect to write a fictional account even though this activity is designed to invite students to write about real events that happened in their lives. Other students will mix fantasy with reality. Regardless of the students' choices, it is important that their decisions be respected and accepted.

Students could be invited to share a selected portion of their rough draft story at Author Sharing Time or read their entire selection at Authors' Chair. Rough drafts can be kept in students' Author's Folders and considered as one of several publications they might rework, edit, and publish in the months to come.

Follow-Up

1. As a variation of this lesson, students can be asked to find pictures of people or objects that remind them of particular experiences. Participants would then draw the setting before writing their selection.

2. Rather than identifying settings that remind them of a personal experience, participants can be asked to find settings that they think would make a good backdrop for a fictional story. Teachers might suggest this option to any participants who seem to have difficulty identifying a personal experience to share.

3. Students can use dioramas, either student-made or commercially made, to create background settings in which to place their characters and stories.

4. A group of students can create a large mural background with moveable characters (characters are cut out and taped onto straws or sticks) to use in creating a group Picture Setting story.

References

Picture Settings was originally developed by Stephen Kucer and Carolyn Burke. See the following source for further information on a related strategy:

Busch, K. 1986. The transmediation of signs: Pictures, cognition, and text. Ph.D. diss., Indiana University, Bloomington.

Poetry in Motion

Introduction

Poetry in Motion encourages readers to give up their accuracy notions about comprehension and instead to see the reading of difficult texts as a learning process. Readers are asked to read and reread the text, assuming that there will be much they won't understand the first time or even the third time through. Each rereading allows them to understand the text in a different way and raises new areas of question and puzzlement.

This activity focuses on poetry for several reasons. One is that in reading poetry, readers need to suspend their inclination to jump to a quick conclusion about *the* meaning of the poem. A certain amount of ambiguity is characteristic of poetry, as poets tend to tell less in poetry than authors do in prose. Poetry thus highlights the process of struggling with meaning. The second is that unless teachers read poetry to their students, students are unlikely to experience poetry as an important part of their lives and to realize that poetry can allow them to see life from new perspectives.

Materials/Procedures

* Multiple copies of a poem
* Three colors of highlighter pens

1. Students are given a photocopy of a poem and asked to read the poem three times over several days.
2. Each time they read the poem, students are asked to mark the poem with a different color of highlighter pen. They are to mark words or expressions that struck them or confused them. They are also to mark shifts in the poem and words or phrases that gained significance on a second or third reading.

323

Is it robin o'clock?
Is it five after wing?
Is it quarter to leaf?
Is it nearly time for spring?

Is it grass to eleven?
Is it flower to eight?
Is it half-past snowflake?
Do we still have to wait?

Is it robin o'clock?
Is it five after wing?
Is it quarter to leaf?
Is it nearly time for spring?

Is it grass to eleven?
Is it flower to eight?
Is it half-past snowflake?
Do we still have to wait?

Is it robin o'clock?
Is it five after wing?
Is it quarter to leaf?
Is it nearly time for spring?

Is it grass to eleven?
Is it flower to eight?
Is it half-past snowflake?
Do we still have to wait?

Figure CC22.1 Highlighting a Poem on Three Different Readings (Mary, Age 10). Poem from Merriam (1985).

As a variation, teachers may provide students with three different copies of the same poem so that they mark each reading on a different copy and then compare the three different markings (see Figure CC22.1).

3. When students finish reading the poem three times, they are asked to write a short narrative describing what happened to them as they read the poem. They are not writing an analysis of the poem's meaning but a description of their own reading process and changes in it as they read and reread the poem.

4. Students share these narratives with one another and discuss how they can use the strategy of rereading and rethinking to deal with other difficult texts.

Teacher's Role

Teachers should participate in the process of reading, marking, writing, and sharing along with the students. Students need to see that adults also do not have instant and total comprehension of what they read. All readers have to work at constructing their own meanings as they read.

Although poetry is a favorite form of young children, older students show increasing dislike of poetry. This is primarily due to the misuse of poetry in the classroom. These misuses include overemphasis on traditional and abstract poems rather than on contemporary poems, neglect of poetry, required memorization of poems, and too-detailed analyses of every poem read. Teachers need to explore the positive ways in which they can incorporate poetry into their classrooms on a daily basis so that readers do not miss the new potentials for knowing that poetry offers. Poetry allows readers to explore the careful choice of words, the power of imagery and associations, the use of rhythm in language, and the role of the writer in communicating feelings.

Poetry in Motion should *not* be the first time poetry is used in the classroom. Teachers need to read poetry aloud to their students daily, and the classroom library should include a collection of poetry books. Poetry is not something that we do once a month or have a unit on once a year. Poetry should be integrated throughout the school day. When teachers read a book aloud to the group, they should also read a related poem. Poems should be integrated into theme units. Because poetry is short, teachers can read poems during transition times in the classroom. Teachers should always have poetry at their fingertips, ready to read. Having a poetry file in which favorite poems have been placed on cards and filed according to our own system of use helps us quickly locate a poem we want at an appropriate moment. It is also helpful to purchase several good poetry anthologies for easy referral.

When reading poetry aloud, do not read in an overly dramatic or singsong fashion. Read slowly in a natural voice, focusing on the meaning of the poem rather on the rhyme. Because poetry is such a condensed use of language, read poems aloud several times. Many poets now have recordings of their own poetry available that teachers can place in the listening center. Students should be encouraged to read poetry together during Shared Reading or uninterrupted reading times. In choosing poetry to read aloud and to add to the classroom library, be sure to have a variety of poetry available. Begin with humorous poetry by poets such as Silverstein and Prelutsky that build on students' immediate interests, but don't stop with humorous poetry. Read a wide assortment of poetry and poets to students.

Follow-Up

1. Students can use this same strategy of reading, rereading, and marking their reading process with other text materials, such as content area texts or short stories.

2. Because poetry involves such a concise and careful use of language, reading poetry to students and inviting them to write their own poetry can help them get beyond the "make it longer" stage of revision in their own writing. When students first begin writing and revising, they tend to focus on adding to their story and making it longer. Once they are able to write fluently and writing lengthier stories is no longer their focus of attention, they need to begin examining how they use language.

   Students also need to be invited to write poetry to encourage them to explore poetry as a unique way of communicating meaning about their world to others. When students first begin to write poetry, encourage them to use free verse and not worry about rhyme. Too early an emphasis on fixed forms of poetry such as haiku or limerick can distort students' perceptions about poetry and focus their attention on counting lines and syllables rather than on content. Teachers should particularly focus students' attention on communicating their mental pictures and feelings as they write poetry.

3. Students should be encouraged to start a poetry journal in which they can experiment with writing poetry. Entries can include ideas for poems, lists of favorite words or phrases, poems, and revisions of poems.

4. Poetry invites response. Students can become involved in choral reading of poetry, in drawing the images that the poem leaves in their minds, in trying different art media to illustrate a favorite poem, in acting out or moving to a particular poem, in finding a piece of music that reflects the mood or action of the poem, or in using a poem as an invitation for their own writing. Poetry should also be used as a focus for exploration in Literature Circles and in Text Sets.

5. Students can do poet studies (see Authors Meeting Authors).

6. Students can put together collections of poetry. They can create their own poetry files of favorite poems, put together books of particular kinds of poetry, or make bulletin board displays of poems related to a particular theme. The collections can also be composed of their own or their classmates' poems.

References

This activity was adapted from Thomas Newkirk by Jerome Harste and Kathy Short. For further discussion on this strategy or on the uses of poetry in the classroom, see:

Calkins, L. M. 1986. Poetry. *The art of teaching writing.* Portsmouth, NH: Heinemann.

Hopkins, L. B. 1987. *Pass the poetry, please!,* rev. ed. New York: Harper & Row.

Koch, K. 1971. *Wishes, lies, and dreams: Teaching children to write poetry.* New York: Random House.

Livingston, M. C. 1985. *The child as poet: Myth or reality?* Boston: Horn Book.

McClure, A. 1984. Children's responses to poetry in a supportive literary context. Ph.D. diss., Ohio State University, Columbus.

Newkirk, T. In press. Writing and thinking: Reclaiming the essay. In J. Harste, ed., *Critical thinking: What we can do,* 1988 NCTE Yearbook. Urbana, IL: National Council of Teachers of English.

Rosenblatt, L. 1984. The poem as event. *College English.* November, 123-128.

Terry, A. 1974. *Children's poetry preferences.* Urbana, IL: National Council of Teachers of English.

Appendix: A Beginning List of Books
for a Poetry Collection

Adoff, A. 1979. *Eats.* New York: Lothrop, Lee, and Shepard.

Adoff, A., ed. 1970. *I am the darker brother: An anthology of modern poems by black Americans.* New York: Macmillan.

Aldis, D. [1925] 1952. *All together.* New York: Putnam.

Behn, H. 1984. *Crickets and bullfrogs and whispers of thunder.* New York: Harcourt Brace Jovanovich.

Brooks, G. 1956. *Bronzeville boys and girls.* New York: Harper & Row.

Ciardi, J. 1964. *You know who.* New York: Lippincott.

Cole, J., sel. 1984. *A new treasury of children's poetry.* Garden City, NY: Doubleday.

Cole, W., ed. 1981. *Poem stew.* New York: Lippincott.

de Paola, T. 1985. *Tomie de Paola's Mother Goose.* New York: Putnam.

Dunning, S., Lueders, E., Smith, H., comps. 1966. *Reflections on the gift of a watermelon pickle and other modern verses.* New York: Scott, Foresman.

Ferris, H., comp. 1957. *Favorite poems: Old and new.* Garden City, NY: Doubleday.

Field, R. 1964. *Poems.* New York: Macmillan.

Fisher, A. 1980. *Out in the dark and daylight.* New York: Harper & Row.

Froman, R. 1974. *Seeing things.* New York: Crowell.

Frost, R. 1959. *You come too.* New York: Holt, Rinehart & Winston.

Giovanni, N. 1985. *Spin a soft black song: Poems for children.* rev. ed. New York: Hill & Wang.

Greenfield, E. 1978. *Honey, I love.* New York: Harper & Row.

Hoberman, M. 1981. *Yellow butter, purple jelly, red jam, black bread.* New York: Viking.

Hopkins, L. B., ed. 1982. *Rainbows are made: Poems by Carl Sandburg.* New York: Harcourt Brace Jovanovich.

———. 1983. *The sky is full of song.* New York: Harper & Row.

Hughes, L. 1969. *Don't turn your back.* New York: Knopf.

Jarrell, R. 1964. *The bat-poet.* New York: Macmillan.

Jones, H., ed. 1971. *The trees stand shining: Poetry of the North American Indians.* New York: Dial.

Kennedy, X. J., & Kennedy, D., sel., 1982. *Knock at a star: A child's introduction to poetry.* Boston: Little, Brown.

Kuskin, K. 1980. *Dogs and dragons, trees and dreams.* New York: Harper & Row.

Larrick, N., ed. 1968. *Piping down the valleys wild.* New York: Delacorte.

Lee, D. 1983. *Jelly bean.* Toronto: Macmillan of Canada.

Lewis, R. 1964. *In a spring garden.* New York: Dial.

Livingston, M. C. 1958. *Whispers and other poems.* New York: Harcourt Brace Jovanovich.

———. 1985. *Celebrations.* New York: Holiday House.

Livingston, M. C., ed. 1972. *Listen children listen.* New York: Harcourt Brace Jovanovich.

Lobel, A. 1983. *The book of pigericks.* New York: Harper & Row.

McCord, D. 1967. *Every time I climb a tree.* Boston: Little, Brown.

——— . 1977. *One at a time: His collected poems for the young.* Boston: Little, Brown.

Merriam, E. 1970. *Finding a poem.* New York: Atheneum.

——— . 1984. *Jamboree.* New York: Dell.

——— . 1985. *Blackberry ink.* New York: Morrow.

Milne, A. A. 1958. *The world of Christopher Robin.* New York: Dutton.

Moore, L. 1982. *Something new begins.* New York: Atheneum.

O'Neill, M. 1961. *Hailstones and halibut bones.* Garden City, NY: Doubleday.

Prelutsky, J. 1984. *The new kid on the block.* New York: Greenwillow.

Prelutsky, J., ed. 1983. *The Random House book of poetry for children.* New York: Random House.

Rosen, M. 1983. *You can't catch me.* New York: Dutton.

Silverstein, S. 1974. *Where the sidewalk ends.* New York: Harper & Row.

——— . 1981. *Light in the attic.* New York: Harper & Row.

Stevenson, R. L. [1885] 1947. *A child's garden of verses.* Illustrated by Tasha Tudor. New York: Oxford University Press.

Worth, V. 1972. *Small poems.* New York: Farrar Straus Giroux.

Readers' Theatre

Introduction

Readers' Theatre focuses on bringing stories and characters alive through oral interpretation. Unlike plays, there is little or no costuming or movement, no stage sets, and no memorized lines. The focus in Readers' Theatre is therefore on the literature, not the actors, and on the readers communicating with the audience through the literature. Literature becomes a living experience for both the readers and the audience through the use of facial expressions, voice, and a few gestures. As groups try several different readings of the same story, these readings highlight multiple interpretations of texts. Readers are helped to see that reading is an active and an open process of constructing meaning.

In contrast to round-robin reading, Readers' Theatre focuses on the meaning of the story, not on pronouncing words correctly. Round-robin reading has no "real" audience, while Readers' Theatre provides a setting for oral reading with an audience who has come to enjoy an oral interpretation of a story. Because readers practice before presenting, Readers' Theatre allows both proficient and less proficient readers to be successful in oral reading.

Materials/Procedures

* Multiple copies of literature or scripts
* A few simple props, such as chairs or stools and hats

1. The piece of literature chosen for Readers' Theatre should have a great deal of dialogue, interesting characters, rich and rhythmic language, and a storyline with suspense or conflict and an element of humor or surprise. Sources of literature

329

include basal readers or trade books. Folktales are especially good sources.

2. The literature can be adapted to make a Readers' Theatre script. The adaptations can include omitting extraneous parts, shortening long speeches or descriptive sections, and using a narrator to make connections between scenes. Most adaptations can be done with only minimal rewriting.

3. Copies of the literature should be available for each reading part. Each reader should use a highlighter to indicate the parts to be read on his or her copy.

4. Readers may decide to stand or sit and decide how they will position themselves in relation to one another.

5. A practice session with a small group as the audience may generate suggestions for revision.

6. Students present the Readers' Theatre. During a performance, readers sit or stand facing the audience and read their parts from the scripts, using their vocal expressions to bring life to the story.

Teacher's Role

The teacher will initially select the literature and help students arrange the selections for Readers' Theatre. Later, students will be able to take over these responsibilities themselves. Teachers should encourage both informal and formal presentations of Readers' Theatre. Informal presentations will be quickly planned and presented to the class, while formal presentations will be more carefully planned and practiced before presentation to the class or to other audiences.

Follow-Up

1. Readers may occasionally use a tape of different types of background music during Readers' Theatre.

2. After students participate in a Readers' Theatre, a class discussion can be held about the success of the program. Readers can describe how they made decisions, the audience can respond to what was and was not effective, and a revised performance may then be held.

3. Students can become involved in writing their own scripts for Readers' Theatre or writing reviews of Readers' Theatre performances for the class newspaper.

4. A Readers' Theatre file can be compiled to list the selection, characters, and storyline for future reference. Actual scripts can also be stored for others to use.

References

The following are good resources on Readers' Theatre:

Busching, B. 1981. Readers theatre: An education for language and life. *Language Arts* 58(3):330-338.

Coger, L. I., & White, M. R. 1973. *Readers theatre handbook: A dramatic approach to literature,* rev. ed. Glenview, IL: Scott, Foresman.

Readers Theatre Script Service. P.O. Box 178333, San Diego, CA 92117.

Sloyer, S. 1982. *Readers theatre: Story dramatization in the classroom.* Urbana, IL: National Council of Teachers of English.

Save the Last Word for Me

Introduction

Reading is an active process in which the reader constructs meaning from a text. Because readers bring differing experiences and knowledge to a reading experience, each reader will construct a different interpretation of a text. Readers need to be encouraged to take an active stance to their reading, asking questions and looking for points of agreement or disagreement with the author as they read. This active stance to reading is facilitated when readers interact with other readers and discuss their differing questions and interpretations of a shared piece of reading.

Less proficient readers often believe that proficient readers understand everything they read and that there is one "right" interpretation of every text. Save the Last Word for Me demonstrates to them that all readers work at constructing their own interpretations of what they read through relating their background experiences to the text as well as through discussing the text with other readers.

Materials/Procedures

* Multiple copies of a text
* 3" X 5" cards or slips of scrap paper

1. Each student individually reads the text.
2. As the students read, they write on the first side of the cards or slips of paper any segments of the text (words, phrases, or sentences) that particularly catch their attention. These segments can be items that they find interesting and want

to discuss later or that they particularly agree or disagree with. Students should also record the page number of that segment.

3. On the other side of the cards or slips of paper, the students write out what they want to say about each quote they have selected. This can include questions and points of agreement or disagreement they have with the text segment (see Figures CC24.1 and CC24.2).

Side 1

"From the earliest preschool learning and throughout life, it is important for people to have the opportunities to present what they know, to share it through language, and in the course of this presentation, to complete the learning." p. 16

Side 2

All our ideas and thoughts are the result of talking with others and they have no "body" till that discussion takes place beyond the internal dialogue of other voices + your own. In sharing, we gain our voice and our sense of knowing.

Figure CC24.1 Card by an Adult for *What's Whole in Whole Language?* (Goodman 1986).

Side 1
pg. 27 "He hadn't even won his heat. There was no cheering at either end of the field. The rest of the boys seemed as stunned as he."

Side 2
Jesse Jesse was scared cause he was beaten in a race by a girl. He was not afraid of the girl. It was the boys he was afraid of. Of what they were going to say.

Figure CC24.2   Card by Angie, Grade 6, for *Bridge to Terabithia* (Paterson 1977).

4. Once students have completed the reading and writing of the cards, they gather in small groups or in a single group to share their cards.

5. Before class discussion, students go through their cards and put them in order from most important to least important in terms of their desire to discuss them. During sharing, if someone else uses the same top quote, the person who has not yet shared will choose his or her next quote.

6. Each student reads the quote on a card to the group. The other members of the group have a chance to react to what

was read. The student who read the quote then has the last word about why that segment of text was chosen and bases the remarks both on what he or she earlier wrote on the back of the card and on the preceding discussion.

Teacher's Role

The teacher will want to introduce this strategy using a fairly short text. The text chosen, whether fiction or nonfiction, needs to be one that has the potential for strong response from students. The teacher should participate in making and sharing cards along with the students. Initially, the teacher will play a major role in demonstrating what can be written on the cards and how to go about discussing the cards with one another.

Follow-Up

1. Students work in groups of three to six. Each student silently reads the text material and then chooses one quotation from the text. The students exchange their quotations with each other, and each person responds to the quotation he or she now has. The student who chose the original quotation is not given the last word but does get to see how someone else responds to the quotation he or she chose.

2. Instead of having an oral discussion, students can pass their cards around with a sheet of paper in a variation of Writing in the Round (see Say Something). Each person chooses one card to pass around the small group. Students read the card and write their comments about the quotation on the piece of paper. The next person responds both to the card and to the comments.

Reference

This activity was originally developed by Carolyn Burke.

CURRICULAR COMPONENT

Say Something

Introduction

Language did not develop because of the presence of one language user but because two language users wished to communicate. Language and language learning are inherently social events. Say Something highlights the social nature of language and demonstrates that understanding develops and evolves from our interactions with others. Participants are able to see that "partnership" enhances meaning, and that as constraints normally operating in reading are altered, so are involvement and the kind of thinking that becomes possible.

Say Something is designed to help readers develop a more functional view of reading. Participants learn to respond in terms of what the passage meant to them and how it does or does not relate to their own experiences, rather than in terms of what they think the teacher wants. This activity also helps readers become aware of alternative reading strategies they can use when they run into difficulty in reading a text.

Materials/Procedures

* Multiple copies of a reading selection
* Overhead projector, clear acetate, overhead pens

1. Students are asked to choose a partner, and each pair is given a single copy of a reading selection.
2. Before reading, each pair of participants is asked to decide whether they will read the selection aloud or silently.
3. Students are informed that as they read the selection, they will discuss what they have read with their partner. After

they read the first several paragraphs, they are to stop to "say something" to their partner about what they have read. Then it is the second person's turn to "say something" about what was read. After each exchange of this sort, the partnership reads the next several paragraphs and again each "says something" to the other before going on to the next paragraph, and so on through the text. Students can comment on what was just read, make predictions about what will happen next, or share experiences related to the selection.

4. When the majority of students have finished reading the selection, the teacher should organize a group discussion by writing a central topic from the reading in the middle of the overhead, circling it twice, and asking students to talk about some of the things the author had to say on the topic. As examples are mentioned, the contributor should be asked to explain what this concept had to do with the topic and how it fits in with the other ideas that the article discussed. Ideas mentioned should be webbed off the topic statement on the overhead, so that a map of the author's ideas and how these relate and interrelate are shown on the overhead.

Teacher's Role

Teachers demonstrate that Say Something is used by successful language users by choosing a partner and participating in this activity with students. Throughout the group discussion, the teacher works at establishing a context in which students feel that their interpretations are accepted and that there is no one "right" answer. Any interpretation is accepted as long as the student can support it. "Why" should be a frequent response.

The teacher should encourage students to challenge and extend the interpretations of other students, rather than stepping in to correct what the teacher perceives as misinterpretations. When divergent interpretations are given, the text may be consulted. It is important to point out, however, that given a certain frame of reference, both interpretations could be viable. If the discussion is not going smoothly, the teacher may want to ask, "What kinds of things did your partner say or relate that helped you better understand this selection?"

After the first several times that Say Something is used with a group, the teacher should engage the students in a group discussion aimed at helping them become aware of how they can use this strategy in their own reading. The students can discuss (1) what reading strategies were used to make sense of this reading, and (2) how and under what conditions students might find Say Something a helpful strategy for them to use as readers in the future. Students should be informed that successful readers use procedures similar to Say Something when they encounter difficulty in reading texts and that if they experience difficulty reading any of the materials for the class, Say Something is an alternative reading strategy they can use to solve their problem.

Follow-Up

1. A group Say Something can be used with a small group of students. Each student has a copy of the text. They look through the entire text as a group and decide where they will stop reading to "say something" to one another. These stopping points are marked with a pencil. Each person then begins reading silently. When a reader comes to a stopping point, the reader stops and waits until the others in the group are also ready. Group members then each say something about the section they just read before going on to read the next section silently.

2. Written conversations can be substituted for oral conversations during Say Something. Writing, however, is more constrained. We have found that it is not wise to introduce this alternative until after students feel free to respond to text at a more personal "what it meant to me" level.

3. Instead of making a group web, each pair of students can write a brief summary/response after reading and discussing the selection. These summaries can then be shared with other pairs who have read the same selection and written their own summaries. Students could also do sketches that are then shared with other pairs.

4. A variation of Say Something used to give responses to writing is Writing in the Round. Writers attach a blank sheet of paper to a draft, asking for responses to their writing. The draft is circulated to three or four different readers. Each reader reads the draft and previous readers' comments and then makes suggestions for revisions of meaning. This same activity can be used to get responses to artwork, projects, and oral reports.

5. A similar procedure, Reading in the Round, involves a student writing a response to a reading selection. This response is circulated among other students who write their own comments about the reading selection and about the reactions already written on the sheet by other readers. Instead of beginning with a response, the sheet could have on it several key statements selected from the reading material. As the sheet is passed around, readers respond to one another and to the key statements.

6. Students should be encouraged to use Say Something whenever they say they are having difficulty understanding what they are reading. This procedure should be continued until students naturally engage in this strategy on their own.

References

Say Something was developed by Jerome Harste, Carolyn Burke, and Dorothy Watson. Writing in the Round was developed by Jeff Ducer and Paul Crowley.

CURRICULAR COMPONENT

Schema Stories

Introduction

Schema Stories is an activity designed to encourage students to concentrate on the overall form and structure of a text. Readers possess certain expectations or schemata relating to the structure of stories, and this strategy aims to make them more aware of the influence of these schemata for readers and writers. Students learn about story structure through their experiences in reading literature. This activity will help to continue the development of a "sense of story" as they discuss the sequence of ideas within a text.

Materials/Procedures

* Narrative text that is cut into parts
* Original copy of the text

1. The teacher should select a text that is narrative in form and has an easily identifiable beginning, plot development, and ending.
2. The key text segments (introduction, episodes, climax, ending, etc.) should be identified and the text cut into parts on the basis of those segments. Cuts should be made either just before or just after the segment. Depending on the text complexity and the readers' abilities, three to ten sections should be created. Each segment must be long enough (at least a complete paragraph) to give the readers something substantial to read, even though they might be reading something from the middle of the text. In the case of longer texts, the teacher may decide to rewrite the chunks to shorten them.

3. The text may be photocopied and cut into sections, overhead transparencies may be made, or text segments may be written on file cards.

4. Each student in the group takes one segment of text and reads it silently, thinking about what might have happened before or after that particular excerpt.

5. Assembling the text begins by asking who thinks he or she has the beginning of the text. That student should read the segment aloud.

6. The other students decide if the beginning has been properly chosen and try to find the next segment. The group continues with each reader reading a segment aloud when he or she thinks it comes next in the text, and with the others listening and agreeing or disagreeing with the reader. Disputes about sequencing will have to be negotiated and resolved by having the students refer to the events in the segments and to what makes sense in terms of their understandings of the story structure and content. Variations of the ordering of the text are accepted as long as they create a story that has unity and makes sense.

7. Once the students have assembled the text to their satisfaction, the entire text is read aloud as a unit, with each person reading his or her segment aloud to the group.

8. The original copy of the text can then be distributed to the students so they can see how their sequence compares to the author's original text.

Teacher's Role

Teachers are responsible for choosing appropriate texts and cutting them into segments that will facilitate students' predictions about what follows or precedes the segment. Cutting the text exactly between segments makes these predictions more difficult, so it is important to cut the segments either right after the beginning of another segment or right before the ending of one segment. The initial texts chosen by teachers for this experience should be ones that students are already familiar with or that have an easily identifiable story structure. Folktales are an excellent beginning source of texts that work well for this activity.

The teacher's primary role during this activity is to support the students' own exploration of text structure. When difficulties arise, the teacher should ask questions that help the students use their existing knowledge of story structure and text content. The teacher might ask, "Is there anything missing after this section? Does it make sense to start this way? What do you know about the general topic of this piece that will help you work out what should come next? Can you think of other stories or texts that are like this one?" The teacher also should encourage students to consider alternative structures and to accept that, at times, more than one response is possible.

Follow-Up

1. Many different kinds of texts can be used to create Schema Stories. Cartoons, poetry, math story problems, recipes, songs, folktales, other narrative stories, and nonfiction texts can be cut into segments that reflect the structure of that particular type of text. For example, selections from the social studies or science text can be cut into chunks that reflect the major organizational pattern of that text. It is important that there be some type of predictable structure to the text that students will be able to use in reassembling the segments. Sources of texts include trade books; old basal readers; science, social studies, or math texts; weekly news magazines, and newspaper articles.

2. A particular variation of Schema Stories is Peanut Butter Fudge. The recipe for Peanut Butter Fudge is divided into chunks, with each chunk written on a separate card (see Figure CC26.1). The ingredients and cooking utensils necessary for completing the recipe are placed on a table or cooking area in the classroom. The cards are passed out to students, who must talk with one another and decide how to sequence the steps in making the fudge. They then make the fudge. This serves as a check on whether their sequencing makes sense and can lead to revisions in their original ordering of the recipe.

    As a follow-up to Peanut Butter Fudge, other recipes as well as other types of texts that involve directions, such as the rules for a game or instructions on how to put together a model or a toy, can be divided into parts.

3. For less experienced and less proficient readers, a Wordless Picture Book or a highly predictable book can be used.

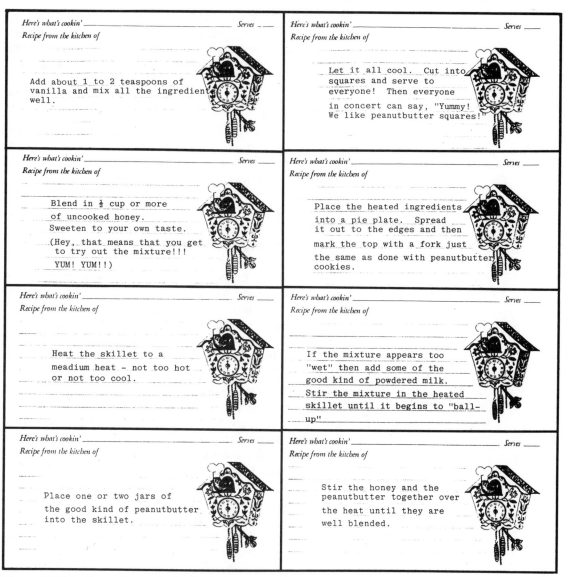

Figure CC26.1 Peanut-Butter Fudge Recipe.

4. Another variation that supports less proficient readers is to allow them to read the original text first and then to reconstruct the text using the text segments.

5. Each student can be given all the parts of the text to be reconstructed. The teacher makes copies of the text and cuts

every text into parts so that each student has a complete set of the segments of the story. Once students have individually or in pairs put the text in the order they feel makes sense, the students compare their reconstructed texts with one another.

6. Instead of cutting the text right before the beginning or end of a segment, the chunks of text can be made by making the cuts directly between the different segments. This usually results in a text that can be constructed in a variety of ways. Students can see how many different ways they can reconstruct the story cards to create various texts that make sense.

7. Blank slots in the story can be provided when the text segments are distributed. Usually only one or two empty slots should be provided. The students should be told that certain parts of the story have been left out, and so there are several blank cards or pieces of paper. They need to discover which sections are missing and place the blanks in the appropriate place as they sequence the text segments. Once they have reconstructed the story, they are asked to write what might be missing from the sections before sharing the whole text with the class.

8. Students can be given the different segments of a comic strip or of a set of sequence pictures from a workbook page to put in order, along with one blank extra segment. They can put this extra segment anywhere they want in relation to the other segments to create a new story. Some type of caption can be written for the extra segment, or the students can write the entire story using their sequence segments as a basis for the story.

9. Students are given the beginning and ending of a short story. They are told that they are going to write a story with another person who has already written the beginning and ending. The students then read the two parts of the story and discuss possible events that could connect the two parts. Each student writes the middle of the story, connecting the two parts in a meaningful way. If an existing story is used as the source of the two parts, the original story can be read to the students after they write their own stories.

10. To help writers become aware of the importance of transitions and words that signal order, have students cut up a

photocopy of one of their own stories and give the pieces to a neighbor to see how their neighbor puts the story together.

References

Schema Stories was originally developed by Dorothy Watson. The version presented here was adapted by Carolyn Burke, Jerome Harste, and Trevor Cairney. Peanut Butter Fudge was developed by Mary Lynn Woods.

Shared Reading

Introduction

Reading is a social activity that involves the construction of meaning. Readers are supported in the reading process when they can share in the reading of meaningful, predictable texts with other readers. This strategy is based on the belief that we learn to read by reading, and that reading can be learned in much the same way as speech is learned. Reading and rereading familiar and predictable stories with others provide successful and enjoyable reading experiences. As students reread stories over and over, they are able to attend to different demonstrations in the stories each time, and they develop a feeling of competence in themselves as readers because they are able to read the stories all the way through fluently. Because the language and structure of these stories become familiar to them, they are able to draw from these stories in understanding new stories that they read and in their writing of stories.

Shared Reading is a useful strategy for all readers, but it is particularly useful for less fluent readers. Less proficient readers need to read in an atmosphere that supports their initial reading experiences and encourages them to take risks and to make predictions based on meaning and structure as they read, rather than focusing their attention on isolated aspects of the reading process.

Materials/Procedures

* Predictable books, both regular size and Big Books
  Several different variations of Shared Reading follow. All variations involve multiple readings of a predictable book with other readers.

Procedure A: Group Read Together Time

1. The teacher introduces the story by reading the title and having the students predict what the story might be about, based on the title and the cover illustration.

2. The teacher then reads the story to the students. Students must be able to see the print as the teacher reads the story. This can be accomplished through having a Big Book with enlarged print so that an entire group can see the print, or through each student having a copy of the story to follow along as the teacher reads. If the teacher is reading from a Big Book, the teacher should point to the words while reading.

3. Students should be encouraged to begin to join in on repeating phrases or sentences as soon as they recognize the predictable parts of the story. With some stories, the teacher may want to pause to let the pupils predict what comes next or to take time to examine how the text and illustrations support each other.

4. After the first reading, students can share their feelings about the story, confirm their predictions, and elaborate on certain parts of the story that they especially liked.

5. If possible, a second reading should immediately follow the discussion. If not, this story should be the first one read during the next Shared Reading period. In the second reading, the students should be encouraged to take more responsibility as they read in chorus the repetitive parts or the words that are highly predictable from the meaning of the story.

6. If the students remain interested in the story, it can be read a third time, with the students taking on still more of the reading in chorus. The number of times a story is reread depends on the response of the group—on whether they are enjoying the story and asking for it during Shared Reading, and on how well they are able to join in reading the story in chorus.

7. The story should then be placed in the library corner for students to read independently or with another child, and in the listening corner for those who still need support in reading the story. The students should be given many opportunities to reread the story so that they are able to read it fluently.

8. Each Shared Reading should involve the children's selection of old favorites that they again want to read together as a

group and introduce new stories, songs, and poems that are predictable.

Procedure B: Partner Reading

1. During uninterrupted reading, students are allowed to choose whether they will read alone or with one or two other children.
2. The sharing of the reading can take different forms: one person can read to the other person, each can read every other page, one person can read the first half of the book and the other can finish the book, each can read a book to the other person, the two can read in unison, the book can be read chorally with each taking different parts, and other variations.
3. Partner reading can occur between students of different grade levels as well as at the same grade level. Students can share books they have read or authored with each other.

Procedure C: Popcorn Reading

1. Each reader should have a copy of the text to be read.
2. One person starts reading aloud, then stops reading at any point.
3. As soon as one reader stops, another person quickly jumps in and takes over. Whoever jumps in first continues reading as long as desired, then suddenly stops, and another reader quickly pops in. Whoever jumps in first gets to continue reading. No one is forced to read, and there is no order determining how the readers take over. If one person is dominating or reads too far, he or she may be asked to let others have a turn.
4. If there is only one copy of the text, the reader simply passes the text on to another person at whatever point he or she chooses to stop reading.

Procedure D: Choral Reading

1. Each student should have a copy of a poem or a predictable book. It's best to begin with a familiar poem or rhyme.

2. The group decides on a choral arrangement for the poem or book: unison, antiphonal, solo, refrain, line-a-group, line-a-child. They also make decisions about voice pitch, inflection, feeling, pace, and pauses.

3. Following the first choral reading, the group discusses the reading and then tries out other possible choral arrangements to see which are the most effective.

4. Instead of reading with a partner, students can read along with a tape recording of the story in the listening center.

5. A small group of students can sit together at a table or on a rug, reading silently from the same text. After a period of time, the group stops and shares their reading with one another. This variation, called Reading Round Table, was developed by Carolyn Burke.

Teacher's Role

The teacher needs to help locate books that are predictable for a particular group of students because they build on familiar reader experiences and because of the text organization. The text organization is predictable because of the language, storyline, and structure rather than because of controlled vocabulary or phonetic regularity. Features such as rhyme, rhythm, familiar sequences, repetitive patterns or refrains, familiar concepts or storylines, and a good match between the text and illustrations can help make a text predictable. Although repetitive patterns characterize predictable books for younger children, predictable books for older children are predictable because they are about familiar topics or issues from a student's daily life, or because they are from a series or genre in which the student has done a lot of reading. Any book that a student has read or listened to several times becomes a predictable book for that student.

Teachers should provide opportunities for students to read texts in unison or to do choral reading. Reading and rereading chorally or in unison provide support for readers who are at different levels of proficiency in reading. During unison reading, some children will be reading the print, while others cannot read the print but can join in on the repeating parts, and still others sit and listen. No one is embarrassed or made to feel inadequate, but everyone simply joins in as able.

Follow-Up

1. Predictable books usually provide story structures that easily lead to a variety of additional activities. These activities should focus attention on the meaning of the story. Some stories may be dramatized as the students read the parts of the characters. Some follow a pattern that can be used to write a new story. Some stories can be cut apart into several meaningful chunks and then students can put the story back together in sequence (see Schema Stories). Other stories can be responded to and interpreted through art or music.

2. The Group Composed Books strategy provides ideas on how to use predictable books as a pattern for writing a class book.

3. Shirley Brice Heath has extended the strategy of partner reading by having videotapes made of fifth-grade students reading to first-grade students. She and the fifth-grade students view the tapes together and decide what is and is not working.

4. In cross-grade partner reading where older students read with the same younger partner over a period of time, the students can be invited to use their knowledge about their partner to write a book for him or her.

5. Read-a-Book-a-Day is a variation that involves tearing apart a paperback copy of a chapter book by chapters. The teacher reads the first chapter to a small group and then gives each person in the group a chapter to read. After the students have read their chapters, they come back together in the group to share what their individual chapters were about and to discuss how their chapters are related and how they fit together. This activity can be used with informational books that have chapters or with fiction books that are episodic stories. Episodic stories have chapters that can be understood fairly well without the other chapters having been read. Instead of each chapter being highly connected to the next, each chapter relates another adventure of the characters. Examples of episodic books are. *Homer Price* (McCloskey 1943), *Wind in the Willow* (Grahame 1940), and *Frog and Toad Together* (Lobel 1972).

References

The person most closely associated with Big Books and Shared Reading is Don Holdaway. Others have also written about predictable books and shared reading and have provided bibliographies of preditable books:

Atwell, M. 1985. Predictable books for adolescent readers. *Journal of Reading* 29(1):18-22.

Bridges, C., et al. 1983. Using Predictable Materials vs. Preprimers to Teach Beginning Sight Words. *Reading Teacher* 36:884-891.

Holdaway, D. 1979. *The foundations of literacy*. Portsmouth, NH: Heinemann.

Holdaway, D. 1982. The big book trend—A discussion with Don Holdaway. *Language Arts* (8):815-821.

Rhodes, L. 1981. I can read! Predictable books as resources for reading and writing instruction. *Reading Teacher* 34(5):511-518.

Appendix A: A Beginning List of Predictable Books

Ahlberg, J., & Ahlberg, A. 1978. *Each peach pear plum*. New York: Viking.

Barchas, S. 1975. *I was walking down the road*. New York: Scholastic.

Becker, J. 1973. *Seven little rabbits*. New York: Walker.

Boone, R. & Mills, A. 1961. *I know an old lady*. New York: Rand McNally.

Brown, M. W. 1947. *Goodnight moon*. New York: Harper & Row.

Brown, M. 1957. *The three billy goats gruff*. New York: Harcourt Brace World.

Brown, R. 1981. *A dark dark tale*. New York: Dial.

Burningham, J. 1971. *Mr. Gumpy's outing*. New York: Holt, Rinehart & Winston.

Carle, E. 1969. *The very hungry caterpillar*. Cleveland: Collins World.

——— . 1977. *The grouchy ladybug*. New York: Crowell.

de Regniers, B. S. 1972. *May I bring a friend?* New York: Atheneum.

Galdone, P. 1970. *The three little pigs*. New York: Clarion.

——— . 1973. *The little red hen*. New York: Scholastic.

Gerstein, M. 1984. *Roll over*. New York: Crown.

Ginsburg, M. 1972. *The chick and the duckling*. New York: Macmillan.

Goss, J. & Harste, J. [1981] 1985. *It didn't frighten me!* Worthington, OH: Willowisp.

Heller, R. 1981. *Chickens aren't the only ones*. New York: Grosset and Dunlap.

Hutchins, P. 1968. *Rosie's walk*. New York: Macmillan.

——— . 1971. *Titch*. New York: Macmillan.

——— . 1982. *Goodnight owl*. New York: Macmillan.

Kent, J. 1971. *The fat cat*. Parents Magazine.

Kraus, R. 1945. *The carrot seed*. New York: Harper & Row.

——— . 1970. *Whose mouse are you?* New York: Collier.

——— . 1986. *Where are you going little mouse?* New York: Greenwillow.

Martin, B. 1970. *Fire! Fire! said Mrs. McGuire*. Holt, Rinehart & Winston.

——— . [1970] 1983. *Brown bear, brown bear, what do you see?* Holt, Rinehart & Winston.

Peek, M. 1985. *Mary wore her red dress and Henry wore his green sneakers.* New York: Clarion.
Tafuri, N. 1984. *Have you seen my duckling?* New York: Greenwillow.
Tolstoy, A. 1968. *The great big enormous turnip.* New York: Franklin Watts.
Wood, A. 1984. *The napping house.* New York: Harcourt Brace Jovanovich.

Appendix B: Predictable Sets of Books

Bill Martin Instant Readers and *Sounds of Language* Reading Series. New York: Holt, Rinehart, & Winston.
Reading Systems and *Reading Unlimited.* Glenview, IL: Scott, Foresman.
Ready to Read Books. New York: Owen.
Rigby Readers. Mount Prospect, IL: Jostens Learning Systems.
Story Box. San Diego: Wright Group.

LINK, 1895 Dudley Street, Lakewood, CO 80215 has LINK PAKS available, which include a copy of a predictable book, along with instructional activities and ideas that can be used with the book.

Appendix C: Books about Environmental Print

Goor, R. & N. 1983. *Signs.* New York: Crowell.
Hoban, T. 1983. *I read signs.* New York: Greenwillow.
——— . 1984. *I walk and read.* New York: Greenwillow.
Hutchins, P. 1980. *The tale of Thomas Mead.* New York: Greenwillow.

Sketch to Stretch

Introduction

Sketch to Stretch helps language users realize that we can create meaning in many communication systems (language, art, movement, music, etc.). By taking what we know in one communication system and recasting it in terms of another system, new signs and new forms of expression are created, and new knowledge generated. This process of recasting is called "transmediation," and is a fundamental process of what it means to be literate.

Sketch to Stretch encourages students to go beyond a literal understanding of what they have experienced. By becoming involved in this strategy, students who are reluctant to take risks or who have dysfunctional notions of language see that not everyone has the same response to a selection. Although much of the meaning is shared, variations in interpretation add to new meanings and new insights. Often, as students draw, they generate new insights of their own. They are faced with a problem because the meanings they had constructed for the selection through language cannot be transferred into a drawing. As they deal with this problem, they usually come to understand the selection at a different level than they initially understood it. Sometimes students discuss and explore aspects of meaning they may have captured in art that they were not aware of having understood verbally.

Materials/Procedures

* Multiple copies of a reading selection
* Pencil, paper, and crayons or colored markers

353

1. Students should be divided into small groups of four or five.
2. After reading the selection, students should think about what they read and then draw a sketch of "what the selection meant to you or what you made of the reading."
3. Students should be told there are many ways of representing the meaning of an experience and they are free to experiment with their interpretation. Students should not be rushed but given ample time to read and draw (see Figures CC28.1, CC28.2, and CC28.3).
4. When the sketches are complete, each person in the group shows his or her sketch to the others in that group. The group participants study the sketch and say what they think the artist is attempting to say.
5. Once everyone has been given the opportunity to hypothesize an interpretation, the artist, of course, gets the last word.
6. Sharing continues in this fashion until all group members have shared their sketches. Each group can then identify one sketch in the group to be shared with the entire class. This sketch is put on an acetate sheet for the overhead projector.

Teacher's Role

Teachers may need to help students focus on interpretation rather than on their artistic talents. Teachers should do their own Sketch to Stretch and share it with the group of students they are working with at an appropriate time. Students often initially have difficulty understanding the directions to "draw what the story means to you," and will draw their favorite scene. Don't give up on the activity. The students will need repeated opportunities to try the activity before they begin to play with the meanings they are creating through sketching and to get beyond their initial limited interpretations of what a sketch should be.

Teachers should discuss (1) why various readers have different interpretations, (2) why there is no correct reading (or sketch) but rather that what each reader focused on depended on the reader's interest and background, and (3) how and under what conditions Sketch to Stretch might be a particularly useful strategy for readers to use (timeline selections or stories, floor plans in mysteries, complex descriptions of cell reproduction, etc.).

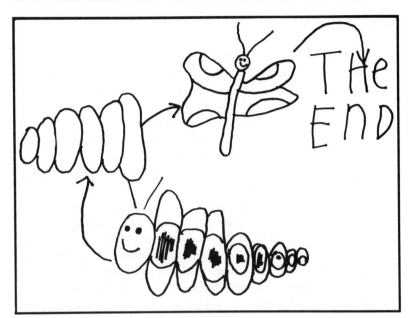

Figure CC28.1 Sketch for *The Very Hungry Caterpillar* (Carle 1969). From Siegel (1984).

Figure CC28.2 Sketch for *Nana Upstairs, Nana Downstairs* (de Paola 1972). From Siegel (1984).

Figure CC28.3 Sketch for *Ira Sleeps Over* (Waber 1972). From Siegel (1984).

Follow-Up

1. Sketches can be compiled and published in a class book (see Bookmaking). In addition, a Message Board could be developed for students to share sketches they make from self-selected books they are reading. These sketches can serve as advertisements for particular books.

2. Students can read different selections that are related in some way (see Text Sets) and make sketches. As they discuss their sketches, they can make hypotheses about how their different selections are related.

3. Students should be encouraged to use Sketch to Stretch as a way of self-monitoring their comprehension during and after reading. Teachers should invite students to use this strategy as one of several strategies they might employ during reading. The strategy of moving to another communication system can involve moving to drama or music in addition to art.

4. Students can be encouraged to include sketches along with their written work, particularly projects, to expand on the interpretation being presented.

5. Once students have written a first draft (or have experienced a writer's block), they can be asked to shift to another communication mode. No priority should be given to moves to art. Students can be asked how else they might represent their meaning, and their choice of pantomime, drama, math, music, or other mode can be honored. Students should return to writing once they have expressed their meaning in an alternate mode. Often they will find that they have gained new insight into the topic at hand.

6. This lesson plan for Sketch to Stretch highlights written language. Art is secondary and seen as supportive of written language growth. However, when the classroom focus is on art, math, science, or some other area, this relationship can be reversed by having students move from art, math, or science to writing or reading and then back to art, math, or science. To this end, students should be helped to see that shifts in communication systems help learners gain new perspectives and insights. Such shifting is one of several strategies that they and other successful language learners might employ in a variety of learning situations.

7. Students can create story maps. A story map pictures the sequence of events that took place within the story.

8. Students can sketch what they think the author looks like after reading a number of books by a particular author, and then compare their sketches.

References

Sketch to Stretch was originally developed by Jerome Harste, Carolyn Burke, Marjorie Siegel, and Karen Feathers. It was the focus of a research study by Marjorie Siegel that is reported in:

Siegel, M. G. 1984. Reading as signification. Ph.D. diss., Indiana University, Bloomington.

Text Sets

Introduction

When readers read two or more texts that are related in some way, they are encouraged to share and extend their comprehension of each text differently than if only one text had been read and discussed. Learning and understanding are processes of making connections. We are able to understand what we read only because of the connections we make between the current book and our past experiences, which include previous books we have read or written. Text Sets highlight the strategy of searching for connections as we read.

As readers make connections between texts, they begin to see the reading event as an experience in itself. A reader can read one text to prepare for reading and better understanding a second text. The focus is not on what readers have to do to get ready to read, but on what happens when readers read one text to facilitate their understanding of other, related texts.

In addition, reading related texts encourages discussion among a group of students in Literature Circles. Because they have read different texts, they have a real reason for sharing their books with one another. Text Sets facilitate the connections they can make in their discussions as they compare and contrast the related texts.

Materials/Procedures

* Two or more texts that have similar characteristics, such as similar themes, text types, topics, and so on (see appendix)

Two different procedures may be used to encourage students to share and extend their understandings of Text Sets.

Procedure A *(everyone reads all the texts in the set)*

1. Everyone reads or listens to the teacher read each of the texts in the text set. Instead of reading the whole text, teachers may read a portion of each text to all the students and then have the students finish each text independently. The important thing is that everyone is familiar with all the texts in the set.

2. The group discusses the similarities and differences of the texts. The group can focus on comparisons such as: "What was the same or different about these stories (narratives)? What information did you find presented in more than one of the texts (expository texts)? What are the similarities in the way these stories or texts were written?"

3. After discussing all the possible similarities and differences, students are asked to identify which ones are of major importance and to identify other texts they may have read or heard earlier that are related to these major similarities.

4. At the end of the discussion of the Text Set, the group can brainstorm ideas for extensions based on the similarities of the books in the Text Set. These extensions can include making comparison charts; writing a drama, Readers' Theatre, or story that fits in the Text Set; making a game or display; or making a mural or diorama (see Literature Response Activities).

Procedure B *(everyone reads different texts)*

1. Each person in the group reads only one or two of the texts from the Text Set. They are told that each will be asked to share what was read and learned from the text with the rest of the group.

2. Students share what they read with the rest of the group. After each person shares, the others ask questions to help clarify what was shared.

3. Students discuss the similarities and differences across the texts as these become apparent. They develop their own categories for these comparisons and share examples from their books.

4. If the discussion lasts over several days, students will often read other books in the Text Set as they become interested in these books or as the group decides everyone needs to read a particular book for the next day's discussion.

5. At the end of the discussion, the group brainstorms ideas for how they can share their Text Set with the class.

Teacher's Role

The major role of the teacher is to gather different kinds of Text Sets together for students to use in these discussions. The teacher also initially leads the discussion until the students understand how to proceed on their own. The teacher can then make decisions about when to join a group.

When first using Text Sets, it is best to limit the number of books in the set to three or four. Later, Text Sets can include a large group of books (6-25) from which students select the books they will discuss. Once students have participated in several Text Sets, they can sometimes be asked to use the library to gather the books for a particular Text Set. Look for unusual kinds of groupings for Text Sets (for example, sets having to do with threes or crowding stories). Also include in the Text Sets all kinds of reading materials, not just literature. Look for environmental print, newspaper or magazine articles, ads, maps, and other materials for the sets.

When teachers ask a group to read two or three books in a Text Set and then meet and discuss these books, the groups develop different strategies for how they conduct these discussions. Some groups read only those two or three books and spend their time drawing comparisons between them. Some groups will decide to take one book or certain subset of books out of the set each day to focus on in the discussion. Some groups continue reading as they discuss so that students have read most or all of the books by the end of their discussion. Some groups generate a list of possible comparisons or questions and then use this list to guide their discussion. Some groups use a Literature Log and begin their discussions each day sharing from their logs. We have found it helpful during the first Text Set discussions to brainstorm possible ways of handling these discussions with students, but then each group develops its own discussion strategy.

Follow-Up

1. Either procedure can be followed up by inviting students to write their own text that would fit in the same Text Set or to develop a drama that uses the characteristics of the Text

Set. If the Text Set involved analyzing illustrations, students could try to use some of the illustrating techniques in their own work. When these are shared in Authors' Circle, other students comment on whether the student has used the major characteristics of the Text Set.

2. Once students have discovered the similarities and differences, they can develop a comparison chart on a large piece of paper by deciding on several categories and then listing the characteristics of each text under those categories. The texts are listed on the side of the chart, and across the top are the categories that the group decides showed similarities and differences across the texts.

   Examples of possible categories are country of origin, names for characters, beginnings, tasks or events, name of protector, villains, magical powers, types of punishments, endings, and illustrations.

   The charts will be more attractive if students fill them in using both words and pictures to record how each text fits in a particular category. A good idea in charting is to give each student a small square of paper to draw or write on and then to glue that square onto the large chart.

3. A Caldecott or Newbery Award Text Set can be created. Students first read through a set of books that won one of these awards in previous years. They use these books to generate criteria for winning the award. The students are then given the books that received the award or an honorable mention for the current year. They are told that these books were nominated for the award and are asked to look through them and decide which book should win the award, and why it should win. Once they have made and defended their choice, they are told which book received the medal. If the book they chose did not win, the students discuss why they think the award was given to another book and decide whether they agree with the committee.

4. Text Sets of three or four books can be put in book bags for students to check out to take home as homework to be read with and to family members.

5. Text Sets are excellent to use in Literature Circles because they facilitate discussion, especially among students who are reluctant to talk (see Literature Circle).

6. Other uses of Text Sets in the classroom include the following: setting up displays of books in Text Sets; reading books

from a Text Set aloud to the class over a period of time; creating a Text Set that builds off of a basal story; and creating Text Sets that are related to math, science, or social studies units.

References

Variations of this activity have been developed by Dorothy Watson, Carolyn Burke, Linda Crafton, Lynn Rhodes, and Kathy Short. A good additional reference is:

Moss, J. 1984. *Focus units in literature.* Urbana, IL: National Council of Teachers of English.

Appendix: Types of Text Sets

Story Variants (different cultural variants of the same story)

Louie, A. 1982. *Yeh-Shen: A Cinderella story from China.* New York: Philomel.
Mbane, P. 1972. *Nomi and the magic fish.* New York: Doubleday.
Perrault, C. 1964. *Cinderella.* Illustrated by Marcia Brown. New York: Scribner.
Steel, F. 1976. *Tattercoats.* Illustrated by Diane Goode. New York: Bradbury.
Whitney, T. P. 1970. *Vasilisa the beautiful.* New York: Macmillan.

Story Versions (same story in different retellings)

de Regniers, B. 1972. *Little red riding hood.* New York: Atheneum.
Galdone, P. 1974. *Little red riding hood.* New York: McGraw-Hill.
Hyman, T. S. 1982. *Little red riding hood.* Boston: Little, Brown.
Zwerger, L. 1983. *Little red cap.* New York: Morrow.

Story Structures (same basic organizational plot structure)

In the following texts, the characters are sequenced according to size:

Carle, E. 1977. *The grouchy ladybug.* New York: Crowell.
Ets, M. 1972. *The elephant in the wall.* New York: Viking.
Tolstoy, A. 1968. *The great big enormous turnip.* New York: Franklin Watts.

In these texts, there is a cumulative pattern where one thing causes another thing to happen:

Aardema, V. 1975. *Why mosquitoes buzz in people's ears.* New York: Dial.
Galdone, P. 1961. *The house that Jack built.* New York: McGraw Hill.
Kaplan, R. 1981. *Jump frog jump.* New York: Scholastic.
Wood, A. 1984. *The napping house.* New York: Harcourt Brace Jovanovich.
Zolotow, C. 1963. *The quarreling book.* New York: Harper & Row.

Themes

In the following texts, the theme is that understanding parts requires understanding of the whole:

Domanska, J. 1974. *What do you see?* New York: Macmillan.
Quigley, L. 1959. *The blind man and the elephant.* New York: Scribner.

In these texts, the theme is the value of individuality:

de Paola, T. 1979. *Oliver Button is a sissy.* New York: Harcourt Brace Jovanovich.
Leaf, M. 1938. *The story of Ferdinand.* New York: Viking.
Pinkwater, D. M. 1977. *The big orange splot.* New York: Scholastic.
Yashima, T. 1955. *Crow boy.* New York: Viking.

A useful resource to locate texts that are thematically similar is:

Lima, C. W. 1982. *A to zoo: Subject access to children's picture books.* New York: Bowker.

Text Types

The following are all "how" and "why" stories:

Aardema, V. 1975. *Why mosquitoes buzz in people's ears.* New York: Dial.
Elkin, B. 1966. *Why the sun was late.* New York: Parents Magazine.
Kipling, R. 1973. *How the rhinoceros got his skin.* New York: Walker.
——— . 1976. *How the camel got his hump.* New York: Spoken Arts.

Other examples of text types would be folktales, fables, tall tales, experiment books, "how to" manuals, and mysteries.

Topics

The following books are about caterpillars:

Carle, E. 1969. *The very hungry caterpillar.* Cleveland: Collins World.
Martin, B. *Ten little caterpillars.* New York: Holt, Rinehart & Winston.
Reidel, M. 1974. *From egg to butterfly.* Minneapolis: Carolrhode Books.

The following books are about puppets:

Boylad, E. 1970. *How to be a puppeteer*. New York: McCall.
Keats, E. J. 1975. *Louie*. New York: Greenwillow.
Ross, L. 1969. *Hand puppets: How to make and use them*. New York: Lothrop, Lee, and Shepard.

The following books are about pigs:

Galdone, P. 1970. *The three little pigs*. New York: Scholastic.
Goodall, J. 1983. *Paddy Pork—Odd Jobs*. New York: Atheneum.
King-Smith, D. 1985. *Babe the gallant pig*. New York: Viking.
Lobel, A. 1982. *The book of pigericks*. New York: Atheneum.
Scott, J. 1981. *The book of the pig*. New York: Putnam.
White, E. B. 1952. *Charlotte's web*. New York: Harper & Row.
Yolen, J. 1987. *Piggins*. New York: Harcourt Brace Jovanovich.

Different Illustrators of the Same Text

Adams, P. 1973. *There was an old lady who swallowed a fly*. New York: Grosset and Dunlap.
Boone, R. & Mille, A. 1961. *I know an old lady*. New York: Rand McNally.
Kellogg, S. 1974. *There was an old woman*. New York: Parents Magazine.
Westcott, N. S. 1980. *I know an old lady who swallowed a fly*. Boston: Little, Brown.

Characters

Any set of books that contains stories about the same set of characters such as:

Ramona, Henry Huggins, and *Ralph* series by Beverly Cleary
Frog and Toad series by Arnold Lobel
George and Martha series by James Marshall
Amelia Bedelia series by Peggy Parish
Nate the Great series by Marjorie Sharmat

Authors or Illustrators

Any set of books written by the same author or illustrated by the same illustrator. For example, a set of books by Tomie de Paola, Pat Hutchins, or Betsy Byars.

Culture

A set of books from a particular culture. This works especially well with sets of folktales, such as a set of folktales from Japan or

Russia. The sets can also include books from a variety of genres. The following books all reflect Japanese culture:

Behn, H., trans. 1964. *Cricket songs: Japanese haiku.* New York: Harcourt Brace Jovanovich.

Hodges, M. 1964. *The wave.* Boston: Houghton Mifflin.

Jacobsen, K. 1982. *Japan.* Chicago: Children's Press.

Mosel, A. 1972. *Funny little woman.* New York: Dutton.

Say, A. 1982. *The bicycle man.* Boston: Houghton Mifflin.

Yagawa, S. 1981. *The crane wife.* New York: Morrow.

Yashima, T. 1955. *Crow boy.* New York: Viking.

———. 1967. *Seashore story.* New York: Viking.

Theme Cycles

Introduction

Theme Cycles allow teachers and students to work together in using reading and writing to learn, and in developing their own units of study. Recently, educators have begun focusing on how students can use reading and writing to explore and learn about their world. The exploration of new ideas always operates on the edge of the known. The knowledge and understandings that learners already have about life is the platform upon which they currently stand and from which they will launch themselves into the future.

Learning needs to connect with, as well as go beyond, what is already known to us. Teachers and students must work together in negotiating curriculum. Teachers bring their knowledge and experiences, including what they have learned from experts and from how others have organized knowledge into fields of study and ways of knowing, to this negotiation. Students bring their own knowledge and experiences with learning and life. The curriculum that results from the coming together of teachers and students reaches toward new potentials for knowing.

Materials/Procedures

* Large sheets of white paper
* Collections of informational materials

1. At the beginning of the school year, students are asked to talk about the things they would like to study during the year. Teachers also share what they are expected to have students study. Two lists of suggested topics are created from

this sharing. Teachers and students then negotiate and settle on a list of potential topics for the year. In some cases, student topics are subsumed under school topics, and in other instances school topics are subsumed under student topics.

2. One topic is chosen for study through negotiation between students and teachers. As part of this discussion, they also discuss the possible reasons *why* they want to learn more about a particular topic.

3. The class talks about the topic and together makes a web with two different sections on a large sheet of butcher paper: "What We Know" and "What We Want to Know." The topic is written in the center and circled. Students begin by telling what they know about the topic. These items are webbed around the title of the topic. On a second section of the web, students add what they want to know about the topic. This second section is used to make a list of possible research questions or problems (see Figure CC30.1).

4. Teachers and students then create a list of books, places, and people to whom they can go to get further information on the topic. They also list materials needed for experiments or classroom centers that will be used to explore the topic. Everyone takes responsibility for collecting these resources and bringing them into the classroom.

5. Students as individuals or groups are asked to select from the list of questions under "What We Want to Know" those they think are most important or that interest them most.

6. Students then engage in whole-group, small-group, and individual learning activities to explore the theme or topic. These activities involve using reading and writing to learn as well as using hands-on activities, art, drama, music, and movement to explore and learn more about the topic.

7. As students learn new information or develop new questions, these are added to the web. There should be many opportunities for the different groups to share informally with one another throughout the study.

8. At the end of the study, students present what they have learned to one another, selecting those ideas that were most interesting or important to them. They may also decide to limit their presentation to a single concept about which they have a lot of information. These presentations may be formal or informal. In lieu of, or in addition to, written and

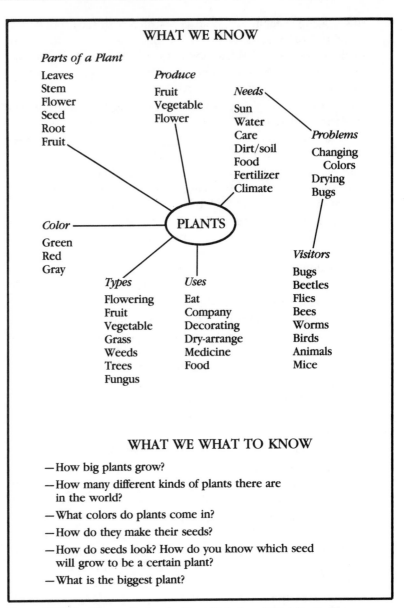

Figure CC30.1   Theme Cycle of a Plant Web, by a Third-Grade Class.

oral reports, students are encouraged to use a variety of presentation forms (diaries or logs, plays, learning centers, demonstrations, murals, drawings, displays, debates, Readers' Theatres, slide shows, etc.).

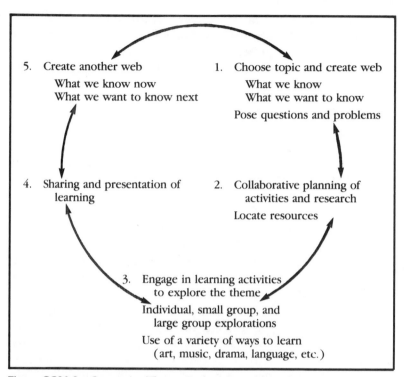

Figure CC30.2 Generative Theme Cycle. Adapted from Bess Altwerger by Kathy G. Short, 1987.

9. Another web with two other sections, "What We Know Now" and "What We Want to Know Next," can be created.

The entire process is illustrated in Figure CC30.2.

Teacher's Role

Because of students' past instructional histories, which may have signaled to them that schools are not concerned with their interests and experiences, teachers may first need to build a supportive classroom context before they can really negotiate with students on curriculum. The list of potential topics created at the beginning of the year is not the final list, but should continue to be negotiated and changed throughout the school year.

Teachers will play a major role in helping to organize the classroom environment to support whole-group, small-group, and individual experiences. Throughout the studies, teachers encourage students to move beyond what they already know by considering new questions, pursuing new kinds of resources, and finding a variety of ways to present their ideas back to the group. This encouragement should take the form of invitations rather than assignments.

Follow-Up

1. Students can use this strategy of listing what they know and what they want to know before reading an individual informational text.

2. If students are dealing with a large quantity of new information, rather than adding to the web, they may want to place their ideas on cards. They can write each idea on a card and then arrange and rearrange these cards into categories. See Generating Written Discourse for further discussion of using this strategy to create a written text.

3. The theme being explored by the class can be based on students' sociopolitical life so that they learn to dialogue critically about their life. They study their own community life to critique and go beyond the stereotypes, limitations, or oppressions that are part of their political realities. This variation is currently being explored by Bess Altwerger, Pam Hoffman, and other teachers in Albuquerque, New Mexico.

4. At several points during the year, students should be involved in expert projects. Expert projects differ from Theme Cycles in that individual students or small groups choose their own topic on which they want to become an expert. These topics do not relate to a broader class topic but are generated from student experiences and interests. These expert projects go through the Theme Cycle process.

5. A variation on expert projects is to have each student list a question he or she has always wondered about. These questions are posted on a Message Board. If other students have information on any of these questions, they write a response. Either the student who posed the question or other class members can choose to pursue any of the questions on the board and then post a response on the board.

6. Multimedia Blitz can be used to introduce students to options they might want to consider for expert projects. The teacher sets up learning centers on different topics around the room

with books, filmstrips, posters, pamphlets, artifacts, and any other materials related to the topics. Students are invited to spend some time exploring these centers and deciding on a topic on which they want to become an expert. They are not limited to the topics in the learning centers. The centers are used to get them thinking about possibilities and about the types of resources they will need to gather. This variation was developed by Susan Robinson.

7. Students in Myriam Revel-Wood's classroom form themselves into Science Clubs for the year. The students use the suggested textbook curriculum for their grade level to form various Science Clubs. Each club must have at least two members. The clubs meet regularly and work by themselves as well as with the teacher in formulating questions, selecting topics of study, conducting investigations, and reporting back to the class on new projects and findings. These clubs last for the entire year.

Shorter clubs are used in social studies. Students form themselves into clubs that last for a six- to eight-week period. Clubs relate to topics that build from the school social studies program. Students engage in field and library research and then present their findings to the group in some way.

8. At the conclusion of a Theme Cycle or expert projects, students can create learning centers and invite other classes in the school to visit the centers. At each center are displays and activities that students in charge of the center have developed to share what they learned. In some schools, several classrooms join together and set up a learning fair in the gym or cafeteria for the entire school to visit.

References

This description of Theme Cycles was adapted from the work of Bess Altwerger and from the "Read-for-Information Guide" developed by Yetta Goodman and Carolyn Burke. For further information see:

Goodman, Y. M. & Burke, C. L. 1980. *Reading strategies: Focus on comprehension.* New York: Owen.

Wordless Picture Books

Introduction

Wordless Picture Books tell a story entirely through the illustrations. The absence of language in these books allows the student to focus on the story taking place in the sequence of pictures rather than concentrating on the words on the page. These books are especially supportive for less proficient readers because of the absence of print, the focus on prediction, and the use of the books for oral and written language storytelling. Students use the pictures, their background experiences regarding the strategies of prediction and confirmation, and their understanding of story structures to construct a story about the book. As students share their stories with one another, they will see how each one constructed a different story from the pictures because of their differing background experiences.

Materials/Procedures

* Wordless books

1. A display of wordless books should be set up in the classroom.
2. The teacher should introduce the books to the students and talk about telling a story without words.
3. One book should be chosen to discuss as a class. First, students should page through the entire book, looking at the pictures and talking about what seems to be going on. Then they can go back through the book and take turns telling a story about the book.
4. Students can look through the books, select one, and make up their own story based on the pictures.

5. Students can share their stories with each other in small groups.

6. Students can then be invited to tape-record their story for others to listen to in the listening center, to write their story and publish it for others to read, or to act out their story for the class.

Teacher's Role

Students often initially do not see wordless books as "real" books because of the absence of words. The teacher needs to choose wordless books carefully based on the age level and interests of the students. Introductions to the books should focus on getting students involved and interested in the books. Wordless books cover a tremendous range of complexity and topics, and so are appropriate for older students as well as for young children.

Teachers sometimes make up booklets that include photocopies of the pictures for the story, with space for students to write their texts below the pictures. These booklets are placed in the Writing-Reading Center for students to use. Students can write about all the pictures from a wordless book or can choose four or five pictures to use in creating their own stories.

Follow-Up

1. Teachers can have all the students individually tell a story orally or in writing about the same wordless book as a way to evaluate language development and understanding of story structure.

2. Students can work in pairs. They can write a story together for a wordless book or they can individually write a story for the same book and then compare their two stories.

3. Students can take turns writing a story about a wordless book by telling the story in a round. The first person writes page one and then passes the book and the story to the second person, who writes page two. The story continues to be passed around the class or small group until it is completed. The writing of the story could also be done between two students who pass the story back and forth to each other after every page.

4. Students can draw or cut out pictures from a magazine to make their own wordless books.

References

The following references provide information on the use of wordless books:

Abrahamson, R. F. 1981. An update of wordless picture books with an annotated bibliography. *Reading Teacher* 34(4):417-421.

Degler, L. S. 1979. Putting words into wordless books. *Reading Teacher* 32(4):399-402.

McGee, L. M., & Tompkins, G. E. 1983. Wordless picture books are for older readers too. *Reading Teacher* 27(2):120-123.

Mid-Missouri TAWL. 1983. *Strategies that make sense: Invitations to literacy for secondary students.* Columbia, MO: Mid-Missouri TAWL.

Appendix: A Beginning List of Wordless Books

Alexander, M. 1970. *Bobo's dream.* New York: Dial

Anno, M. 1977. *Anno's journey.* New York: Collins.

Briggs, R. 1978. *The snowman.* New York: Random House.

Carle, E. 1971. *Do you want to be my friend?* New York: Collins.

de Paola, T. 1978. *Pancakes for breakfast.* New York: Harcourt Brace Jovanovich.

Goodall, J. 1968. *The adventures of Paddy Pork.* New York: Harcourt Brace Jovanovich.

——— . 1979. *The Story of an English Village.* New York: Atheneum.

Hoban, T. 1981. *Take another look.* New York: Greenwillow.

——— . 1983. *I read signs.* New York: Greenwillow.

Hutchins, P. 1971. *Changes, changes.* New York: Macmillan.

Krahn, F. 1978. *The great ape.* New York: Penguin.

Mayer, M. 1974. *Frog goes to dinner.* New York: Dial.

——— . 1975. *One frog too many.* New York: Dial.

Ormerod, J. 1981. *Sunlight.* New York: Lothrop.

——— . 1982. *Moonlight.* New York: Lothrop.

Spier, P. 1977. *Noah's ark.* New York: Doubleday.

——— . 1982. *Peter Spier's rain.* New York: Doubleday.

Turkle, B. 1976. *Deep in the forest.* New York: Dutton.

Ward, L. 1973. *The silver pony.* Boston: Houghton Mifflin.

Written Conversation

Introduction

Although written language differs from oral language, what children know about oral language can be used to support their move into writing. Written Conversation builds on this support by making minimal distinctions between oral language and written language. Not only does oral language support written language, but reading and writing support each other. In Written Conversation, what one language participant writes is read by the second participant and can be used to support what that participant writes, and vice versa.

Written Conversation provides an informal writing environment in which students and teachers are encouraged to explore meaning with each other. Because the focus is on informal communication with another person, Written Conversation is supportive in helping language users overcome their insecurities about putting their ideas down on paper and in drawing their attention to consideration of audience. It is a natural activity in a classroom where a degree of quiet is expected during certain periods of the day.

Materials/Procedures

* Paper (any scrap will do) and a pencil

1. The first participant writes a question on a sheet of paper and hands the paper and the pencil to the second participant.

2. The second participant reads the question, writes a response to it, and returns the paper to the first participant. The activity proceeds in this fashion, with the participants changing roles in asking questions and making responses until the conversation is terminated by one of the participants (see Figures CC32.1, CC32.2, and CC32.3).

375

Figure CC32.1   Written Conversation between an Adult and a Four-Year-Old (Mills 1986).

Transcription:

What did you do this weekend?
Museum
What did you do?

I went on a canoe trip.
I went to Lake Michigan today.

Figure CC32.2   Written Conversation between an Adult and a Six-Year-Old.

Transcription:

Hi.
Hi.
My name is Diane.
My name is Lillie.
I am 21 years old.
I am 6 years old.
I like ice cream.
I like ice cream too.
I like to read.
Let's read to Erin.
I love you.

Glen, do you have a girl friend?
No.
Why not?
I don't like girls!
Why not?
Because they get me in trouble!
How do they do that?

They write letters to you
and they talk to you
when you are not supposed to!

Figure CC32.3 Written Conversation between Two Nine-Year-Olds (Special Education).

Teacher's Role

Written Conversation can be introduced as a natural way for class members (including the teacher) to exchange comments and yet not disturb others who are working. The teacher might wait to introduce the activity until after the classroom has become noisy and students are complaining that they can't concentrate. In introducing the activity, the teacher should stress that Written Conversation is just like oral conversation, except that instead of talking orally with a neighbor or friend, they will do their talking on paper.

There are several different ways that teachers can introduce this activity to their classes. Some teachers have announced a "Written Conversation Day" during which students can do as much talking as they wish, but only on paper rather than orally. Other teachers begin by having a public conversation with one student using the overhead projector. Students are then asked to pair up and have similar conversations with each other. Another strategy is simply for the teacher to begin informally sitting next to various children and having a Written Conversation, and then encouraging them to try this activity with others.

Teachers must make every effort to engage in Written Conversations with students as frequently as possible, often electing a Written Conversation over an oral conversation if such a choice can be made. Teachers should also encourage students to engage in Written Conversations with one another whenever appropriate.

Teachers will want to adjust the rules for Written Conversation for young children whose writing is unconventional and difficult for others to read. Each participant, whether adult or child, writes a message and then reads whatever was written to the other participant.

Follow-Up

1. Written Conversations can be used instead of comprehension activities such as worksheets or question-and-answer discussions with the teacher. After reading a selection, students can be asked to discuss, via Written Conversation, their understanding of a selection with another student. Although these conversations could be collected by the teacher, the activity is best used and introduced to students as simply a device they can use to organize their thinking before engaging in a group discussion.

2. Students can read different variations of the same story and then engage in Written Conversations with one another to compare the similarities and differences in their versions. For example, students could read different Cinderella variants (see Text Sets).

3. Students can be invited to have a Written Conversation with another student on a topic they are going to write about. Once they have had their conversation and written their draft, they should be asked to share their feelings about how having a Written Conversation facilitated their writing. Other students should be invited to try this strategy before writing a first draft on a topic of their choice.

4. Written Conversation can be used to discuss disputes and disruptive behavior in the class or on the playground. Having students write about what happened often calms tempers and gives students time to organize and support their view of the experience.

Reference

Written Conversation was initially developed by Carolyn Burke.

Bibliography

Alexander, L. 1968- .The Prydain Chronicles (series). New York: Dell. (Titles include *The book of three; The black cauldron; The castle of Llyr; Taran Wanderer; The high king.*)

Aliki. 1986. *How a book is made.* New York: Crowell.

Anderson, R. C. & Pearson, P. D. 1984. *A schema-theoretic view of basic processes in reading comprehension.* Technical Report No. 306. Champaign, IL: University of Illinois, Center for the Study of Reading.

Arnheim, R. 1954. *Art and visual perception.* Berkeley: University of California Press.

Atwell, M. 1980. The evolution of text: The interrelationship of reading and writing in the composing process. Ph.D. diss., Indiana University, Bloomington.

——— . 1985. Predictable books for adolescent readers. *Journal of Reading* 29(1): 18-22.

Atwell, N. 1984. Writing and reading literature from the inside out. *Language Arts* 61(3): 240-252.

——— . 1987. *In the middle: Writing, reading, and learning with adolescents.* Portsmouth, NH: Boynton/Cook-Heinemann.

Audubon Field Guides. Garden City, NY: Doubleday.

Banks, L. R. 1981. *The Indian in the cupboard.* Garden City, NY: Doubleday.

Barnes, D. 1975. *From communication to curriculum.* New York: Penguin.

Big Books from Down Under (series). 1986- . Crystal Lake, IL: Rigby Education. (Big Books are also now available from several other U.S. publishers, including Scholastic and Owen.)

Blos, J. 1979. *A gathering of days: A New England girl's journal, 1830–32.* New York: Scribner.

Brown, D. [1971] 1984. *Bury my heart at wounded knee.* New York: Simon & Schuster.

Buck, P. S. 1986. *The big wave.* New York: Harper & Row.

Burke, C. L. 1984. Figure introduced in graduate coursework. Indiana University.

——— . 1985a. *A natural curriculum.* Videotape. In J. C. Harste (host & developer) & E. Jurewicz (producer & director), The Authoring Cycle: Read Better, Write Better, Reason Better (videotape series). Portsmouth, NH: Heinemann.

——— . 1985b. Personal communication.

——— . 1986. An amateur model of literacy. Speech given at the World

Congress on Reading, International Reading Association, London.

Calkins, L. M. 1986. *The art of teaching writing.* Portsmouth, NH: Heinemann.

Carle, E. 1969. *The very hungry caterpillar.* Cleveland: Collins World.

Choose Your Own Adventure Series. 1979-   . New York: Bantam. (*The cave of time* by E. Packard; *Journey under the sea* by R. A. Montgomery; *By balloon to the Sahara* by D. Terrman; *Space and beyond* by R. A. Montgomery; *The mystery of chimney rock* by E. Packard: *Your code name is Jonah* by E. Packard; *The third planet from Altair* by E. Packard; *Deadwood City* by E. Packard; *Who killed Harlowe Thrombey?* by E. Packard; *The lost jewels of Nabooti* by R. A. Montgomery; *Mystery of the Maya* by R. A. Montgomery.)

Cleary, B. 1983. *Dear Mr. Henshaw.* New York: Morrow.

Clyde, J. A. 1986. A collaborative venture: Exploring the socio-psycholinguistic nature of literacy. Ph.D. diss., Indiana University, Bloomington.

Commire, A. 1971-   . Something about the Author (series). Detroit: Gale.

Cullinan, B. E., et al. 1981. *Literature and the child.* New York: Harcourt Brace Jovanovich.

de Paola, T. 1972. *Nana upstairs, Nana downstairs.* New York: Putnam.

Dixon, F. W. 1933-   . Hardy Boys Mystery Stories (series). New York: Grosset and Dunlap. (Titles include *The Viking symbol mystery; The tower treasure; The house on the cliff; The secret of the old mill; The missing chums; Hunting for hidden gold;* and many more.)

Doake, D. 1986. *Whole language principles and practices in reading development with special emphasis on reading recovery* (videotape). Ontario, Canada: Scholastic-TAB Publications.

Donaldson, M. 1978. *Children's minds.* New York: Norton.

Eisner, E. W. 1982. *Cognition and curriculum.* New York: Longman.

Fleck, L. [1935] 1979. *Genesis and development of a scientific fact.* Chicago: University of Chicago Press.

Gardner, H. 1980. *Artful scribbles.* New York: Basic.

Golden Book Field Guides. New York: Western.

Goodman, K. 1986. *What's whole in whole language?* Portsmouth, NH: Heinemann.

Goodman, K., Smith, E. B., Meredith, R., & Goodman, Y. M. 1987. *Language and thinking in school.* 3d ed. New York: Owen.

Goodman, Y. M., Burke, C. L., & Sherman, B. 1980. *Strategies in reading: Focus on comprehension.* New York: Holt, Rinehart & Winston.

Goor, R., & Goor, N. 1983. *Signs.* New York: Crowell.

Goss, J. L., & Harste, J. C. [1981] 1985. *It didn't frighten me!* Worthington, OH: Willowisp.

Grahame, K. 1940. *Wind in the willow.* New York: Scribner.

Graves, D. 1983. *Writing: Teachers and children at work.* Portsmouth, NH: Heinemann.

——. 1984. *A researcher learns to write.* Portsmouth, NH: Heinemann.

——. 1985. *A natural curriculum.* In J. C. Harste (developer & host) &

E. Jurewicz (producer & director), The Authoring Cycle: Read Better, Write Better, Reason Better (videotape series). Portsmouth, NH: Heinemann.

Graves, D., & Hansen, J. 1983. The author's chair. *Language Arts* 60(2): 176-183.

Hakes, D. T. 1980. *The development of metalinguistic abilities in children.* New York: Springer-Verlag.

Halliday, M. A. K. 1985. *Three aspects of children's language development: Learn language, learn about language, learn through language.* Mimeograph. Department of Linguistics, University of Sydney.

Harste, J. C. 1986. What it means to be strategic: Good readers as informants. Paper presented at the National Reading Conference, Austin, Texas.

Harste, J. C., Burke, C. L., & Woodward, V. A. 1981. *Children, their language and world: Initial encounters with print.* Final Report NIE-G-79-0132. Bloomington: Indiana University, Language Education Department.

———. 1983. *The young child as writer-reader and informant.* Final Report NIE-G-80-0121. Bloomington: Indiana University, Language Education Department.

Harste, J. C. (host & developer), & Jurewicz, E. (producer & director). 1985. The Authoring Cycle: Read Better, Write Better, Reason Better (videotape series). Portsmouth, NH: Heinemann.

Harste, J. C., Pierce, K., & Cairney, T. 1985. *The authoring cycle: A viewing guide.* Portsmouth, NH: Heinemann.

Harste, J. C., & Stephens, D. 1985. *Toward practical theory: A state of practice assessment of reading comprehension instruction.* Final Report USDE-C-300-83-0130. Bloomington: Indiana University, Language Education Department.

Harste, J. C., Woodward, V. A., & Burke, C. L. 1984. *Language stories & literacy lessons.* Portsmouth, NH: Heinemann.

Hemingway, E. 1952. *The old man and the sea.* New York: Macmillan.

Hepler, S. I. 1982. Patterns of response to literature: A one-year study of a fifth and sixth grade classroom. Ph.D. diss., Ohio State University, Columbus.

Hickman, J. 1981. A new perspective on response to literature: Research in an elementary school setting. *Research in the Teaching of English* 13(4): 343-354.

Hoban, T. 1983. *I read signs.* New York: Greenwillow.

———. 1984. *I walk and read.* New York: Greenwillow.

Holdaway, D. 1979. *The foundations of literacy.* Portsmouth, NH: Heinemann.

Hopkins, L. B. 1969. *Books are by people.* New York: Citation.

———. 1974. *More books by more people.* New York: Citation.

Hulett, Joycelin, ed. 1982. *Whole language activities for a comprehension centered language program.* Columbia, MO: University of Missouri.

Hutchins, P. 1968. *Rosie's walk.* New York: Macmillan.

———. 1980. *The tale of Thomas Mead.* New York: Greenwillow.

Keene, C. 1930- . Nancy Drew Mystery Stories (series). New York: Grosset and Dunlap. (Titles include *The bungalow mystery; The secret of the old clock; The hidden staircase; The mystery of Lilac Inn; The secret of Shadow Ranch; The secret of Red Gate Farm;* and many more.)

Kellogg, S. 1973. *The island of the Skog.* New York: Dial.

Kellogg, S. (narrator), & Blantz, J. (writer). 1976. *How a picture book is made: The island of the Skog.* Slides/audiotape. Weston, CT: Weston Woods.

Kucer, S. 1983. Using text comprehension as a metaphor for understanding text production: Building bridges between reading and writing. Ph.D. diss., Indiana University, Bloomington.

Lewis, C. S. 1950- . The Chronicles of Narnia (series). New York: Macmillan. (Titles include *The lion, the witch, and the wardrobe; The voyage of the Dawn Treader; The silver chair; The horse and his boy; The magician's nephew; The last battle.*)

Lobel, A. 1972. *Frog and toad together.* New York: Harper & Row.

McCloskey, R. 1943. *Homer Price.* New York, Viking.

McGovern, A. 1979. *Little humpback whale.* New York: Scholastic.

MacLachlan, P. 1985. *Sarah plain and tall.* New York: Harper & Row.

Martin, B., Jr. [1970] 1983. *Brown bear, brown bear, what do you see?* New York: Holt, Rinehart & Winston.

Merriam, E. 1977. *Ab to zogg.* New York: Macmillan. (Other books include *Fresh paint: New poems,* 1986; *A word or two with you,* 1981; *The birthday door,* 1986 [Morrow]; *Jamboree,* 1984 [Dell]; *A sky full of poems,* 1986 [Dell].)

———. 1985. *Blackberry ink.* New York: Morrow.

Mid-Missouri TAWL. 1983. *Strategies that make sense: Invitations to literacy for secondary students.* Columbia, MO: Mid-Missouri TAWL.

Mills, H. A. 1986. Evaluating literacy: A transactional process. Ph.D. diss., Indiana University, Bloomington.

Moll, L., & Diaz, S. 1987. A socio-cultural approach to the study of Hispanic children. In A. Allen, ed., *Library services for Hispanic children.* Phoenix, AZ: Oryx Press.

Murray, D. 1984. *Write to learn.* New York: Holt, Rinehart & Winston.

Neisser, U. 1976. *Cognition and reality.* San Francisco: Freeman.

Newman, J. 1983. *Whole language activities.* Department of Education Monographs on Learning and Teaching. Halifax, Nova Scotia: Dalhousie University.

Newsroom. 1984. Minneapolis, MN: Springboard Software.

Paterson, K. 1977. *Bridge to Terabithia.* Illustrated by Donna Diamond. New York: Crowell.

Peterson's Field Guides. Boston: Houghton Mifflin.

Piaget, J. 1976. *The grasp of consciousness: Action and concept in the young child.* Cambridge: Harvard University Press.

Pierce, K. M. 1986. Curriculum as collaboration: Toward practical theory. Ph.D. diss., Indiana University, Bloomington.

Rhodes, L. 1981. I can read! Predictable books as resources for reading and writing instruction. *Reading Teacher* 34(5): 511-518.

——. 1983. *Extended literature activities*. Denver: University of Colorado.

Rowe, D. W. 1986. Literacy in the child's world: Preschoolers' explorations of alternate sign systems. Ph.D. diss., Indiana University, Bloomington.

Ruwe, M. 1971. *Ten little bears*. Illustrated by D. Csanady. Glenview, IL: Scott, Foresman.

Rylant, C. 1986. *The relatives came*. New York: Bradbury.

Scibior, O. S. 1986. Reconsidering spelling development: A sociopsycholinguistic perspective. Ph.D. diss., Indiana University, Bloomington.

Short, K. G. 1986. Literacy as a collaborative experience. Ph.D. diss., Indiana University, Bloomington.

Short, K. G., & Burke, C. L. 1988. Creating curricula which foster thinking. In J. C. Harste, ed., *Critical thinking*. Urbana, IL: National Council of Teachers of English.

Shreve, S. 1984. *The flunking of Joshua T. Bates*. New York: Knopf.

Siegel, M. G. 1984. Reading as signification. Ph.D. diss., Indiana University, Bloomington.

Smith, E. B., Goodman, K., & Meredith, R. 1978. *Language and thinking in school*. 2d ed. New York: Holt, Rinehart & Winston.

Smith, F. 1981. Demonstrations, engagement, and sensitivity: A revised approach to the language arts. *Language Arts* 52(1): 103-112.

——. 1982. *Understanding reading*. 3d ed. New York: Holt, Rinehart & Winston.

Spiro, R. J., Vispoel, W. L., Schmitz, J., Samarapungavan, A., & Boerger, A. In press. Knowledge acquisition for application: Cognitive flexibility and transfer in complex content domains. In B. C. Britton, ed., *Executive control processes*. Hillsdale, NJ: Erlbaum.

Stein, N. L., & Glenn, C. G. 1978. An analysis of story comprehension in elementary school children. In R. O. Freedle, ed., *Advances in discourse processing*, vol. 2, *New Directions*. Norwood, NJ: Ablex.

Tolstoy, A. 1971. *The great big enormous turnip*. Glenview, IL: Scott, Foresman.

Trelease, J. 1985. *The read-aloud handbook*. rev. ed. New York: Penguin.

Vargus, N. R. 1982. Letter writing over time: Socio-cognitive constraints in transition. Ph.D. diss., Indiana University, Bloomington.

Vygotsky, L. S. [1934] 1962. *Thought and language*. Cambridge: MIT Press.

——. 1978. *Mind and society*. Ed. M. Cole, V. John-Steiner, S. Scribner, & E. Sonberman. Cambridge: Harvard University Press.

Waber, B. 1972. *Ira sleeps over*. Boston: Houghton, Mifflin.

Watson, D. J. 1978. Reader selected miscues: Getting more from sustained silent reading. *English Education* 10(1): 75-85.

———. 1982. What is a whole-language reading program? *The Missouri Reader* 7(1): 8-10.

White, E. B. 1952. *Charlotte's Web*. New York: Harper & Row.

Suggested Reading

Atwell, N. 1987. *In the middle: Writing, reading, and learning with adolescents.* Portsmouth, NH: Boynton/Cook-Heinemann.

Baghban, M. 1984. *Our daughter learns to read and write: A case study from birth to three.* Newark, DE: International Reading Association.

Barnes, D. 1975. *From communication to curriculum.* New York: Penguin.

Barton, B. 1986. *Tell me another.* Portsmouth, NH: Heinemann.

Baskwill, J., & Whitman, P. 1986. *Whole language sourcebook.* Richmond Hill, MO: Scholastic-TAB Publications.

Bissex, G. L. 1980. *GNYS AT WRK: A child learns to write and read.* Cambridge: Harvard University Press.

Buchanan, E., ed. 1980. *For the love of reading.* Winnipeg, Canada: C. E. L. Group. (Order from Orin Cochran, 14 Regula Place, Winnipeg, Manitoba, R2W 2P9.)

Butler, A., & Turbill, J. 1984. *Towards a reading-writing classroom.* Portsmouth, NH: Heinemann.

Calkins, L. M. 1983. *Lessons from a child.* Portsmouth, NH: Heinemann.

———. 1986. *The art of teaching writing.* Portsmouth, NH: Heinemann.

Cambourne, B., & Turbill, J. 1987. *Coping with chaos.* Portsmouth, NH: Heinemann.

Cochrane, O., Cochrane, D., Scalena, S., & Buchanan, E. 1984. *Reading, writing and caring.* New York: Owen.

DeFord, D. E. 1981. Literacy: Reading, writing and other essentials. *Language Arts* 58(6): 652-658.

Edelsky, C., & Smith, K. 1984. Is that writing—or are those marks just a figment of your curriculum? *Language Arts* 61(1): 24-32.

Ferreriro, E., & Teberosky, A. 1982. *Literacy before schooling.* Portsmouth, NH: Heinemann.

Gillis, C., et al. In press. *Whole language strategies for secondary students.* New York: Owen.

Goodman, K. S. 1983. The solution is the risk: A response to "A Nation at Risk." *SLATE Newsletter.* Urbana, IL: National Council of Teachers of English. (Reprinted in January 1984, *Education Digest.*)

———. 1986. *What's whole in whole language?* Bright Idea Book Series. Portsmouth, NH: Heinemann.

Goodman, K. S., Smith, E. B., Meredith, R., & Goodman, Y. M. 1987. *Language and thinking in school.* 3d ed. New York: Owen.

Goodman, Y. M. 1978. Kid watching: An alternative to testing. *Journal of National Elementary School Principals* 57(4): 22-27.

——— . 1980. *Initial encounters with print.* Videotape. In D. Strickler (producer & director), Reading Comprehension (videotape series). Portsmouth, NH: Heinemann.

Goodman, Y. M., & Burke, C. L. 1980. *Reading strategies: Focus on comprehension.* New York: Owen.

Goodman, Y. M., Watson, D., & Burke, C. L. 1987. *Reading miscue inventory: Alternative procedures.* New York: Owen.

Graves. D. 1983. *Writing: Teachers and children at work.* Portsmouth, NH: Heinemann.

Halliday, M. A. K. 1975. *Learning how to mean: Explorations in the development of language.* London: Edward Arnold.

Hansen, J. 1987. *When writers read.* Portsmouth, NH: Heinemann.

Hansen, J., Graves, D. (developers), Whitney, J., & Hubbard, R. (writers & producers). 1986. The Reading and Writing Process (videotape series). Portsmouth, NH: Heinemann.

Hansen, J., Newkirk, T., & Graves, D. M. 1985. *Breaking ground: Teachers relate reading and writing in the elementary school.* Portsmouth, NH: Heinemann.

Hall, N. 1987. *The emergence of literacy.* Portsmouth, NH: Heinemann.

Harste, J. C., Woodward, V. A., & Burke, C. L. 1984. *Language stories & literacy lessons.* Portsmouth, NH: Heinemann.

Heath, S. B. 1983. *Ways with words.* Cambridge, England: Cambridge University Press.

Holdaway, D. 1979. *The foundations of literacy.* Portsmouth, NH: Heinemann.

Jaggar, A., & Smith-Burke, M. T., eds. 1985. *Observing the language learner.* Newark, DE: International Reading Association.

King, M., & Rental, V. 1979. Toward a theory of early writing development. *Research in the Teaching of English* 13(1): 243-253.

Linfors, J. 1987. *Children's language and learning.* 2d ed. Englewood Cliffs, NJ: Prentice-Hall.

McVitty, W., ed. 1986. *Getting it together: Organizing the reading-writing classroom.* Portsmouth, NH: Heinemann.

Newkirk, T., & Atwell, N., eds. 1988. *Understanding writing: Ways of observing, learning, and teaching.* 2d ed. Portsmouth, NH: Heinemann.

Newman, J. 1984. *The craft of children's writing.* Bright Idea Book Series. Ontario, Canada: Scholastic-TAB Publishers. (Distributed in the United States by Heinemann, Portsmouth, NH.)

——— . 1985. *Whole language: Theory in use.* Portsmouth, NH: Heinemann.

Meek, M. 1982. *Learning to read.* London: Bodley Head.

Milz, V. 1980. *The comprehension-centered classroom: Setting it up and making it work.* Videotape. In D. J. Strickler (producer & director), Reading Comprehension (videotape series). Portsmouth, NH: Heinemann.

Paley, V. G. 1981. *Wally's stories.* Cambridge: Harvard University Press.

Pearson, P. D., & Tierney, R. J. 1984. On becoming a thoughtful reader: Reading like a writer. In A. C. Purves & D. Niles, eds., *Becoming readers in a complex society,* Part 1 of the *Eighty-third Yearbook of the National Society for the Study of Education.* Chicago: University of Chicago Press.

Perl, S., & Wagner, N. 1986. *Through teachers' eyes: Portraits of writing teachers at work.* Portsmouth, NH: Heinemann.

Rhodes, L. 1981. I can read! Predictable books as resources for reading and writing instruction. *Reading Teacher* 34(5): 511-518.

Rhodes, L. K. 1983. Organizing the elementary classroom for effective language learning. In U. H. Hardt, ed., *Teaching reading with the other language arts.* Newark, DE: International Reading Association.

Rhodes, L. K., & Hill, M. W. 1983. Home-school cooperation in integrated language arts. In B. A. Bushing & J. I. Schwartz, eds., *Integrating the language arts in the elementary school.* Urbana, IL: National Council of Teachers of English.

Rosen, H. 1984. *Stories and meanings.* London: National Association for the Teaching of English.

Shanklin, N. K. L. 1981. *Relating reading and writing: Developing a transactional theory of the writing process.* Monographs in Language & Reading Studies. Bloomington, IN: School of Education Publications Office, Indiana University.

Sherman, B. W. 1979. Reading for meaning. *Learning* 60(1): 41-44.

Short, K. G. 1985. A new lens for reading comprehension: Comprehension processes as critical thinking. In A. Crismore, ed., *Landscapes: A state-of-art assessment of reading comprehension research, 1974–1984.* USDE-C-300-83-0130. Bloomington: Indiana University, Language Education Department.

Sims, R. 1980. *Children's literature in a comprehension-centered reading program.* Videotape. In D. J. Strickler (director & producer), Reading Comprehension (videotape series). Portsmouth, NH: Heinemann.

Smith, E. B., Goodman, K. S., & Meredith, R. 1978. *Language and thinking in school.* 2d ed. New York: Holt, Rinehart & Winston.

Smith, F. 1978. *Reading without nonsense.* New York: Teachers College Press.

——. 1984. *Learning to be a critical thinker.* Victoria, Canada: Abel.

——. 1987. *Insult to intelligence.* New York: Arbor House.

Taylor, D. 1983. *Family literacy: Young children learning to read and write.* Portsmouth, NH: Heinemann.

Taylor, D., & Strickland, D. 1986. *Family storybook reading.* Portsmouth, NH: Heinemann.

Teale, W. H. 1986. Emergent literacy: Reading and writing in early childhood. Invited review of research presented at the Annual Meeting of the National Reading Conference, Austin. (*1987 Yearbook of the National Reading Conference,* J. Readance & S. Baldwin, eds. Rochester, NY: National Reading Conference.)

Trelease, J. 1985. *The read-aloud handbook,* rev. ed. New York: Penguin.

Turbill, J. 1983. *Now, we want to write!* Portsmouth, NH: Heinemann.

———, ed. 1982. *No better way to teach writing!* Rozelle, Australia: Primary English Teaching Association. (Distributed in the United States by Heinemann, Portsmouth, NH.)

Watson, D. J. 1980. *Learning about the reader.* Videotape. In D. Strickler (producer & director), Reading Comprehension (videotape series). Portsmouth, NH: Heinemann.

———. 1980. *Strategies for a comprehension-centered reading program.* Videotape. In D. Strickler (producer & director), Reading Comprehension (videotape series). Portsmouth, NH: Heinemann.

———. 1982. What is a whole language program? *The Missouri Reader* 7(1): 8-10.

———, ed. In press. *Ideas with insights: K-6 language arts.* Urbana, IL: National Council of Teachers of English.

Wells, G. 1986. *The meaning makers: Children learning language and using language to learn.* Portsmouth, NH: Heinemann.

Index

Aardema, V., 301, 317, 363
Abrahamson, R., 374
Adams, P., 364
Adoff, A., 327
Adults as authors, 15
Ahlberg, A., 317, 351
Ahlberg, J., 351
Aldis, D., 327
Alexander, L., 171, 302, 381
Alexander, M., 374
Aliki, B., 90, 262, 381
Alison, 3
Alternate communication systems,
    10, 11, 318-22, 353-57
  in Literature Response Activities,
    151
Altwerger, B., 369, 370, 371
Amy, language story, 83
Anderson, H., 301
Anderson, R., 5, 381
Anno, M., 374
Anomalies, 215-18
  examples, 217
  follow-up, 216
  materials and procedures, 215-16
  rationale, 215
  teacher's role, 216
  worksheet, 218
Armstrong, W., 303
Arnheim, R., 14, 381
Art, 33-37
Artists, 196-98
Assessing progress, 230
Atwell, M., 82, 141, 351, 381
Atwell, N., 62, 80, 159, 231, 289,
    292, 387, 388
Audience, 13
Audubon Field Guides, 382
Author of the Week Program, 235
Author Sharing Time, 16
  curricular description, 122-24
Author study, 236

Author's Folder, 20, 227-31
  and Classroom Newspaper, 247
  curricular description, 64-68
  and evaluation, 228-30
  follow-up, 230-31
  fostering self-evaluation, 230
  materials and procedures, 228-29
  rationale, 227
  teacher's role, 229-30
Authoring
  in content areas, 177, 181-211
  as learning, 5
Authoring cycle
  curricular components, 213-379
  curricular description, 18-25
  as curricular framework, 10, 33,
    55, 105-7
  curricular model, 19
  getting started, 51-103
  key elements, 52-54
  as learning cycle, 9-18, 36-37
  and publishing, 19-25
  videotape series, ix
Authors and authorship, 5
Authors Meeting Authors, 232-37
  and Author of the Week Program,
    235
  curricular description, 127,
    145-50
  follow-up, 235-36
  and Group Composed Books, 235
  and Literature Circles, 233
  materials and procedures, 232-33
  parent involvement, 235
  rationale, 232
  and Readers' Theatre, 233
  teacher's role, 234-35
  writing opportunities, 235
Authors' Chair, 46, 219-20
  and Authors' Circle, 124
  curricular description, 124-28
  follow-up, 220

Authors' Chair (*continued*)
  materials and procedures, 219-20
  rationale, 219
  teacher's role, 220
  and Work Time, 219
Authors' Circle, 20, 221-26
  and Authors' Chair, 124
  curricular description, 68-80,
    80-82
  and drama, 226
  follow-up, 225-26
  introducing, 70
  materials and procedures, 222-24
  rationale, 221-22
  and Readers' Theatre, 226
  teacher's role, 224-25
  and Text Sets, 361
Authorship
  and functionality, 11
  variety of, 18

Babbit, N., 303
Baghban, M., 387
Baldwin, S., 389
Banks, L., 171, 303, 381
Barchas, S., 351
Barnes, D., 13, 17, 299, 381, 387
Barton, B., 387
Basal readers
  moving away from, 243
  and Readers' Theatre, 137
Baskwill, J., 387
Baylor, B., 267
Beard, R., 196
Becker, J., 351
Behn, H., 327, 365
Beth, language story, 6-7
Big Books, 381
Bilingual, 266
Bishop, C., 303
Bissex, G., 387
Blantz, J., 90, 262, 384
Bleich, D., 316
Blos, J., 282, 285, 381
Blume, J., 317
Board games, 306
Bobbie, language story, 22-23
Boerger, A., 385
Book Sales, 166, 306
Bookmaking, 93, 238-42
  and Group Composed Books, 240
  follow-up, 240-41

materials and procedures, 238-39
rationale, 239
teacher's role, 239-40
and Young Authors Conference,
  240
Books
  about caterpillars, 363-64
  character series, 364
  about environmental print, 352
  about pigs, 364
  on poetry, 327-28
  about puppets, 364
Boone, R., 351, 364
Botell, M., 317
Bouffler, C., 226
Boyd, language story, 102
Boylad, E., 363
Brainstorming, 275
Brian, language story, 22-23
Bridges, C., 350
Briggs, R., 374
Brink, C., 267
Britton, B., 385
Brooks, G., 327
Brown, D., 171, 381
Brown, M., 351
Brown, R., 351
Buchanan, E., 387
Buck, P., 171, 381
Bulla, R., 301
Burke, C., ii, ix, x, xi, 3, 5, 16, 19,
    33, 40, 51, 62, 67, 100, 102,
    105, 118, 134, 169, 190-91,
    226, 251, 262, 276, 312, 322,
    325, 339, 345, 357, 362, 371,
    379, 381, 382, 383, 385, 388
Burnett, F., 303
Burningham, J., 351
Burton, F., 267
Busch, K., 322
Busching, B., 331, 389
Butler, A., 387
Byars, B., 303, 364

Cairney, T., ix, xi, 345, 383
Caldecott Award, text set, 361
Calkins, L., 226, 231, 262, 298, 326,
    382, 387
Cambourne, B., 387
Carle, E., 142, 277, 301, 351, 355,
    362, 363, 374, 382

Carrick, C., 301
Cartoons, 342
Celebrating authorship, 92-99, 238-42
Chapter books, 302-4
Character sketch, 56-57
  examples, 59, 60
Children, as curricular informants, 4-9
Childress, A., 317
Choice, 61-62, 203-5, 243
Choose Your Own Adventure, 126, 141, 382
Choose Your Own Story, 243-45
  curricular description, 64
  follow-up, 244-45
  materials and procedures, 243-44
  rationale, 243
  teacher's role, 244
  and writing, 244
Choral reading, 348-49
Ciardi, J., 327
Classroom Library, curricular description, 128-31
Classroom Logs, 159, 290
Classroom Magazine, 249
Classroom Newspaper, 246-52
  adaptations, 247
  and Author's Folder, 247
  curricular description, 128, 235
  example, 250
  and Family Stories, 247
  follow-up, 249-52
  and Getting to Know You, 247
  materials and procedures, 246-47
  rationale, 246
  teacher's role, 248-49
  and units of study, 247
  various roles, 247
Classroom organization, 63-64, 311-12
Cleary, B., 147, 172, 236-37, 282, 285, 303, 364, 382
Cloning an Author, 253-56
  curricular description, 101, 151
  follow-up, 253
  and Generating Written Discourse, 256
  and Literature Response Activities, 307
  materials and procedures, 253-55
  rationale, 253

teacher's role, 255
  variations, 255-56
  and writing, 256
Clyde, J., xi, 198, 252, 262, 382
Cochrane, D., 387
Cochrane, O., 387
Coerr, E., 303
Coger, L., 331
Cole, J., 327
Cole, M., 385
Collaboration, 15-16, 206-7
Collage, 306
Collier, C., 303
Collier, J., 303
Commercials, 278
Commire, A., 146, 237, 382
Community Logs, 159
Comparison charts, 306
Compartmentalization, and curriculum, 122
Complexity, and language learning, 13
Comprehension
  and flow charts, 245
  and maps, 245
  as patterns that connect, 358
  and Poetry in Motion, 323
  and Save the Last Word for Me, 332
  strategy instruction, 215-18, 243-45, 253-56, 293-304, 306, 316, 336-39, 340-45
  and timelines, 245
  using drama, 244
  using gameboards, 244
Comprehension-centered curriculum, tenets, 208-10
Computer software, for classroom newspaper, 252
Computers, 95
Content area writing, and Generating Written Discourse, 270-71
Context, 53
Convention, 13, 84
Coody, B., 308
Cooney, B., 267, 302
Cooking, 306
Cooney, B., 267, 302
Copeland, K., 159
Corey
  example, 281
  language story, 25-33

Cousins, P., 377
Crafton, L., 362
Crismore, A., 389
Crowley, P., 225, 230, 339
Cullinan, B., 147, 308, 382
Cumulative pattern books, 363
Cumulative writing folders, 230
Curricular tenets, 208-10
Curriculum, 48
    function of, 51
    as negotiated, 48-49
    status of, 51

Danny, language story, 185-87
de Paola, T., 147, 267, 302, 327,
    355, 363, 364, 374, 382
de Regniers, B., 351, 362
DeFord, D., 387
Degler, L., 374
Demonstrating authorship, 14-16
Demonstrations, 14-17, 118
    and modeling, 14
Dialogue journals, 156, 282
    example, 174, 281
Diaz, S., 266-67, 384
Dioramas, 306
Discussion, 16
    how to stimulate, 299-301
Displays, 306
Dixon, F., 141, 382
Doake, D., 143, 382
Domanska, J., 363
Donaldson, M., 9
Drama, 226, 245, 306, 317
Ducer, J., 339
Dunning, S., 327

Edelsky, C., 387
Editing
    and conventions, 87-88
    and publishing, 91
Editors' responsibility, 20
Editors' Table, 257-62
    and Authors' Circle, 258
    curricular description, 57, 82-92
    follow-up, 261-62
    materials and procedures, 258-60
    rationale, 257
    teacher's role, 260-61

Eisner, E., 7, 9, 11, 12, 18, 382
Elkin, B., 363
Empowerment, 54
Engagement, 118
Environmental print walks, books,
    and recipes, 190-96
Environmental Print Books, 182
    examples, 192
Environmental Print Recipes, 182
    examples, 193-95
Environmental Print Walks, 182
Erickson, F., 317
Estes, E., 303
Ets, M., 362
Evaluation, 20-25, 65-67, 227-29,
    286-92, 373
Experiencing authorship, 11-14
Expert Projects, 370
Expository text, 272
Extending the cycle, 33-37,
    181-211
Extensive reading, 293

Family Stories, 263-67
    and Classroom Newspaper, 247
    curricular description, 59
    example, 264
    follow-up, 265-66
    materials and procedures, 263-64
    and original research, 266
    rationale, 263
    and social studies, 265
    teacher's role, 265
    and units of study, 265-66
Feathers, K., 357
Ferreriro, E., 387
Ferris, H., 327
Field, R., 327
Fisher, A., 327
Fisher, E., 237
Fitzhugh, L., 285
Fleck, L., xi, 382
Flow charts, 245
Folktales, 342
Form and function, 13
Fox, P., 303
Frank, A., 285
Freschet, B., 302
Fritz, J., 303
Froman, R., 327
Functionality, 11

Galdone, P., 302, 351, 362, 363, 364
Gameboards, 244
Gardner, H., 14, 382
Generating Written Discourse, 268-73
  and Cloning an Author, 256
  and content area writing, 270-71
  curricular description, 101, 184, 189, 256
  example, 271
  follow-up, 270-71
  materials and procedures, 269-70
  rationale, 268-69
  as a research tool, 272
  teacher's role, 270
  and Theme Cycles, 370
Generativeness, 18
George, J., 303
Gerstein, M., 351
Getting to Know You, 274-76
  and Classroom Newspaper, 247
  curricular description, 55-64
  examples, 59-60
  materials and procedures, 274-75
  rationale, 274
  as a research tool, 276
  teacher's role, 275-76
Gillis, C., 387
Ginsburg, M., 351
Giovanni, N., 327
Glenn, C., 8
Golden Book Field Guides, 382
Goodall, J., 364, 374
Goodman, K., 100, 382, 385, 387, 389
Goodman, Y., 67, 100, 371, 382, 387-88
Goor, N., 382
Goor, R., 196, 352, 382
Goss, J., 136, 351, 382
Grahame, K., 350, 382
Graves, D., 7, 62, 121, 122, 124, 220, 226, 231, 262, 382, 388
Greenfield, E., 304, 327
Griffin, S., 242
Group Composed Bookmaking, procedures and materials, 241
Group Composed Books, 277-79
  and Authors Meeting Authors, 235
  and Bookmaking, 240
  curricular description, 64, 145, 192, 240
  example, 278
  follow-up, 279
  materials and procedures, 277-78
  rationale, 277
  and Readers' Theatre, 279
  and Shared Reading, 279, 350
  teacher's role, 278-79
Group Read Together Time, 347-48

Hakes, D., 383
Hakes, T., 8
Hall, N., 388
Halliday, M. A. K., 179, 383, 388
Hansen, J., 124, 220, 388
Harste, J., ii, ix, 3, 5, 16, 40, 51, 105, 118, 134, 136, 146, 169, 190-91, 197, 218, 251, 256, 267, 279, 317, 326, 337, 339, 345, 351, 357, 381, 382, 383, 385, 388
Harste, J. M., 193-96, 201-2
Harvey, B., 285
Hazen, B., 302
Heath, S., 266, 388
Heine, D., 284
Heller, R., 351
Hemingway, E., 171, 383
Hepler, S., 124, 299, 383
Hickman, J., 124, 131, 152-53, 383
Hill, M., 389
History, example, 177
Hoban, T., 196, 352, 374, 383
Hoberman, M., 327
Hodges, M., 302, 365
Hoffman, P., 370
Holdaway, D., 143, 350-51, 383, 388
Homework, 155, 361
Hopkins, L., 146, 237, 326, 327, 383
Hubbard, R., 388
Huck, C., 299
Hughes, L., 327
Hulett, J., x, 383
Hunter, M., 303
Hutchins, P., 109, 196, 265, 267, 277, 351, 352, 364, 374, 383
Hyman, T., 362

I Recommend File, 235
Illustrators, 232-37, 364
  and the I Recommend File, 235
  and Wordless Picture Books, 372
Informal writing, 280-85, 375
Information books, 128
Innocenti, R., 302
Instant Readers, 352
Instructional history, 369
Intensive reading, 293
Interaction, 16
Interpretation, 332
Intertextuality, 358
Interviewing, 233-34, 274-76
  an author/illustrator, 232-34
Invitations, 15, 62, 99-102, 136,
  169-79, 306

Jacobsen, K., 365
Jaggar, A., 388
Japanese Culture Books, 365
Jarrell, R., 327
Jennifer, 3
Jenny, example, 163
John-Steiner, V., 385
Jones, H., 327
Journal entries, 173
  example, 281
  Tyler, 41-48
Journals, 280-85
  construction, 154-55
  curricular description, 63-64,
    153-60
  follow-up, 283-84
  materials and procedures, 280
  rationale, 280
  teacher's role, 282-83
  variations, 283-84
Jump Rope Jingles, 193, 278
Jurewicz, E., ix, 197, 381, 383
Juster, N., 303

Kammi, language story, 132-33
Kaplan, R., 363
Kauffman, G., ii, ix, x, 18, 25, 58,
  59, 89, 105-15, 121, 130, 148,
  152, 157, 159-60, 203-7, 267,
  299
  character sketch, 60

Keats, E., 302, 363
Keene, C., 141, 383
Keith, language story, 23
Kellogg, S., 90, 262, 364, 384
Kennedy, D., 327
Kennedy, X., 327
Kent, J., 351
King, M., 388
King-Smith, D., 364
Kingman, L., 237
Kipling, R., 363
Koch, K., 326
Krahn, F., 374
Kraus, R., 351
Kucer, S., 271, 273, 322, 384
Kuskin, K., 327

Language activities
  as invitations, 15
  open-ended, 14-15
Language as social, 336
Language learning
  and audience, 13
  and complexity, 13
  as context specific, 53
  and convention, 13
  form and function, 13
  and functionality, 11
  and generativeness, 18
  and meaning, 52
  multimodal nature, 53
  and perspective, 53
  and reflexivity, 54
  as search for unified meaning, 52
  and social interation, 12
  as a social process, 48-49
  text in context, 12
  and transmediation, 12
Language story
  Alison & Jennifer, 3
  Amy, 83
  Beth, 6-7
  Bobbie, 22-23
  Boyd, 102
  Brian, 22-23
  Corey, 25-33
  Danny, 185-87
  "ferret vs parrot", 23
  Kammi, 132-33
  Keith, 23

Mai Xia, 23
Marvin, 85
Michelle, 3
Mudhi, 320
"Smashed Toe", 25-33
Talking Egg Books, 147
Tuck, 46-48
Tyler, 41-48
Larrick, N., 327
Lasky, K., 267
Lawson, R., 267
Leaf, M., 363
Learning, as patterns that connect, 53
Learning centers, 306
   and Theme Cycles, 370-71
Learning Logs, 286-92
   curricular description, 64, 159
   follow-up, 289-90
   as form of Journal, 284
   and Literature Circles, 289
   and Literature Response Activities, 307
   materials and procedures, 286-88
   rationale, 286
   teacher's role, 288-89
Lee, D., 327
LeGuin, U., 303
L'Engle, M., 303
Letitia, example, 179
Letter to an Author, example, 236
Letter writing, 235
Letters to the editor, 22-24
Levinson, R., 267
Lewis, C., 171, 303, 384
Lewis, R., 327
Life experiences, 54-61
Lima, C., 363
Linfors, J., 388
LINK, 352
Lionni, L., 302, 317
Literacy, 3-4
   and reflexivity, 9
Literature, depth and variety, 113-14
Literature Circles, 293-304
   and Authors Meeting Authors, 232
   curricular description, 34, 105-15, 151

getting started, 108-9
and Learning Logs, 289
and Literature Response Activities, 306
materials and procedures, 294-96
and Poetry in Motion, 326
rationale, 293
role of teacher, 109-10, 296-98
and Text Sets, 361
variations, 114-15
Literature Logs
   curricular description, 64
   examples, 287, 290
   as form of Learning Log, 289
   and Literature Response Activities, 306
Literature Response Activities, 305-8
   curricular description, 107, 112-13, 150-60
   follow-up, 307
   and Learning Logs, 307
   and Literature Circles, 306
   and Literature Logs, 306
   materials and procedures, 305-6
   rationale, 305
   and Readers' Theatre, 306
   and Save the Last Word for Me, 307
   and Say Something, 307
   and Sketch to Stretch, 306-7
   teacher's role, 307
Livingston, M., 304, 326, 327-28
Lobel, A., 302, 328, 350, 364, 384
Louie, A., 362
Lowry, L., 303
Lueders, E., 327
Luenn, N., 302

MacLachlan, P., 265, 267, 303, 384
Magazines, 170-71
Mai Xia, language story, 23
Managing editor, 100, 261
Mapping, 245
Maps, 245
Marshall, J., 364
Martin, B., 126, 142, 351, 363, 384
Maruki, T., 302
Marvin, language story, 85
Math Logs, 290

Math story problems, 342
Mattson, C., 132-33
Mayer, M., 302, 374
Mbane, P., 362
McCloskey, R., 267, 350, 384
McClure, A., 326
McCord, D., 304, 328
McGee, L., 374
McGovern, A., 254, 384
McKenzie, M., 279
McKinley, R., 303
McVitty, W., 388
Meaning, 52
Mechanics, 228-29, 257-62
Meek, M., 388
Meredith, R., 100, 382, 385, 387, 389
Merriam, E., 148-49, 152, 304, 324, 328, 384
Message Board, 309-12
    curricular description, 63-64, 164-65, 173-74
    examples, 175, 310
    follow-up, 311
    materials and procedures, 309
    rationale, 309
    and Sketch to Stretch, 356
    teacher's role, 310
    and Theme Cycles, 370
Meta-cognition, 323-28
Michelle, 3
Mid-Missouri TAWL, x, 374, 384
Miles, M., 302
Mille, A., 351, 364
Mills, H., 121, 231, 279, 376, 384
Milne, A., 328
Milz, V., 93, 147, 191-92, 241-42, 388
Mine, Yours, and Ours, 313-17
    follow-up, 314
    materials and procedures, 314
    rationale, 313-14
    and Sketch to Stretch, 316
    teacher's role, 314
Mobiles, 306
Moll, L., 266-67, 384
Montgomery, R., 382
Moore, L., 328
Mosel, A., 365
Moss, J., 308, 362

Mudhi, language story, 320
Multimedia Blitz, 183-87
    and Theme Cycles, 370
    and Units of Study, 370
Murals, 306, 322
Murray, D., 384

Narrative, 313-17
Natural language environments, 119
Neisser, U., 5, 384
Ness, E., 302
Newbery Award, text sets, 361
Newkirk, T., 231, 326, 388
Newman, J., x, 384, 388
Newspaper in Education Week, 251
Newsroom, 384
Niles, D., 389
Nursery rhymes, 278

O'Brien, R., 303
O'Dell, S., 303
O'Keefe, T., 159
O'Neill, M., 328
Open-ended activities, 14-15
Oral interpretation, 329
Ormerod, J., 374

Packard, E., 382
Paley, V., 388
Papier-mâché, 306
Parent involvement, 198-202
    and Authors Meeting Authors, 235
Parents' Day, 93, 198-202
Parents' Night, 239
Parish, P., 364
Parker, M., 237
Partner Reading, 348
Pat, character sketch, 59
Pattern books, 277-78
Patterson, K., 171, 303, 384
Peanut Butter Fudge, 342-43
    curricular description, 199
Pearson, P. D., 5, 381, 389
Peek, M., 351
Peer learning, 15-16
Pen Pals, 63, 64, 160-63
    curricular description, 160-65
    example, 163

Perl, S., 252, 389
Perrault, C., 302, 362
Personal Journals, curricular
    description, 153-60, 172-73
Perspectives, 313-14
  books that compare, 317
  and language learning, 53
Peterson's Field Guides, 384
Photo Group Composed Books, 279
Photographs, 279
Piaget, J., 8, 384
Picture books, 301-2
Picture Setting, 318-22
  curricular description, 63
  example, 320
  follow-up, 321-22
  materials and procedures, 318-19
  rationale, 318
  teacher's role, 319-20
Pierce, K., ix, xi, 292, 315, 317,
    383, 384
Pinkwater, D., 363
Play Dough Recipe, 195
Poetry, 304, 342
  example, 324
Poetry file, 324-25
Poetry in Motion, 323-28
  curricular description, 127
  follow-up, 325-26
  materials and procedures, 323-24
  rationale, 323
  teacher's role, 324-25
Popcorn Reading, 348
  curricular description, 144
Posters, 306, 311
Pragmatic effect, as curricular
    criterion, 103
Predictable books, 140-45, 342,
    350
  bibliography, 351-52
  sets available, 352
Prelutsky, J., 304, 328
Private journals, 282
Publication program, importance,
    246
Publishing
  alternatives to writing, 266, 276
  curricular description, 19-25,
    92-99
  options, 249-51
  within the curriculum, 221-22

Puppet shows, 306
Purves, A., 389

Quigley, L., 363

Raskin, E., 303
Rawls, W., 303
Read-a-Book-a-Day, 350
Read-for-Information-Guide, 371
Readance, J., 389
Readers' Theatre, 329-31
  and Authors Meeting Authors,
    233
  and Authors' Circle, 226
  curricular description, 64, 136-40
  follow-up, 330-31
  and Group Composed Books, 279
  and Literature Response Activities,
    306
  materials and procedures, 329-30
  rationale, 329
  script service, 331
  teacher's role, 330
Reading
  as authoring, 33-37, 105-15
  as search for unified meaning,
    253
  as social, 346
Reading and writing
  differences between, 9
  to learn, 5, 366
Reading as authoring, curricular
    description, 105-15
Reading in the Round, and Say
    Something, 339
Reading Round Table, 144
Reading Systems, 352
Reading to children, 125-26
Reading Unlimited, 352
Ready to Read, 352
Recipes, 342
Reed, L., 284
Reflective journals, 284
Reflexivity, 3, 54, 286-92
Reidel, M., 363
Rental, V., 388
Researching
  and Getting to Know You, 272

Researching (*continued*)
involving children, 265, 266, 272, 291, 316
and Mine, Yours, and Ours, 316
using Generating Written Discourse, 272
using Learning Logs, 291
Revel-Wood, M., ii, ix, x, 64, 93, 154, 159, 162, 164, 169-79, 187-90, 273, 371
Revision, 80-82
first graders, 74-75
kindergarten, 132-33
Rhodes, L., x, 141, 351, 362, 384-85, 389
Richard, family story, 264
Rigby Readers, 352
Risk-taking, 243
Robinson, S., ii, ix, x, 93, 156, 164, 183-87, 197, 245, 251, 371
Roller TV Shows, 306
Rosen, H., 317, 389
Rosen, M., 328
Rosenblatt, L., 326
Ross, L., 363
Rough drafts
handling, 228
importance, 17
Rowe, D., ii, xi, 13, 18, 118-19, 198, 262, 385
Ruwe, M., 385
Rylant, C., 265, 267, 303, 385

Samarapungavan, A., 385
Save the Last Word for Me, 332-35
curricular description, 151
examples, 333-34
follow-up, 335
and Literature Response Activities, 307
materials and procedures, 332-33
rationale, 332
and Say Something, 335
teacher's role, 335
Say Something, 336-39
curricular description, 67, 151
follow-up, 338-39
and Literature Response Activities, 307
materials and procedures, 336-37
rationale, 336

and Save the Last Word for Me, 335
teacher's role, 337-38
and Writing in the Round, 338
Say, A., 365
Scalena, D., 387
Schema Stories, 340-45
curricular description, 101
follow-up, 342-45
materials and procedures, 340
rationale, 340
teacher's role, 341-42
Schmitz, J., 385
School literacy, 11
Schwartz, J., 389
Scibior, O., 102, 385
Science Clubs, 187-90
and Theme Cycles, 371
Science Logs, 159, 289
Scott, J., 364
Scribner, S., 385
Sculpture, 306
Self-editing, 80-82
Semantic editing, 87
curricular description, 257-62
Semantic mapping, 177-78
Sendak, M., 302
Shanklin, N., 291-92, 389
Shared Reading, 346-52
curricular description, 64, 140-45
follow-up, 350
and Group Composed Books, 279
materials and procedures, 346-49
rationale, 346
teacher's role, 349
Sharing, and authoring, 219-20
Sharmat, M., 364
Sherman, B., 67, 100, 382, 389
Sherri, character sketch, 59
Shoebox biographies, 276
Short, K., ii, ix, 18, 33, 105-15, 148, 262, 267, 279, 299, 317, 326, 362, 385, 389
Shreve, S., 385
Shuy, R., 284
Siegel, M., 12, 355, 357, 385
Sign systems, 3
function, 4
Silverstein, S., 328
Sims, R., 389
Sketch to Stretch, 353-57

curricular description, 107
examples, 355
follow-up, 356-57
and Literature Response Activities, 306-7
materials and procedures, 353-54
and Mine, Yours, and Ours, 316
rationale, 353
teacher's role, 354
Sloan, G., 299
Sloyer, S., 331
Smashed toe, language story, 25-33
Smith, D., 303
Smith, E. B., 100, 327, 382, 385, 387, 389
Smith, F., 14, 118, 385, 389
Smith, K., 107, 299, 387
Smith, R., 303
Smith-Burke, M., 388
Social interaction, 274
and language learning, 12
Social nature, of language learning, 48
Social studies, 316
and Theme Cycles, 371
Social Studies Clubs, 187-90
Somers, A., 308
Sonberman, E., 385
Songs, 278, 342
Sounds of Language, 352
Speare, E., 303
Spelling, 58, 88
Spier, P., 302, 374
Spiro, R., 385
Staton, J., 284
Steel, F., 362
Steffel, N., 242
Steig, W., 302
Stein, N., 8
Stephens, D., xi, 51, 383
Steptoe, J., 302
Stevenson, M., 68
Stevenson, R., 328
Stolz, M., 317
Stories, importance, 313-14
Story Box, 352
Story maps, 356
Story structures, 362-63
Story variants, 362
Story versions, 362
Strategic reading, 127

Strategies, 229
Strategy instruction, curricular description, 99-102
Strategy lessons, 99-102
Strickland, D., 220, 389
Strickler, D., 388, 389, 390
Supportive classroom environments, 117-67
Tafuri, N., 352
Talking Egg Books, language story, 147
Taylor, D., 220, 389
Taylor, M., 267, 303
Taylor, T., 303
Teachers as authors, 15
Teaching, as curriculum development, 39-49
Teaching and learning, as a relationship, 54
Teale, W., 389
Teberosky, A., 387
Ten Little Bear Stories, 74-75
Tension, 215
Terry, A., 326
Test Sets, 304
Text in context, and language learning, 12
Text macrostructure, 268-73
Text Sets, 358-65
and Authors' Circle, 361
curricular description, 298
follow-up, 360-62
and Literature Circles, 361
materials and procedures, 358-60
and Poetry in Motion, 326
rationale, 358
and Sketch to Stretch, 357
teacher's role, 360
types of, 362-65
Text shuffle, 270-71
Text structure, 340
Text types, how and why stories, 363
Text world, 253
Thank-you notes, 235
Theme books, 363
Theme Cycles, 366-71
example, 368
follow-up, 370-71
and Learning Centers, 370-71

Theme Cycles (*continued*)
  materials and procedures, 366-69
  model, 369
  and Multimedia Blitz, 370
  organizing for instruction, 187-90
  rationale, 366
  and Science Clubs, 371
  in science, 371
  in social studies, 371
  teacher's role, 369-70
Theme resource books, 363
Theoretical base, for authoring
    cycle, 208-10
Think-Me-a-Poem, 199
Thought collective, xi
Tierney, R. J., 389
Timelines, and comprehension, 245
Tolstoy, A., 142, 352, 362, 385
Tompkins, G., 374
Topic books, 363-64
Transmediation, and language
    learning, 12
Traveling stories, 279
Trelease, J., 127, 220, 385, 390
Tuck, language story, 46-48
Turbill, J., 387, 390
Turkle, B., 317, 374
Tyler, language story, 41-48

Uchida, Y., 267
Uninterrupted reading and writing
  curricular description, 41-48
  importance, 61
  role in authoring, 61-64
Units of study
  as authoring, 33-37
  and Classroom Newspaper, 247
  curricular description, 183-87,
    202-7
  and Family Stories, 265-66
  follow-up, 370-71
  getting started, 183-87
  materials and procedures, 366-69
  ocean vs dinosaur, 203-5
  organizing for instruction, 187-90
  rationale, 366
  teacher's role, 369-70

Valuing authorship, why important,
    16-18
Van Allsburg, C., 302

Vandergrift, K., 299-300
Vargus, N., 123, 162, 385
Variation, and language learning, 17
Video newspaper, 251
Videotapes, Authoring Cycle Series,
    ix
Viorst, J., 317
Vispoel, W., 385
Voight, C., 304
Vygotsky, L., 8, 12, 385

Waber, B., 302
Waber, C., 355
Wagner, N., 389
Walking journals, 284
Ward, L., 302, 374
Watson, D., x, 56, 99, 339, 345,
    362, 385, 388, 390
Webbing
  and comprehension, 306
  curricular description, 177-78
Weiss, H., 242
Wells, G., 317, 390
Westcott, N., 364
White, E. B., 141, 364, 385
White, M., 331
Whitehead, R., 308
Whitman, P., 387
Whitney, J., 388
Whitney, T., 362
Wilde, O., 302
Wilder, L., 267
Wilson, N., 252
Wintle, J., 237
Wood, A., 352, 363
Woods, M., ii, ix, x, 39-49, 64, 88,
    93, 120, 155, 165, 199-201,
    251, 276, 284, 345
Woodward, V., ii, ix, xi, 3, 5, 16,
    118, 134, 169, 190-91, 383,
    388
Woolsey, D., 267
Wordless Picture Books, 372-74
  bibliography, 374
  curricular description, 64, 342
  follow-up, 373-74
  materials and procedures, 372-73
  rationale, 372
  teacher's role, 373
  and Writing-Reading Center, 373

Work Time
  and Authors' Chair, 219-20
  curricular description, 63-64,
    120-22
Worth, V., 328
Worthington, J., 308
Writing in the Round
  curricular description, 79
  and Save the Last Word for Me,
    335
  and Say Something, 338
Writing opportunities, and Authors
  Meeting Authors, 235
Writing-Reading Center
  curricular description, 64, 132-36
  diagram, 135
  and Wordless Picture Books, 373
Written Conversation
  curricular description, 40-41,
    284, 338, 375-79

examples, 376-77
follow-up, 378-79
materials and procedures, 375
rationale, 375
teacher's role, 377-78

Yagawa, S., 365
Yashima, T., 302, 363, 365
Yoder, K., 107, 159-60
Yolen, J., 302, 304, 317, 364
Young Authors Conferences
  and Bookmaking, 240
  curricular description, 98, 202,
    240

Zolotow, C., 302, 363
Zwerger, L., 362